Using Time Line®

Stephen Nelson

Que Corporation
LEADING COMPUTER KNOWLEDGE

Using Time Line

Copyright ©1990 by Que® Corporation

All rights reserved. Printed in the United States of America. No part of this book may be used or reproduced in any form or by any means, or stored in a database or retrieval system, without prior written permission of the publisher except in the case of brief quotations embodied in critical articles and reviews. Making copies of any part of this book for any purpose other than your own personal use is a violation of United States copyright laws. For information, address Que Corporation, 11711 N. College Ave., Carmel, IN 46032.

Library of Congress Catalog No.: 90-62071

ISBN 0-88022-602-1

This book is sold *as is*, without warranty of any kind, either express or implied, respecting the contents of this book, including but not limited to implied warranties for the book's quality, performance, merchantability, or fitness for any particular purpose. Neither Que Corporation nor its dealers or distributors shall be liable to the purchaser or any other person or entity with respect to any liability, loss, or damage caused or alleged to be caused directly or indirectly by this book.

93 92 91   8 7 6 5 4 3 2

Interpretation of the printing code: the rightmost double-digit number is the year of the book's printing; the rightmost single-digit number, the number of the book's printing. For example, a printing of 90-1 shows that the first printing of the book occurred in 1990.

Using Time Line covers Time Line Version 4.0 and earlier versions.

Publishing Director
Lloyd J. Short

Acquisitions Editor
Karen A. Bluestein

Product Director
Shelley O'Hara

Editors
reVisions Plus, Inc.

Technical Editor
Robert I. Murray

Indexer
Hilary Adams
Jill Bomaster

Book Design and Production
Dan Armstrong
Claudia Bell
Brad Chinn
Don Clemons
Denny Hager
Charles Hutchinson
Betty Kish
Bob LaRoche
Cindy L. Phipps
Joe Ramon
Dennis Sheehan
Bruce Steed

Composed in Garamond and OCRB
by Que Corporation

ABOUT THE AUTHOR

Stephen Nelson

Stephen Nelson, a certified public accountant, provides financial consulting and computer-based financial modeling services to a variety of forms and investors—principally in the areas of real estate and manufacturing.

Mr. Nelson's past experience includes a stint as the treasurer and controller of Caddex Corporation, a venture-capital-funded start-up software development company and an early pioneer in the electronic publishing field, and, prior to that, as a senior consultant with Arthur Andersen & Co. There, he provided financial and systems consulting services to clients in a variety of industries.

Mr. Nelson has authored more than 30 articles on financial management and modeling for national publications, including *Lotus Magazine* and *INC Magazine*. He is author of Que's *Using Harvard Project Manager*, *Using DacEasy* and *Using Quicken*, and the author and architect of *Business Forecasting and Planning with Microsoft Excel*, a collection of spreadsheet templates published by Microsoft Press.

Mr. Nelson holds a Bachelor of Science in Accounting from Central Washington University and a Master's in Business Administration with a finance emphasis from the University of Washington.

CONTENTS AT A GLANCE

Introduction 1

Part I: Covering the Basics

Chapter 1:   A Primer on Project Management 9
Chapter 2:   Installing and Starting Time Line 29
Chapter 3:   Getting Started with Time Line 57

Part II: Using Advanced Project Management Tools

Chapter 4:   Managing Project and Task Details 91
Chapter 5:   Identifying and Allocating Resources and Costs 133
Chapter 6:   Monitoring Project Progress, Resources, and Costs .. 159

Part III: Managing the System

Chapter 7:   Customizing Gantt, PERT, and Tree Chart Screens .. 177
Chapter 8:   Printing Reports 201
Chapter 9:   Working with the Time Line Files 255
Chapter 10: Using the Time Line's Utilities and
             Macros Features 289
Chapter 11: Protecting against System Disasters 317

Index 327

TABLE OF CONTENTS

Introduction 1
    What Is Time Line? 2
    When To Use Time Line 2
    When Not To Use Time Line 4
    What Is in This Book? 4

I   Covering the Basics

1   A Primer on Project Management 9
    What Is a Project? 9
    What Is Project Management? 10
        Organizing the Pieces Making Up the Project 10
        Showing the Timing of the Tasks 12
            Estimating Task and Project Durations 12
            Using Start and Finish Dates and Times 15
        Identifying and Allocating Project Resources 19
        Monitoring Project Time, Resources, and Costs 21
    How Does Time Line Help? 22
        Using Time Line To Organize Projects 22
        Using Time Line To Show Timing 23
        Using Time Line To Manage Resources 24
        Using Time Line To Monitor a Project 26
    Chapter Summary 26

2   Installing and Starting Time Line 29
    Installing Time Line 23
    Reviewing the READ.ME DOC file 40
    Starting Time Line Version 4.0 41
    Configuring Time Line for Your Computer 42
        Using Video To Describe Your Monitor 43
        Using Printer To Describe Your Report Printer 46
        Using Graphics To Describe Your Graphics
            Printer or Plotter 49
        Deciding on a Date Format 52

    Deciding on a Disk File Format 53
    Describing Your Mouse 54
    Saving Your Options 55
  Chapter Summary 56

3 Getting Started with Time Line 57

  Creating a Simple Project 57
    Introducing a Sample Project 57
    Choosing Menu Options 59
    Creating a Project Calendar 59
        Standard Workday 62
        Standard Workweek 63
        Standard Week Begins 63
        Standard Year Begins 64
        Precision 64
        Format End Dates 64
    Adding Tasks 65
    Editing and Deleting Tasks 68
    Moving Around in a Large Project 69
        Using Key Combinations 69
        Using Search 70
    Moving Tasks Around 71
    Recognizing Task Dependencies 71
        Defining Dependencies 72
        Removing Dependencies 75
  Un-Doing and Re-Doing 75
  Erasing the Project 76
  Saving the Project 76
  Retrieving the Project 78
  Printing a Project Report 79
    Printing a Graphics Gantt Chart 80
    Printing a Textual PERT Chart 82
  Using Time Line's On-Line Help 82
  Using the Assist Menu's Help, New Schedule, and
    Tutorial Options 84
    Using the Assist Menu's Help 84
    Using the Assist Menu's New Schedule Option 86
    Using the Assist Menu's Tutorial 88
  Chapter Summary 88

II Advanced Project Management Tools

4 Managing Project and Task Details 91

More on Adding Tasks 91
  Using Subtasks and Summary Tasks 91
    Creating Subtasks and a Summary Task 92
    Changing Subtasks to Tasks 96
    Deleting Subtasks and Summary Tasks 97
    Hiding and Unhiding Subtasks 97
    Moving around in a Project with Subtasks 98
    Subtasks and Dependencies 99
  Using Milestones 99
    Defining a Milestone 99
  Using Keywords, WBS Codes, and OBS Codes 101
    Entering Keywords 101
    Entering WBS Codes 101
    Using WBS Codes To Search for Tasks 102
    More on Using the WBS Manager 103
      Defining a WBS Numbering Scheme 103
      Erasing WBS Codes 106
      Checking WBS Codes 107
      Transferring the Contents of another Field to the
        WBS Code Field 108
      Renumbering Tasks 110
    Entering OBS Codes 110
    Linking Tasks to Another File 110
    Creating Schedule Links 111
    Task Links 113
    Removing a Link 114
  Using the Other Tasks Menu Options 114
    Copying Tasks 115
    Documenting Tasks with Notes 115
    Form 117
More on Defining Projects 117
  Using the Options Form 117
    Collecting Project Level Information 118
    Setting the As-of Date 119
    Selecting the Date Display 119
    Choosing the Task Form Version 120
    Choosing a Recalculation Method 120
    Deciding on Undo and Redo Limits 121

    Forcing Future Tasks After the As-of Date 121
    Turning Sound On and Off 121
    Controlling PERT Charts 121
  Using the Journal To Document the Project 122
More on Defining Dependencies 125
  Defining Partial Dependencies 125
  Reviewing Task Dependencies 127
    Showing the Dependencies 127
    Listing the Dependencies with the Dependency Box. 127
    Correcting Dependencies from the Dependency Box 129
  Understanding and Correcting Circular Dependencies 129
    Correcting When Recalculation Is Automatic 130
    Correcting When Recalculation Is Manual 130
Chapter Summary 131

5 Identifying and Allocating Resources and Costs 133

Expanding the Sailboat Project 133
Working With Resources 135
  Identifying Resources 135
  Allocating Resources 139
  Reviewing Resource Allocations 143
    Using a Gantt Chart To Display Allocations 143
    Using a Histogram To Review Allocations 144
  Adjusting Resource Allocations 147
    Manually Leveling Resources 147
    Automatically Adjusting Allocations 148
Using Effort-Driven Scheduling 149
Working With Costs 150
  Identifying Costs 151
  Budgeting for Costs 153
Allocating Resources and Costs to Summary Tasks 157
Chapter Summary 158

6 Monitoring Project Progress, Resources, and Costs 159

Setting the Baseline 159
Monitoring Actual Project Time 163
Monitoring the Actual Resource Usage 166
Monitoring the Actual Costs 168
Using the Assist Update Option 171
Chapter Summary 174

III Managing the System

7 Customizing Gantt, PERT, and Tree Chart Screens 177

Using the Sort Option 177
    Picking a Sort Key 177
    Sorting the Tasks 181
    Using the Filter Option 181
Selecting Tasks and Subtasks with a Filter 182
    Highlighting Tasks and Subtasks with a Filter 184
    Creating Your Own Filters 186
    Editing and Deleting Filters 190
Using the Layout Option 190
    Using a Predefined Layout 192
    Creating a Custom Gantt Chart or PERT/Tree Layout 196
    Editing and Deleting Layouts 200
Chapter Summary 200

8 Printing Reports 201

Using Time Line's Text Reports 201
    A Few Words about Strips 203
    Controlling Printing with the Form Option 204
    Printing a Text Report 209
    Printing a Gantt Chart 209
    Printing the Tasks Report 211
    Printing a Detail Report 214
    Printing a Status Report 218
    Printing an Assignment Report 223
    Printing a Cross Tab Report 226
    Printing a Resource Report 231
    Printing a Histogram Report 233
    Printing a PERT and Tree Charts 238
Printing Graphical Gantt and PERT Charts 241
    Simple Printing of Gantt and PERT Charts 241
    Completing the Graphics/Gantt Chart Form 244
        The Layout Name Field 244
        The Palette Name Field 245
        The Title & Legend Field 245
        The Print On Field 245
        The Corners, Borders, Horizontal Grid, and Vertical Grid Field 246
        The Extra Spacing and Through Outline Level Fields 246

The Baseline Bar and Always Show Actuals Fields 246
The Scale and Gantt Section Is Fields 247
The Date Range Fields 247
The Task Bar Labels Field 248
Completing the Graphics/PERT Chart Form 248
The Layout Name Field 249
The Palette Name Field 249
The Title & Legend Field 250
The Task Box Style, Corners, and Shadows Fields 250
The Dependency Line Style, Corners, and Shadows
  Fields 250
The Periodic PERT Fields 251
The Time Period Field 251
The Arrange Tasks by Field 251
The Eliminate Empty Time Periods to Save Space Field 251
Completing the Graphics Chart Size Form 252
The Force to One Page Field 252
The Resize to Pages Across and Pages Down Fields 253
The Reduce/Enlarge To Field 253
The Preview on Screen Field 253
Chapter Summary 253

9 Working with the Time Line Files 255

Covering the Basics of File Management 255
Saving a Project for the First Time 256
Resaving a Project 258
Renaming and Relocating Project Files 259
Retrieving the Project 260
Erasing Files 262
Backing up Project Files 264
Restoring Project Files 266
Advanced File Management Operations 267
Combining Files 267
Exporting Time Line Files 271
Importing Files 275
Importing Time Line Version 2 and 3 Files 276
Importing Spreadsheet and Database Files 277
Importing Outline Files 280
Working with Files on a Network 286
Chapter Summary 287

10 Using Time Line Utilities and Macro Features 289

Tapping the Time Line Utilities 289
    The Exit to DOS Option 289
    Stats 292
    DOS Date and Time 293
    TL 3.0 Config 294
Speeding Things Up With Macros 295
    What Is a Macro? 295
    Illustrating Some Simple Macros 296
    Saving and Reusing Macros 299
    Some Tips for Writing Simple Macros 301
    Reviewing the Other Macro Menu Options 303
        The Erase Option 304
        The Configure Option 304
        The Halt Option 305
        The Insert Option 305
            The Macro Option 306
            The Secondary Macro Option 306
            The Input Pause Option 307
            The Choices Option 307
            The Dialog Options 308
            The Pause Option 309
            The Link Option 310
    Editing Macros 310
    Some Tips for Writing More Complex Macros 314
    Chapter Summary 315

11 Protecting against System Disasters 317

Defining a Few Basic Terms 318
Preventing Hardware Disasters 318
    Dealing with Dirty Power 319
    Hard Disk Failures 319
    Floppy Disk Problems 320
Reviewing and Preventing Software Disasters 321
    Recovering Deleted Files 321
    Protecting against Viruses 322
        What Are Viruses? 322
        Where Do Viruses Come From? 323
        Detecting Viruses and Disinfecting Disks 323
    Working with Beta Software 324
    Chapter Summary 324

Index 327

ACKNOWLEDGMENTS

Special thanks to Barbara Gress at Symantec Corporation for all her help.

Trademark Acknowledgments

Que Corporation has made every effort to supply trademark information about company names, products, and services mentioned in this book. Trademarks indicated below were derived from various sources. Que Corporation cannot attest to the accuracy of this information.

1-2-3, Lotus and Symphony are registered trademarks of Lotus Development Corporation.

dBASE, dBASE III, and dBASE IV are registered trademarks of Ashton-Tate Corporation.

Microsoft, MS-DOS, Microsoft Excel, and Microsoft Word are registered trademarks of Microsoft Corporation.

Quattro is a registered trademark of Borland International, Inc.

Time Line is a registered trademark of Symantec Corporation.

WordPerfect is a registered trademark of WordPerfect Corporation.

WordStar is a registered trademark of WordStar Corporation.

CONVENTIONS USED IN THIS BOOK

The conventions used in this book have been established to help you learn to use the program quickly and easily.

Names of menus, menu options, screens, and screen options are written with initial capital letters. Words and letters that the user types are written in *italic* or set off on a separate line. On-screen messages are written in a `special typeface` and capitalized as they appear on-screen.

Introduction

On project managers' office walls, you sometimes see posters that list the five stages of a project as

1. Enthusiasm for the goal
2. Disillusionment with the progress
3. Search for the guilty
4. Persecution of the innocent
5. Praise for the nonparticipants

Unfortunately, the poster isn't so much a joke as it is a commentary on the way many projects are organized and the reasons many projects fail. Microcomputer-based project management software packages represent, in a sense, a response to these problems. And this book, *Using Time Line*, can help you profit from a specific software package: Time Line 4.0.

If you're considering using a microcomputer-based project management package like Time Line, if you already have decided to install Time Line and want a little extra help in getting started with the package, or if you're using Time Line and want a reference source with a different focus than the Time Line user's manual, *Using Time Line* will help. In this book, you will find a wealth of information on the latest version of the Time Line program, organized by project management activity.

Using Time Line

What Is Time Line?

Time Line is a complete set of project-management tools you can use to manage projects more successfully. The package allows you to use many of the standard approaches to defining projects and organizing the tasks that make up a project, including Program Evaluation and Review Technique (PERT), Gantt charts, Tree charts, and several variations on these approaches. The package lets you monitor the actual progress and costs of a project and compare these to the planned progress and costs. The package also lets you allocate and monitor the people and equipment resources used by a project. All in all, Time Line can automate many of the tasks integral to modern project management.

By using Time Line, you can have essentially the same tools available to you that in the past have been available only to large corporations and government agencies with huge computers and extremely expensive project-management software.

When To Use Time Line

Time Line is a powerful project-management system that probably can provide you with most and maybe all of the tools and techniques you need for successfully managing projects. At one end of the spectrum are the Time Line users who manage projects with hundreds or thousands of tasks and as many resources. At the other end of the spectrum are the Time Line users who barely-but-profitably-tap into Time Line's features and functions in order to think more clearly about organizing simple yet important projects.

Your use may fall somewhere in between the two extremes. Regardless of where your use falls, you will find that a project-management system like Time Line delivers five general benefits:

Using a project-management system lets you answer the question "What is a project?"

> That may seem implicit. Perhaps even obvious. Unfortunately, all too often the people whose commitment and involvement is required for project success don't agree on key points such as who will manage the project, when will it start, when will it finish, and how much will it cost. Even when your use is very basic, going through the steps of using a project-management package like Time Line lets you answer this fundamental question.

Using a project-management system lets you answer the question "How will the project be accomplished?"

Answering this question organizes the various pieces of the project. In essence, answering this question requires breaking a project down into the subprojects or tasks that make up a project. Sometimes, these subprojects or tasks may need to be broken down into even smaller pieces. You also need to identify the dependencies among the individual pieces. A project-management package like Time Line provides you with a series of tools that make answering this question much easier.

Using a project-management system lets you answer the question "When will the project and the parts of the project be completed?"

Typically, the process of scheduling tasks and scheduling project start and finish dates represents an essential step in managing a project. Clearly, you need to know when your project should start and when it should be finished. You also need to know when tasks that are part of a project need to start and whether you can delay certain tasks with no adverse effects. You also need to know when to hire people required for a project and when to schedule delivery dates for equipment needed for a project. Usually, if you use a project-management system to answer how the project will be accomplished, the system automatically answers when the project and the parts of the project will be completed.

The resource-management feature of more powerful microcomputer-based project-management systems like Time Line lets you answer the question "Who or what will do the work?"

Sometimes, answering the three previous questions—what, how, and when—is all you need. However, for projects where successfully managing people and equipment is necessary, Time Line provides a resource-management feature. In short, Time Line's resource-management feature lets you ensure that the people and equipment you need for completing a project on time and within your budget are available when you need them.

Using Time Line lets you answer the question, "How is the project progressing compared to what I planned?"

In general, one of the basic ways you manage a project is to compare what was planned to what actually happens. Sometimes people view these comparisons as negative. The idea, however, is that if you're following your original plan in terms of time spent, resources used, or costs incurred, it means that you're moving toward successful completion of the project. And if you're not following your original plan, it means you're not moving toward successful completion of the project—which you usually benefit by learning as soon as possible.

When Not To Use Time Line

As mentioned earlier, you probably can use Time Line to perform project management for very large projects—perhaps those with several hundred and even several thousand pieces. At some point, however, you may have a larger project than can be performed using a microcomputer-based package like Time Line. (With 650K of free memory—memory that isn't used by DOS or Time Line—you can theoretically have up to 2,000 tasks.) In that case, you probably need a minicomputer-based package that allows for tens or hundreds of thousands of pieces to make up the whole project. Those packages can cost thousands of dollars. If you think you're probably a candidate for a larger, minicomputer-based project management package, try this suggestion: Experiment with Time Line to develop a list of the requirements you have for your project management system. Then use that list as a basis for beginning your search for a more expensive package. Minicomputer manufactures can provide you with lists of the project-management software that run on the minicomputer you have available.

What Is in This Book?

Using Time Line is divided into three parts.

Part 1, "Covering the Basics," gives you the basic information you will need to begin using Time Line productively.

Chapter 1, "A Primer of Project Management," covers the basics of project management. Learning and using a project management system is much like learning to drive a car. A significant investment of time, and sometimes money, is involved. Just as you need to learn about speed limits, road signs, and driving laws before driving a car, you need to learn about project management in order to use any full-fledged project-management system. Chapter 1 describes what projects are, what project management is, and how Time Line helps you manage projects.

Chapter 2, "Installing and Starting Time Line," outlines the steps necessary to install and begin using Time Line successfully. The chapter describes how to install Time Line, select menu options, enter data into screen fields within the Time Line system, and provide information to the program about the monitor and printer you will use. The chapter also describes how to start Time Line.

Chapter 3, "Getting Started with Time Line," describes the basic steps for creating a simple project. This chapter describes how to define project tasks and the relationships between tasks, how to save and retrieve project files, and how to print two basic project management reports. This chapter also describes some of the features that Time Line provides for new users.

Part II, "Using Advanced Project-Management Tools," provides you with information you will need to tap into Time Line's advanced project management features.

Chapter 4, "Managing Project and Task Details," explains how to use the Schedule menu options to describe and define more complex projects and tasks. The chapter goes into detailed discussions of many of the topics introduced in Chapter 3.

Chapter 5, "Identifying and Allocating Resources and Costs," describes how to identify project resources, show when they are available, and allocate them to projects. The chapter also describes how to identify and budget for project costs.

Chapter 6, "Monitoring Project Progress, Resources, and Costs," describes the steps you follow to track actual project progress, resource usage, and cost spending. The chapter also describes how you compare this actual data with whatever was originally planned.

Part III, "Managing the System," gives you the information you need to address system issues: how to change the way screens look, how to print and plot project reports, and how to manage the project data files Time Line creates.

Chapter 7, "Customizing Gantt, Pert, and Tree Chart Screens," describes how to use the Sort, Filter, and Layout menu options to change the appearance of the Gantt, Pert, and Tree chart screens in Time Line. You can use these options also to control the data that appears on reports. In effect, Chapter 7 gives you the background information to fine-tune and customize the way you use Time Line—a handy feature that may mean you can get exactly what you want from the package.

Chapter 8, "Printing Reports," examines how to use each of the Report and Graphics menu options for printing reports. Communicating the project's organization and progress to project participants amounts to one of the big benefits of a project-management system. Chapter 8 outlines the mechanics of generating the Time Line textual and graphical reports you can use to do this. This chapter also includes examples of the different reports that Time Line generates.

Chapter 9, "Working with the Time Line Files," examines basic file management activities such as how to save, retrieve, erase, backup and restore project files. This chapter also covers some of the more advanced file management activities such as how to use Time Line's file combine, import, and export features.

Chapter 10, "Using Time Line Utilities and Macro Features," describes how to benefit from each of the menu options on Time Line's Utilities menu. These options amount to handy tools you can use to make working with Time Line easier and faster. In fact, one of the Time Line utilities, Macros, even gives you the ability to customize the operation of Time Line.

Chapter 11, "Protecting against System Disasters," covers some general information about how to prevent system disasters—or at least minimize their impact. This information doesn't just apply to Time Line and project management, but rather to any computer application. This information is important to include at this point because system disasters can make it more difficult and, sometimes, even impossible to use Time Line for better managing important projects.

Part I

Covering the Basics

Includes

A Primer on Project Management

Installing and Starting Time Line

Getting Started with Time Line

1

A Primer on Project Management

If you're new to project management, the whole subject can be rather confusing. There are the new terms, the many behind-the-scenes calculations, and usually the complexities of the project you want to better manage.

To begin using project management as the powerful tool it really is, you need to strip away the clutter, learn the language, and review the arithmetic. This chapter helps you accomplish this objective—preparing you to use project management—by asking and answering three questions:

1. What is a project?
2. What is project management?
3. How does Time Line help?

When you finish this chapter, you should be able to determine whether you really want to use Timeline for a particular project and, if so, how you want to use Timeline.

What Is a Project?

Because people use various definitions of the word *project*, starting off with a common definition is best. A project is an activity that has a definite start and definite finish, that produces some measurable result, and that requires time, money, and resources to reach completion. Although that definition amounts to a rather abstract description, usually projects tend to be concrete and easy to identify. For example, building a skyscraper, writing a book, installing a computer, and making a movie all are projects. Each has a definite start and a definite finish. Each produces some measurable result. Each requires time, money, and resources.

What Is Project Management?

Although the term *management* often refers to activities that are highly subjective and qualitative, the term *project management* actually refers to four activities related to making sure that you successfully complete a project:

1. Organizing and showing the individual pieces making up a project

2. Showing the timing of tasks: both the time required to complete tasks and the time tasks start and stop

3. Identifying and allocating the resources you need to complete a project

4. Comparing what is planned to happen with what actually happens. Usually, comparisons are made in three areas: time spent, money spent, and resources required.

For an example of these four components of project management, suppose that you decide to paint the inside of your apartment. The following section explains how you could set up your project.

Organizing the Pieces Making Up the Project

Even for a small project like painting the inside of your apartment, you may benefit by breaking the project into pieces and noting any relationships among the pieces. You may, for example, list six steps for the painting project:

1. Washing off the walls you will paint

2. Plugging any holes with putty or spackle

3. Taping window and door frames to protect them

4. Buying the paint and brushes you need

5. Painting the walls

6. Cleaning up after you finish

Each of the steps is called a *task*. Clearly, some tasks can be performed at the same time. For example, the first four tasks—washing, plugging, taping, and buying—can probably occur in any order. If someone helps, these tasks can even occur at the same time.

Some tasks, however, need to be performed after you complete another task. For example, you need to complete the first four tasks before you can begin to paint. And you need to complete the fifth task (painting) before you start the sixth task (cleaning up). These relationships are called *dependencies* because one task depends on another. These relationships are also called *links* because the start of one task is linked to the finish of another task. When two tasks depend on each other, the task that must be finished first is called a *predecessor*. The task that must follow the predecessor is called a *successor*.

Some tasks consist of still smaller tasks or pieces. For example, the cleaning up task may be broken into four additional tasks:

1. Locate any paint spills and remove

2. Clean the paint brushes

3. Remove the tape from around the window and door frames

4. Put away the remaining paint and paint brushes

When a task represents part of another task, it is called a *subtask*. Creating lists of tasks and subtasks is one of the ways you can organize the pieces of a project. Other ways are available, too.

For example, you can organize project information with a PERT chart (see fig. 1.1). Figure 1.1 graphically depicts the six main tasks you need to complete in the imaginary painting project.

PERT is an acronym for *Program Evaluation and Review Technique*. PERT charts show the tasks and the task dependencies of a project.

A PERT chart also shows the relationships among tasks. For example, in figure 1.1, the boxes containing task names show the pieces of the project. The lines connecting the boxes show the order in which the tasks must be performed.

Listing project tasks and using PERT charts typically make projects easier and more successful. One benefit is that you ensure that you will remember what you need to do to complete the project.

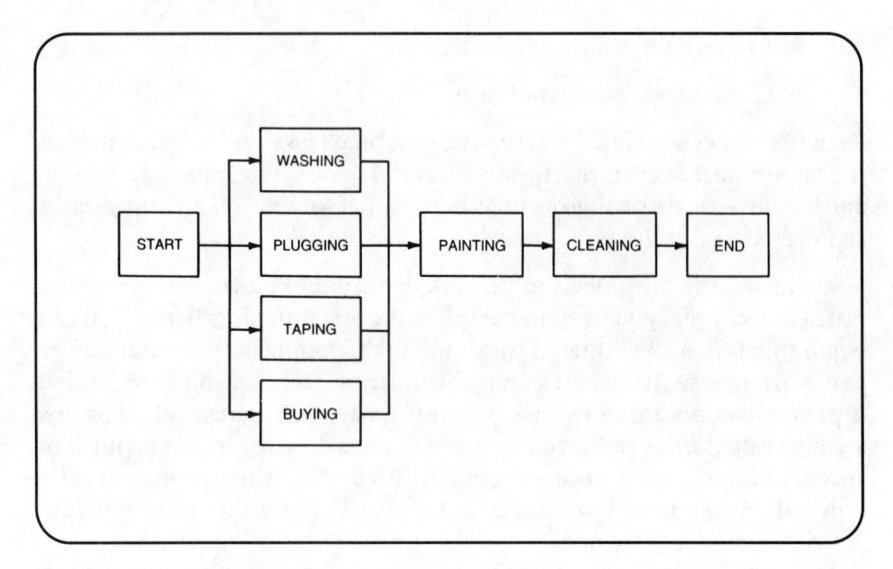

Fig. 1.1. An example Pert Chart.

Another benefit is that with PERT charts, you can visually organize and inspect the relationships among tasks. After reviewing figure 1.1, for example, you may decide that other dependencies or links exist. Certainly, PERT charts make reviewing task dependencies easier.

These two benefits become more important when you manage projects with even more tasks. Part of the reason is that missing a task or dependency is easier when more tasks are involved. Another reason is that when you have large projects, you often tap the skills of more people. If you manage a project with several dozen, several hundred, or several thousand people, achieving project success requires that everyone knows what the project entails and the order in which tasks should be completed.

Showing the Timing of the Tasks

Showing the timing of tasks is the second part of the project-management activity. The timing of tasks consists of two parts: figuring how much time a task takes and figuring when a task starts and finishes.

Estimating Task and Project Durations

Your first step in showing the timing of tasks is to estimate the amount of time each of the tasks will take. Suppose that you decide to organize the painting project, using the six main tasks.

You may make the following estimates:

Washing—three hours

Plugging—one hour

Taping—one hour

Buying—half an hour

Painting—four hours

Cleaning—half an hour

The time taken to complete a task is called its *duration*. For example, the duration of the washing task equals three hours, and the duration of the plugging task equals one hour.

Some pieces of a project aren't really tasks at all, because their duration equals zero. When the duration of a piece equals zero, the piece is called a *milestone*. Typically, milestones represent events that don't require work. For example, the Start and End boxes in figure 1.1 represent milestones.

After you estimate task durations, you can determine how long the project will take to finish by identifying the paths through a project on a PERT chart. To move from the start of the project to the end of the project, you must follow a path. For example, the first path is to start the project, move to the washing task, move to the painting task, and then move to the cleaning task.

Figure 1.1 shows four paths, or routes, through the PERT chart:

Path 1: Washing–Painting–Cleaning

Path 2: Plugging–Painting–Cleaning

Path 3: Taping–Painting–Cleaning

Path 4: Buying–Painting–Cleaning

If the term *path* still seems confusing, place your finger on the Start box in figure 1.1 and trace the lines that connect the Start box to the Washing box, the Washing box to the Painting box, the Painting box to the Cleaning box, and the Cleaning box to the End box. What you trace with your finger is the first of the four paths.

Each path has a duration that equals the total of the individual task durations making up the path. You can calculate the path durations of the four tasks as follows:

Duration of path 1:

> Washing duration + Painting duration + Cleaning duration
> 3 hours + 4 hours + 0.5 hour = 7.5 hours

Duration of path 2:

> Plugging duration + Painting duration + Cleaning duration
> 1 hour + 4 hours + 0.5 hour = 5.5 hours

Duration of path 3:

> Taping duration + Painting duration + Cleaning duration
> 1 hour + 4 hours + 0.5 hour = 5.5 hours

Duration of path 4:

> Buying duration + Painting duration + Cleaning duration
> 0.5 hour + 4 hours + 0.5 hour = 5 hours

When you know the durations of each of the paths through the project, you know how long the project will take to finish. The path with the longest duration, called the *critical path*, shows how long the project will take to finish, which is the project duration. In the case of the four paths through the painting project, the critical path is the first one, Washing-Painting-Cleaning, which takes 7.5 hours. The project duration, then, equals 7.5 hours.

Project-management systems like Time Line calculate the durations of each of the paths through a project, identify the critical path, and give the project duration. In the simple painting project, making the required calculations isn't much work. But when projects include hundreds of tasks and dozens of paths, the time savings are enormous.

At this point, you may be asking yourself why you would want to go to the work of estimating durations so you can calculate the critical path. You usually will want to know your project's critical path for three reasons.

First, because the duration of the critical path equals the duration of the project, identifying the critical path lets you estimate when you will finish the project. In the case of the painting project, because the critical path equals 7.5 hours, you know that once you start the project, it will take at least 7.5 hours to complete.

Second, if you know which tasks are on the critical path, you know which tasks cannot be delayed without delaying the project. For example, the painting task is on the critical path. If painting takes longer than 4 hours, your project takes longer than 7.5 hours.

Chapter 1: A Primer on Project Management

Third, if you know which tasks aren't on the critical path, you know which tasks can be delayed without delaying the project. For example, the buying task isn't on the critical path. So, to some extent, the buying task can be delayed without delaying the project. The amount of time a task can be delayed without delaying the project is called *slack*. To determine the actual amount of slack, you need to know when a task can start and when a task must finish, which is the subject of the next section.

Using Start and Finish Dates and Times

Start and finish dates and times comprise a second aspect of the timing of tasks. Four dates or times are to be calculated for each task: early start, early finish, late start, and late finish. The *early start* shows the earliest date or time you can begin work on a task. The *early finish* shows the earliest date or time you can expect to complete a task. The *late start* shows the latest date or time you can begin work on a task without delaying the project. The *late finish* shows the latest date or time you can complete a task without delaying the project. Does any of this information—knowing when tasks need to be initiated and completed—help? Yes, especially if you have a large number of tasks in the project, because tracking a large number of tasks is more difficult.

The arithmetic for calculating start and finish dates and times isn't difficult, but it is rather tedious. Thankfully, Time Line performs the arithmetic for you. However, because you use the start and finish dates in your decision making, you should understand the calculations. To calculate the start and finish dates for tasks and for the project, do the following steps:

1. Identify when you will start the project. Suppose that in the painting example, you decide you will start next Saturday at 8 a.m. The project start time, then, equals 8 a.m.

2. Calculate the finish time of the project by adding the durations of all the tasks in the critical path to the project start:

    8 a.m. (project start)
    + 3 hours (duration of washing task)
    + 4 hours (duration of painting task)
    + 0.5 hours (duration of cleaning task)
    = 3:30 p.m. (early finish time of project)

3. Starting with the first task in each path, calculate the early start of each task in each path by adding the duration of the predecessor task to the early start time of the predecessor task. For the first task in a path, because there is no predecessor task, use the project start. This sounds confusing, but it

isn't. For example, make the calculations to determine the early starts for the tasks in the first path, washing–painting–cleaning:

Early start of washing task:

> 8 a.m. (project start)
> + 0 hours (no predecessor task)
> = 8 a.m. (early start of washing task)

Early start of painting task:

> 8 a.m. (early start of washing task)
> + 3 hours (duration of washing task)
> = 11 a.m. (early start of painting task)

Early start of cleaning task:

> 11 a.m. (early start of painting task)
> + 4 hours (duration of painting task)
> = 3 p.m. (early start of cleaning task)

In a similar fashion, you also can calculate the early starts of tasks in each of the remaining paths. The only twist is when a task appears on more than one path. For example, the two tasks painting and cleaning appear in all four paths for the painting project:

> Path 1: Washing–Painting–Cleaning
> Path 2: Plugging–Painting–Cleaning
> Path 3: Taping–Painting–Cleaning
> Path 4: Buying–Painting–Cleaning

So you end calculating an early start for the painting and cleaning tasks for each of the four paths through the project. The obvious question is, which of the four early starts is correct? The answer is that when you calculate more than one early start, the latest early start is the correct one.

This sounds tricky, but really it's not. Take the case of the first four tasks in the painting project. If you make the calculations of the painting task's early start for each of the four paths, you get these four early starts:

Path 1:

> 8 a.m. + 3 hours washing = 11 a.m. early start painting

Path 2:

>8 a.m. + 1 hour plugging = 9 a.m. early start painting

Path 3:

>8 a.m. + 1 hour taping = 9 a.m. early start painting

Path 4:

>8 a.m. + 0.5 hour buying = 8:30 a.m. early start painting

4. Calculate the early finish of each task by adding the duration of the task to the early start of the task. For example, to calculate the early finish of the washing task, add the early start of the washing task (8 a.m.) to the duration of the washing task (3 hours). The early finish of the washing task equals 11 a.m.

In this example, the latest of the early starts is 11 a.m., which is when the washing task finishes. Because you cannot start painting until you finish washing, picking the latest of the early start dates means you're sure that you have completed the predecessor tasks that finish last.

Figure 1.2 shows the early start and finish times you would calculate for the painting project as part of steps 3 and 4.

Task Name	Task Duration	Early Start	Early Finish
Washing	3.00	8:00 AM	11:00 AM
Plugging	1.00	8:00 AM	9:00 AM
Taping	1.00	8:00 AM	9:00 AM
Buying	0.50	8:00 AM	8:30 AM
Painting	4.00	11:00 AM	3:00 PM
Cleaning	0.50	3:00 PM	3:30 PM

Fig. 1.2. The early start and finish times.

5. Starting with the last task in the each of the paths, calculate the late finish of each task in each path by subtracting the duration of the successor task from the late finish date of the successor task. For the last task in a path, because there is no successor task, use the project finish. For example, make the calculations to determine the late finishes for the tasks in the first path, washing–painting–cleaning:

Late finish of cleaning task:

> 3:30 p.m. (project finish)
> – 0 hours (no successor task)
> = 3:30 p.m. (late finish of washing task)

Late finish of painting task:

> 3:30 p.m. (late finish of cleaning task)
> – 0.5 hour (duration of cleaning task)
> = 3 p.m. (late finish of painting task)

Late finish of washing task:

> 3 p.m. (late finish of painting task)
> – 4 hours (duration of painting task)
> = 11 a.m. (late finish of washing task)

In a similar fashion, you also can calculate the late finishes of tasks in each of the remaining paths. But as with calculating the early starts, however, there is a twist: When a task appears on more than one path, you end up calculating several late finishes. For example, the two tasks painting and cleaning appear in all four paths for the painting project:

Path 1: Washing–Painting–Cleaning
Path 2: Plugging–Painting–Cleaning
Path 3: Taping–Painting–Cleaning
Path 4: Buying–Painting–Cleaning

So you must calculate four late finish times for the painting and cleaning tasks for each of the four paths through the project. In this example, you end up calculating the same late finish times because the two tasks that lay on all four paths are the last two tasks on each. Often, however, you will calculate different latest finishes. And when you do, use the earliest late finish.

6. Calculate the late start of each task by subtracting the duration of the task from its late finish. For example, to calculate the late start of the buying task, subtract the buying task

duration, 0.5 hour, from the late finish of the buying task, which figure 1.3 shows as 11 a.m. Figure 1.3 also shows the latest start and finish times you would calculate for the painting project as part of steps 5 and 6.

Task Name	Task Duration	Late Start	Late Finish
Washing	3.00	8:00 AM	11:00 AM
Plugging	1.00	10:00 AM	11:00 AM
Taping	1.00	10:00 AM	11:00 AM
Buying	0.50	10:30 AM	11:00 AM
Painting	4.00	11:00 AM	3:00 PM
Cleaning	0.50	3:00 PM	3:30 PM

Fig. 1.3. The latest start and finish times.

7. Calculate the difference between the early and late start or the difference between the early and late finish. Either calculation produces the same result because the task duration determines the difference between the early start and finish and between the late start and finish. Figure 1.4 shows these differences calculated both ways. The difference equals the amount of slack in a task—the amount that a task start or finish can be delayed without delaying the project. Tasks on the critical path show zero slack, which means any delay in completing that task delays the project. However, it is helpful to know, for example, that you can delay the buying task start as much 2.5 hours without delaying the project.

Identifying and Allocating Project Resources

Identifying and allocating the resources you require to complete a project represent the third aspect of project management. Typically, you need both people and equipment to complete tasks. And because resources are limited, you usually need to organize your projects with an eye to the available resources.

Task Name	Task Duration	Early Start	Early Finish	Late Start	Late Finish	Slack Time
Washing	3.00	8:00 AM	11:00 AM	8:00 AM	11:00 AM	0.00
Plugging	1.00	8:00 AM	9:00 AM	10:00 AM	11:00 AM	2.00
Taping	1.00	8:00 AM	9:00 AM	10:00 AM	11:00 AM	2.00
Buying	0.50	8:00 AM	8:30 AM	10:30 AM	11:00 AM	2.50
Painting	4.00	11:00 AM	3:00 PM	11:00 AM	3:00 PM	0.00
Cleaning	0.50	3:00 PM	3:30 PM	3:00 PM	3:30 PM	0.00

Fig. 1.4. Calculating slack.

Take the imaginary project of painting your apartment. If you add up the durations of all the tasks, the project in total requires 10 hours of time from one or more persons. That's a resource. If you have cathedral ceilings, the project probably requires ladders and scaffolding. Those are resources, too. Because projects usually require resources—both people and equipment— you want to make sure that your plans assume realistic use of any resources.

Here are the steps to recognizing the resources required for a project:

1. List the resources you have available.
2. Allocate the resources needed to project tasks.
3. Adjust for any discrepancies between the resources you have available and the resources you need.

In listing the available resources, include both people and equipment. In the painting project, your people resources probably include yourself and perhaps a helpful friend. Your equipment resources may include a ladder, paint brushes, a roller, and drop cloths to protect your furniture from paint. You can actually create a resources list from this information:

Me
My best friend
A 10-foot ladder
Two paint brushes
A paint roller
Two 10-by-16-foot drop cloths

In allocating resources, you commit a resource to a task and, as a result, take it off the list of available resources. If you allocate your best friend to the task of washing the walls, for example, remove him or her from the resources list. If you allocate the use of the ladder for plugging holes with putty and spackle, remove the ladder from the resources list.

After you complete the first two steps of recognizing project resources, you need to resolve any discrepancies between what the project needs and what you actually have available to allocate. Essentially, you want to verify that neither of the following two error conditions exists:

1. Resource shortages
2. Resource overallocations

Resource shortages refer to situations in which you need a resource for a task, but the resource is not available. If your painting project calls for you to complete the painting within the 7.5-hour project duration, you need more than one person because the project amounts to 10 hours of work.

Resource overallocations refer to situations in which you allocate a resource to different tasks that need to use the resource at the same time. If your painting project calls for the ladder to be used simultaneously—by you when you plug holes and by your best friend when he or she washes walls—a resource overallocation exists. Both of you cannot use the ladder at once.

With only a handful of tasks and a short list of resources, identifying and allocating resources is probably not worth the effort. Many projects, however, involve hundreds of tasks and resources. In these cases, forgetting about one resource or inadvertently overallocating a resource is all too easy.

Monitoring Project Time, Resources, and Costs

The fourth component of project management consists of monitoring the actual time spent on tasks, the actual resources used by tasks, and the actual costs of a project. Traditionally, you monitor these three characteristics—time, resources, and cost—by comparing what you planned with what actually occurs.

Sometimes this business of comparing planned figures with actual figures gives you unfavorable results. Unfortunately, the comparisons often show that the project is progressing more slowly, is using more resources, and is costing more money than you originally planned. However, the comparisons provide you with an early warning system. And, often, the early warnings give you time to remedy problems when they are little rather than big.

How Does Time Line Help?

Time Line includes features that help you with each of the four components of project management you just examined. Essentially, Time Line provides you with a collection of screens and reports that perform one or more of the four components. This section gives a few examples.

Note: Many screens and reports perform two and sometimes even three of the four components of project management. In fact, you cannot rigidly categorize most screens or reports as belonging to only one component of project management.

Using Time Line To Organize Projects

Time Line provides two views of a project that are particularly helpful for organizing the tasks that make up a project:

1. Tree charts
2. PERT charts

Note: Chapters 3 and 4 describe each of these approaches in more detail.

Tree charts show the tasks of a project by picturing a project as an upside-down tree diagram (see figure 1.5). If a task has subtasks, the subtasks branch out of the task boxes.

PERT charts, as noted earlier, provide an excellent format for visually showing the tasks of a project and the order in which the tasks need to be completed. Figure 1.6 shows an example of a PERT chart that Time Line might draw to show the painting project task. This chart resembles the handmade PERT chart shown in figure 1.1.

When Time Line draws a PERT chart, the task names are shown inside the boxes representing tasks. For example, Wash is a task. (None show the painting the apartment project, but if that project had milestones, they would also show inside the boxes.)

```
            Schedule Name  :
            Responsible    :
            As-of Date     : 25-Apr-90  8:00a      Schedule File :


                                :==========:
                                |Project   |
                                :==========:
                   /--------------------+----------------------------------\
         :==========: :==========: :==========: :==========: :==========: :==========:
         |Wash      | |Plug      | |Tape      | |Buy       | |Paint     | |Clean     |
         :==========: :==========: :==========: :==========: :==========: :==========:
         TIME LINE Tree Diagram Report, Strip 1
```

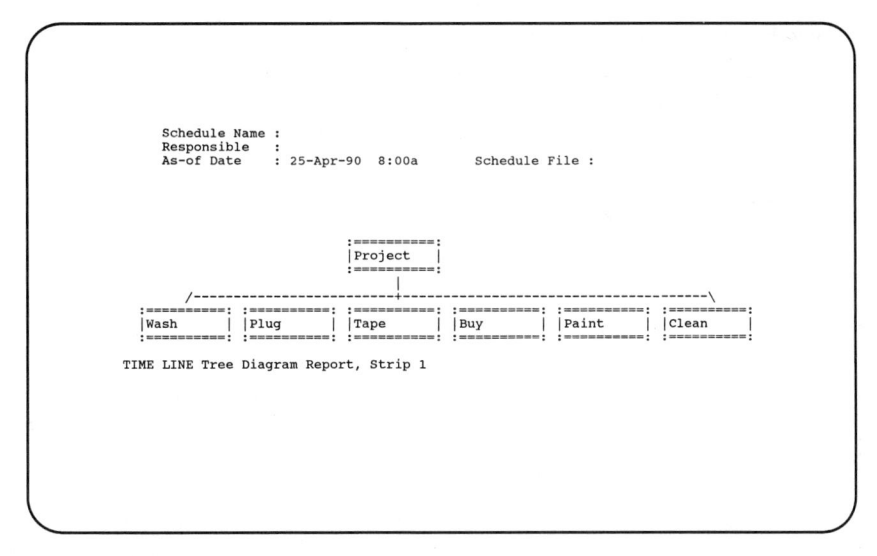

Fig. 1.5. An example of a Time Line tree chart.

```
            Schedule Name  :
            Responsible    :
            As-of Date     : 25-Apr-90  8:00a      Schedule File :




         :==========:        :==========:   :==========:
         |Wash      |---///|Paint     |-|Clean     |
         :==========:    UUU:==========:   :==========:
                         |||
                         |||
         :==========:    |||
         |Plug      |---/||
         :==========:    ||
                         ||
         :==========:    ||
         |Tape      |----/|
         :==========:     |
                          |
         :==========:     |
         |Buy       |-----/
         :==========:
         TIME LINE PERT Diagram Report, Strip 1
```

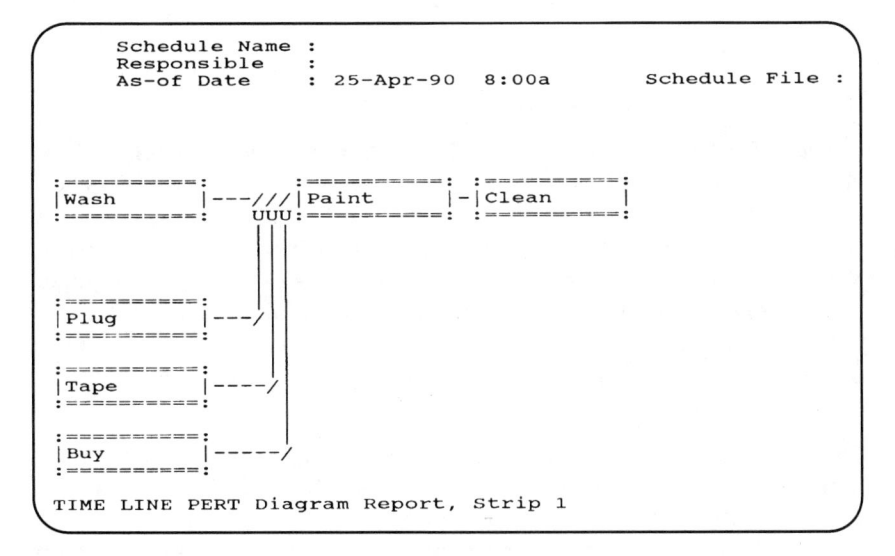

Fig. 1.6. An example of a Time Line PERT chart.

Using Time Line To Show Timing

Time Line provides another approach for creating projects: Gantt charts. Although Gantt charts represent a helpful way to organize the pieces of a project, they also represent powerful method to show the timing of the various pieces of a project.

Gantt charts show the tasks of a project as solid, horizontal bars plotted against a time-scale to show how long tasks take, when tasks start, and when tasks finish. Figure 1.7 shows a Gantt chart.

```
Schedule Name :
Responsible   :
As-of Date    : 25-Apr-90  8:00a        Schedule File :


                                             90
                                             Apr
Task Name                 Resources  Status  25         26
   Wash                                 C    XXX         .
   Plug                                      X--         .
   Tape                                      X--         .
   Buy                                       X--         .
   Paint                                C       | XXXX  .
   Clean                                C       |       X.
-----------------------------------------------------------------
XXXXX Detail Task       ##### Summary Task      ***** Baseline
xxXXX (Progress)        ==### (Progress)         >>>  Conflict
XXX-- (Slack)           ###-- (Slack)           ..XXX Resource delay
Progress shows Percent Achieved on Actual         M   Milestone
----------------- Scale: 60 minutes per character --------------
TIME LINE Gantt Chart Report, Strip 1
```

Fig. 1.7. An example Time Line Gantt chart.

The list of tasks shown on the left side of the screen gives you task names. You control which additional information you want to show. Figure 1.7 shows the first resource allocated to the task and a status flag of **C** if the task is on the critical path. The task bars, which are made up of **X**s indicate how long the task takes. In figure 1.7, each **X** represents an hour, but this might be different on another Gantt chart. Time Line provides a legend at the bottom of the chart. (Right now this information won't make a lot of sense if you're not familiar with Time Line, but in a few chapters, you'll understand all of this.)

The other valuable feature of Time Line Gantt charts is that they show slack time for tasks with a dashed line drawn from the end of the bar, which represents the early finish date or time to the late finish date or time. In figure 1.7, for example, because the plug, buy, and tape tasks all contain slack, you see a dashed line showing the slack time.

Chapters 3 and 4 examine how to create Gantt charts in more detail.

Using Time Line To Manage Resources

Time Line also provides screens and reports that allow you to manage project resources. To verify that you have remembered to allocate resources to each of the tasks making up a project, you can print an Assignment Report (see fig. 1.8).

```
Schedule Name  :
Responsible    :
As-of Date     : 25-Apr-90  8:00a       Schedule File :


                                     Resource        Total
Task Name                            Name            Hours
------------------------------------ ----------      ------------
Wash                                 Ladder             3
                                     Me                 3
                                     My friend          3

Plug                                 Me                 1
                                     Ladder             1

Tape                                 My friend          1

Buy                                  Me                 1

Paint                                Me                 4
                                     My friend          4
                                     Ladder             4
                                     Brushes            4

Clean                                Me                 1
```

Fig. 1.8. *The Assignment Report shows the resources allocated to a task.*

This report shows you the resource allocations you have made for each task. If tasks need resource allocations, the tasks should appear on this report. If they don't, you know you have additional allocations to make.

To verify that you haven't overallocated a resource, you can print a histogram, which plots use of a resource in a bar chart. By comparing allocated resources with the actual resources available, you can ascertain whether you're planning to use more of a resource—a person or some piece of equipment—than is available.

Figure 1.9 shows an example of a histogram. The pound symbols show how much of a resource is allocated to a task. The vertical axis of the histogram is represented by the numbers to the right of each task name. The actual resources allocated is shown by bars made up of pound symbols. Each pound symbol (#) represents one-half unit of the resource on the vertical time scale and one hour of the project on the horizontal time scale. So if the pound symbol bars show more resource being used than exists, you know you've allocated more of a resource than exists. The resource named "Me", for example, shows three full units being allocated for the first hour of the project—which means you've scheduled yourself for more work than you can perform.

```
Schedule Name  :
Responsible    :
As-of Date     : 25-Apr-90  8:00a         Schedule File :


                90
                Apr
                25        26
Brushes      1   .   ####
           0.5.     ####
             0   --------

Ladder       2   #
           1.5#
             1   #######
           0.5#######
             0   --------

Me           3   #
           2.5#
             2   #
           1.5#
             1   ########
           0.5########
             0   --------

My friend    2   #
           1.5#
             1   #######
           0.5#######
             0   --------

TIME LINE Histogram Report showing Total Work Hours / Max. Level
```

Fig. 1.9. An example of a Time Line histogram.

Chapter 5 examines in more detail the steps for identifying and allocating project resources.

Using Time Line To Monitor a Project

The fourth and final component of project management is monitoring project time, cost, and resources by comparing what you planned to use with what you actually use. Time Line allows you to collect a complete set of planned and actual project time, cost, and resources information. You should be able to monitor carefully any of the three factors.

Most of the figures shown earlier provide methods of monitoring project time, cost, and resources by letting you also include actual time, resource, or cost data on a report along side the planned time, resource, or cost data.

Chapter 6 describes in detail the steps for doing all of this.

Chapter Summary

This chapter described what a project is and identified the four components of project management: organizing the pieces that make up a project; showing the timing of the project tasks; identifying and allocating project resources; and monitoring project time, cost, and resources. This chapter also described how you can use Time Line to help with each of these four components.

Chapter 2, "Installing and Starting Time Line," examines the next step: installing Time Line on your computer.

2

Installing and Starting Time Line

Using your computer to better manage important projects isn't difficult. You will need to take a few preliminary steps, however. Specifically, you will need to install the Time Line software, learn a few basics about selecting menu options and filling screen fields, and provide some information to Time Line about the monitor you're using and about any printer or plotter you will use to produce reports.

This chapter examines each of these prerequisite steps. First, you will work through the steps of installing Time Line on your system. Then you will learn the basics of selecting menu options and entering information on the screen. Finally, you will learn about the procedures for making the system settings.

Installing Time Line

To install Time Line, you must meet the following minimum hardware requirements:

1. IBM XT, AT, PS/2 or compatible
2. 640K of memory
3. Hard disk with at least 6 megabytes of free space and one 5.25-inch or 3.5-inch floppy drive
4. MS-DOS or PC DOS Version 3.0 or above
5. Monochrome or color monitor

Part I: Covering the Basics

To install Time Line on your hard disk, do the following:

1. Turn on your computer and monitor; then make sure that your system has the correct date and time set. (Type date at the C:\> prompt to reset the date, if necessary. Type time at the C:\> prompt to reset the time. On many DOS systems, date and time are displayed automatically as part of the startup procedure.) You will need at least 512K of free, or available, memory to install and later run Time Line. You can check your available memory by typing chkdsk at the C:\> prompt (see fig. 2.1). If you don't have the necessary available memory, unload any memory resident programs like Sidekick or PC Tools Deluxe that use up your computer's memory.

```
C:\>chkdsk

 31344640 bytes total disk space
    55296 bytes in 3 hidden files
    92160 bytes in 38 directories
 18710528 bytes in 1293 user files
 12486656 bytes available on disk

   655360 bytes total memory
   536912 bytes free

C:\>
```

Fig. 2.1. Verify that you have 512K of available memory with the DOS CHKDSK command.

2. Insert the Time Line disk labeled #1 Install Disk in the floppy drive and type a:install at the C:\> prompt. The installation program briefly displays the words Time Line on your screen and then the Welcome screen shown in fig. 2.2 appears. The Welcome screen tells you that the installation program will install Time Line 4.0 on your system, ask a series of questions about your computer and the way you will use Time Line, and copy the program files from the floppy disks to your hard disk. Press F10 to continue.

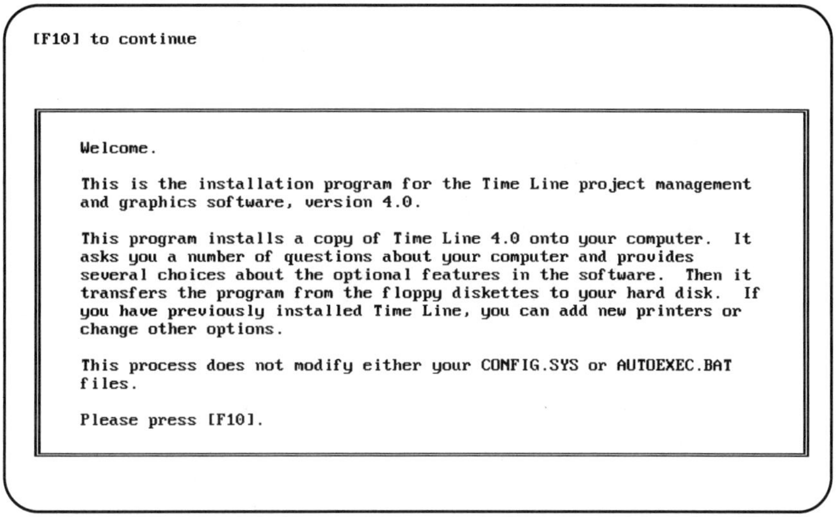

Chapter 2: Installing and Starting Time Line **31**

```
[F10] to continue


    ┌──────────────────────────────────────────────────────────────┐
    │ Welcome.                                                     │
    │                                                              │
    │ This is the installation program for the Time Line project management
    │ and graphics software, version 4.0.                          │
    │                                                              │
    │ This program installs a copy of Time Line 4.0 onto your computer.  It
    │ asks you a number of questions about your computer and provides
    │ several choices about the optional features in the software.  Then it
    │ transfers the program from the floppy diskettes to your hard disk.  If
    │ you have previously installed Time Line, you can add new printers or
    │ change other options.                                        │
    │                                                              │
    │ This process does not modify either your CONFIG.SYS or AUTOEXEC.BAT
    │ files.                                                       │
    │                                                              │
    │ Please press [F10].                                          │
    └──────────────────────────────────────────────────────────────┘
```

Fig. 2.2. The Welcome screen.

   3. The Install program alerts you that the installation process will take from 10 to 25 minutes, depending on the speed of your computer, and that you that you can stop the installation at any time by pressing ESC (see fig. 2.3). Press F10 to continue.

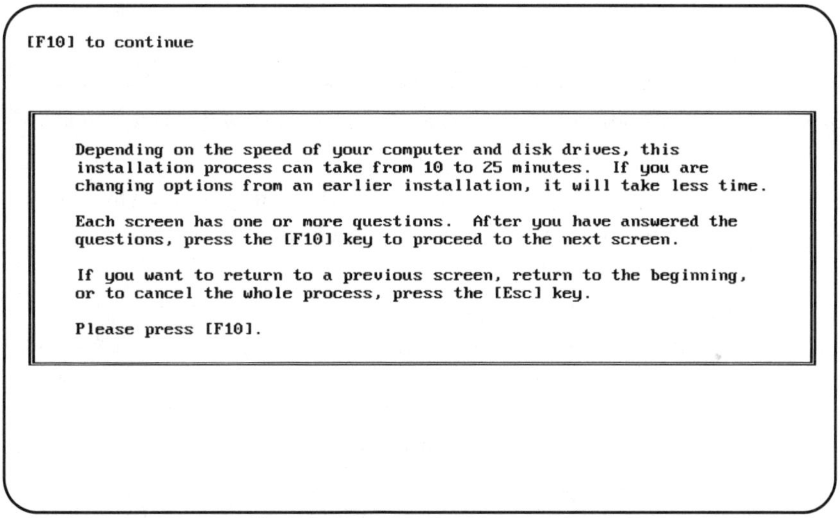

```
[F10] to continue


    ┌──────────────────────────────────────────────────────────────┐
    │ Depending on the speed of your computer and disk drives, this
    │ installation process can take from 10 to 25 minutes.  If you are
    │ changing options from an earlier installation, it will take less time.
    │                                                              │
    │ Each screen has one or more questions.  After you have answered the
    │ questions, press the [F10] key to proceed to the next screen.
    │                                                              │
    │ If you want to return to a previous screen, return to the beginning,
    │ or to cancel the whole process, press the [Esc] key.         │
    │                                                              │
    │ Please press [F10].                                          │
    └──────────────────────────────────────────────────────────────┘
```

Fig. 2.3. Install alerts you the installation will take from 10 to 25 minutes.

Part I: Covering the Basics

4. The Install program asks whether you are installing Time Line 4.0 for the first time or changing options you set during a previous installation (see fig. 2.4).

   Highlight the words First Time using the right and left arrow keys if Time Line 4.0 isn't already installed on your computer or you want to add yourself as a user to an existing LAN installation of Time Line 4.0.

   Highlight the words Change Options if Time Line 4.0 is already installed but you want to change the printer or graphics output device.

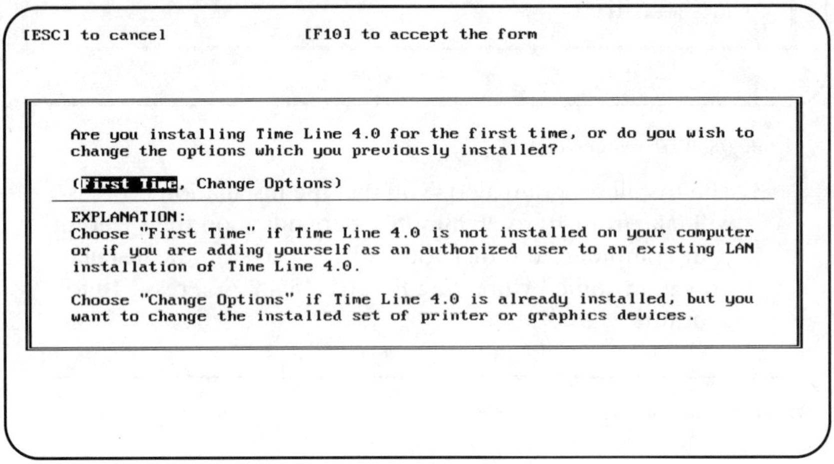

```
[ESC] to cancel              [F10] to accept the form




    Are you installing Time Line 4.0 for the first time, or do you wish to
    change the options which you previously installed?

    (First Time, Change Options)

    EXPLANATION:
    Choose "First Time" if Time Line 4.0 is not installed on your computer
    or if you are adding yourself as an authorized user to an existing LAN
    installation of Time Line 4.0.

    Choose "Change Options" if Time Line 4.0 is already installed, but you
    want to change the installed set of printer or graphics devices.
```

Fig. 2.4. Install asks whether you are installing Time Line 4.0 for the first time or changing previous installation options.

   Press Enter or F10 when the correct installation description, First Time or Change Options, is highlighted and you're ready to continue.

5. The Install program asks whether you are installing Time Line 4.0 as a single user on your hard disk or subdirectory on a network, if you are installing Time Line 4.0 on a local area network (LAN), or if you are adding a user to the list of authorized users on an existing network version of Time Line 4.0 (see fig. 2.5).

   Highlight the words Own Use using the right and left arrow keys if Time Line 4.0 is to be installed for a single user.

   Highlight the words LAN Server if you are a network administrator installing Time Line 4.0 on the network.

Chapter 2: Installing and Starting Time Line **33**

Highlight the words Add User to LAN if Time Line is already installed on a network and you want to add an authorized user.

Press Enter or F10 when the correct selection, Own Use, LAN Server, or Add User to LAN, is highlighted and you're ready to continue.

```
[ESC] to cancel            [F10] to accept the form


  Are you installing Time Line onto a computer for your own use, onto a
  LAN server, or adding a user to a copy of Time Line installed on a LAN?

  (Own Use, LAN Server, Add User To LAN)

  EXPLANATION:
  Choose "Own Use" if you are a single user installing the program either
  onto your hard disk or onto your user area of a network.

  Choose "LAN Server" if you are a LAN Administrator installing the
  program onto a network server for shared use.

  Choose "Add User To LAN" if you want to add your name to a list of
  authorized users of an existing LAN version of Time Line 4.0.
```

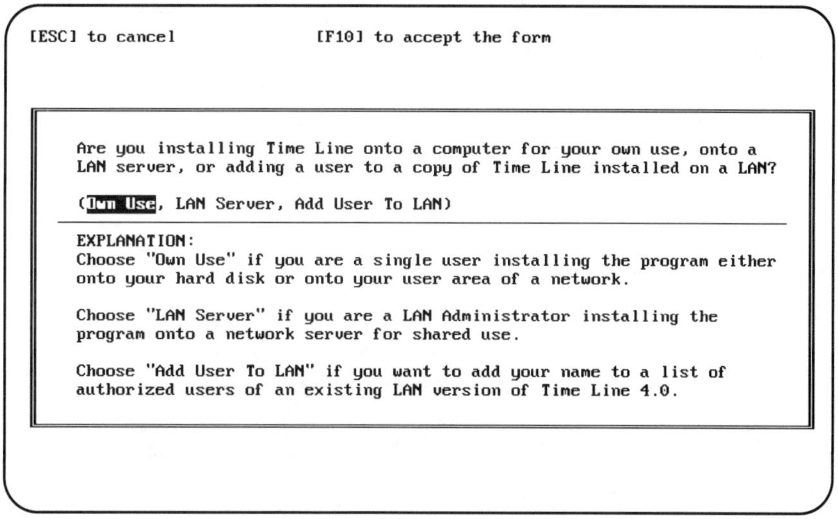

Fig. 2.5. Install asks whether you are installing Time Line 4.0 as a single user, on a LAN, or to add a user to a LAN.

6. The Install program asks for a user name (see fig. 2.6). You can use up to 28 characters including letters, numbers, and blanks, but use the shortest name possible. In a local area network, you will use this name to identify yourself when starting Time Line. Press Enter or F10 when you're ready to continue.

7. The Install program asks for the serial number of your copy of Time Line (see fig. 2.7). The ten-page booklet that came with your software, named *Getting Started*, shows the serial number on its first page. Enter the serial number using the number keys. If you make a mistake, use the arrow keys to move the curser so it rests on the correct number and type the correct number. Press Enter or F10 when you're ready to continue.

Part I: Covering the Basics

```
[ESC] to cancel              [F10] to accept the form



    Please enter a name.  If you are using Time Line on a LAN, you will
    use this name (or unique identifier) when starting Time Line.

    We recommend a unique short name.  Only A-Z, 0-9, and spaces are
    allowed in your Time Line user name.

    Your name: [STEVE NELSON           ]

    EXPLANATION:
    Your user name ensures that you can run Time Line 4.0 in a multiple-
    user environment.  Any copy of Time Line may be given multiple-user
    capabilities, so Install asks you for a user name even if you will be
    the only user of the software now.
```

Fig. 2.6. Install asks for a user name.

```
[ESC] to cancel              [F10] to accept the form



    Page One of your "Getting Started" booklet contains your unique serial
    number.

    Please enter that serial number here:

    A     B     C     D     E     F
    [30000-00000-00000-00000-00000-00000]

    EXPLANATION:
    Your copy of Time Line will be encoded with this number.
```

Fig. 2.7. Install asks for your serial number.

8. The Install program asks for directory in which the program files should be stored (see fig. 2.8). The default directory is C:\TL4; but you can change this simply by typing a different disk and directory. If the directory you enter doesn't already exist, the Install program creates it.

One piece of advice: You probably don't want to install Time Line 4.0 in the same directory as a previous version of Time Line—just so you can keep the two versions separate if you're planning to continue working with both for a while. Press F10 when you're ready to continue.

Note: Throughout the rest of this book, I will assume you named the Time Line 4.0 directory TL4 and that it resides on the C disk. If you use another name that better fits your requirements, remember to replace your disk and directory name wherever you see C:\TL4.

```
[ESC] to cancel              [F10] to accept the form



    The Time Line program files are stored in a directory on your hard
    disk.  The default drive and directory for Time Line 4.0 is C:\TL4.
    This is probably right for you.  However, if the software should be
    in a different drive and directory, you may change it.

    Drive and directory:

    [C:\TL4\                                            ]

    EXPLANATION:
    A default drive and directory are shown above.  If you want to change
    it, enter the directory name you have chosen and press [F10].  To
    accept the default, press [F10].

    The install program can create a new directory for you.
```

Fig. 2.8. *Install asks for the disk and directory in which the program files should be stored.*

9. The Install program asks which graphics devices—printers and plotters—you will use to produce Time Line 4.0 graphics reports (see fig. 2.9). Mark the graphics devices as either yes or no by using the up and down arrow keys to highlight the device and then the left and right arrow keys to high the appropriate answer, yes or no. Don't select graphics devices you won't ever use—or will use only infrequently. Each graphics device marked yes uses roughly 100 kilobytes of disk space for the device driver. Press F10 to continue.

Part I: Covering the Basics

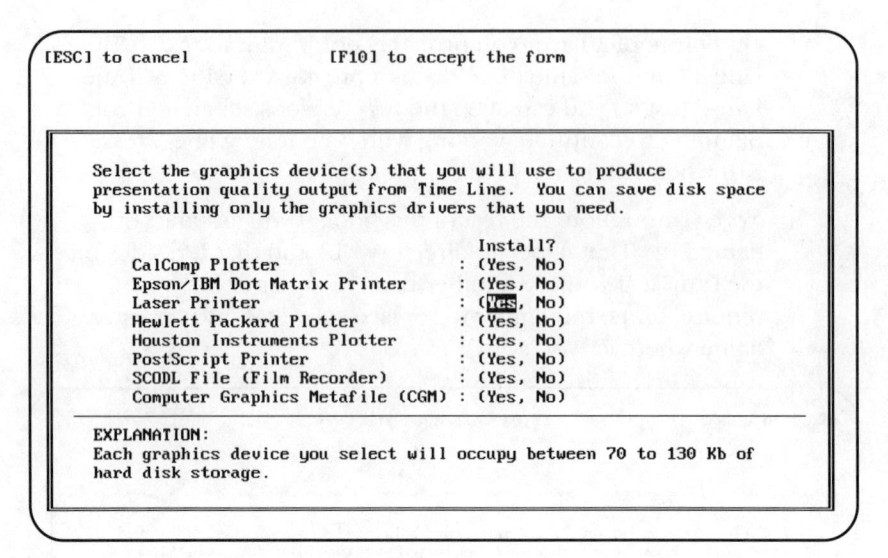

```
[ESC] to cancel            [F10] to accept the form

┌─────────────────────────────────────────────────────────────┐
│                                                             │
│   Select the graphics device(s) that you will use to produce│
│   presentation quality output from Time Line.  You can save disk space
│   by installing only the graphics drivers that you need.    │
│                                         Install?            │
│            CalComp Plotter            : (Yes, No)           │
│            Epson/IBM Dot Matrix Printer : (Yes, No)         │
│            Laser Printer              : (Yes, No)           │
│            Hewlett Packard Plotter    : (Yes, No)           │
│            Houston Instruments Plotter : (Yes, No)          │
│            PostScript Printer         : (Yes, No)           │
│            SCODL File (Film Recorder) : (Yes, No)           │
│            Computer Graphics Metafile (CGM) : (Yes, No)     │
│                                                             │
│   EXPLANATION:                                              │
│   Each graphics device you select will occupy between 70 to 130 Kb of
│   hard disk storage.                                        │
│                                                             │
└─────────────────────────────────────────────────────────────┘
```

Fig. 2.9. *Install asks which graphics devices you will use to produce Time Line 4.0 text reports.*

10. The Install program asks which printers you will use to produce text reports (see fig. 2.10). Mark the printer devices as either yes or no by using the up and down arrow keys to move the highlight to the answers for a device and then the left and right arrow keys to highlight the appropriate answer, yes or no. Press F10 to continue.

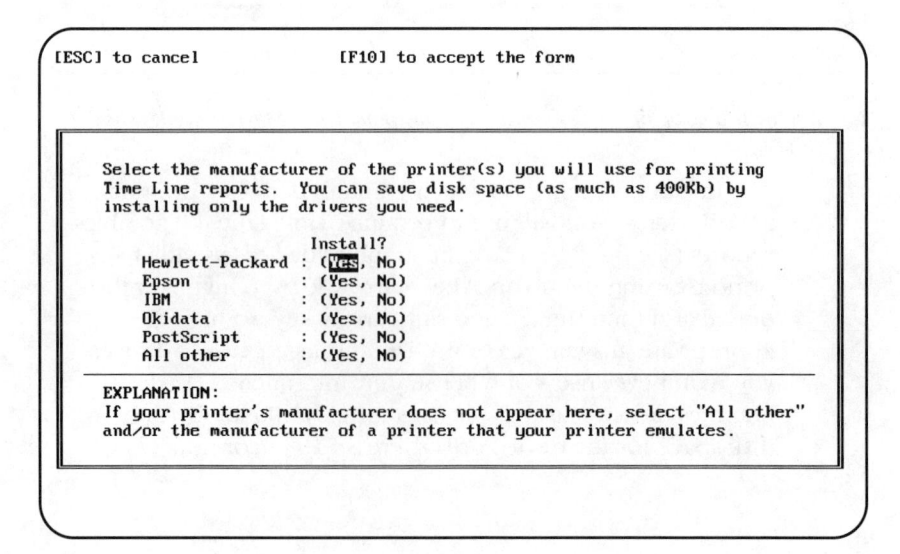

```
[ESC] to cancel            [F10] to accept the form

┌─────────────────────────────────────────────────────────────┐
│                                                             │
│   Select the manufacturer of the printer(s) you will use for printing
│   Time Line reports.  You can save disk space (as much as 400Kb) by
│   installing only the drivers you need.                     │
│                     Install?                                │
│       Hewlett-Packard : (Yes, No)                           │
│       Epson           : (Yes, No)                           │
│       IBM             : (Yes, No)                           │
│       Okidata         : (Yes, No)                           │
│       PostScript      : (Yes, No)                           │
│       All other       : (Yes, No)                           │
│                                                             │
│   EXPLANATION:                                              │
│   If your printer's manufacturer does not appear here, select "All other"
│   and/or the manufacturer of a printer that your printer emulates.
│                                                             │
└─────────────────────────────────────────────────────────────┘
```

Fig. 2.10. *Install asks which printers you will use to produce Time Line 4.0 text reports.*

Chapter 2: Installing and Starting Time Line 37

11. (Optional) The Install program asks whether your monitor is monochrome or color (see fig. 2.11). Highlight the words Monochrome or Color, using the right and left arrow keys. Press Enter or F10 when the correct monitor description is highlighted and you are ready to continue.

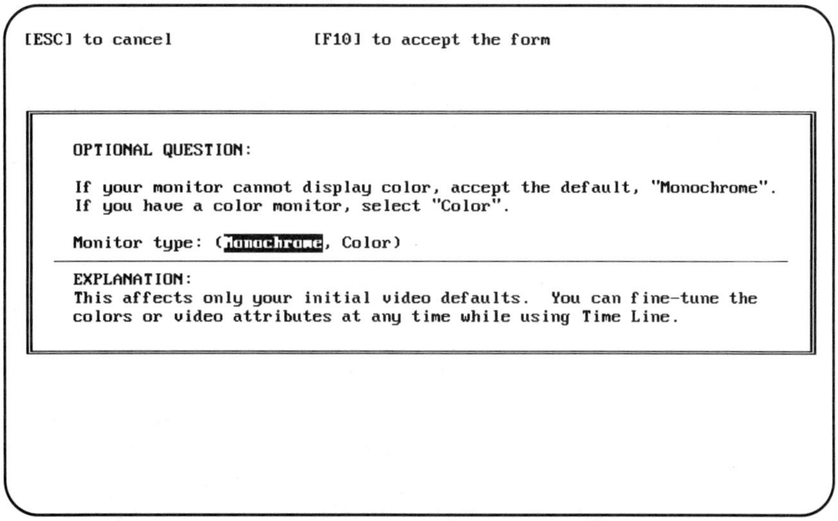

```
[ESC] to cancel              [F10] to accept the form


  ┌─────────────────────────────────────────────────────────────────┐
  │                                                                 │
  │  OPTIONAL QUESTION:                                             │
  │                                                                 │
  │  If your monitor cannot display color, accept the default, "Monochrome".
  │  If you have a color monitor, select "Color".                   │
  │                                                                 │
  │  Monitor type: (Monochrome, Color)                              │
  │  EXPLANATION:                                                   │
  │  This affects only your initial video defaults.  You can fine-tune the
  │  colors or video attributes at any time while using Time Line.  │
  │                                                                 │
  └─────────────────────────────────────────────────────────────────┘
```

Fig. 2.11. Install asks whether your monitor is monochrome or color.

12. (Optional) The Install program asks whether you want to compress the display (see fig. 2.12). Normally, a monitor displays 25 lines on a screen. With an EGA monitor, you can display 43 lines on a screen. And with a VGA monitor, you can display 50 lines on a screen. If your computer possesses either an EGA or a VGA monitor, select Compressed using the left and right arrow keys to see more information on the screen. (The figures throughout this book use the Normal — 25 lines per screen—setting because it's easier on your eyes.) Press Enter or F10 to continue.

13. The Install program tells you that it's ready to copy the appropriate program files to the Time Line 4.0 directory (see fig. 2.13). Highlight the word Proceed and press Enter to continue with the installation.

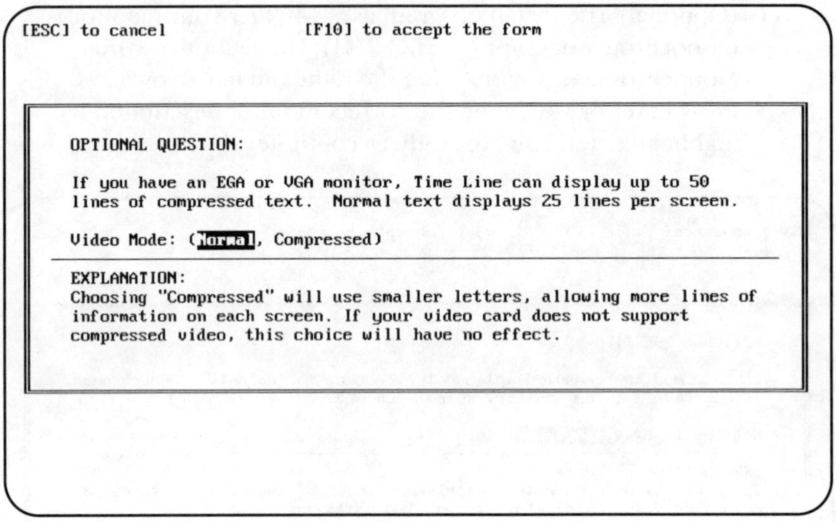

Part I: Covering the Basics

```
[ESC] to cancel            [F10] to accept the form


    OPTIONAL QUESTION:

    If you have an EGA or VGA monitor, Time Line can display up to 50
    lines of compressed text.  Normal text displays 25 lines per screen.

    Video Mode: (Normal, Compressed)

    EXPLANATION:
    Choosing "Compressed" will use smaller letters, allowing more lines of
    information on each screen. If your video card does not support
    compressed video, this choice will have no effect.
```

Fig. 2.12. Install asks whether you want to compress the display.

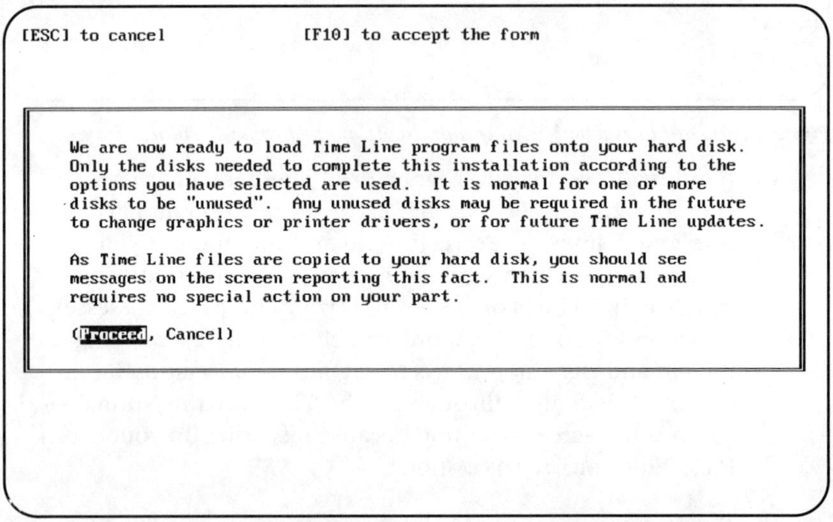

```
[ESC] to cancel            [F10] to accept the form


    We are now ready to load Time Line program files onto your hard disk.
    Only the disks needed to complete this installation according to the
    options you have selected are used.  It is normal for one or more
    disks to be "unused".  Any unused disks may be required in the future
    to change graphics or printer drivers, or for future Time Line updates.

    As Time Line files are copied to your hard disk, you should see
    messages on the screen reporting this fact.  This is normal and
    requires no special action on your part.

    (Proceed, Cancel)
```

Fig. 2.13. Install tells you that it's ready to copy the appropriate program files to the Time Line 4.0 directory.

14. The Install program briefly displays a one-line message on the screen that tells you it's creating and checking the directories it will use for Time Line 4.0. Next, the Install program displays the Time Line Install box which tells you to insert the diskette labeled Time Line Disk 2 (see fig. 2.14).

Chapter 2: Installing and Starting Time Line 39

Insert the diskette, and then select Proceed to continue with the installation. As the Install program copies the program files from the diskette, it will display messages on the screen about searching and exploding files. This is normal. Time Line 4.0 uses a file compression tool called PKUNZIP to store compressed versions of the program file which need to be uncompressed, or exploded, so that you can use them. When the Install program finishes copying one diskette to the hard disk, it prompts you for another. Depending on your installation settings, you may not be prompted to insert every disk.

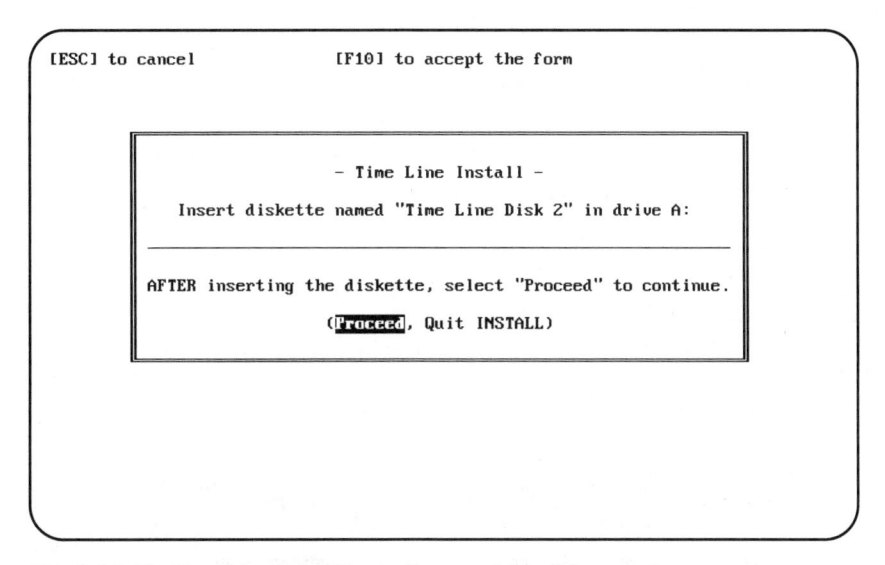

```
[ESC] to cancel          [F10] to accept the form




            ┌─────────────────────────────────────────────┐
            │           - Time Line Install -             │
            │  Insert diskette named "Time Line Disk 2" in drive A: │
            │                                             │
            │─────────────────────────────────────────────│
            │ AFTER inserting the diskette, select "Proceed" to continue. │
            │             (Proceed, Quit INSTALL)         │
            └─────────────────────────────────────────────┘
```

Fig. 2.14. The Time Line Install box tells you which diskette to insert next.

15. When the Install program finishes, it displays a message box which says Time Line version 4.0 installation is complete, gives the two ways you can use to start Time Line 4.0, and tells you to read the READ.ME file (see fig. 2.15). Press F10 to continue.

16. The Install program then displays a screen which reminds you to register your purchase so that you'll receive announcements of product updates and other related information (see fig. 2.16). This screen also gives you several phone numbers you can call if you have problems operating the software. Congratulations! You've installed Time Line 4.0. Press F10 to return to the DOS prompt. But before you start Time Line, take a few minutes to review the READ.ME file—something I'll describe how to do next.

Part I: Covering the Basics

```
[F10] to continue

Installation complete.

    ┌─────────────────────────────────────────────────────────────┐
    │                                                             │
    │   Time Line Version 4.0 is now installed.                   │
    │                                                             │
    │   To run Time Line, type "TL" after moving to your user     │
    │   directory, "C:\TL4\".                                     │
    │                                                             │
    │   If you are creating large schedules and do not require    │
    │   the Time Line macros feature, start Time Line by typing   │
    │   "TLNOMAC" (this saves approximately 18K of memory, which  │
    │   can be used to store additional schedule information.)    │
    │                                                             │
    │   A READ.ME file is in "C:\TL4\INSTALL\".                   │
    │   Use a text editor or the DOS type command to view this    │
    │   file.  It contains the latest information about Time      │
    │   Line 4.0 along with tips and tricks that may enhance      │
    │   your productivity.  You can also use the notepad          │
    │   feature of Time Line to import this file for viewing.     │
    │   For information on fine-tuning the performance of Time    │
    │   Line, see Appendix J in the Time Line manual.             │
    │                                                             │
    └─────────────────────────────────────────────────────────────┘
```

Fig. 2.15. The Installation complete screen.

```
[F10] to continue

Installation complete.

    ┌─────────────────────────────────────────────────────────────┐
    │                                                             │
    │   Don't forget to register your copy of Time Line in order  │
    │   to receive notification of upgrades, the Symantec         │
    │   newsletter, and important product information.            │
    │                                                             │
    │   Symantec offers training and consulting services, and     │
    │   unlimited technical support.  If you need technical       │
    │   assistance for Time Line and you are located within the   │
    │   USA or Canada, call 415/898-1919.                         │
    │   For Symantec Customer Service, call 408/253-9600.         │
    │                                                             │
    │   If you are located outside the USA and Canada, contact    │
    │   your local Symantec office or distributor for product     │
    │   support.  For information about the Symantec office or    │
    │   distributor in your area, call 408/253-9600.              │
    │                                                             │
    └─────────────────────────────────────────────────────────────┘
```

Fig. 2.16. Install reminds you to register your purchase and gives you several telephone numbers to call for technical support of the product.

Reviewing the READ.ME file

Software developers use the READ.ME file to give you important, late-breaking news on using a product. Typically, the READ.ME file contains information somebody realized only too late should have been included in the documentation, features that were added at the last minute, and notes on some problems the software developer's technical support people have identified. You really should review the READ.ME file. To do so, you can retrieve the file by using a word processing application like Microsoft Word or WordPerfect, by using the Notepads feature available in Time Line (described in Chapter 4), or by using the DOS TYPE command. The quickest way to review the READ.ME file is to use the DOS TYPE command.

To use the DOS TYPE command, enter the following line at the DOS prompt (C:\>):

TYPE C:\TL4\INSTALL\READ.ME

DOS then displays and scrolls through the entire READ.ME file on the screen. To stop the scrolling, press the Ctrl key and the S key simultaneously. To restart the scrolling, again press Ctrl-S. Getting used to the mechanics of using Ctrl-S to control scrolling takes a little time, but try using Ctrl-S a few times and you'll soon become proficient. (By the way, you can also use the DOS TYPE command and Ctrl-S to review the READ.ME files for other application programs.)

Starting Time Line Version 4.0

There are two ways to start Time Line 4.0: with the macros feature and without the macros feature. To start Time Line 4.0 so that you can use the macros feature, move to C:\TL4 by typing CD TL4 at the C:\> prompt. Then type TL to start Time Line 4.0. The program takes a few seconds to load, and then you see the starting Time Line 4.0 screen (see fig. 2.17).

To start Time Line 4.0 without the macros feature—which, at this point, is probably what you want to do—move to TL4 directory, and then type TLNOMAC to start the program. If you know you won't use the macro feature (described in Chapter 10, "Using the Time Line Utilities"), start Time Line without the macro feature because doing so saves memory—about 18K— you will then be able to use for project information.

Time Line displays the screen shown in figure 2.17 for a few seconds and then, if you haven't used Time Line before and saved a schedule, it displays the Getting Started screen shown in figure 2.18. (The next chapter explains the Getting Started screen in detail.) To exit from the Getting Started screen, press Q. Time Line next displays the Configure menu at the top of the screen, which is described next (see fig. 2.19).

Part I: Covering the Basics

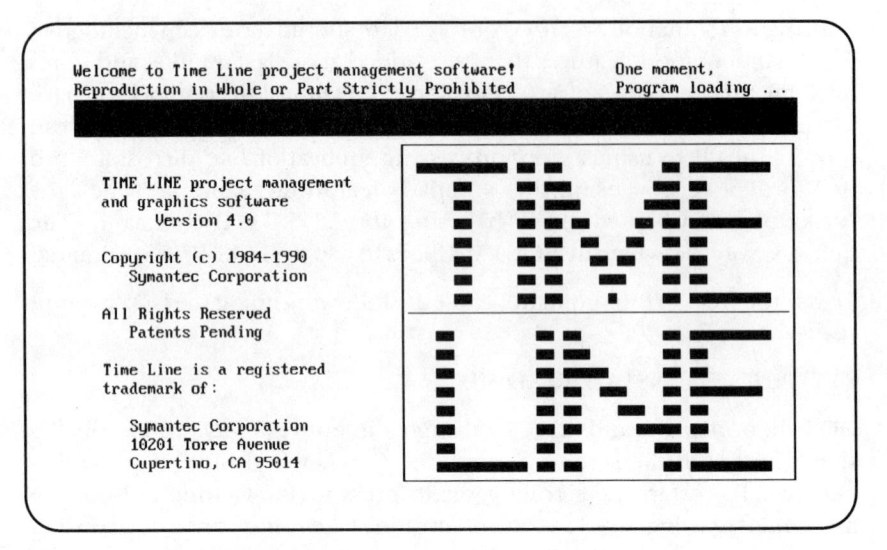

```
Welcome to Time Line project management software!      One moment,
Reproduction in Whole or Part Strictly Prohibited      Program loading ...


         TIME LINE project management
         and graphics software
                Version 4.0

         Copyright (c) 1984-1990
              Symantec Corporation

         All Rights Reserved
             Patents Pending

         Time Line is a registered
         trademark of:

              Symantec Corporation
              10201 Torre Avenue
              Cupertino, CA 95014
```

Fig. 2.17. The Time Line 4.0 screen.

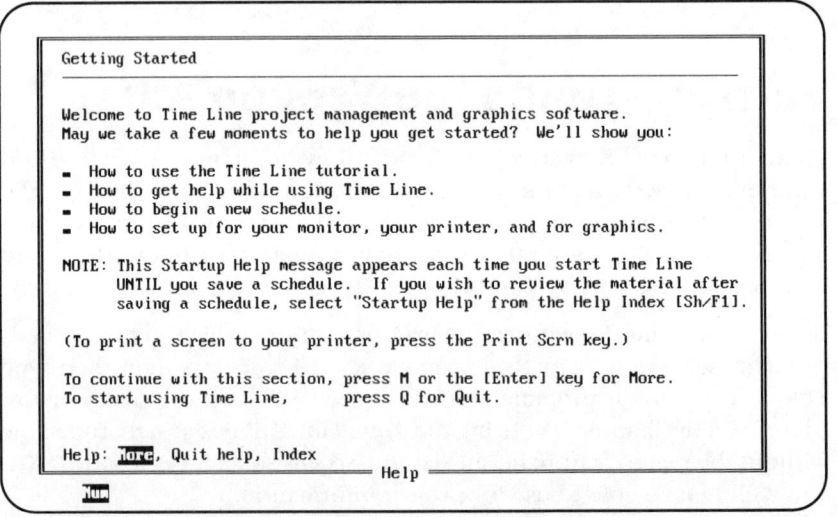

```
Getting Started

Welcome to Time Line project management and graphics software.
May we take a few moments to help you get started? We'll show you:

  ■ How to use the Time Line tutorial.
  ■ How to get help while using Time Line.
  ■ How to begin a new schedule.
  ■ How to set up for your monitor, your printer, and for graphics.

NOTE: This Startup Help message appears each time you start Time Line
      UNTIL you save a schedule.  If you wish to review the material after
      saving a schedule, select "Startup Help" from the Help Index [Sh/F1].

(To print a screen to your printer, press the Print Scrn key.)

To continue with this section, press M or the [Enter] key for More.
To start using Time Line,        press Q for Quit.


Help: More, Quit help, Index
                                  Help
```

Fig. 2.18. Time Line displays the Getting Started screen after the copyright screen until you save a schedule.

Configuring Time Line for Your Computer

Even after you install Time Line, you will need to specifically describe your computer and the printers and plotters you will use. To do so, you use the

Chapter 2: Installing and Starting Time Line **43**

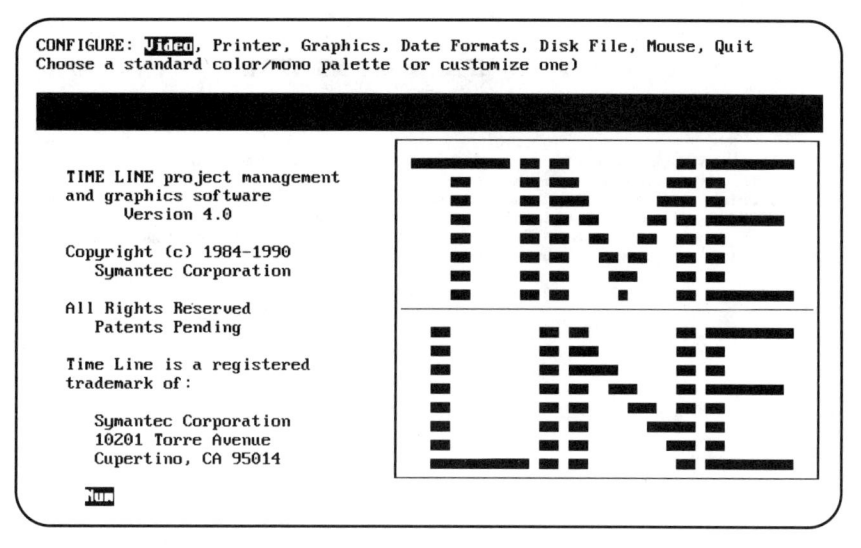

```
CONFIGURE: Video, Printer, Graphics, Date Formats, Disk File, Mouse, Quit
Choose a standard color/mono palette (or customize one)



        TIME LINE project management
        and graphics software
              Version 4.0

        Copyright (c) 1984-1990
            Symantec Corporation

        All Rights Reserved
            Patents Pending

        Time Line is a registered
        trademark of:

            Symantec Corporation
            10201 Torre Avenue
            Cupertino, CA 95014

        Num
```

Fig. 2.19. The Configure means at the top of the screen.

Configure menu options: Video, Printer, Graphics, Date Formats, Disk File, and Mouse.

Using Video To Describe Your Monitor

What Time Line refers to as the "video" component of your system is actually made up of two things: the video monitor that shows the Time Line screens and menus you work with, and the video controller card inside your computer that, in effect, operates the video monitor. It isn't difficult to do, but because there's quite a bit of variety in the video component of computers, you need to tell Time Line a little bit about your particular computer. To do so, follow these steps:

1. Select the Video option from the Configure menu. Time Line displays a screen which asks which kind of computer you have (see fig. 2.20).

2. Pick your computer from the list by using the arrow keys to highlight your computer and by then pressing Enter. If your computer isn't on the list, pick either IBM PC, AT, 'compatible,' or Other.

3. (Optional) The two last options on the list of computers—Customize and Video Options—let you change the appearance of the Time Line screens. You shouldn't need to use

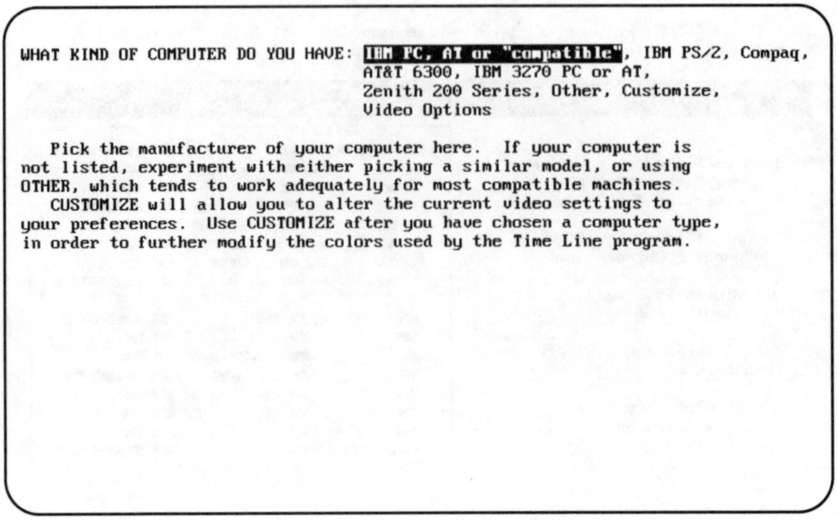

Part I: Covering the Basics

```
WHAT KIND OF COMPUTER DO YOU HAVE: IBM PC, AT or "compatible", IBM PS/2, Compaq,
                                    AT&T 6300, IBM 3270 PC or AT,
                                    Zenith 200 Series, Other, Customize,
                                    Video Options

   Pick the manufacturer of your computer here. If your computer is
not listed, experiment with either picking a similar model, or using
OTHER, which tends to work adequately for most compatible machines.
   CUSTOMIZE will allow you to alter the current video settings to
your preferences. Use CUSTOMIZE after you have chosen a computer type,
in order to further modify the colors used by the Time Line program.
```

Fig. 2.20. The Configure Video screen.

these two options, and I won't spend a lot of time describing them here. But just for your information, Customize displays submenus which list the various pieces of each screen—cursors, text, messages, and so forth—and which let you choose which color the indicated piece of the screen should appear in. (I won't describe the Customize option more than that here: You can have more fun experimenting with the colors than reading about them anyway.)

The Video Options Menu Option simply asks three questions. The first question is Would you prefer fast or clean? The default answer is fast, but if you have video display problems, such as a screen not appearing or looking funny when it does, try the clean setting. The second video options question is Reprogram the 6845 video controller? The default answer is no, but if you want Time Line to display brighter colors, try selecting yes. (By the way, some other software programs won't work or won't work well if you reprogram the video controller). The third video options question is whether Time Line should attempt whenever it's in graphics preview mode to Automatically detect the video adapter? The default answer is yes. If you mark no, Time Line uses whatever video adapter you specify during the configuration. (Chapter 8, "Printing Reports," describes the graphic preview mode.)

Chapter 2: Installing and Starting Time Line **45**

4. Time Line next displays a screen which asks what kind of monitor you have: Monochrome, Color, or Other (see fig. 2.21). Pick a monitor type by using the arrow keys to highlight the type of monitor you have and by then pressing Enter. Most probably, you will select either Monochrome or Color. You shouldn't need to pick Other unless you have an IBM 3270 monitor, a gas plasma monitor, or a liquid crystal display monitor. The Other option simply lists these additional choices.

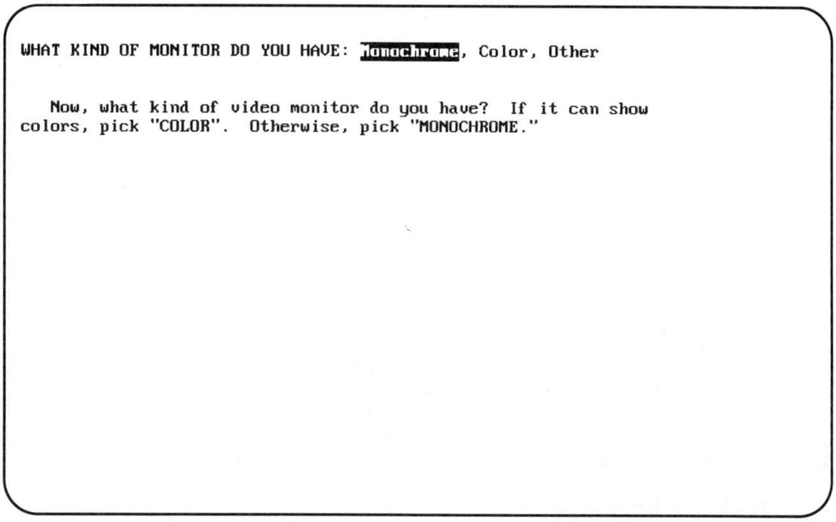

```
WHAT KIND OF MONITOR DO YOU HAVE: Monochrome, Color, Other

  Now, what kind of video monitor do you have?  If it can show
colors, pick "COLOR".  Otherwise, pick "MONOCHROME."
```

Fig. 2.21. The What Kind of Monitor screen.

5. Time Line displays a screen which asks you to identify your video controller—which is the same thing as your video card (see fig. 2.22). Use the arrow keys to highlight your selection and then press Enter. If your monitor is monochrome, your video controller card is either Monochrome, Hercules Monographics, or CGA—probably Monochrome. If your monitor is color, the video controller card is either CGA, EGA, VGA, or MCGA and probably is either EGA or VGA. If you don't know that kind of video controller card your computer uses, refer to the documentation that came with the computer, or experiment with different video controller settings.

6. Time Line displays a message box which asks if you've finished setting up, or describing, your computer's video display. Use the arrow keys to highlight yes and then press Enter. If you instead want to repeat the video configuration

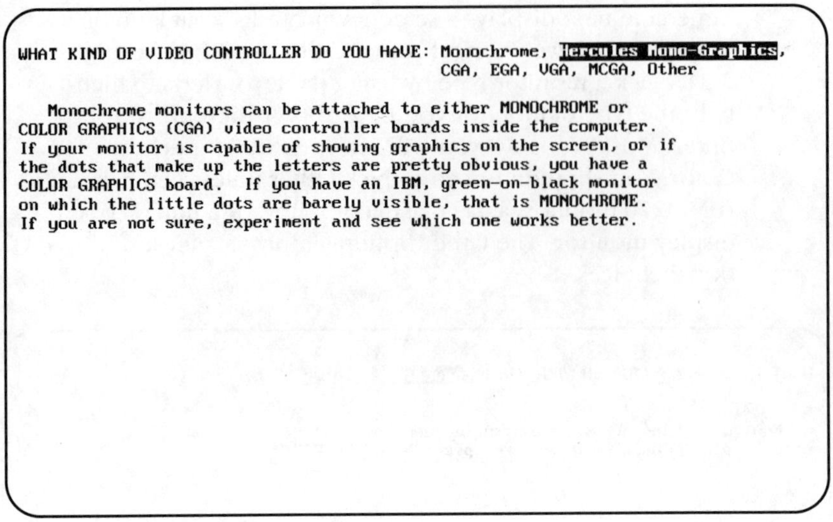

Part I: Covering the Basics

```
WHAT KIND OF VIDEO CONTROLLER DO YOU HAVE: Monochrome, Hercules Mono-Graphics,
                                            CGA, EGA, VGA, MCGA, Other

    Monochrome monitors can be attached to either MONOCHROME or
 COLOR GRAPHICS (CGA) video controller boards inside the computer.
 If your monitor is capable of showing graphics on the screen, or if
 the dots that make up the letters are pretty obvious, you have a
 COLOR GRAPHICS board.  If you have an IBM, green-on-black monitor
 on which the little dots are barely visible, that is MONOCHROME.
 If you are not sure, experiment and see which one works better.
```

Fig. 2.22. The What Kind of Video Controller screen.

process, answer no. Time Line returns you to the screen which asks which kind of computer you have. (Refer to step 1 and see figure 2.20.)

Using Printer To Describe Your Report Printer

During the installation of Time Line, you identify which printer you will ultimately use to print text reports. Time Line also needs to know a few other things, however, such as how your printer connects to your computer and what size and style of characters the printer should use. To do so, follow these steps:

1. Select Printer from the Configure menu. Time Line displays the Printer Devices list box (see fig. 2.23). The printer devices listed will conform to whatever you selected during the installation.

2. Use the up- and down-arrow keys to mark the printer and printer setting you will use for the text reports. If the list of printer devices takes up more than one box, you can use the PgUp and PgDn keys to see other parts of the list. Only the print options for the printer you selected appear. If you have questions about the various options, refer to the manual that

Chapter 2: Installing and Starting Time Line

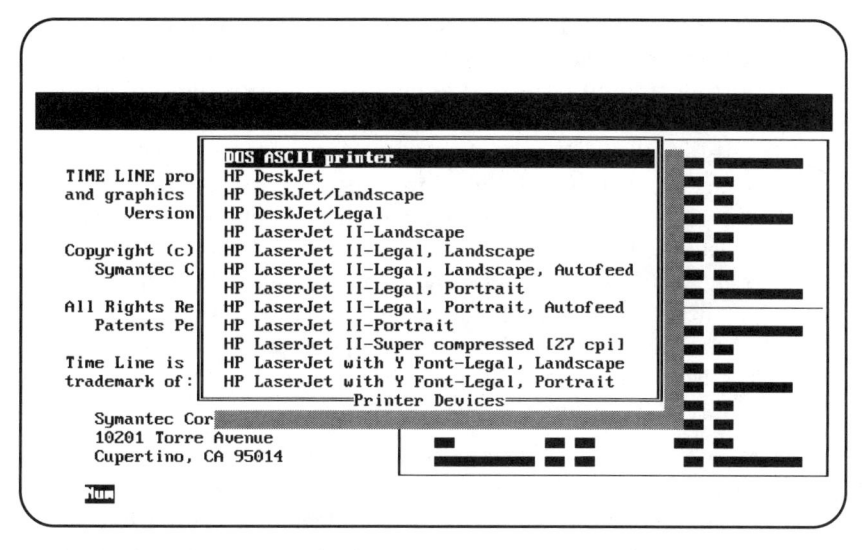

Fig. 2.23. The Printer Devices list box.

came with your printer. After you mark the printer setting, press Enter. Time Line displays the Setup Communications Form like that shown in figure 2.24. You use the Setup Communications Form screen to describe how your printer connects to your computer. The Setup Communications Form looks more complicated than it is. Don't let it worry you.

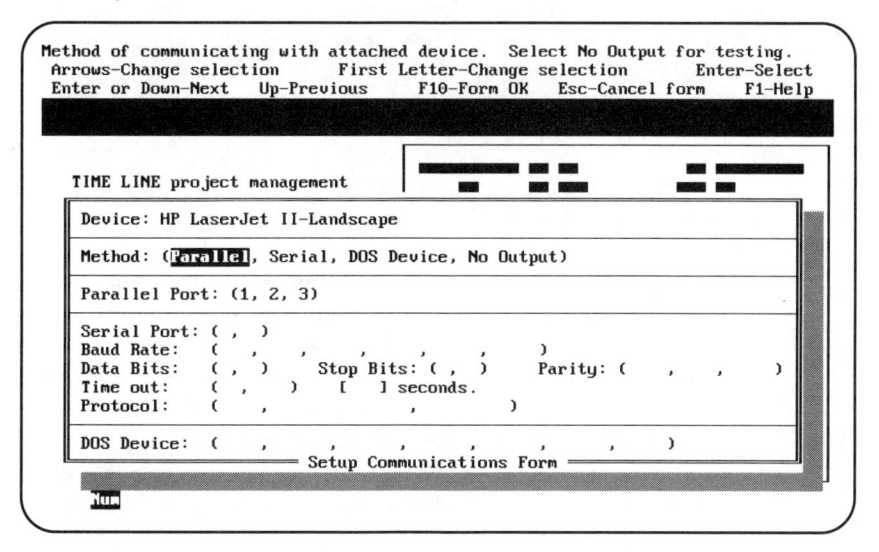

Fig. 2.24. The Setup Communications Form screen.

3. Use the up- and down-arrow keys to mark the Method setting. Then use the right- and left-arrow keys to mark the port, or communication channel, that connects the printer to the computer, or type the first letter of the setting you want to select. If you don't already know which port you will be using, follow the cable that connects the printer to the computer. The socket into which the cable plugs will usually be labeled Parallel 1, Parallel 2, Serial 1, or Serial 2. If the socket is labeled Parallel-something, you mark the method as Parallel. And if the socket is labeled Serial-something, you mark Serial. The DOS Device setting is usually for networks. The No Output setting causes Time Line not to send the report to the printer.

Note: You don't need to understand the difference between parallel and serial communications, but since we're on the subject you might want to know a little about parallel and serial communications. These terms refer to the way the data is sent from the computer to the printer; with parallel communications, eight bits of data can be sent at one time, while with serial communications, only one bit of data can be sent at a time. Parallel communications are faster, so if you have a choice with your printer, go with the parallel method.

4. (Optional). If you marked the Method as parallel, use the up- and down-arrow keys to move the curser to the Parallel setting. Then use the right- and left-arrow keys to indicate which parallel port is used: 1, 2, or 3; or type the number of the port. If you followed the printer cable to the socket it plugs into on the back of your computer, you should know the actual port number.

5. (Optional). If you marked the Method as serial, use the up- and down-arrow keys to move the curser to the Serial port setting and then mark which serial port is used: 1 or 2. There are also a variety of other fields—data bits, stop bits, parity, time out, seconds, and protocol—you use to describe the rules and conventions that the printer and computer should use for serial communications. I'm not going to spend time here describing the significance and history of each of these settings because you don't need to know anything about them to correctly set them. All you need to know is what your printer expects or wants—which you can get from the printer's user manual. So find the printer user's manual and look up the section that describes how to connect the

Chapter 2: Installing and Starting Time Line **49**

printer. What you want to find is the paragraph that gives you the precise serial communication settings, or protocol. When you've found the settings, use the arrow keys to mark the appropriate serial settings.

6. (Optional). If you marked the Method as DOS Device, use the up- and down-arrow keys to move the curser to the DOS Device setting and then mark which DOS port is used: PRN, LPT1, LPT2, LPT3, COM1, COM2, or AUX.

7. Press F10 to save the printer configuration, or description.

Using Graphics To Describe Your Graphics Printer or Plotter

You also identify the printer or plotter you will use to print text reports. To do so, follow these steps:

1. Select Graphics from the Configure menu. Time Line displays the Graphics Devices list box (see fig. 2.25).

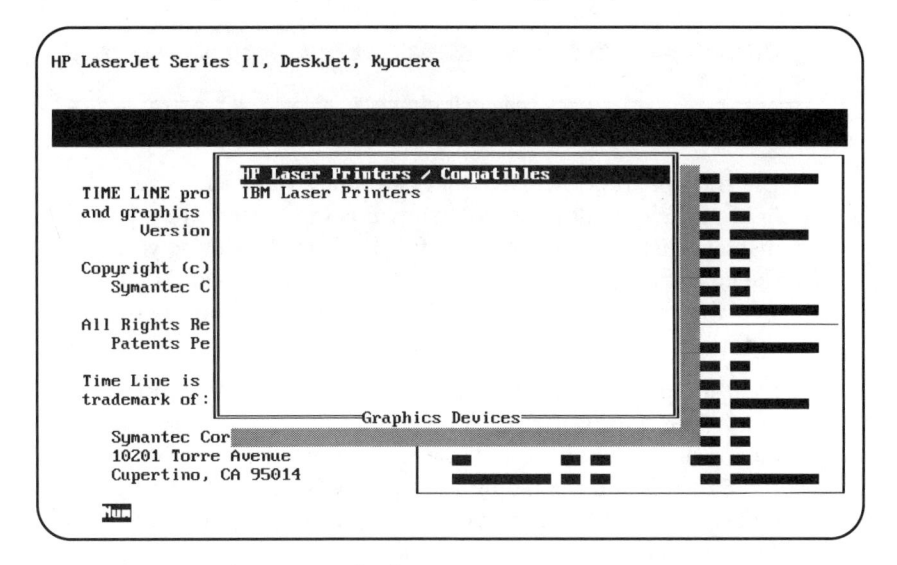

```
HP LaserJet Series II, DeskJet, Kyocera




                              ┌─HP Laser Printers / Compatibles─┐
            TIME LINE pro     │ IBM Laser Printers              │
            and graphics      │                                 │
                  Version     │                                 │
                              │                                 │
            Copyright (c)     │                                 │
               Symantec C     │                                 │
                              │                                 │
            All Rights Re     │                                 │
              Patents Pe      │                                 │
                              │                                 │
            Time Line is      │                                 │
            trademark of:     │                                 │
                              └──────Graphics Devices───────────┘
            Symantec Cor
            10201 Torre Avenue
            Cupertino, CA 95014

  Num
```

Fig. 2.25. The Graphics Devices list box.

2. Just as for describing your report printer, use the up- and down-arrow keys to mark the printer or plotter. Only the printers and plotters you selected appear. After you mark the printer or plotter, press Enter. Time Line displays the Graphics Setup Form like that shown in figure 2.26. You use the

Graphics Setup Form screen to describe such things as the size of paper used for graphics reports, how the graphics report should be arranged on a page, and which resolution, or output quality, you want. (*Note:* The screen you see may vary slightly from that shown in figure 2.26. Time Line collects information specific to the graphics device.)

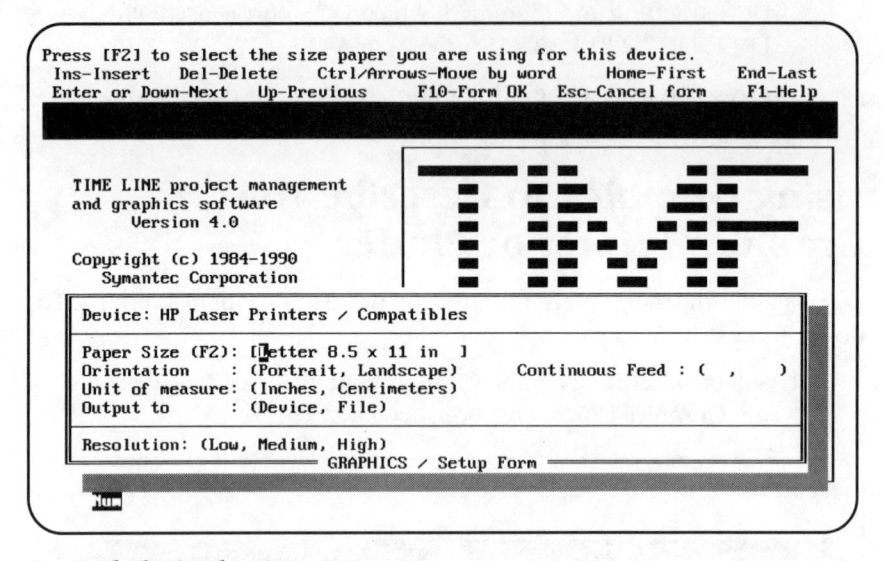

```
Press [F2] to select the size paper you are using for this device.
  Ins-Insert    Del-Delete    Ctrl/Arrows-Move by word    Home-First    End-Last
  Enter or Down-Next    Up-Previous    F10-Form OK    Esc-Cancel form    F1-Help


     TIME LINE project management
     and graphics software
           Version 4.0

     Copyright (c) 1984-1990
         Symantec Corporation

    ┌─────────────────────────────────────────────────────────────────────┐
    │ Device: HP Laser Printers / Compatibles                             │
    │                                                                     │
    │ Paper Size (F2): [Letter 8.5 x 11 in ]                              │
    │ Orientation    : (Portrait, Landscape)    Continuous Feed : ( , )   │
    │ Unit of measure: (Inches, Centimeters)                              │
    │ Output to      : (Device, File)                                     │
    │                                                                     │
    │ Resolution: (Low, Medium, High)                                     │
    └══════════════════════ GRAPHICS / Setup Form ════════════════════════┘
     Num
```

***Fig. 2.26.** The Graphics Setup Form screen.*

3. Use the up- and down-arrow keys to mark the paper size field. If the default paper size shown isn't correct, press F2 to display a list of the paper sizes for the graphics device you selected during the installation. Then use the up- and down-arrow keys to mark the desired paper size and then press Enter.

4. Use the up- and down-arrow keys to mark the orientation field. Type P for portrait, and type L for landscape. *Portrait* means on an 8.5-by-11-inch piece of paper, the paper's width is 8.5 inches and the height is 11 inches. *Landscape* means that on an 8.5-by-11-inch piece of paper, the paper's width is 11 inches and the height is 8.5 inches.

5. Use the up- and down-arrow keys to mark the Unit of measure setting to calibrate the paper size settings. Then type I for inches, and type C for centimeters.

6. Use the up- and down-arrow keys to mark the Output To setting to indicate whether you want Time Line to generate a

Chapter 2: Installing and Starting Time Line   51

graphics report that will be printed or plotted or you want Time Line to generate a graphics file. Type D to print or plot the graphics report, and type F to create a graphics file.

7. Use the up- and down-arrow keys to mark the Resolution setting field. Resolution refers to the crispness and precision of the graphics reports that Time Line creates. Low resolution produces poorest output quality, but it takes the least time to create. High resolution produces the best output quality, but it takes the most time to create. Medium resolution is the default setting.

8. After you set the Resolution, press F10. Time Line displays the Setup Communications Form which you use to describe how your printer connects to your computer (refer to fig. 2.24).

9. Completing the Setup Communications Form for a graphics printer or plotter works the same way as completing the Form for a report printer. Use the up- and down-arrow keys to mark the Method setting. Then use the right- and left-arrow keys to mark the port, or communication channel, that connects the printer to the computer; or type the first letter of the setting you want to select.

10. If you marked the Method as parallel, use the up- and down-arrow keys to move the curser to the Parallel setting. Then use the right- and left-arrow keys to indicate which parallel port is used: 1, 2, or 3; or type the number of the port. If you followed the printer or plotter cable to the socket it plugs into on the back of your computer, you should know the actual port number.

11. If you marked the Method as serial, use the up- and down-arrow keys to move the curser to the Serial port setting and then mark which serial port is used: 1 or 2. There are also a variety of other fields—data bits, stop bits, parity, time out, seconds, and protocol—you use to describe the rules and conventions that the printer and computer should use for serial communications. Look up the section in the printer or plotter user's manual that describes how to connect the printer or plotter. What you want to find is the paragraph that gives you the precise serial communication settings, or protocol. Using the arrow keys, mark the appropriate serial settings.

12. If you marked the Method as DOS Device, use the up- and down-arrow keys to move the curser to the DOS Device setting and then mark which DOS port is used: PRN, LPT1, LPT2, LPT3, COM1, COM2, or AUX.

13. Press F10 to save the graphics printer or plotter configuration, or description.

Deciding on a Date Format

A basic part of Time Line, and of any project management system, is that it works with dates: The system collects dates, calculates dates, and monitors planned and actual dates. For this reason, Time Line gives you a choice of how it should display, or format, dates. To choose a date format:

1. Select Date Formats from the Configure menu. Time Line displays the Format box which gives examples of the six date formats (see fig. 2.27).

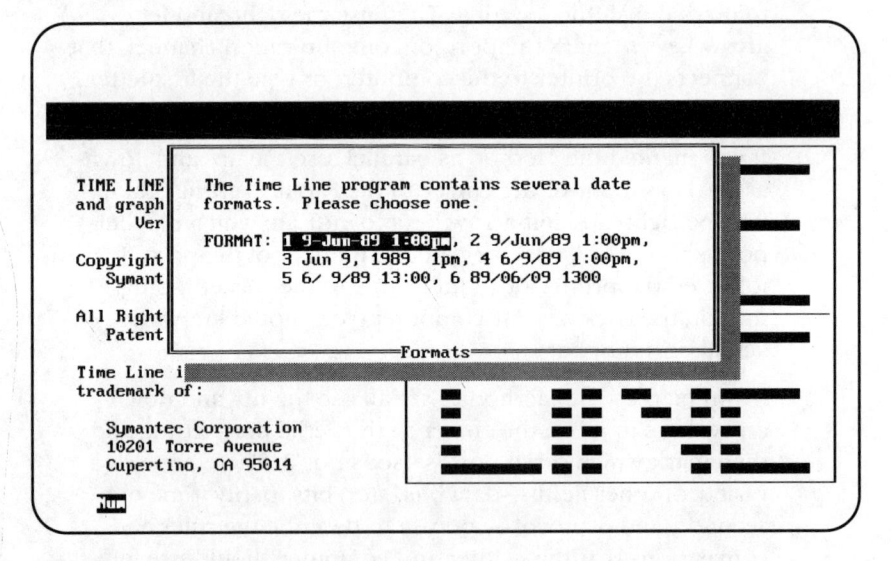

Fig. 2.27. The Format box.

2. Use the up- and down-arrow keys to mark one of the date formats, or type the number in front of the date format. There's nothing tricky here. Just pick the date style, or format, that you use for dates and, therefore, want Time Line to also use.

3. Press F10 or Enter to set the marked date format.

Deciding on a Disk File Format

Most people will work with the project management files that Time Line creates inside of Time Line. Project management files will be created, updated, and printed using Time Line. However, some users may want to use the files created by Time Line in other programs—typically so they can be printed or plotted using another computer or another software program. For these users, Time Line provides flexibility in the structure and characters used for the files. If you need this flexibility—and most users don't—follow these steps:

1. Select Disk File from the Configure menu. Time Line displays the File Formats box (see fig. 2.28).

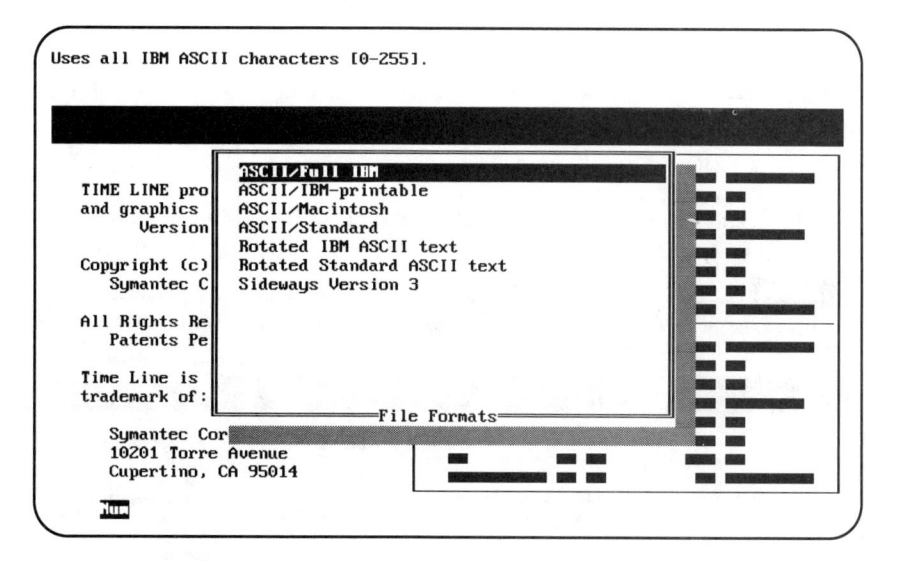

Fig. 2.28. The File Formats box.

2. Use the up- and down-arrow keys to mark one of the seven file formats, or structures.

3. Press F10 or Enter to set the marked format.

The default file format is ASCII/Full IBM which means Time Line uses the complete IBM extended character set when it created files. If you're unsure of the file format you want, mark ASCII/Full IBM. To determine that you want another file format, look at the requirements of whatever it is that will use the files you create with Time Line. ASCII/IBM printable creates files that use only characters that can be printed. ASCII/Macintosh creates files that can more easily be used by an Apple Macintosh. ASCII/Standard creates

Part I: Covering the Basics

files that only use characters in the standard ASCII character set. Rotated IBM ASCII text creates files using the full IBM character set that can more easily be printed using a sideways printing utility such as Sideways. Rotated Standard ASCII text creates files using the standard ASCII character set that can more easily be printed using a sideways printing utility. Sideways Version 3 creates file specifically for printing with version 3 of the Sideways utility.

Describing Your Mouse

If you are a mouse user, you should know that Time Line gives you control over a couple aspects of mouse operation: how slowly you can double-click, and how slow or fast Time Line will scroll with the mouse. By default, Time Line makes two default settings which are fine for most people. If you find, however, that you want to be able to double click, or scroll faster or slower, use the Mouse Configure option.

To use the Mouse option:

1. Select Mouse from the Configure menu. Time Line displays the Mouse Control Form screen (see fig. 2.29).

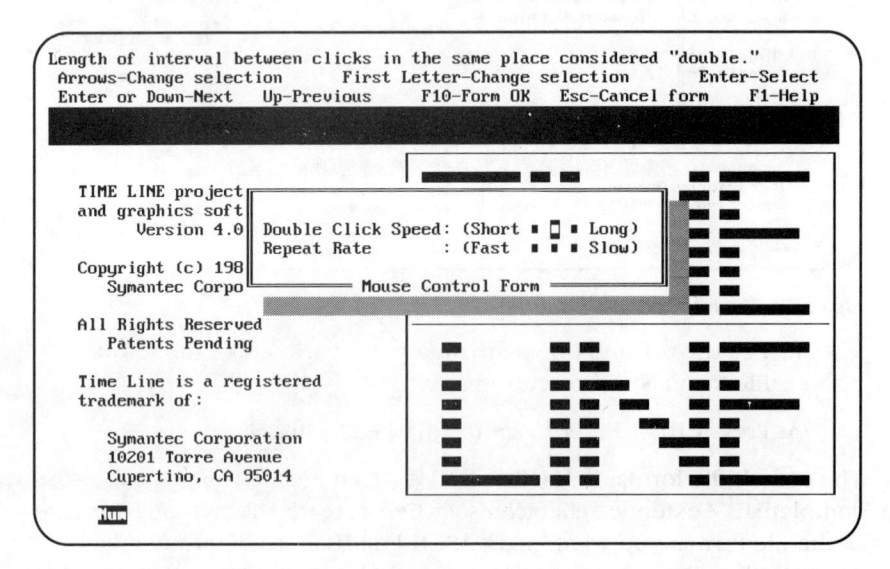

Fig. 2.29. The Mouse Control Form screen.

2. Use the up- and down-arrow keys to mark the Double Click setting. Then use the right- and left-arrow keys to indicate how slow or how fast two clicks on the same location need to

be to considered a double-click. (If you're new to a mouse, don't worry about this. You won't have already developed a speed and style with which you work the mouse.) The default double-click speed is set to the medium button.

3. Use the up- and down-arrow keys to mark the Repeat Rate box. Then use the right- and left-arrow keys to indicate how slow or how fast Time Line should scroll. The default repeat rate setting is for the fastest possible scrolling, but you can slow this down by selecting a button to the right of the Fast button.

4. Press F10 to set the marked mouse control settings.

Saving Your Options

After you finish defining the mouse control settings, Time Line next displays the main Time Line screen with the menu bar activated. (The *menu bar* is the list of options at the top of the screen.) To save all your configure options, you'll need to follow these steps:

1. Press F to access the File menu.

2. Press S to initiate a Save operation. Time Line will display the No Name box which indicates you haven't created and named a project schedule (see fig. 2.30).

3. To save the options, use the arrow keys to highlight options only and then press Enter.

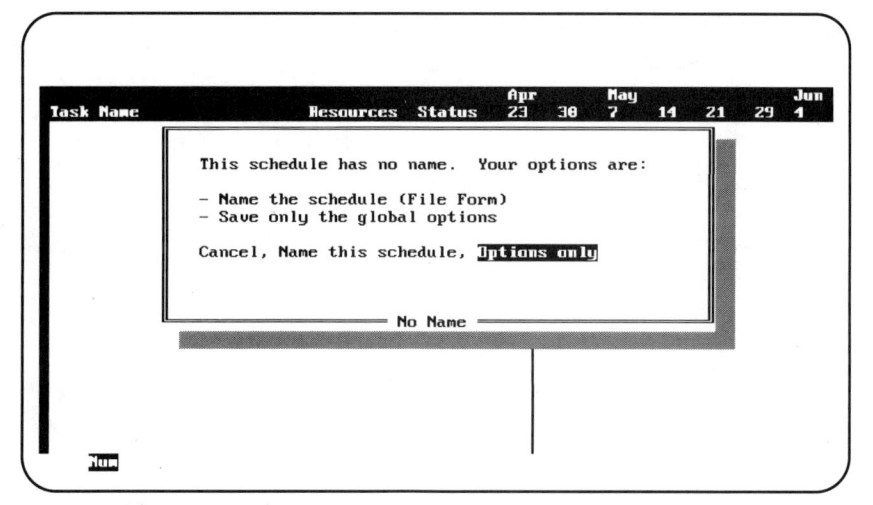

Fig. 2.30. The No Name box.

4. (Optional) To leave the Time Lime program, reactivate the menu bar by pressing / (slash) and then pressing Q to select the Quit program option. Time Line will ask you to confirm you want to leave, answer Yes.

Chapter Summary

This chapter described how to install, start, and configure Time Line 4.0. If you're ready to get started with Time Line, the next chapter, "Getting Started with Time Line," examines the steps to using Time Line to create and monitor a simple project. Chapter 3 also covers how to select menu options, fill and edit screen fields, and how to use the on-line help feature—things you'll need to know in order to get going on computer-based project management.

3

Getting Started with Time Line

Even if you're new to project management, you will find Time Line easy to use—once you learn the basics covered in this chapter. The chapter covers everything you need to know to begin using Time Line for simple project management: how to create a simple project, how to use several of the assist menu options, and how to print, save, and retrieve projects. After you read this chapter, you should be able to begin using Time Line productively. For those users who only need the basic project management functions, this chapter covers the core features you will most often use.

Creating a Simple Project

To begin, start Time Line. Because you haven't yet saved a project, Time Line will display the initial copyright notice screen and then the main Time Line screen with the menu bar showing, or activated. Figure 3.1 shows the main project creation screen.

Introducing a Sample Project

Suppose that you are in the business of building sailboats. Each sailboat represents a project, and each project takes roughly five steps. First, you build a fiberglass hull. After you complete the hull and it dries, you build bulkheads, install an engine, and build the deck and cockpit. After the bulkheads are finished, you can install the rigging.

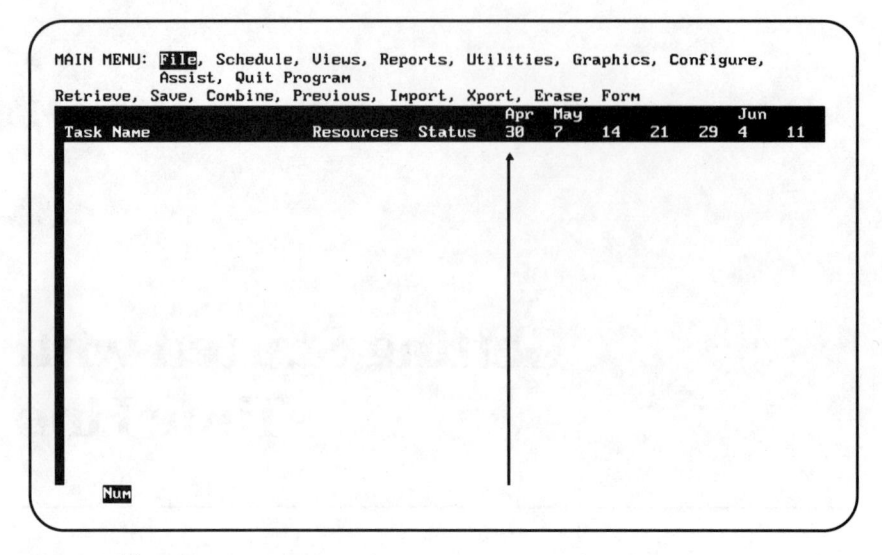

```
MAIN MENU: File, Schedule, Views, Reports, Utilities, Graphics, Configure,
           Assist, Quit Program
Retrieve, Save, Combine, Previous, Import, Xport, Erase, Form
                                          Apr  May                Jun
Task Name                Resources Status 30   7    14   21   29  4    11
```

Fig. 3.1. The project creation screen.

In a real boat-building business, of course, the task durations for the project of building a sailboat would depend on factors like the type of rigging, the size of the boat, and the size and type of engine. However, for purposes of this chapter, let's assume that laying the hull takes a week, that building the bulkheads takes four days, that installing the engine takes four hours, that laying the decks takes a week, and that both the interior and the rigging take three days each.

Your project, then, may be stated as a simple list of six tasks:

1. Lay hull—one week
2. Build bulkheads—four days
3. Install engine—four hours
4. Lay deck—one week
5. Finish interiors—three days
6. Rig—three days

Several dependencies exist in this scenario. First, before you can do anything else, you must lay the hull because you build the bulkheads inside it, install the engine in it, and lay the deck on top of it. A second dependency—perhaps not so clear—is that before you can rig the sailboat by adding winches and installing a mast, halyards, and the like, you need to complete the deck. Third, to finish the interiors, you must first build the bulkheads, install the engine, and lay the deck.

Note: This simple project is used as the basis of illustrations and examples throughout the rest of the book. Accordingly, you may want to follow along with the steps for creating the project. These steps are described later in the chapter.

Choosing Menu Options

The project creation screen should show the main menu, or menu bar, along the top of the project creation screen as shown in figure 3.1. If the menu is not displayed, press / to activate the main menu. You can select menu options from the Time Line main menu at least two different ways. One way is to type the first letter of the option you want to select. For example, you can press F to select the File option, press S to select the Schedule option, press V to select the Views option, and so forth. A second way to select options is to highlight the option you want to select. Initially, the File option is highlighted when the menu first appears, but you can use the up-, down-, left-, and right-arrow keys to move the highlight. When the option you want to select is highlighted, press Enter.

After you choose a menu option, Time Line may display another menu, called a *submenu* because it's a menu under a menu; or it may display a screen you fill in with data. To deselect, or back off, a menu or a screen, press the Esc key. You can also use Esc to remove the main menu, or deactivate the menu bar.

Creating a Project Calendar

The first step is setting up any project to be managed is to identify the time period—days, months, and years—over which the project will occur. Within Time Line, you identify the time period by defining the calendar. Typically, this represents the first step you take in setting up a new project. The five steps for creating a project calendar are

1. Select the Schedule option from the main menu. If the main menu isn't already displayed, press / to activate the menu bar.

2. Select the Calendar option from the Schedule menu. After you select the Calendar option, the Calendar submenu shows, listing four options: Workhours, Dates, Settings, and Quit.

3. To set the working hours (the hours each day of the week during which work goes on), select the Workhours option. Time Line displays the Workhours screen (see fig. 3.2).

Part I: Covering the Basics

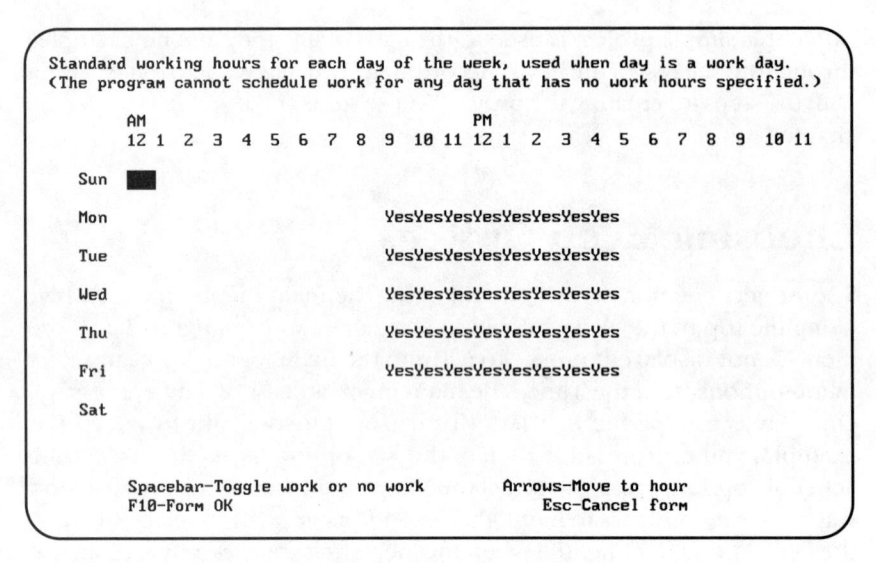

```
Standard working hours for each day of the week, used when day is a work day.
(The program cannot schedule work for any day that has no work hours specified.)
              AM                            PM
              12 1  2  3  4  5  6  7  8  9 10 11 12 1  2  3  4  5  6  7  8  9 10 11
        Sun   ██
        Mon                                 YesYesYesYesYesYesYesYes
        Tue                                 YesYesYesYesYesYesYesYes
        Wed                                 YesYesYesYesYesYesYesYes
        Thu                                 YesYesYesYesYesYesYesYes
        Fri                                 YesYesYesYesYesYesYesYes
        Sat


        Spacebar-Toggle work or no work     Arrows-Move to hour
        F10-Form OK                         Esc-Cancel form
```

Fig. 3.2. The Workhours screen with the default working hours.

The default, or initial setting, is for working hours to run from 9:00 a.m. to 5:00 p.m. Monday through Friday. Time Line uses a horizontal row to represent a day: Sunday is the first row, Monday is the second row, Tuesday is the third row, and so forth. Time Line uses columns to represent the twenty-four hours in each day. 12:00 a.m. is the first column, 1:00 a.m. is the second column, 2:00 a.m. is the third column, and so forth. Time Line indicates a working hour by displaying the word Yes in the intersection of the row that represents the day of the week and the column that represents the hour of the day.

You can change the default settings by using the arrow keys to move to a day's hour and then pressing the Spacebar. The Spacebar toggles between Yes, which indicates a working hour, and a blank space, which indicates a non-working hour.

Figure 3.3 shows a modified Workhours form screen so the working day starts as 8:00 a.m., breaks from 12:00 p.m. to 1:00 p.m. for lunch, and then ends at 5:00 p.m. (I use the workhours specified by figure 3.3 in the examples throughout this chapter; so if you're following along, make these changes to your workhours, too.) To save your changes on the Workhours screen, press F10. To exit from the screen without saving your changes, press Esc. If you press F10 or Esc, Time Line redisplays the Calendar submenu.

Chapter 3: Getting Started with Time Line

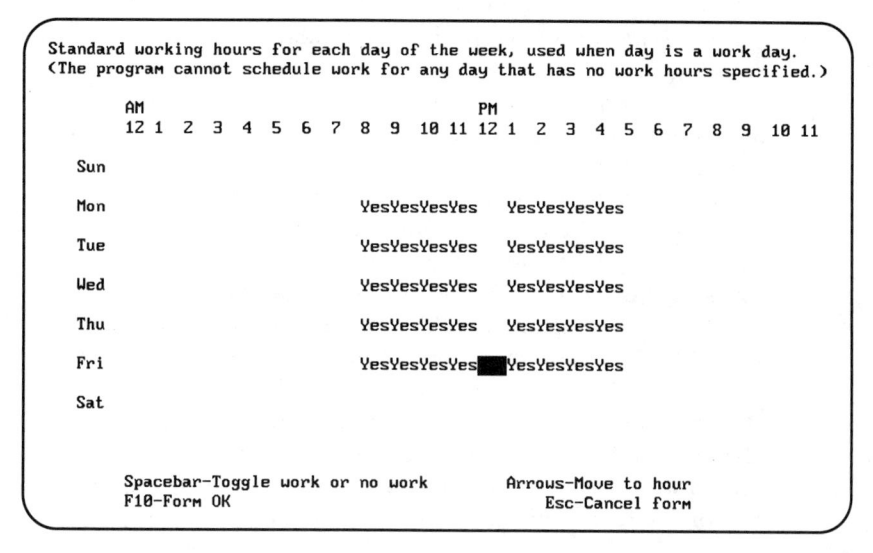

```
Standard working hours for each day of the week, used when day is a work day.
(The program cannot schedule work for any day that has no work hours specified.)
        AM                              PM
        12 1  2  3  4  5  6  7  8  9 10 11 12 1  2  3  4  5  6  7  8  9 10 11
   Sun
   Mon                         YesYesYesYes    YesYesYesYes
   Tue                         YesYesYesYes    YesYesYesYes
   Wed                         YesYesYesYes    YesYesYesYes
   Thu                         YesYesYesYes    YesYesYesYes
   Fri                         YesYesYesYes█   YesYesYesYes
   Sat

        Spacebar-Toggle work or no work    Arrows-Move to hour
        F10-Form OK                        Esc-Cancel form
```

Fig. 3.3. The Workhours screen modified to show the day starting at 8:00am and with lunch break from 12:00pm to 1:00pm.

4. To set the dates during which work will occur, select the Dates option from the Calendar submenu. This submenu should be displayed if you just completed the Workhours screen. Time Line then displays the Date screen, which is just a calendar (see fig. 3.4).

```
April  1990
Sun        Mon       Tue       Wed       Thu       Fri       Sat
1          2         3         4         5         6         7
No Work                                                      No Work
8          9         10        11        12        13        14
No Work                                                      No Work
15         16        17        18        19        20        21
No Work                                                      No Work
22         23        24        25        26        27        28
No Work                                                      No Work
29         30
No Work

Spacebar-Toggle work or no work                 Arrows-Move to date
Tab-Next month    Shift/Tab-Prev month     F10-Form OK   Esc-Cancel form
```

Fig. 3.4. The Date screen showing every Saturday and Sunday as "no-work" days.

Use the Dates form screen to show holidays and other non-working days. By default, Saturday and Sunday are "no work" days, and Monday through Friday are "work" days. Time Line also shows the standard U.S. holidays as "no work" days: New Year's Day, Martin Luther King Day, President's Day, Memorial Day, Independence Day, Labor Day, Columbus Day, Veterans Day, Thanksgiving, and Christmas. You can change this by using the arrow keys to move to a day and then pressing the Spacebar. The Spacebar toggles between no work, which indicates a holiday, and blank which indicates a workday. Time Line shows one month on a screen at a time. To move to the next month, press Tab or PgDn. To move to the previous month, press Shift-Tab or PgUp. To save your changes on the Date form screen, press F10. To exit from the screen without saving your changes, press Esc. If you press F10 or Esc, Time Line redisplays the Calendar submenu.

Note: Before Time Line can schedule work on a day, the day must be a workday and must have work hours assigned. For example, in order for work to occur on Wednesday, April 4, Wednesday must have hours assigned to it and April 4 must be a workday.

5. Define the overall calendar by selecting the Settings option from the Calendar submenu. Time Line displays the Calendar Settings Form screen (see fig. 3.5). Use the Calendar Settings Form screen to set the number of days in a normal workday, the number of days in the normal workweek, the first day of the normal workweek, the first month of the scheduling year, and the smallest time unit used to schedule. You also use the Calendar Settings Form screen to tell Time Line how to report the ending date of a task. To move between the fields, use the up- and down-arrows. To move between the various portions of the box the fields appear in, use Tab and Shift-Tab.

Standard Workday

The Standard Workday field sets the number of working hours in the normal workday. Usually, a workday is eight hours, so you enter 8. Enter the figure as a whole number. Time Line uses your input to convert task durations entered in days to hours.

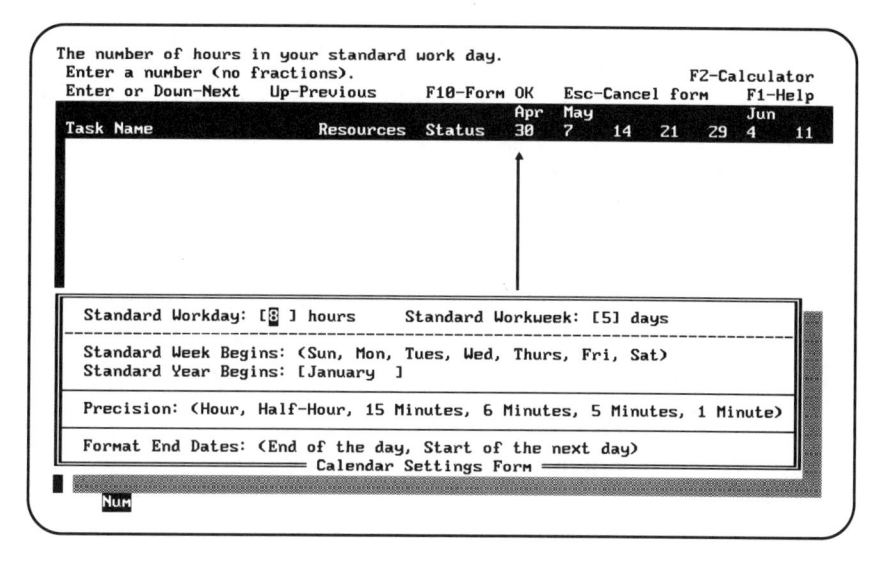

```
The number of hours in your standard work day.
 Enter a number (no fractions).                              F2-Calculator
 Enter or Down-Next    Up-Previous    F10-Form OK  Esc-Cancel form   F1-Help
                                          Apr  May              Jun
 Task Name                Resources Status 30   7   14   21  29  4   11
 ┌──────────────────────────────────────────────────────────────────┐
 │ Standard Workday: [8] hours     Standard Workweek: [5] days      │
 │------------------------------------------------------------------│
 │ Standard Week Begins: (Sun, Mon, Tues, Wed, Thurs, Fri, Sat)     │
 │ Standard Year Begins: [January  ]                                │
 │ Precision: (Hour, Half-Hour, 15 Minutes, 6 Minutes, 5 Minutes, 1 Minute) │
 │ Format End Dates: (End of the day, Start of the next day)        │
 └═══════════════════════ Calendar Settings Form ═══════════════════┘
 Num
```

Fig. 3.5. The Calendar Settings Form screen.

Standard Workweek

The Standard Workweek field sets the number of days in a normal workweek. Enter the figure—from 1 to 7—as a whole number. Time Line uses your input to convert task durations entered in months and weeks to days or hours.

Note: To schedule more work per day, increase the standard workday figure; and to schedule more work per week, increase the standard workweek figure. Then when you leave the Calendar Settings Form screen, answer Yes to the `Keep durations` message. Finally, add work hours by using the Workhours screen (refer to fig. 3.2).

Time Line uses the standard workweek value to determine the average number of days in a month which, in turn, the program uses to convert tasks with monthly durations to daily or hourly durations. If the standard workweek is 1 day, the days per month is 4. If the standard workweek is 2 days, the days per month is 9. If the standard workweek is 3 days, the days per month is 13. If the standard workweek is 4 days, the days per month is 17. If the standard workweek is 5 days, the days per month is 22. If the standard workweek is 6 days, the days per month is 26. And, finally, if the standard workweek is 7 days, the days per month is 30.

Standard Week Begins

The Standard Week Begins field sets the first day of the week. Usually, the first day is Monday, which is the default setting. To set another day as the first day of the week, type the first letter of the day name: S for Sunday, M for Monday, T for Tuesday, W for Wednesday, and so forth. Because two letters start two days start with the same letter—Sunday and Saturday, and Tuesday and Thursday—typing an S toggles between Sunday and Saturday and typing a T toggles between Tuesday and Thursday.

Standard Year Begins

The Standard Year Begins field sets the first month of the fiscal year so that Time Line knows how to group information on reports that show annual information. Usually, fiscal years match calendar years so the default first month is January. To set another month as the first month of the year, type the full month name—February, March, April, and so on—or the first three characters of the month name—Feb, Mar, Apr and so on.

Precision

The Precision field sets the smallest unit of time used in Time Line. Time Line rounds task durations to the precision you specify. So if the precision is set to 1 hour and you enter a duration of 1.25 hours, Time Line rounds the duration to 1 hour. The default precision setting is an hour, and Hour allows for up to a twenty-five year schedule.

Smaller time units increase your scheduling precision but reduce the possible schedule length: Half-hour allows up to fifteen years, both 5 Minutes and 6 Minutes allow up to three years, and 1 Minute allows up to six months. To set a different smallest-time-unit, type the first letter or number of the time-unit name: H for Hour, H for Half-hour, 1 for 15 Minutes, 6 for 6 Minutes, and so forth. (Typing an H toggles between Hour and Half-hour.)

Format End Dates

The Format End Date field sets how a task that finishes at the very end of a workday is scheduled: at the end of the workday or at the beginning of the next workday. The default setting is End of the Day. To use the Start of the (next) Day setting, type an S. This calendar setting doesn't affect scheduling calculations.

To save your changes on the Calendar Settings Form screen, press F10. To exit from the screen without saving your changes, press Esc. If you press F10 or Esc, Time Line redisplays the Calendar submenu. To leave the calendar submenu, press Q for quit or Esc.

Chapter 3: Getting Started with Time Line **65**

Adding Tasks

After you define the project calendar, the next step is to add the tasks that make up the project. There are six tasks you add for the sailboat project. The steps you use are the same for each.

1. Press the Ins key to display the Task Form screen (see fig. 3.6), or activate the menu bar by pressing / and then select Schedule from the main menu, Tasks from the Schedule submenu, and Add from the Tasks submenu. There are many fields on the Task Form screen, but don't worry about them for now. You only need to enter or mark three of the fields: Name, Type, and Duration.

Tip Remember that you select menu options either by typing the first letter of the option name or by using the arrow keys to first highlight the option name and then pressing Enter. Remember, too, that you can back off a menu by pressing Esc.

```
This 30-character name identifies the task in the outline.
Ins-Insert    Del-Delete    Ctrl/Arrows-Move by word    Home-First    End-Last
Enter or Down-Next    Up-Previous    F10-Form OK    Esc-Cancel form    F1-Help
                                            Apr   May                    Jun
Task Name                Resources  Status  30    7     14    21    29   4    11
                                            ?
                                            ↑

  Name       : [█                    ]           Keyword: [              ]
  Note (F2): [                                                            ]
  Type       : <Fixed, ASAP, ALAP>    WBS:  [                              ]
  Driven by: <Duration, Effort>       OBS:  [                              ]
  Duration : [0    ] <Mi, H, D, W, Mo>  Priority:[2  ] Link to file (F2):[ ]
  Effort     : [0    ] <Mi, H, D, W, Mo> ─── Resources/Costs ───
  Status     : <Future, Started, Done)  [        ] [        ] [        ]
  Start      : [30-Apr-90  9:00am]      [        ] [        ] [        ]
  End        : [30-Apr-90  9:00am]      [        ] [        ] [        ]
   ─ Achievements and Expenditures ─    [        ] [        ] [        ]
  Basln:   100 % <No Baseline>          [        ] [        ] [        ]
  ..............................       [        ] [        ] [        ]
  Achvd: [0    ]% 0 days          $0   [        ] [        ] [        ]
  Spent:      0 % 0 days          $0   [        ] [        ] [        ]
                                   ═ Task Form ═
 Num
```

Fig. 3.6. *The Task Form.*

2. Enter the name for the task. The task name field is the first field on the Task Form screen, and Time Line first positions the cursor on this field when it displays the screen. Use up to thirty characters including letters, numbers, and special symbols for the task name. Time Line allows duplicate names, and it allows you to change names later.

The characters you type appear at the current position of the cursor, the flashing underline mark. What you type replaces, or overwrites, the current field contents. If you want to insert a character or word rather than overwriting it, press the Ins key before you type. To remove the character on which the cursor rests, press the Del key. To remove the character behind the cursor, press the backspace key. To move to the beginning of the field, press Home. To move to the end of the field, press End. To move to the beginning of the next word, press Ctrl-right-arrow. To move to the beginning of the previous word, press Ctrl-left-arrow. When you finish entering the name for the task, press the down arrow once to move the cursor to the Type field.

Tip The rules and mechanics of entering and editing text in the task name field also apply to other text fields in Time Line: Ins inserts the next characters you type. Del removes the character over the cursor. Backspace removes the character behind the cursor. Home moves the cursor to the beginning of the field. End moves the cursor to the end of the field. Ctrl-right-arrow and Ctrl-left-arrow move the cursor to the next word or the previous word.

3. (Optional) Enter a description of the task in the Notes field. The description can be anything you want. The Notes field on the Task Form is 60 characters long, but if that doesn't provide enough space, press F2 while the cursor is positioned on the Note field. Time Line opens a notepad (see fig. 3.7) which you can use to more fully document a task. To close the notepad and save your notes, press F10. If you use a notepad, Time Line displays the first line of the notepad in the Notes field. (Chapter 4, "Managing Project and Task Details," describes the notepad feature in more depth.)

4. Enter the type of the task. There are three possibilities: Fixed, ASAP, and ALAP. ASAP is an acronym for "as soon as possible." ASAP indicates that a task should start as soon as any predecessor tasks are complete. ALAP is an acronym for "as late as possible." ALAP indicates that a task should start as late as it can without delaying the project's completion. Fixed indicates a task should start or end on a specific date. The first task of the sailboat project, for example, might be fixed. Or if a sailboat had been promised to a customer by a certain date, the last task of the sailboat project might be fixed. If a

```
Ins-Insert      Del-Delete     F3-Delete line       Sh/F9-Delete to end of line
F7-Read file    F8-Write file  F9-Reformat      F10-Note OK  Esc-Cancel    F1-Help
                                            Apr  May                  Jun
Task Name                   Resources Status  30   7    14   21   29   4    11
                                         ?
```

Name   : [Lay hull   ]   Keyword: [   ]

Note (F2):

The Lay hull task will be started as soon as we receive a ten percent deposit from the customer and a signed purchase order.

Type   :
Driven by:
Duration :
Effort   :
Status   :
Start   :
End   :
— Achieve
BasIn: 10
Achvd: [0
Spent:

— Lay hull —

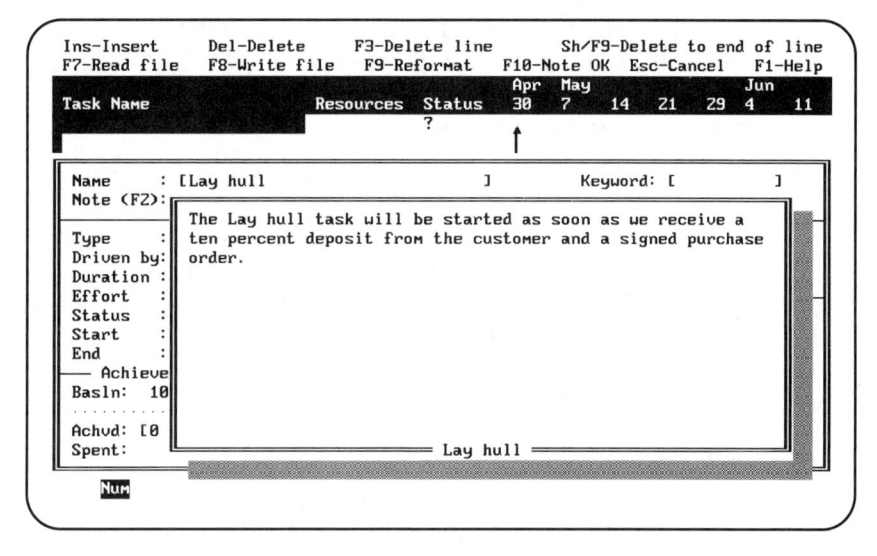

Num

Fig. 3.7. The notepad box lets you more fully describe a task.

    task type is fixed, you also enter the start date or the completion date. To define the type of task, type the first letter of the type name: F for fixed, A for ASAP, and A for ALAP. (Typing an A toggles between the ASAP and ALAP choices.) In the sailboat example, the first task should be fixed with a start date equal to the current date, and the other five tasks should be ASAP. When you finish defining the type of task, press the down-arrow key to move the cursor to the Duration field.

5. Enter the duration of the task. Entering the duration is a two-part process. First, enter the number of time units inside the brackets. Then press the down-arrow key to move the type of time units and type the first letter of the type of time units you use to calibrate the task duration. Mi indicates minutes. H indicates hours. D indicates days. W indicates weeks. Mo indicates months. Because both minutes and months start with the same letter, typing an M toggles between these two choices. When you finish centering the duration, press the down-arrow key to move the cursor to the center field.

6. Mark the status of the task as either Future, Started, or Done. The default status is Future. Future indicates that work on the task hasn't begun. Started indicates that work on the task has begun but hasn't finished. Done indicates that the work on the task has been completed. Time Line shows tasks that

have been started and tasks that have been completed differently on the Gantt chart to indicate their status. (Chapter 6, "Monitoring Project Progress, Resources, and Costs" talks more about the status of tasks.)

7. (Optional) As long as the status of a task is Future, Time Line calculates the start date for you as the first date in the future when all the predecessor tasks have been completed. However, if you mark a task as started, you need to enter the date on which work on a task begins. For this, use the Start Date field. If you mark a task as done, you will need to record the date work on the task began and the date work ended using the Start Date and End Date field. (Chapter 6, "Monitoring Project Time, Resources, and Costs" also talks more about this.)

Note: If you specified the task type as Fixed, Time Line needs two of the following three pieces of information: the Start Date, End Date, or Duration. With two of these pieces of information, the program can and does calculate the other. With the Start Date and the Duration, for example, Time Line can calculate the End Date. With the End Date and the Duration, it can calculate the Start Date. And with the Start and End Dates, it can calculate the Duration.

When you finish marking the status, press F10 to save your work. To define the other five tasks of the sailboat, repeat steps 1 through 7 five more times, using the task names and task durations given earlier in the chapter.

Figure 3.8 shows the sailboat project viewed in a Gantt chart after entering the six sailboat tasks. Because you've entered the six tasks sequentially, Time Line assumes they should be performed sequentially.

Time Line marks the selected task by highlighting it. At the top the screen, Time Line shows a variety of information about the selected task including the task name, the task type, the duration, and the calculated start and finish dates and times for the task.

Editing and Deleting Tasks

As part of adding the six tasks that make up the sailboat project, you may erroneously enter a task or inadvertently enter an extra task...so now you need to know how to edit and delete tasks. To edit an existing task, position the cursor on the task using the up- and down-arrow keys. Up arrow moves the cursor to the previous task and the down arrow moves the cursor to the next task. Then press Ctrl-F2 or activate the main menu by pressing / and then select Schedule from the main menu, Tasks from the Schedule

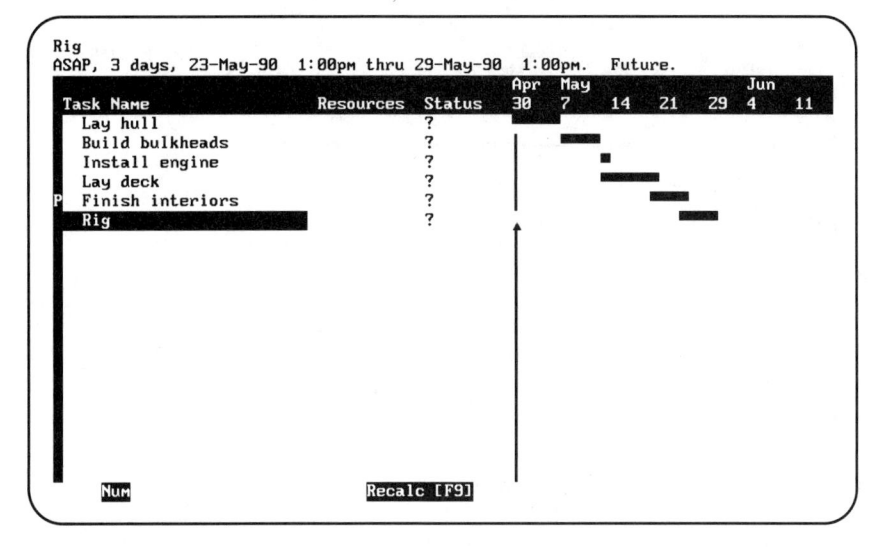

```
Rig
ASAP, 3 days, 23-May-90  1:00pm thru 29-May-90  1:00pm.  Future.
                                              Apr  May              Jun
    Task Name              Resources  Status  30   7    14   21  29  4   11
      Lay hull                          ?
      Build bulkheads                   ?
      Install engine                    ?
      Lay deck                          ?
    P Finish interiors                  ?
      Rig                               ?


    Num                             Recalc [F9]
```

Fig. 3.8. The sailboat project viewed in a Gantt chart after entering the six sailboat tasks.

submenu, and Edit from the Tasks submenu. Time Line displays the Task Form screen with the selected task. Make any needed changes, and then press F10.

To delete an existing task, position the cursor on the task, using the up- and down-arrow keys; then pressing Del. Or, alternatively, activate the main menu by pressing /, select Schedule from the main menu, Tasks from the Schedule submenu, and Delete from the Tasks submenu. Time Line displays a message box, like the one shown in figure 3.9, alerting you that it's about to delete a task and asking whether you want to continue. To delete the task, press Enter. If you don't want to delete the task, type C for cancel.

Moving Around in a Large Project

When a project includes only a handful of tasks, the up- and down-arrow keys are usually adequate for moving through the list of project tasks. However, as the list of tasks grows larger and larger, there are other key combinations for moving to different tasks and even a menu option for moving quickly to a different task.

Using Key Combinations

Time Line provides several key combinations. If you've been constructing the sailboat project by following along, try out these key combinations:

Part I: Covering the Basics

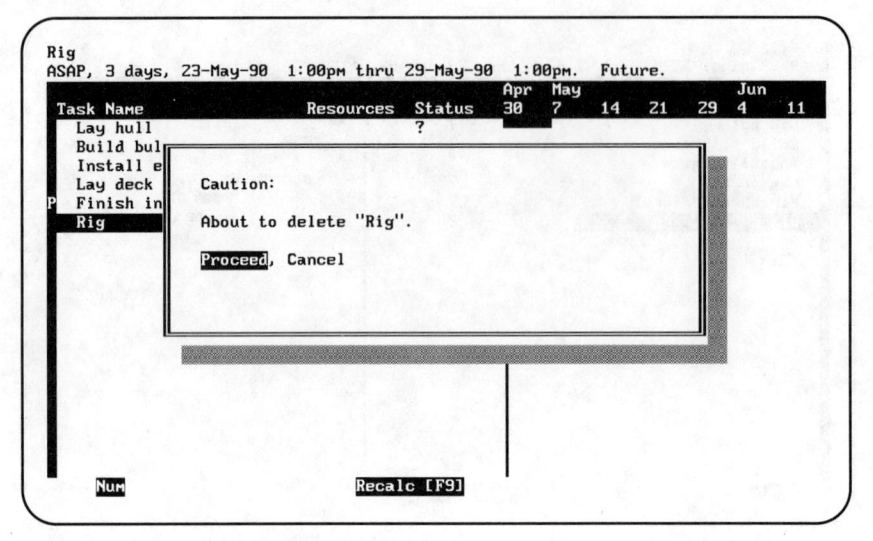

```
Rig
ASAP, 3 days, 23-May-90  1:00pm thru 29-May-90  1:00pm.  Future.
                                              Apr  May              Jun
Task Name              Resources  Status      30   7    14   21  29  4    11
    Lay hull                        ?
    Build bul┌─────────────────────────────────┐
    Install e│                                 │
    Lay deck │ Caution:                        │
  P Finish in│                                 │
    Rig      │ About to delete "Rig".          │
             │                                 │
             │ Proceed, Cancel                 │
             │                                 │
             └─────────────────────────────────┘


      Num                        Recalc [F9]
```

Fig. 3.9. The Delete message box.

Press this key	To move the cursor
PgUp	Up an entire screen
PgDn	Down an entire screen
* - up arrow[1] * - Home * - PgUp	To the first task in project
* - down arrow * - End * - PgDn	To the last task in project

[1] Press and hold the asterisk key (*) while pressing the second key.

Using Search

Time Line also provides a menu option you can use to make searching and then selecting tasks easier: the Task menu's Search option. To use the Search option, follow these steps:

1. Activate the menu bar and select Schedule Tasks Search, or press F5. Time Line displays a QuickPick box which lists each of the tasks in the project.

2. Type the first character or characters of the task you want to find, and Time Line lists all the tasks that match what you

typed. So with the Sailboat project, if you typed *lay*, the QuickPick would show two tasks: lay hull and lay deck.

3. Using the arrow keys, highlight the task you want to select, and then press Enter. Time Line selects the Gantt chart task you selected from the QuickPick box.

Tip The same rules for selecting tasks in a QuickPick box also apply to other list boxes in Time Line, such as those for picking a file or resource from a list.

Moving Tasks

Ultimately, Time Line will arrange your tasks in the order which they must start. Time Line will know this order after you define any dependencies (described in the next section). In the meantime, however, you can move tasks around by simultaneously pressing the Shift key and the up-arrow or down-arrow key on the numeric keypad. To move the selected task up a row in the list of tasks, press Shift-down-arrow. To move the selected task down a row, press Shift-up-arrow. If your keypad has separate arrow keys, those will not work for moving a task—you must use the up-arrow and down-arrow keys on the numeric keypad for this purpose.

Recognizing Task Dependencies

To actually complete the definition of the project, there's one final set of steps—defining the dependencies between the tasks. As mentioned earlier, Lay hull needs to precede Build bulkheads, Install engine, and Lay deck. Similarly, Lay deck needs to precede Rig. And Build bulkheads, Install engine, and Lay deck all need to precede Finish interior. In all, then, there are seven dependencies:

Predecessor	*Successor*
1. Lay hull	Build bulkheads
2. Lay hull	Install engine
3. Lay hull	Lay deck
4. Lay deck	Rig
5. Build bulkheads	Finish interior
6. Install engine	Finish interior
7. Lay deck	Finish interior

Defining Dependencies

To finish describing the organization of the project, you'll need to recognize these seven dependencies. To define dependencies, work through these five steps:

1. (Optional) Change the view of the project to a PERT chart. Activate the menu bar, select Views from the main menu, and then select PERT from the View submenu. Time Line redisplays the sailboat project as a PERT chart.

Tip PERT charts are extremely handy—and probably the most efficient way—for seeing task dependencies. Consider using them when you define dependencies. (PERT charts show each task as a small box. Although the boxes are small, not all of the boxes may show on a screen at the same time. When this is the case, use the arrow keys to move the cursor to another task so Time Line displays it.)

2. Use the arrow keys to highlight the predecessor task in a dependency and then press the Spacebar. Time Line marks the task with a P to indicate it will be the predecessor task in a dependency. For the first dependency, Lay hull to Build bulkheads, you highlight Lay hull as the predecessor (see fig. 3.10).

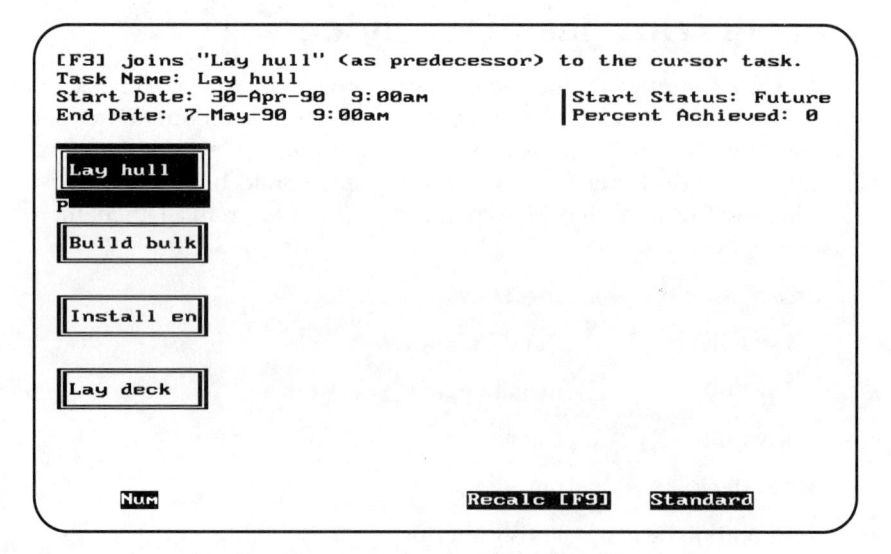

```
[F3] joins "Lay hull" (as predecessor) to the cursor task.
Task Name: Lay hull
Start Date: 30-Apr-90  9:00am          Start Status: Future
End Date: 7-May-90  9:00am             Percent Achieved: 0

    ┌─────────────┐
    │Lay hull     │
    └─────────────┘
    P
    ┌─────────────┐
    │Build bulk   │
    └─────────────┘

    ┌─────────────┐
    │Install en   │
    └─────────────┘

    ┌─────────────┐
    │Lay deck     │
    └─────────────┘


      Num                         Recalc [F9]    Standard
```

***Fig. 3.10.** The Lay hull task marked as the predecessor in the first dependency.*

3. Use the arrow keys to highlight the successor task in a dependency. For the first dependency, Lay hull to Build bulkheads, you highlight Build bulkheads as the successor.

Note: As an alternative to first marking the predecessor task, you can instead highlight the successor task in step 2 and press the Spacebar twice so Time Line marks the task with an S to indicate it will be the successor task in a dependency. Then in step 3, you highlight the predecessor task.

4. Press F3 or activate the main menu bar by pressing /, and then select Schedule from the main menu, Dependencies from the Schedule submenu, and Join from the Dependencies submenu. When you complete the definitions of the first dependency, the sailboat project viewed in a PERT chart should resemble figure 3.11.

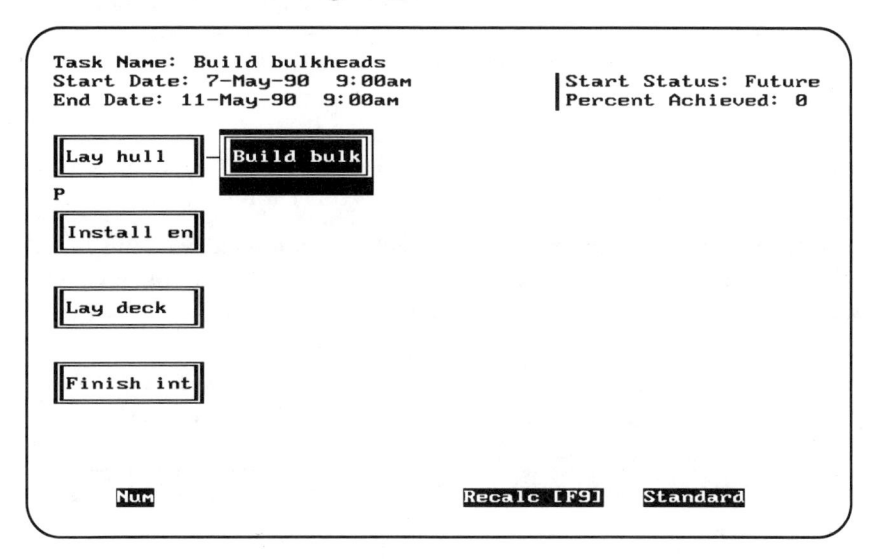

```
Task Name: Build bulkheads
Start Date: 7-May-90   9:00am              Start Status: Future
End Date:  11-May-90   9:00am              Percent Achieved: 0

   ┌────────┐   ┌────────┐
   │Lay hull│───│Build bulk│
   └────────┘   └────────┘
  P
   ┌────────┐
   │Install en│
   └────────┘

   ┌────────┐
   │Lay deck│
   └────────┘

   ┌────────┐
   │Finish int│
   └────────┘


        Num                        Recalc [F9]    Standard
```

Fig. 3.11. The sailboat project viewed in a PERT chart after defining the first dependency.

Repeat steps 2 through 4 to define each of the six remaining dependencies. When you complete the definitions of each of the seven dependencies, press F9 so Time Line recalculates. The sailboat project displayed in a PERT chart should resemble figure 3.12. At this point, you've accomplished the first two components of project management: Organizing the pieces that make up a project, and showing the timing of tasks.

Part I: Covering the Basics

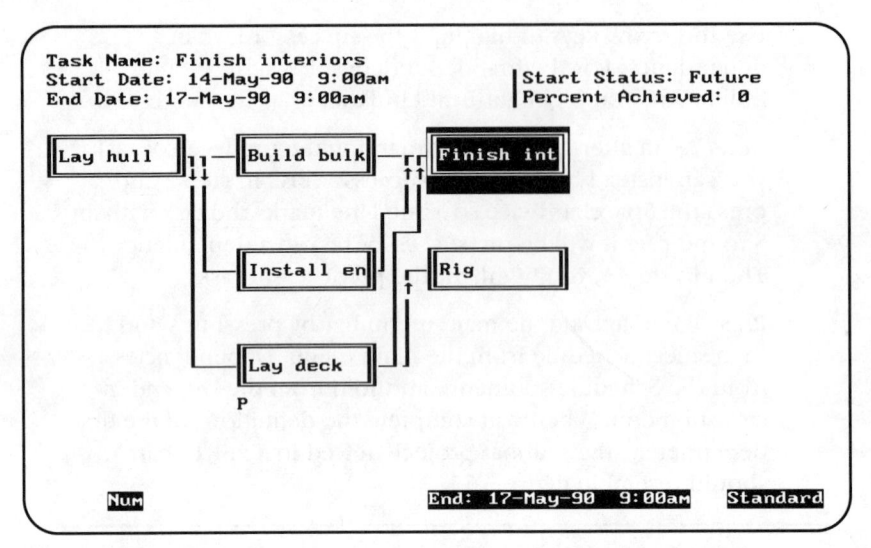

```
Task Name: Finish interiors
Start Date: 14-May-90  9:00am          Start Status: Future
End Date:  17-May-90  9:00am           Percent Achieved: 0
```

Fig. 3.12. The sailboat project viewed in a PERT chart after defining all the seven dependencies.

Note: If you used long task names, like some of those used for the sailboat project, the entire task name may not fill in the PERT chart box. For example, Build bulkheads is cut off so it says `Build Bulk`.

To return to the Gantt chart view of the sailboat project, activate the menu bar, select Views from the main menu, and then select Gantt from the View submenu. Time Line redisplays the sailboat project as a Gantt chart (see fig. 3.13).

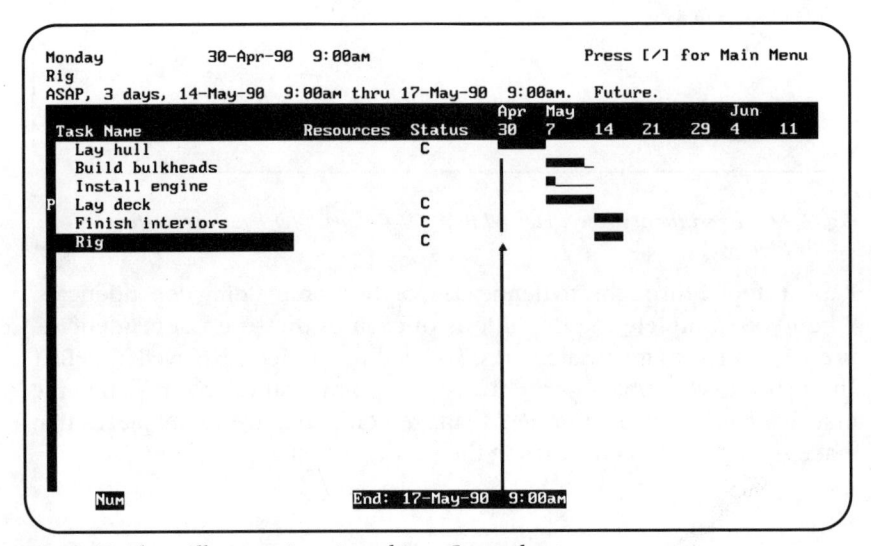

Fig. 3.13. The sailboat project viewed in a Gantt chart.

Removing Dependencies

If you make a mistake and define a dependency you don't want, remove the dependency by following these five steps:

1. (Optional) Change the view of the project to a PERT chart. Activate the menu bar, select Views from the main menu, and then select PERT from the View submenu.

2. Use the arrow keys to highlight the predecessor task in the dependency and then press the Spacebar. Time Line marks the task with a P to indicate it will be the predecessor task in a dependency.

3. Use the arrow keys to highlight the successor task in the dependency.

4. Activate the main menu by pressing /. Then select Schedule, Dependencies, and Unjoin.

To return to the Gantt chart view of the sailboat project, activate the menu bar, select Views from the main menu, and then select Gantt from the View submenu.

Undoing and Redoing

Time Line provides two handy tools for people who make mistakes: Undo and Redo. Undo returns the project to the condition it was in before the most recent menu operation. So if you erroneously added a task, for example, you could use Undo to remove the task. Or if you accidently deleted a task, you could use Undo to replace the task. By default, you can undo up to the last ten menu operations. To use Undo, activate the menu bar by pressing /, and then select Schedule 1-Undo. Alternatively, simultaneously press Alt-F10.

Redo, in effect, undoes Undo. That sounds confusing but really it's not. Say you thought you had erroneously added a task and then used Undo to remove the task. If you then realized that you really should have added the task, you could use Redo to add the task again. Like Undo, the default is that you can redo up to the last ten menu operations. To use Redo, activate the menu bar by pressing / and then select Schedule 2-Redo. Alternatively, simultaneously press Ctrl-F10.

Erasing the Project

Sometimes you'll find that you want to recreate a schedule you're working on from scratch—perhaps, for example, it'll be easier to just start over rather than work with what you've already done. To erase the project correctly stored in memory, follow these steps:

1. Activate the menu bar by pressing slash (/).
2. Then select Schedule and then Erase. Time Line will ask whether you really want to delete the schedule. (The program won't delete the calendar, only the tasks.)
3. Highlight Proceed and press Enter.

Note: Erasing a project only removes it from memory. If you saved the project to disk, described next, it still resides on your disk.

Saving the Project

After you finish creating a calendar, adding tasks, and defining task dependencies, you'll want to save the project. To save the project, take the following three steps:

1. Activate the menu bar and select the File option. Then select the Save option from the File submenu.
2. Time Line displays the No Name box (see fig. 3.14). The No Name box gives you the choice of canceling the Save operation, naming the schedule and saving it, or saving only the global options. Time Line highlights the Name this Schedule field automatically, so you can simply press Enter to select this option. Chapter 9 explains more about working with Time Line files.
3. Time Line displays the File Save Form at the bottom of the screen (see fig. 3.15). In the DOS File field, type the file name you want to use. Whatever you type needs to be a valid DOS file name.

   In the DOS file extension field, Time Line displays the characters T$0 which it will use as file extension. You can, however, choose to use another file extension by entering three different characters. File extensions can use all the same characters as file names.

Chapter 3: Getting Started with Time Line

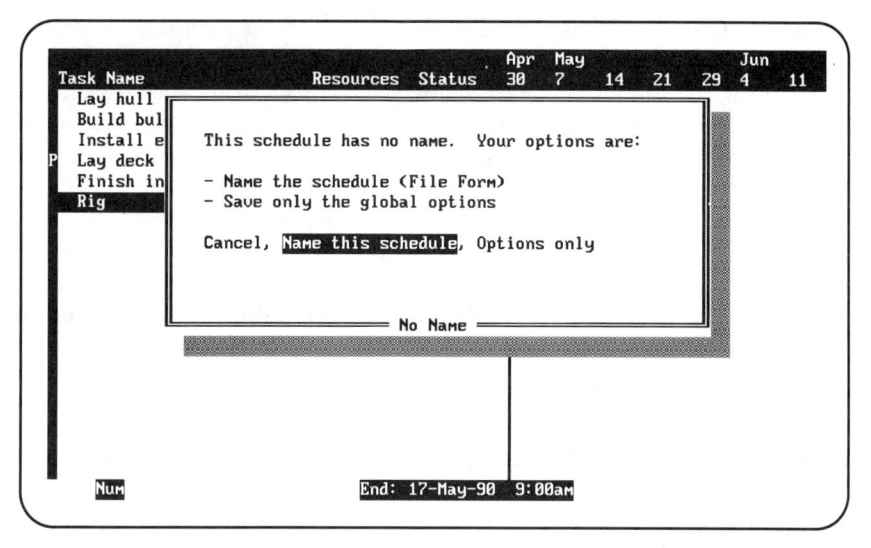

Fig. 3.14. The No Name box.

Tip Valid DOS file names can be up to eight characters long, use letters and numbers but not blanks, and can use several symbols including the following::
` ~ ! @ # $ % ^ & ( ) _ - { } `

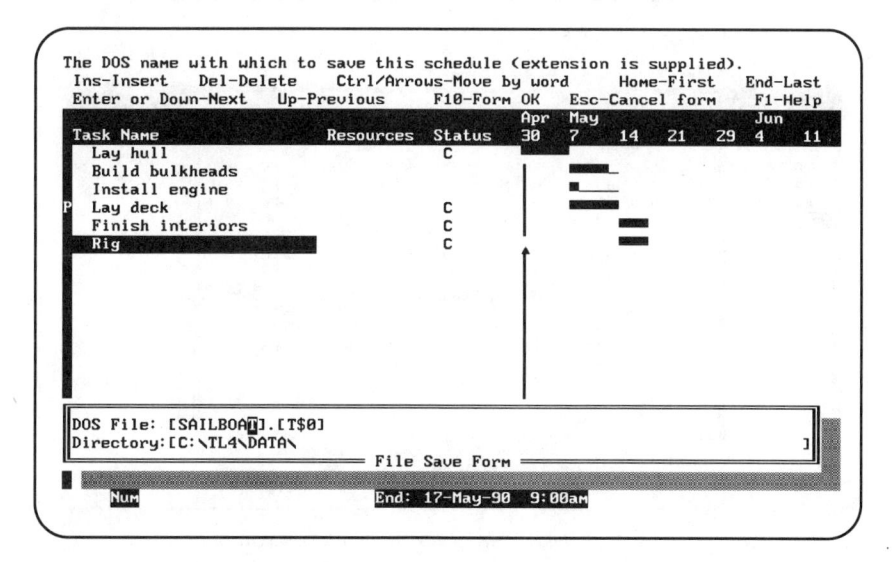

Fig. 3.15. The File Save Form.

Part I: Covering the Basics

In the Directory field, Time Line displays the default pathname used to store Time Line files, C:\TL4\DATA. You can change this if you want by replacing the default entry with some new entry. Whatever you enter, however, needs to be a valid pathname. The drive letter must represent a valid disk drive, the directory must already be defined on that disk drive, and the subdirectory must be defined and located in the directory. When the File Save Form box is complete, press F10 to save the project using the specified name in the indicated directory. You'll briefly see a message at the top of the screen that tells you that Time Line is saving the options; then a message box appears in the middle of the screen telling you Time Line is saving the schedule.

Retrieving the Project

Once you save a project, you'll also need to know how to retrieve a project. The steps to do so aren't difficult. If you just saved the Sailboat project files, you can follow along by taking the following steps:

1. Activate the menu bar by pressing /. Select File from the main menu, and select Retrieve from the File submenu. Time Line displays the Directory List screen (see fig. 3.16). The screen shows all the projects in the default directory, C:\TL4\DATA.

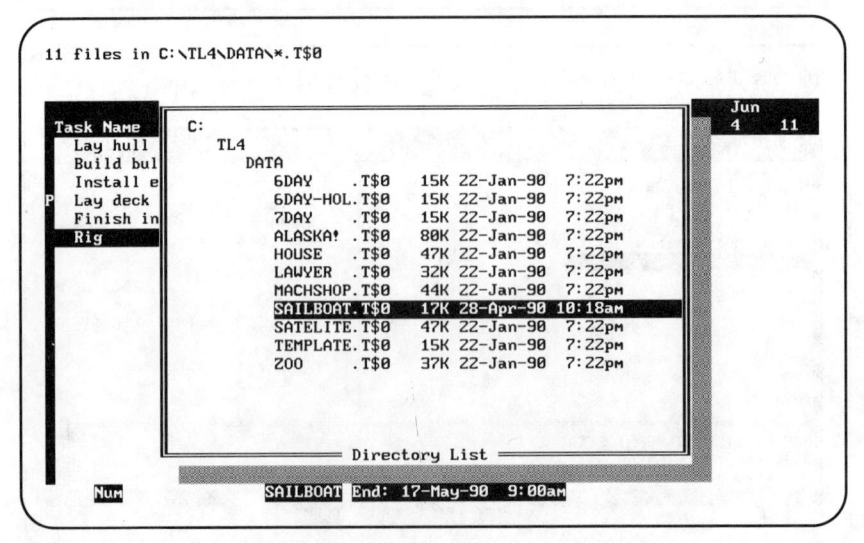

```
11 files in C:\TL4\DATA\*.T$0

Task Name          C:
  Lay hull           TL4
  Build bul            DATA
  Install e              6DAY      .T$0   15K  22-Jan-90   7:22pm
  Lay deck               6DAY-HOL.T$0   15K  22-Jan-90   7:22pm
  Finish in              7DAY      .T$0   15K  22-Jan-90   7:22pm
  Rig                    ALASKA!  .T$0   80K  22-Jan-90   7:22pm
                         HOUSE    .T$0   47K  22-Jan-90   7:22pm
                         LAWYER   .T$0   32K  22-Jan-90   7:22pm
                         MACHSHOP.T$0   44K  22-Jan-90   7:22pm
                         SAILBOAT.T$0   17K  28-Apr-90  10:18am
                         SATELITE.T$0   47K  22-Jan-90   7:22pm
                         TEMPLATE.T$0   15K  22-Jan-90   7:22pm
                         ZOO      .T$0   37K  22-Jan-90   7:22pm

                         ====== Directory List ======
  Num              SAILBOAT  End: 17-May-90  9:00am
```

Fig. 3.16. Time Line displays the Directory List screen when you select File Retrieve.

2. Use the arrow keys to highlight the project you want to retrieve. When the project is highlighted, press Enter.

Note: Time Line includes several example project files in the default directory, but you can use the QuickPick technique described earlier for selecting task for selecting files, too.

3. If you previously retrieved a project or started to create a project, Time Line displays the message box shown in figure 3.17. It alerts you that retrieving a new file will erase the schedule already stored in memory. To continue, select Erase Schedule in Memory by typing an E or by using the arrow keys to highlight Erase Schedule in Memory and then pressing Enter. (*Note:* Erasing the schedule in memory doesn't erase the schedule saved on disk.) Time Line retrieves the project and then displays it.

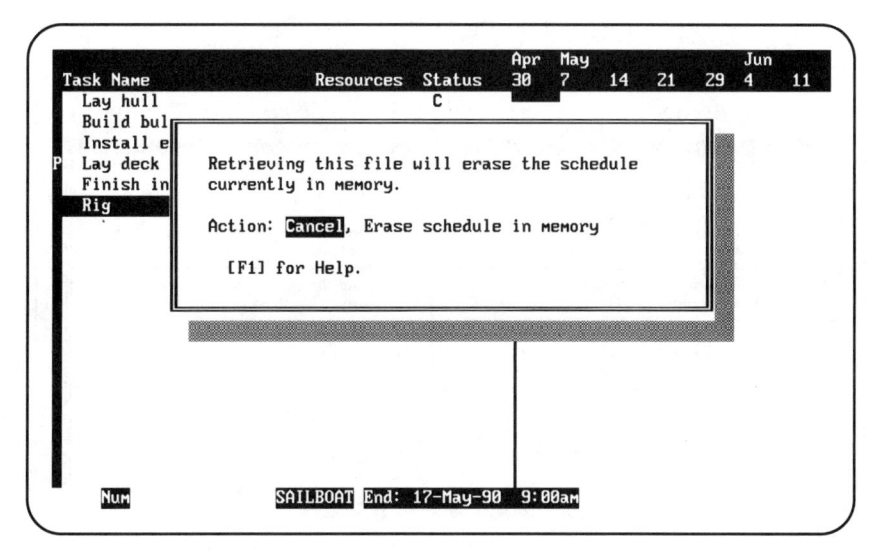

Fig. 3.17. *The message box that alerts you Time Line will erase the current project when it retrieves the new project.*

Printing a Project Report

Chapter 8, "Printing Reports," talks in detail about how to print the twelve textual reports and the two graphics charts that Time Line provides, so I won't go into great detail here. However, it's helpful to know from the start how to print the paper version of the two screen views of a project: the Gantt chart and the PERT chart.

Printing a Graphics Gantt Chart

Four steps are required to print a graphics Gantt Chart. (Chapter 8 describes the four steps in more detail, so you may want to refer there for all the little nuances and subtleties.) This procedure describes how to generate quickly the graphics Gantt chart.

1. Activate the menu bar by pressing /. Select the Graphics option (which displays the Graphics submenu), and then select the Gantt chart option from the Graphics submenu.

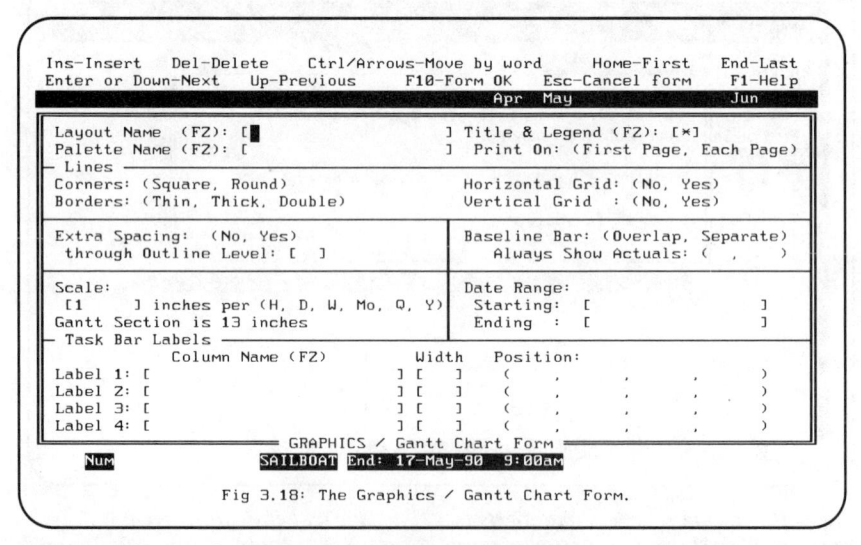

2. Time Line displays the Graphics/Gantt Chart Form screen (see fig. 3.18). Press F10 to accept the default settings. (For instructions on completing the Graphics/Gantt Chart Form screen, refer to Chapter 8, "Printing Reports.")

```
Ins-Insert    Del-Delete    Ctrl/Arrows-Move by word    Home-First    End-Last
Enter or Down-Next    Up-Previous    F10-Form OK    Esc-Cancel form    F1-Help
                                                    Apr    May              Jun

Layout Name  (FZ): [               ] Title & Legend (FZ): [×]
Palette Name (FZ): [               ] Print On: (First Page, Each Page)
─ Lines ─
Corners: (Square, Round)              Horizontal Grid: (No, Yes)
Borders: (Thin, Thick, Double)        Vertical Grid  : (No, Yes)

Extra Spacing:  (No, Yes)             Baseline Bar: (Overlap, Separate)
 through Outline Level: [ ]              Always Show Actuals: (  ,  )
Scale:                                Date Range:
[1     ] inches per (H, D, W, Mo, Q, Y)  Starting: [              ]
Gantt Section is 13 inches                Ending  : [              ]
─ Task Bar Labels ─
             Column Name (FZ)      Width    Position:
Label 1: [                   ]   [    ]    (   ,     ,     ,     )
Label 2: [                   ]   [    ]    (   ,     ,     ,     )
Label 3: [                   ]   [    ]    (   ,     ,     ,     )
Label 4: [                   ]   [    ]    (   ,     ,     ,     )
                            ═══ GRAPHICS / Gantt Chart Form ═══
   Num           SAILBOAT End: 17-May-90  9:00am

              Fig 3.18: The Graphics / Gantt Chart Form.
```

Fig. 3.18. *The Graphics/Gantt Chart Form screen.*

3. Time Line displays the Graphics/Chart Size Form screen (see fig. 3.19). Press F10 to accept the default size. (For instructions on completing the Graphics/Chart Size Form screen, refer to Chapter 8, "Printing Reports.")

4. Time Line displays several messages on the screen that tell you it is in the process of creating the report. Then Time Line displays an on-screen version of the printed Gantt chart (see fig. 3.20). Not all of the chart will appear on the screen, so use the arrow keys to see the different halves of the chart. To print the report, press F10 again.

Chapter 3: Getting Started with Time Line 81

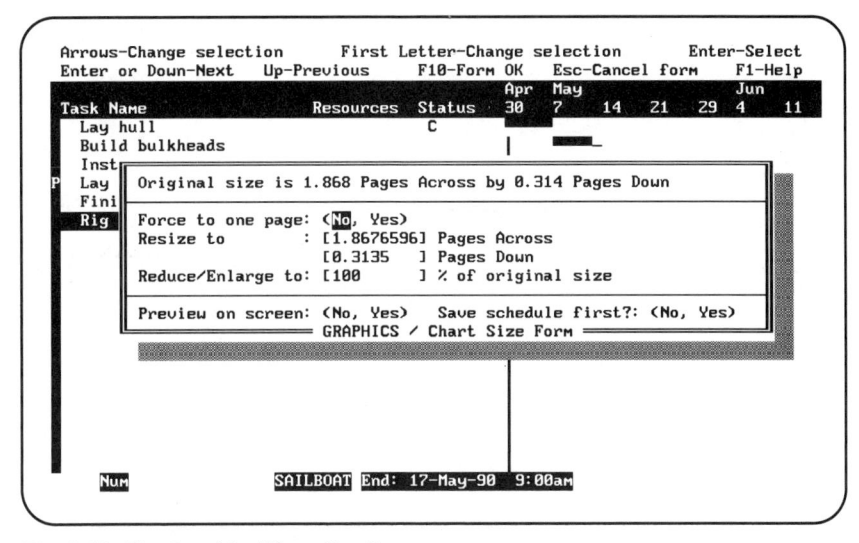

Fig. 3.19. The Graphics/Chart Size Form screen.

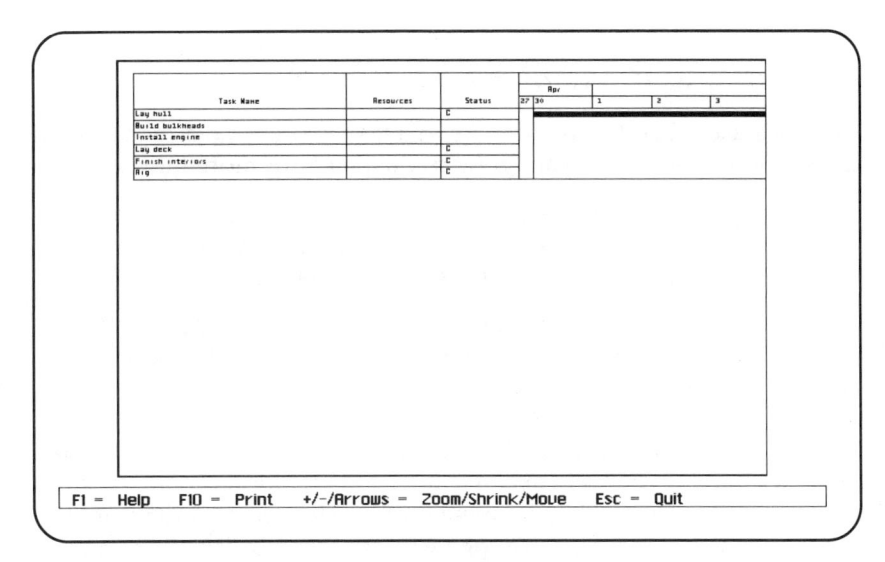

Fig. 3.20. The on-screen version of the printed Gantt chart.

Time Line again displays messages that tell you it's writing the report. Because creating graphics reports takes more time than printing a regular text reports, you'll probably have to wait longer that usual for the report to print. Figure 3.21 shows the printed graphics report.

Note: The Gantt chart for the sailboat project actually takes two pages, so you'll need to tape or paste the two halves together.

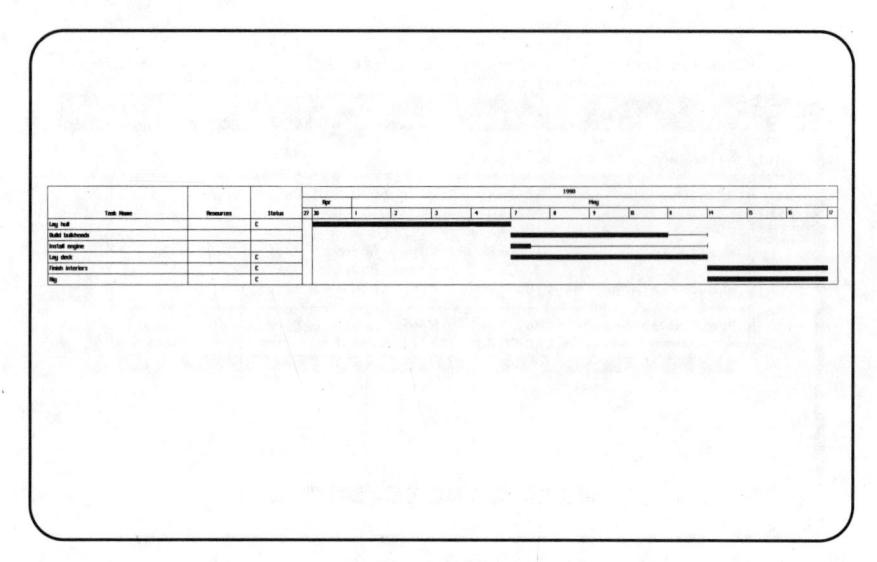

Fig. 3.21. The graphics Gantt chart for the sailboat project.

Printing a Textual PERT Chart

To print a textual PERT Chart report, you take two steps described in the paragraphs that follow. (Again, refer to Chapter 8 for more information.)

1. Activate the menu by pressing /. Select the Reports option (which displays the Reports submenu), and then select the PERT chart option from the Reports submenu.

2. Time Line displays the Ready to print report box (see fig. 3.22). To print the textual version of the PERT report, select Go. To quit, type Q or press Esc.

Figure 3.23, which shows the printed textual version of the PERT chart, illustrates the differences between textual and graphical reports. Textual reports use characters from the regular ASCII character set to create the project management reports. Graphics reports actually draw lines, boxes, and create shading to create the project management reports.

Using Time Line's On-Line Help

From any screen within Time Line, the function key F1 taps an on-line help feature. Time Line's help is context sensitive. In effect, then, you have a reference manual you can access simply by pressing F1. Time Line even opens the on-line "reference manual" to the right page. If you press F1

Chapter 3: Getting Started with Time Line 83

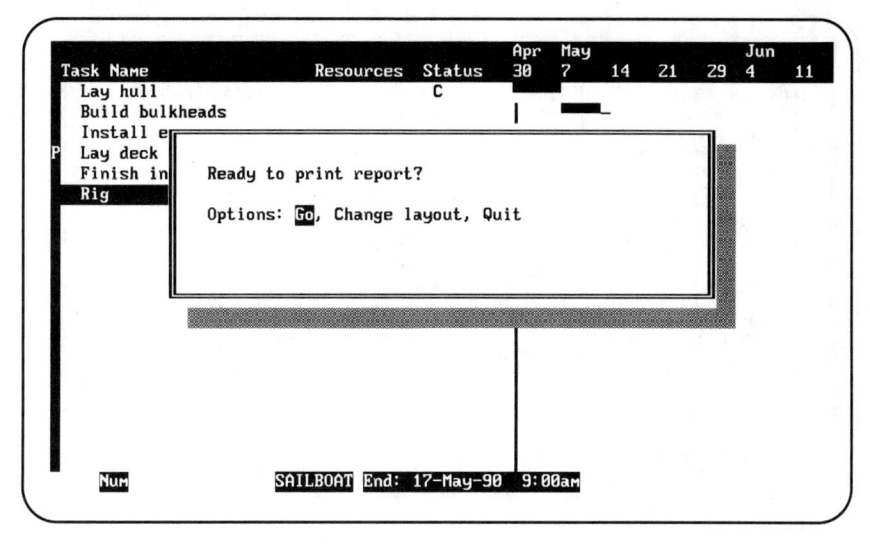

```
                                            Apr  May              Jun
Task Name              Resources  Status     30   7   14   21  29  4   11
    Lay hull                        C
    Build bulkheads                      |      ▬▬
    Install e┌─────────────────────────────────────────┐
    Lay deck │                                         │
    Finish in│  Ready to print report?                 │
P   Rig      │                                         │
             │  Options: Go, Change layout, Quit       │
             │                                         │
             └─────────────────────────────────────────┘

  Num              SAILBOAT  End: 17-May-90  9:00am
```

Fig. 3.22. The Ready to print report box.

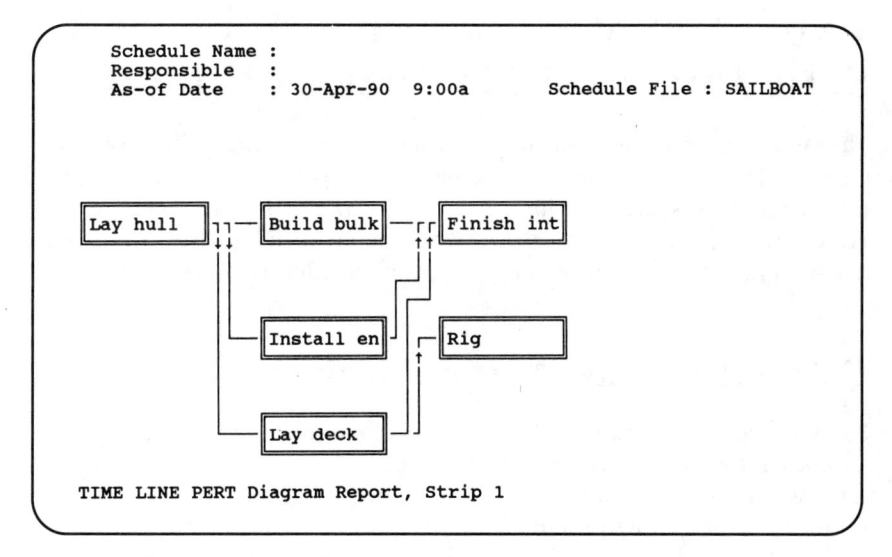

```
    Schedule Name    :
    Responsible      :
    As-of Date       : 30-Apr-90  9:00a        Schedule File : SAILBOAT



       ┌─────────┐     ┌───────────┐     ┌────────────┐
       │ Lay hull│─┐┐──│ Build bulk│──┌┌─│ Finish int │
       └─────────┘ ↓↓  └───────────┘  ↑↑ └────────────┘
                   │                  │
                   │    ┌───────────┐ │  ┌────────────┐
                   └────│ Install en│─┘┌─│ Rig        │
                        └───────────┘  ↑ └────────────┘
                                       │
                        ┌───────────┐  │
                        │ Lay deck  │──┘
                        └───────────┘

    TIME LINE PERT Diagram Report, Strip 1
```

Fig. 3.23. The printed textual version of the PERT chart.

while the Sailboat project is displayed, for example, you get a screenful of information about the Gantt chart view of a project including keys you use to add, edit, and delete tasks, the symbols used, and various other information (see fig. 3.24).

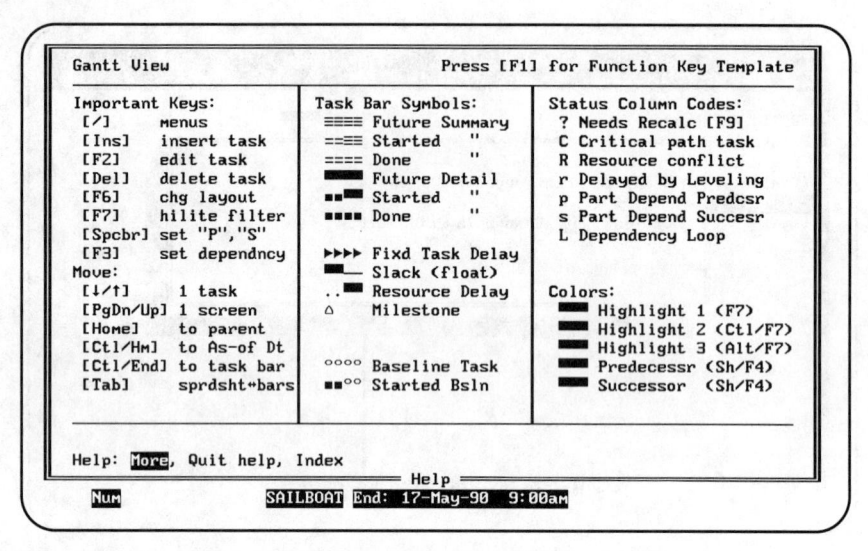

```
Gantt View                            Press [F1] for Function Key Template
Important Keys:      Task Bar Symbols:         Status Column Codes:
[/]    menus        ==== Future Summary        ? Needs Recalc [F9]
[Ins]  insert task  ==== Started    "          C Critical path task
[F2]   edit task    ==== Done       "          R Resource conflict
[Del]  delete task  ■■■■ Future Detail         r Delayed by Leveling
[F6]   chg layout   ■■■■ Started   "           p Part Depend Predcsr
[F7]   hilite filter ■■■■ Done     "           s Part Depend Succesr
[Spcbr] set "P","S"                            L Dependency Loop
[F3]   set dependncy ►►►► Fixd Task Delay
Move:                ■■── Slack (float)
[↓/↑]   1 task       ..■ Resource Delay        Colors:
[PgDn/Up] 1 screen   △   Milestone             ■ Highlight 1 (F7)
[Home]  to parent                              ■ Highlight 2 (Ctl/F7)
[Ctl/Hm] to As-of Dt                           ■ Highlight 3 (Alt/F7)
[Ctl/End] to task bar oooo Baseline Task       ■ Predecessr (Sh/F4)
[Tab]   sprdsht↔bars ■■oo Started Bsln         ■ Successor  (Sh/F4)

Help: More, Quit help, Index
                                       Help
Num                SAILBOAT End: 17-May-90 9:00am
```

Fig. 3.24. Time Line displays a help screen whenever you press F1.

Using the Assist Menu's Help, New Schedule, and Tutorial Options

The Assist menu option on the main menu bar provides three options which are of interest to new Time Line users. If you feel comfortable with the material presented in this chapter and in Chapter 1, "A Primer on Project Management," you probably won't need much help from these two Assist menu options—but you may occasionally find them helpful.

Using the Assist Menu's Help

Help is the first option on the Assist submenu. Help displays three additional options: Presenting Time Line, Index, and Quit. Quit simply returns you to the previous view of the project. Presenting Time Line and Index give you information that can make using Time Line easier.

Presenting Time Line walks you through a short introduction to the Time Line product by displaying nine screens that provide a variety of general information about operating the software and about project management. For example, the first screen welcomes you to Time Line and alerts you that at any time you can press F1 to display a screen with information about what you're trying to do (see fig. 3.25). To be quite candid, you don't need to take the time to go through the Presenting Time Line screens if you've read Chapter 1 and this chapter.

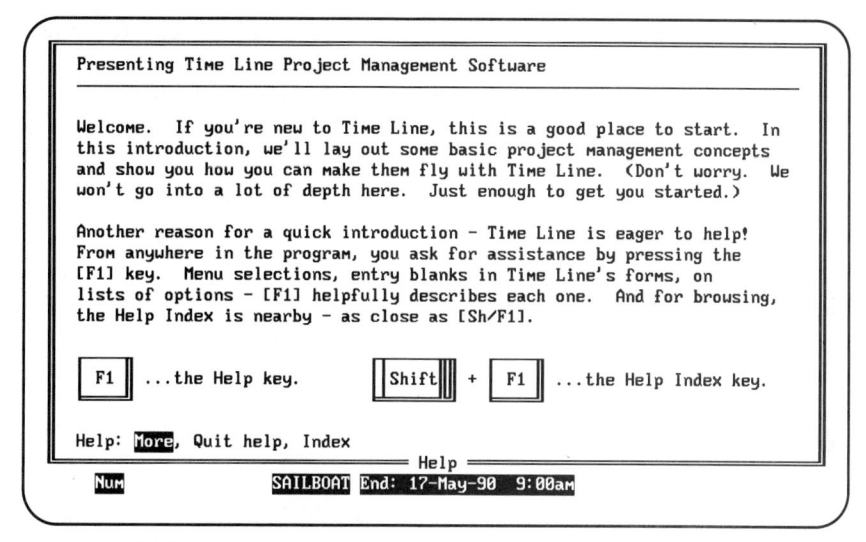

```
┌─────────────────────────────────────────────────────────┐
│ ┌─────────────────────────────────────────────────────┐ │
│ │ Presenting Time Line Project Management Software    │ │
│ │                                                     │ │
│ │ Welcome.  If you're new to Time Line, this is a good place to start.  In │ │
│ │ this introduction, we'll lay out some basic project management concepts │ │
│ │ and show you how you can make them fly with Time Line.  (Don't worry.  We │ │
│ │ won't go into a lot of depth here.  Just enough to get you started.) │ │
│ │                                                     │ │
│ │ Another reason for a quick introduction - Time Line is eager to help! │ │
│ │ From anywhere in the program, you ask for assistance by pressing the │ │
│ │ [F1] key.  Menu selections, entry blanks in Time Line's forms, on │ │
│ │ lists of options - [F1] helpfully describes each one.  And for browsing, │ │
│ │ the Help Index is nearby - as close as [Sh/F1]. │ │
│ │                                                     │ │
│ │   [F1]  ...the Help key.      [Shift] + [F1]  ...the Help Index key. │ │
│ │                                                     │ │
│ │ Help: More, Quit help, Index                        │ │
│ │ ════════════════════════ Help ═════════════════════ │ │
│ │  Num        SAILBOAT End: 17-May-90  9:00am         │ │
│ └─────────────────────────────────────────────────────┘ │
└─────────────────────────────────────────────────────────┘
```

Fig. 3.25. The first page of the Presenting Time Line series of screens.

Index is the second option on the Help menu. Index displays an alphabetized list of help topics (see fig. 3.26). You can also press Shift-F1 to gain access to the help index. To use the index, highlight the topic on which you want help. To move through the list one item at a time, use the up- and down-arrow keys. To move through the list a screenful at a time, use the PgUp and PgDn keys. To see the available help on the selected topic, press Enter or F10.

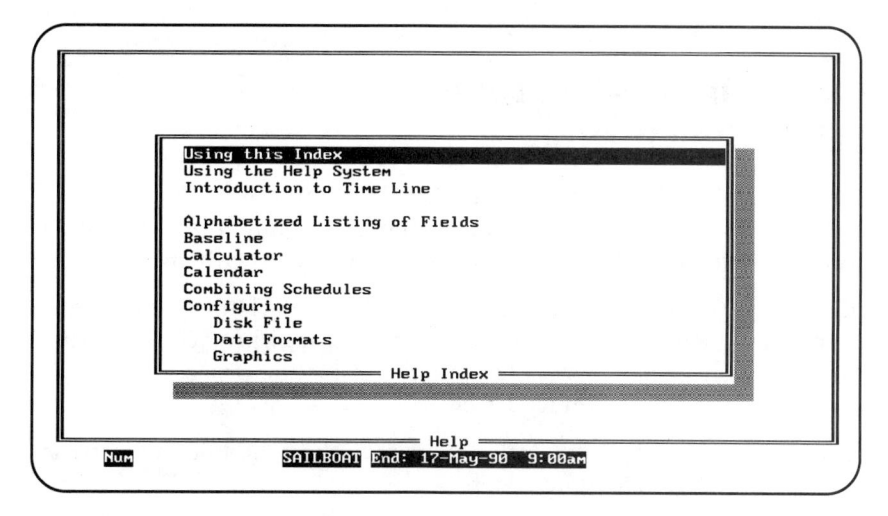

```
┌─────────────────────────────────────────────────────────┐
│                                                         │
│         ┌─────────────────────────────────────┐         │
│         │ Using this Index                    │         │
│         │ Using the Help System               │         │
│         │ Introduction to Time Line           │         │
│         │                                     │         │
│         │ Alphabetized Listing of Fields      │         │
│         │ Baseline                            │         │
│         │ Calculator                          │         │
│         │ Calendar                            │         │
│         │ Combining Schedules                 │         │
│         │ Configuring                         │         │
│         │     Disk File                       │         │
│         │     Date Formats                    │         │
│         │     Graphics                        │         │
│         │ ════════════ Help Index ══════════  │         │
│         └─────────────────────────────────────┘         │
│                        ════════ Help ═══════════        │
│  Num        SAILBOAT End: 17-May-90  9:00am             │
└─────────────────────────────────────────────────────────┘
```

Fig. 3.26. The Help Index screen.

As discussed earlier, Time Line also provides a useful feature called QuickPick which lets you select an item or several items from the list by typing the first character or characters. (You don't need to worry about capitalization.) To see any topics that relate to tasks, for example, you could type *task*. Time Line would then display all the topics that start with the word *task* (see fig. 3.27).

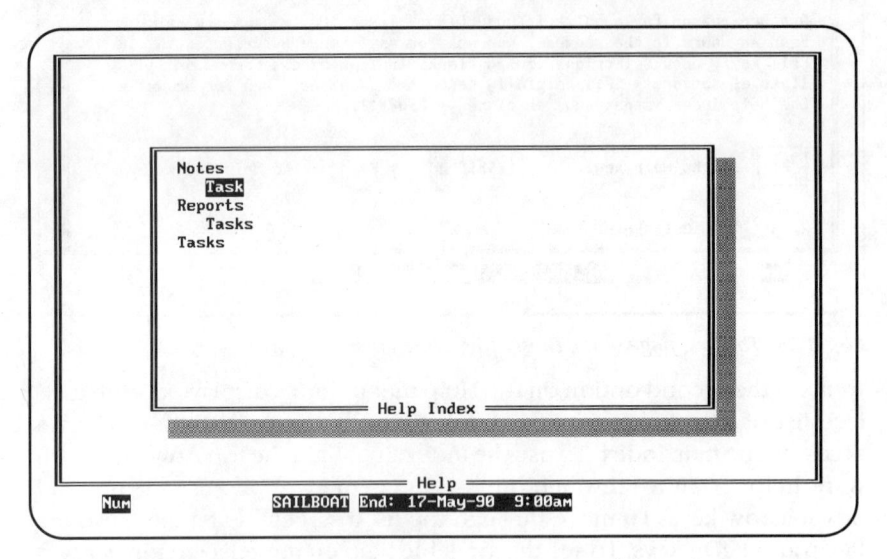

Fig. 3.27. QuickPick lets you type the first letter or letters of the topics you want to see.

Using the Assist Menu's New Schedule Option

Time Line also provides a special menu option that walks you through many of the steps for creating a new project schedule. I didn't discuss it earlier because, until you understand the basics, it's a little overwhelming to use.

However, if you feel comfortable with the basic mechanics of choosing menu options, creating a project calendar, and saving a project, you can use the Assist Menu's New Schedule option to make the process of initially setting up a new project much faster.

To use the New Schedule Option, first save the schedule currently in memory and then follow these steps:

    1. Activate the menu bar by pressing /, and then select Assist New Schedule. Time Line displays two message boxes—one

tells you that New Schedule creates a brand new schedule, and then other asks whether you want to proceed. To continue, select Yes.

2. Time Line next asks whether you want to specify a file name for the project schedule. Select Yes and Time Line displays the File form box, in which you enter a DOS file name for the project. (This procedure was explained earlier in the chapter.) When you complete the File form box, press F10.

3. Time Line next asks whether you want to change holidays and working hours. If you do, select Yes and Time Line displays the calendar submenu, which you use as described earlier in the chapter to create a project calendar. When you're finished defining the project calendar, select Quit from the calendar submenu.

4. Time Line next asks whether you want to enter resources and costs. Select No. ("Defining and Using Resources and Costs," in the next section of the book, provides more advanced descriptions of these items. If you did want to define resources and costs, you'd do so by following the steps described in Chapter 5, "Identifying and Allocating Resources and Costs.")

5. Next, Time Line asks whether you want to enter schedule information or change options. Select No. (If you did want to enter schedule information or change options, you would do so by following the steps described in Chapter 4, "Managing Project and Tasks Details.")

6. Next, Time Line asks whether you want to alter the Gantt Chart Layouts. Select No. (If you did want to alter the Gantt Chart Layouts, you would do so by following the steps described in Chapter 7, "Customizing Screens.")

7. Finally, Time Line asks whether you want to make any additional changes to the schedule. If you answer Yes, Time Line steps through the same series of message boxes referenced in steps 1 through 6. If you answer No, Time Line stops the New Schedule Option and displays the Gantt Chart project screen.

Using the Assist Menu's Tutorial

Time Line provides an on-line tutorial which you can access by activating the menu bar and then selecting Assist Tutorial. If you went through the material covered in this chapter and in Chapter 1, you probably don't need to go through the tutorial. However, if you feel you would benefit from a little more hand-holding, walk through the tutorial's five lessons. They will give you another description of the same basics I've already covered here. Hearing the same information a different way, however, may answer any questions you still have.

Chapter Summary

This chapter describes how to create a simple project, how to print a couple of example reports, and how to save and retrieve the project information. With this information, there's a good chance you now know everything you need for managing the projects—especially if your needs primarily relate to the first two components of project management: organizing the tasks that make up a project and showing the timing and interrelationships.

If what I've described thus far meets your needs, skip ahead to the third section of this book, "Managing the System." Part III includes five chapters—Chapter 7, "Customizing Screens," Chapter 8, "Printing Reports," Chapter 9, "Working with Time Line Files," Chapter 10, "Using the Time Line Utilities," and Chapter 11, "Protecting against System Disasters."

If your project management needs won't be met using the functions described in this chapter, go on to Part II, "Advanced Project Management Features." Part II covers a series of topics related to helping you get more from Time Line. Chapter 4, "Managing Project and Task Details," is probably the best place to start. That chapter gives more information on defining projects, tasks, and dependencies.

Part II

Advanced Project Management Techniques

Includes

Managing Project and Task Details

Identifying and Allocating Resources and Costs

Monitoring Project Progress, Resources, and Costs

4

Managing Project and Task Details

The preceding chapter, "Getting Started with Time Line," describes the basic steps for using Time Line to perform the first two components of project management: organizing the pieces that make up a project, and showing the timing of those pieces, or tasks. But given the power of a computer to collect and arrange project and task information, you can go much further than what Chapter 3 describes. This chapter gives you a tour of the other Time Line features you can use to bolster the basic project management functionality described earlier in the book.

More on Adding Tasks

Chapter 3 covers the basics of adding tasks to a schedule. And you may need only the functions described there. But you can and should consider doing more. This section describes what summary tasks and milestones are and how you use them, how the various views of a project schedule show slack and the critical path, how and why you use WBS codes and OBS codes, and how you link tasks together.

Using Summary Tasks and Subtasks

Summary tasks are tasks that are made up of other tasks. In the case of the sailboat project, for example, each of the six tasks added as part of defining the project may, in fact, really be comprised of still other smaller tasks. Time

Line takes this factor into account by letting you create summary tasks and subtasks. The best way to explain and illustrate the concepts of summary tasks and subtasks is with an example. Assume that the sixth sailboat task (rig) consists of three smaller tasks: installing the winches, the masts, and the halyards. Rig, then, is the summary task. And winches, masts, and halyards are the subtasks.

Creating Subtasks and a Summary Task

To create a subtask, follow these seven steps:

1. Select the summary task and then press Ins to access to the Task Form screen. Define the subtask in the same way that you defined the summary task: give it the name *Winches*, classify its type as ASAP, and estimate its duration as 1 day. Figure 4.1 shows a completed Task Form for adding the subtask Winches. Press F10 when you complete the Task Form.

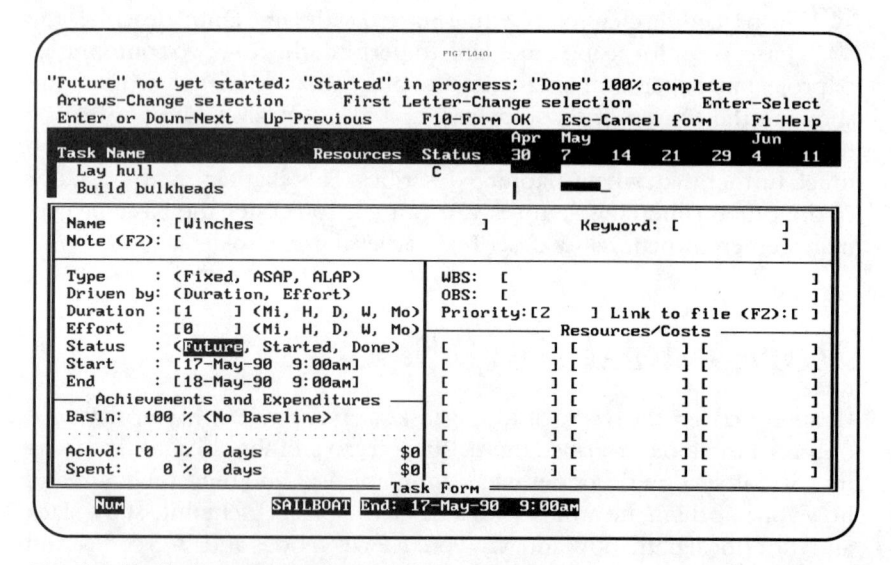

Fig. 4.1. The Task Form completed for adding a subtask.

2. To tell Time Line that Winches is a subtask, activate the menu bar and then select Schedule, Tasks, and then Indent. Or, alternatively, press Shift-right-arrow. Use the right-arrow on the numeric keypad for this. If you use arrow keys, they will not work. Time Line indents the task named Winches under the summary task Rig (see fig. 4.2). In a similar fashion, define the subtasks for Masts and Halyards. For both Masts

and Halyards, the type should be "ASAP", and the duration should be 1 day. As long as you add the two new subtasks under the indented Winches subtasks, Time Line automatically indents them so they align with the task they are added under.

Note: If you indent a summary task, Time Line indents the summary task's subtasks.

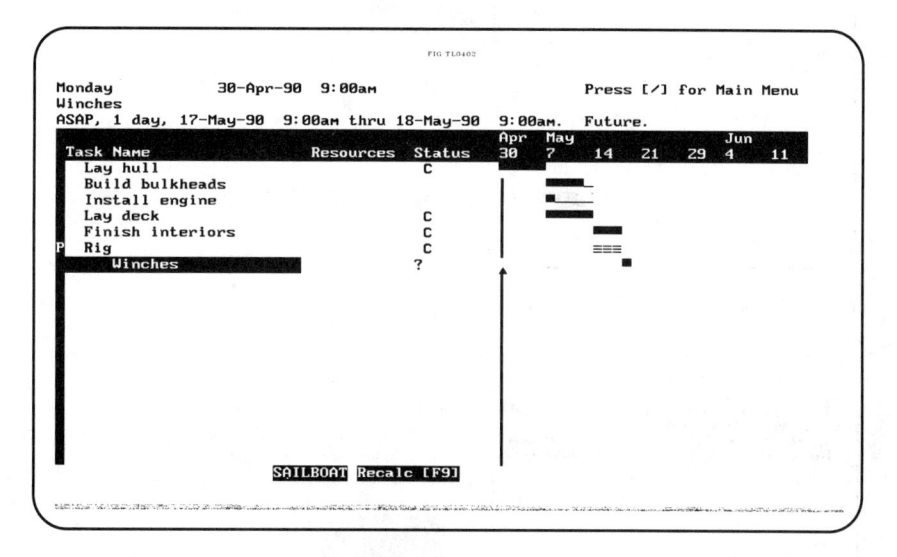

```
                                   FIG TL0402

Monday           30-Apr-90   9:00am                Press [/] for Main Menu
Winches
ASAP, 1 day, 17-May-90  9:00am thru 18-May-90  9:00am.  Future.
                                              Apr  May              Jun
 Task Name               Resources  Status    30   7    14   21  29  4   11
     Lay hull                          C
     Build bulkheads
     Install engine
     Lay deck                          C
     Finish interiors                  C
 P   Rig                               C
         Winches                       ?




                        SAILBOAT  Recalc [F9]
```

Fig. 4.2. *Time Line indents a subtask.*

3. (Optional) Most probably, dependencies exist between subtasks just as they exist between tasks themselves. To identify subtask dependencies, follow the same steps as you do to identify task dependencies. In this case, change the view of the project to a PERT chart. Activate the menu bar, select Views from the main menu, and then select PERT from the View submenu. Time Line redisplays the sailboat project as a PERT chart (see fig. 4.3).

4. Use the arrow keys to highlight the predecessor task in a dependency and then press the Spacebar. Assume for the purpose of the illustration that Winches must be completed before Masts and that Masts must be completed before Halyards. Time Line marks the task with a P to indicate it will be the predecessor task in a dependency. For the first dependency, Winches to Masts, you highlight Winches as the predecessor (see fig. 4.4).

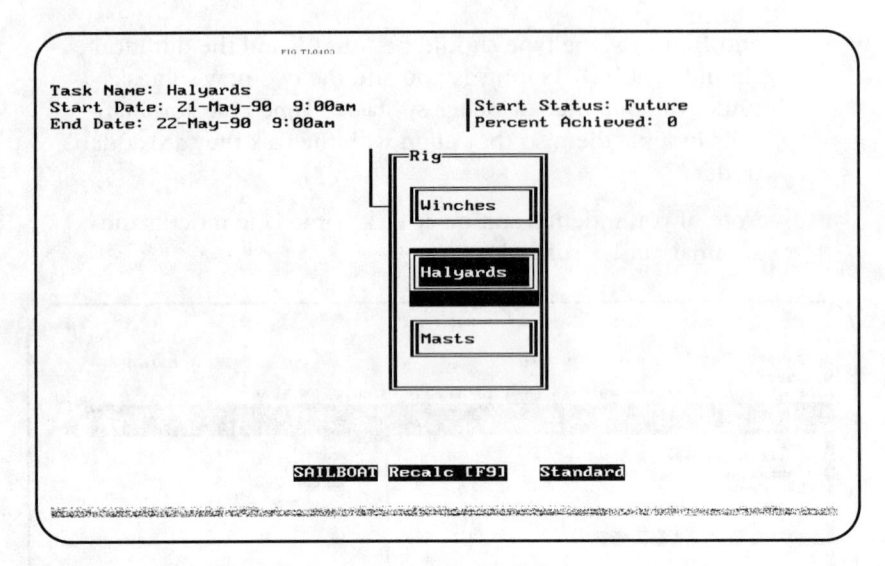

94 Part II: Advanced Project Management Techniques

Fig. 4.3. The sailboat project viewed in a PERT chart.

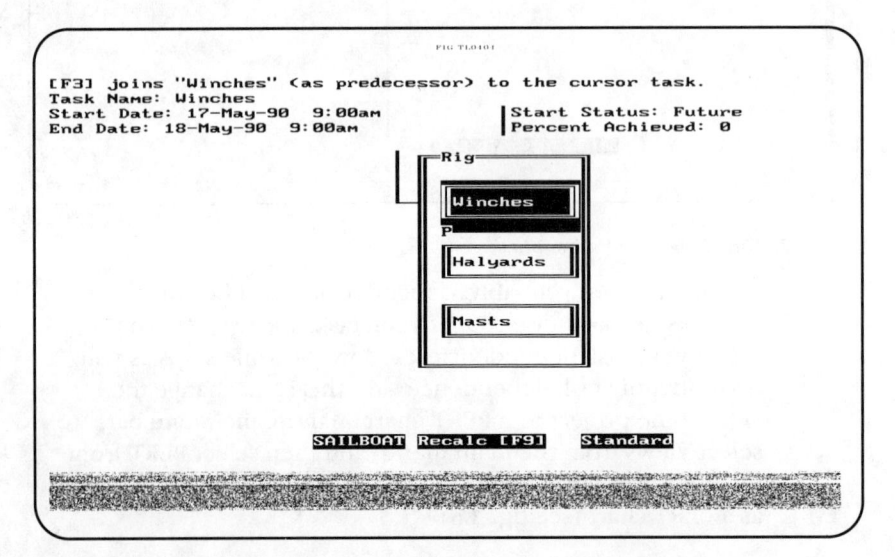

Fig. 4.4. The Winches subtask marked as the predecessor in the first dependency.

5. Use the arrow keys to highlight the successor task in a dependency. For the first dependency, Winches to Masts, you highlight Masts as the successor.

6. Activate the menu bar by pressing /. Then select Schedule from the main menu, Dependencies from the Schedule submenu, and Join from the Dependencies submenu. Repeat

steps 4 through 6 to define the other dependency. When you complete the definitions of the two dependencies, the Rig summary task should resemble figure 4.5.

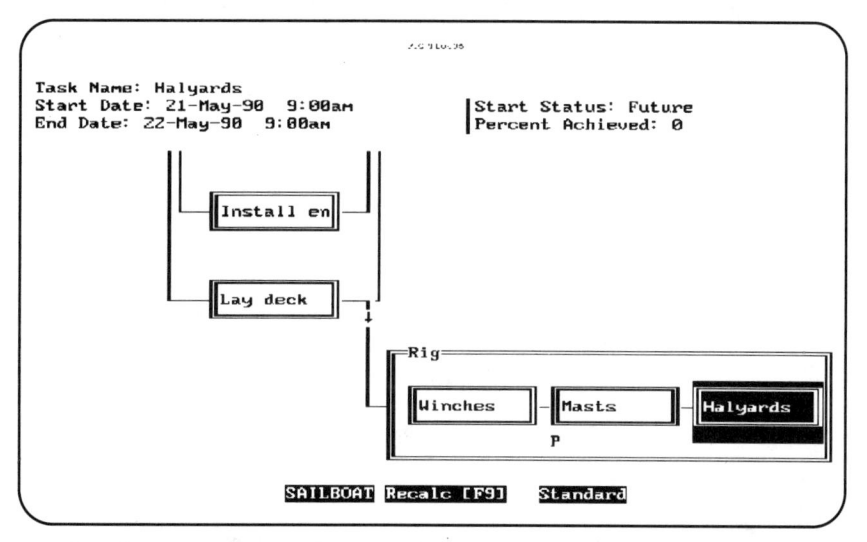

Fig. 4.5. The Rig summary task, viewed in a PERT chart after defining the dependencies.

7. (Optional) To return to the Gantt chart view of the sailboat project, activate the menu bar, select Views from the main menu, and then select Gantt from the View submenu.

   When you complete creating the summary and subtasks, Time Line redisplays the sailboat project as a Gantt chart (see fig. 4.6). As figure 4.6 shows, the duration of the summary task equals the critical path of the subtasks. And to identify summary tasks, Time Line displays the bar representing the duration of the summary task in a different pattern.

8. (Optional) The Tree chart view of a project graphically shows the relationships between summary and subtasks. To view the Rig summary task and its subtasks from this perspective, activate the menu bar and then select Views Tree. Time Line displays the project as shown in figure 4.7. Tasks are shown in boxes, and subtasks are displayed under the summary tasks. To move between tasks, use the arrow keys.

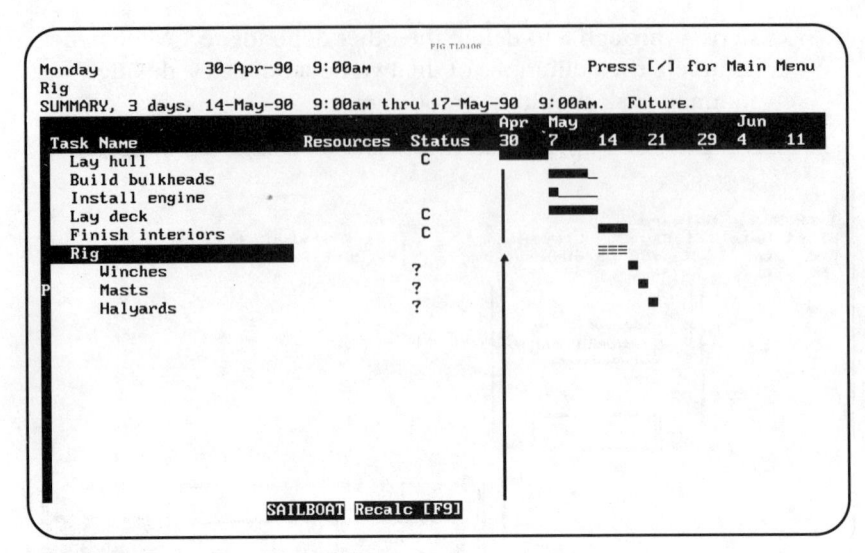

Fig. 4.6. The sailboat project viewed in a Gantt chart.

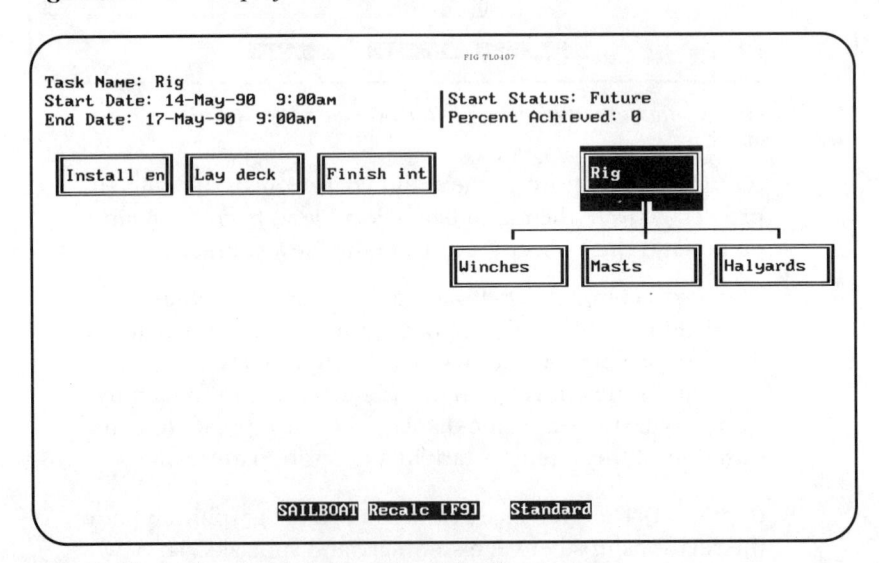

Fig. 4.7. The sailboat project viewed in a Tree chart.

Changing Subtasks to Tasks

To change a subtask into a task and remove it from a summary task, you follow a similar process except in reverse. When the project is displayed in a Gantt view, follow these steps:

    1. Select the task by using the arrow keys.

2. Activate the menu bar, and then select Schedule, Tasks, and then Outdent. Or, alternatively, press Shift-left-arrow. Again, you need to use the arrow key on the keypad. If you outdent a summary task, Time Line also outdents the summary task's subtasks.

3. (Optional) If there are dependencies that no longer exist or are appropriate, activate the menu bar, select Schedule, Dependency, and Unjoin.

Deleting Subtasks and Summary Tasks

Deleting subtasks and summary tasks works roughly the same way as for any other task. You use the Tasks menu Delete option or the Del key. Time Line displays a message box that asks you to confirm you want to delete the selected task. And if you do want to delete the task, select the Proceed option. If you're deleting a summary task, Time Line also displays a second message box that asks you to confirm you want to delete the subtasks. And you can answer Cancel or Proceed to the delete subtasks question.

Hiding and Unhiding Subtasks

You can hide the subtasks that make up a summary task. To do this, select the summary task and then press the - key. If a summary task has hidden subtasks, Time Line displays the + symbol in front of the Summary task (see fig. 4.8). To redisplay hidden subtasks, select the summary task with hidden subtasks and then press the + key.

You can also hide and unhide more than one summary task's subtasks. To hide all the subtasks in the schedule, press * * -. To unhide all the previous hidden subtasks in the schedule, press * * +.

When a project has more than one level of subtasks such as is shown in figure 4.9, you can collapse, or hide, the subtasks below a summary task by pressing either - or * -. If you press * to collapse the subtasks below the selected summary task, pressing + uncollapses only the first level of subtasks. If you press - to collapse the subtasks, pressing + uncollapses all the subtasks. To uncollapse all the subtasks—regardless of how you collapsed them in the first place, press * +.

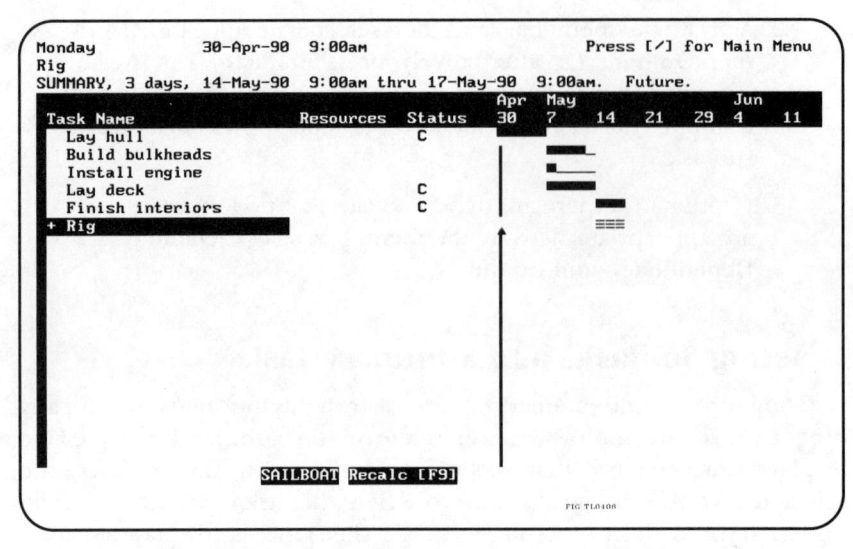

Part II: Advanced Project Management Techniques

```
Monday          30-Apr-90   9:00am                Press [/] for Main Menu
Rig
SUMMARY, 3 days, 14-May-90  9:00am thru 17-May-90  9:00am.  Future.
                                         Apr  May                  Jun
Task Name              Resources  Status  30   7    14   21   29   4    11
    Lay hull                        C
    Build bulkheads
    Install engine
    Lay deck                        C
    Finish interiors                C
+   Rig




                        SAILBOAT Recalc [F9]
```

Fig. 4.8. Time Line indicates when a summary task has hidden subtasks by displaying the + symbol in front of the summary task.

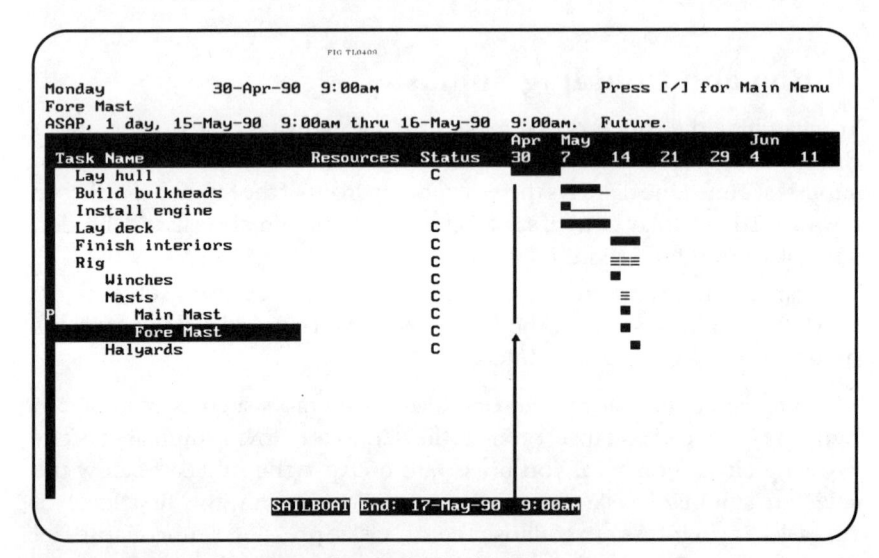

```
Monday          30-Apr-90   9:00am                Press [/] for Main Menu
Fore Mast
ASAP, 1 day, 15-May-90  9:00am thru 16-May-90  9:00am.  Future.
                                         Apr  May                  Jun
Task Name              Resources  Status  30   7    14   21   29   4    11
    Lay hull                        C
    Build bulkheads
    Install engine
    Lay deck                        C
    Finish interiors                C
    Rig                             C
        Winches                     C
        Masts                       C
            Main Mast               C
            Fore Mast               C
        Halyards                    C



                        SAILBOAT End: 17-May-90  9:00am
```

Fig. 4.9. A project may have subtasks with subtasks.

Moving around in a Project with Subtasks

If a project has subtasks, there are several additional key combinations for moving around the task lists:

Key	Action
Home	Moves to the summary task of the subtask where the cursor is currently positioned
End	Moves to the last task at the same level. Or if you're already at the last task at the same level, end moves to the next level
Ctrl-PgUp	Moves up to the next task at the same level
Ctrl-PgDn	Moves down to the next task at the same level
* Ctrl-PgUp	Moves to the first task at the current level
* Ctrl-PgDn	Moves to the last task at the current level

Subtasks and Dependencies

You can use subtasks in dependencies just like any other task. The steps for defining a subtask dependency mirror those for defining a task dependency. There is one thing, however, that you can't do: you can't define a dependency between a summary task and one of the summary task's subtasks. So in the sailboat project example, you can't set the Masts subtask as being dependent on Rig. But that makes sense because a task shouldn't be dependent on itself—even indirectly.

Using Milestones

Milestones are tasks with zero duration. You can create milestones by simply adding a task and specifying the duration as zero. In a sense, milestones represent check points. You can use them to ensure that a project progresses according to schedule. Some people even refer to milestones as the foundation of a project, because milestones tend to anchor a project to a specific time frame. In the example of the sailboat project, receiving a customer order might constitute a milestone—and the event that triggers construction of the sailboat. Another milestone might be delivery of the finished sailboat to the customer.

Defining a Milestone

Defining a milestone requires three simple steps:

1. Press Ins to gain access to the Task Form screen. Define the milestone in the same way that you define tasks: give it a name such as *Order*, classify its type, and enter the duration

Part II: Advanced Project Management Techniques

as 0. Figure 4.10 shows a completed Task Form screen for adding the milestone for a customer order. Press F10 when you complete the Task Form screen.

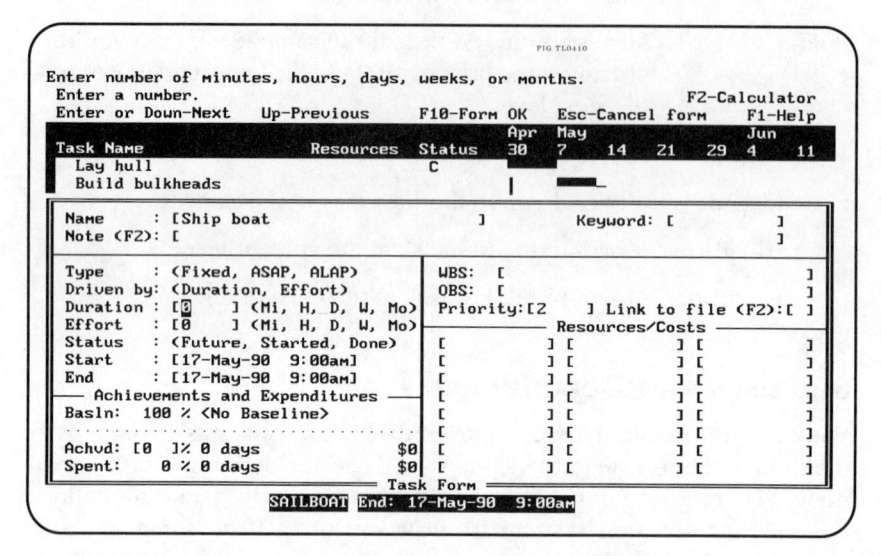

```
                                                      FIG TL0410
Enter number of minutes, hours, days, weeks, or months.
  Enter a number.                                      F2-Calculator
  Enter or Down-Next    Up-Previous      F10-Form OK   Esc-Cancel form    F1-Help
                                          Apr May                    Jun
Task Name                    Resources   Status  30   7   14   21   29   4   11
        Lay hull                          C
        Build bulkheads                     I
  ┌─────────────────────────────────────────────────────────────────────────┐
  │ Name      : [Ship boat                 ]        Keyword: [           ] │
  │ Note (F2): [                                                         ] │
  │                                                                        │
  │ Type      : (Fixed, ASAP, ALAP)        WBS: [                        ] │
  │ Driven by: (Duration, Effort)          OBS: [                        ] │
  │ Duration  : [0  ] (Mi, H, D, W, Mo)    Priority:[2 ] Link to file (F2):[ ]│
  │ Effort    : [0  ] (Mi, H, D, W, Mo)  ── Resources/Costs ──────────────│
  │ Status    : (Future, Started, Done)    [    ] [     ] [     ]       ] │
  │ Start     : [17-May-90  9:00am]        [    ] [     ] [     ]       ] │
  │ End       : [17-May-90  9:00am]        [    ] [     ] [     ]       ] │
  │ ── Achievements and Expenditures ──    [    ] [     ] [     ]       ] │
  │ Basln:  100 % (No Baseline)            [    ] [     ] [     ]       ] │
  │ ..........................             [    ] [     ] [     ]       ] │
  │ Achvd: [0  ]% 0 days             $0    [    ] [     ] [     ]       ] │
  │ Spent:   0 % 0 days              $0    [    ] [     ] [     ]       ] │
  └──────────────────────────── Task Form ─────────────────────────────────┘
                        SAILBOAT End: 17-May-90  9:00am
```

Fig. 4.10. The Task Form screen completed for adding a milestone.

2. To identify the task that the milestone must precede or follow, define a dependency. In the Ship Boat example, the milestone would follow completion of the final two tasks, Rig and Finish interiors. When the milestone precedes another task, use the arrow keys to highlight the milestone and then press the Spacebar. Time Line marks the milestone with a P to indicate it will be a predecessor milestone in a dependency.

3. Use the arrow keys to highlight the task that follows the milestone. For the first milestone, Customer order, you highlight Lay hull as the successor.

4. Activate the main menu by pressing /. Then select Schedule, Dependencies, and then Join. Repeat steps 5 through 7 to define each milestone.

When you complete a definition for the Ship boat milestone, the sailboat project displayed in a Gantt chart should resemble figure 4.11. As figure 4.11 shows, Time Line displays the milestones as triangles on a Gantt chart.

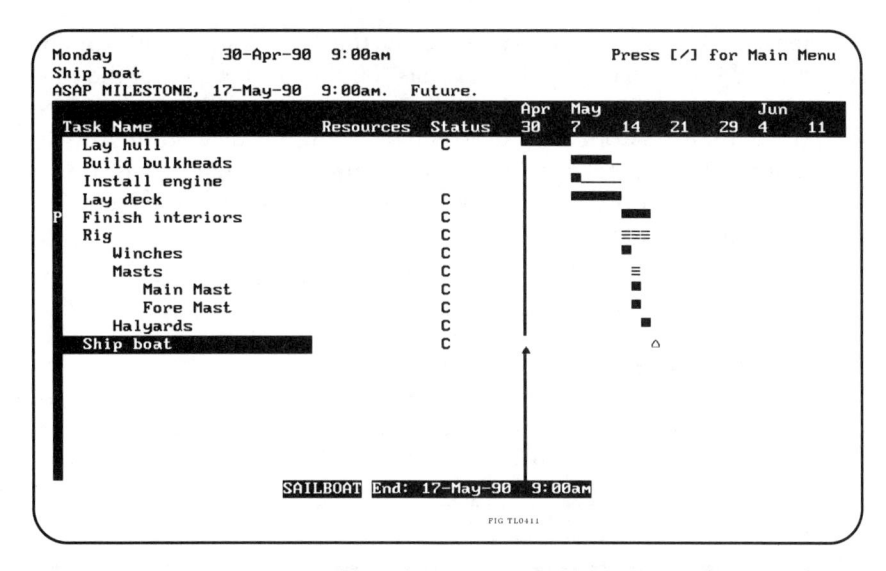

```
Monday          30-Apr-90   9:00am                    Press [/] for Main Menu
Ship boat
ASAP MILESTONE, 17-May-90   9:00am.   Future.
                                                Apr  May             Jun
Task Name                  Resources   Status    30  7    14   21  29  4    11
   Lay hull                              C
   Build bulkheads                                    ▬_
   Install engine                                     ▬
   Lay deck                              C
 P Finish interiors                      C
   Rig                                   C             ≡≡≡
      Winches                            C             ▬
      Masts                              C              ≡
         Main Mast                       C              ▬
         Fore Mast                       C               ▬
      Halyards                           C               ▬
   Ship boat                             C                        △




                            SAILBOAT End: 17-May-90  9:00am
                                        FIG TL0411
```

Fig. 4.11. The Gantt chart updated to include two milestones.

Using Keywords, WBS Codes, and OBS Codes

The Task Form screen provides three optional fields that give you the opportunity to collect additional information about the tasks that make up a project: Keywords, WBS Codes, and OBS Codes. You can also use these three fields to sort and filter the tasks that appear on the screen. (Chapter 7, "Customizing Screens," describes how to sort and filter the tasks that appear in a screen.)

Entering Keywords

The Keyword field provides ten characters of space to further describe or classify a task. Time Line will display the Keyword on the Gantt chart screen if you tell it to by using the Layout Form screen (described in Chapter 7). You can also use the Keyword field to sort or filter tasks (also described in the Chapter 7.) You enter keywords by accessing the Task Form screen, using the arrow keys to move to the Keyword field, and typing the keyword.

Entering WBS Codes

WBS Codes number the tasks in a project. WBS is an acronym for *Work Breakdown Structure*, a system for numbering the tasks in a project. The first task is 1, the second is 2, the third is 3, and so on. If task 1 has subtasks,

Part II: Advanced Project Management Techniques

the first subtask is 1.1, the second is 1.2, the third is 1.3, and so on. You can use the WBS code to extract a task or tasks from a project to another file. Enter WBS codes by accessing the Task Form screen, using the arrow keys to move to the WBS Code field, and then by typing the keyword. The Assist menu option WBS Manager provides tools for quickly assigning WBS Codes to all the tasks in a project. To use the WBS Manager to enter the WBS Codes, follow these steps:

1. Activate the menu bar by pressing /. Select Assist, WBS Manager, and Number Blank Tasks.

2. Time Line displays the Number Blank Tasks box (see fig. 4.12). The program asks which tasks you want to number. Select the All Tasks option and press Enter. Time Line numbers the tasks in the project.

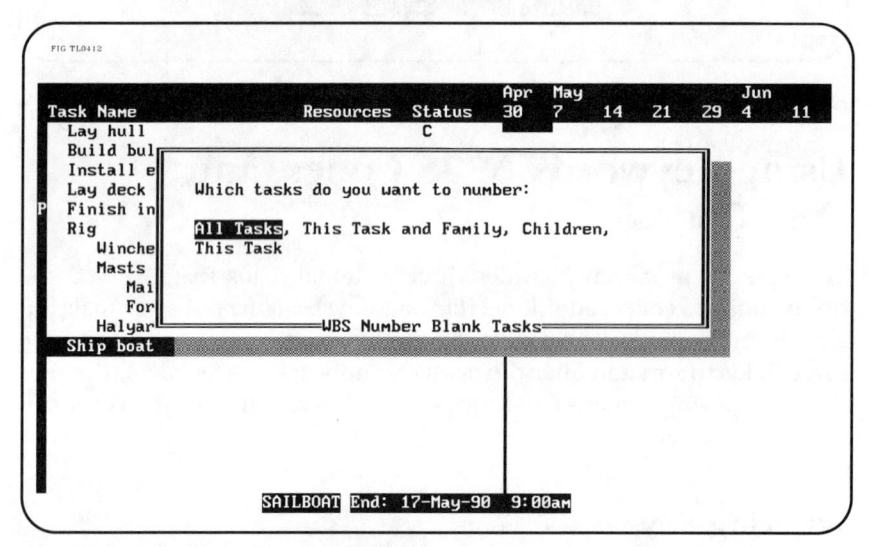

Fig. 4.12. The WBS Number Blank Tasks box.

Using WBS Codes To Search for Tasks

One handy thing to remember if you start using WBS Codes is that just as you can search for tasks based on their task names, you can also search for tasks based on their WBS Codes. To search for a task based on it's WBS Code, follow these steps:

1. Press Shift-F5. Time Line displays a QuickPick box which lists each of the WBS Codes in the project (see fig. 4.13).

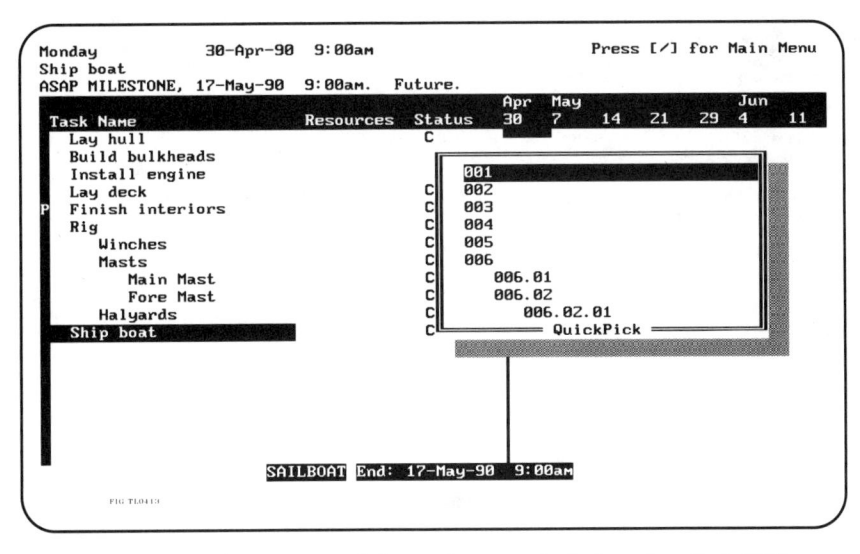

```
Monday          30-Apr-90   9:00am              Press [/] for Main Menu
Ship boat
ASAP MILESTONE, 17-May-90   9:00am.   Future.
                                          Apr  May              Jun
  Task Name               Resources Status 30   7    14   21  29  4     11
     Lay hull                          C
     Build bulkheads
     Install engine                       ┌─────────────────────────────┐
     Lay deck                          C  │ 001                         │
   P Finish interiors                  C  │ 002                         │
     Rig                               C  │ 003                         │
        Winches                        C  │ 004                         │
        Masts                          C  │ 005                         │
           Main Mast                   C  │ 006                         │
           Fore Mast                   C  │    006.01                   │
        Halyards                       C  │    006.02                   │
     Ship boat                         C  │       006.02.01             │
                                          │════════ QuickPick ══════════│
                                          └─────────────────────────────┘


                            ▐SAILBOAT▌ End: 17-May-90   9:00am
```

Fig. 4.13. Time Line lets you search for and move to tasks based on their WBS codes.

   2. Type the first number or numbers of the WBS Code of the task you want to find, and Time Line lists all the WBS Codes that match what you typed.

   3. Using the arrow keys, highlight the WBS Code you want to select and then press Enter. Time Line selects the Gantt chart task you selected from the QuickPick box.

More on Using the WBS Manager

If you do use the WBS Manager to enter WBS Codes, there are a few additional features it provides—and about which you probably want to know. The WBS Manager allows you to create a customized WBS numbering scheme, to review WBS Codes for errors, to remove the WBS Codes already entered for a project, and to transfer the contents of, say, the OBS Code field to the WBS Code field, or vice versa. To use the WBS Manager, you first activate the menu bar, select Assist, and then WBS Manager. Time Line displays the WBS Manager submenu which lists eight options: Form, Both Verify and Renumber, Verify, Number Blank Tasks, Renumber, Erase, Transfer, and Quit (see fig. 4.14).

Defining a WBS Numbering Scheme

Time Line gives you complete flexibility over how it numbers tasks with the WBS Manager. You can control the number of digits used, how codes are formatted, and even direct that letters be used in place of or along side the digits.

Part II: Advanced Project Management Techniques

```
WBS: Form, Both Verify and Renumber, Verify, Number Blank Tasks, Renumber,
     Erase, Transfer, Quit
WBS Form Manager
                                              Apr  May              Jun
  Task Name              Resources  Status    30   7    14   21    29  4    11
    Lay hull                          C
    Build bulkheads                   
    Install engine                    
    Lay deck                          C
  P Finish interiors                  C
    Rig                               C
      Winches                         C
      Masts                           C
        Main Mast                     C
        Fore Mast                     C
      Halyards                        C
    Ship boat                         C

                            SAILBOAT End: 17-May-90  9:00am
FIG TL0414
```

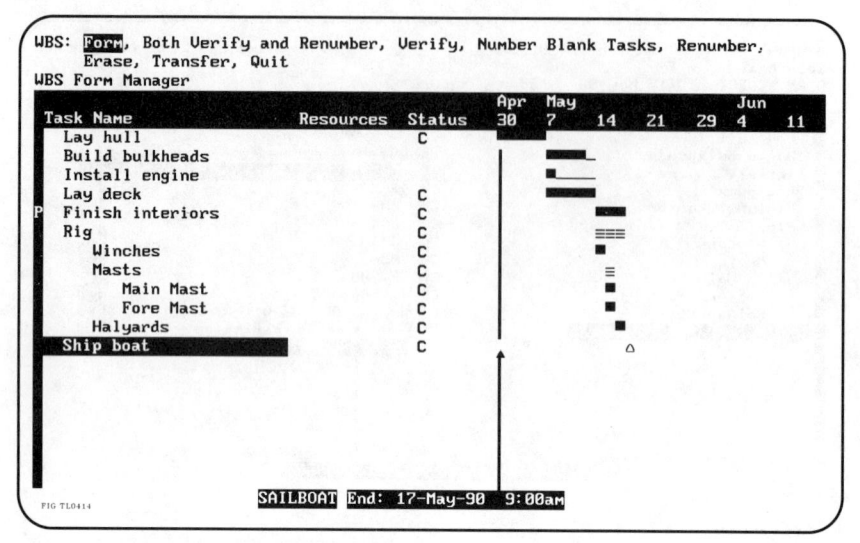

Fig. 4.14. The WBS Manager submenu.

To specify the rules by which Time Line should create the WBS codes:

1. Select the Form menu option. Time Line displays the WBS Manager Form screen, which lets you specify the numbering system that should be used.

2. (Optional) Enter a WBS Code Prefix. The Prefix field lets you specify a letter or number that you want to precede all WBS Codes. By default, the Prefix field is blank.

3. (Optional) Review the character count. The Character count field shows the total characters—letters or numbers—that Time Line will use for the longest WBS code based on the current numbering system. The maximum WBS Code length is 30, so by comparing the character count value to 30, you'll know whether your numbering system must use shorter codes or may use longer codes.

For each task level in a project, you specify seven parameters to control how Time Line creates WBS Codes. The first task level in the sailboat project consists of the tasks: Lay hull, Build bulkheads, Install engine, Lay deck, Finish Interiors, and Rig. The second task level consists of the first level's subtasks. In the sailboat example, this consists of the Rig subtasks: Winches, Masts and Halyards. The third task level consists of the second task level's subtasks. In the Sailboat example, the third level tasks are the Masts subtasks: Main

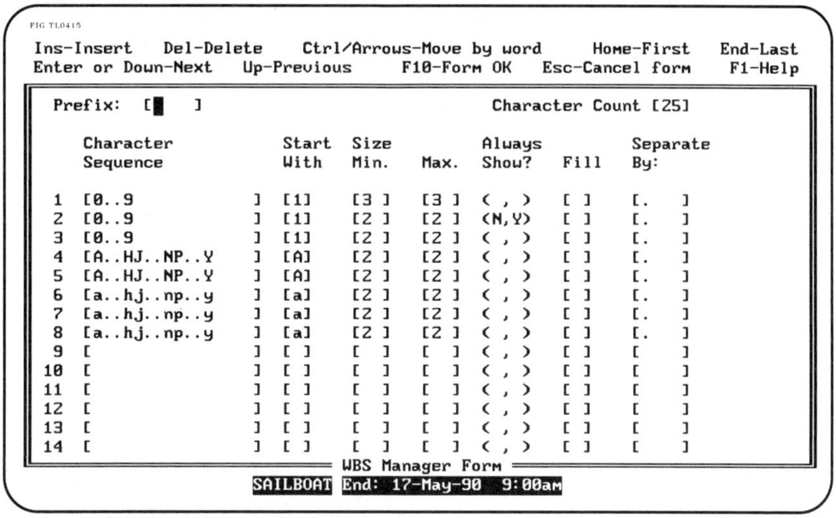

Chapter 4: Managing Projects and Task Details 105

```
 Ins-Insert    Del-Delete    Ctrl/Arrows-Move by word    Home-First    End-Last
 Enter or Down-Next    Up-Previous    F10-Form OK    Esc-Cancel form    F1-Help

   Prefix:  [ ]                                Character Count [25]

        Character              Start  Size           Always        Separate
        Sequence               With   Min.   Max.    Show?  Fill   By:
    1   [0..9           ]      [1]    [3 ]   [3 ]   ( , )   [ ]    [.    ]
    2   [0..9           ]      [1]    [2 ]   [2 ]   (N,Y)   [ ]    [.    ]
    3   [0..9           ]      [1]    [2 ]   [2 ]   ( , )   [ ]    [.    ]
    4   [A..HJ..NP..Y   ]      [A]    [2 ]   [2 ]   ( , )   [ ]    [.    ]
    5   [A..HJ..NP..Y   ]      [A]    [2 ]   [2 ]   ( , )   [ ]    [.    ]
    6   [a..hj..np..y   ]      [a]    [2 ]   [2 ]   ( , )   [ ]    [.    ]
    7   [a..hj..np..y   ]      [a]    [2 ]   [2 ]   ( , )   [ ]    [.    ]
    8   [a..hj..np..y   ]      [a]    [2 ]   [2 ]   ( , )   [ ]    [.    ]
    9   [               ]      [ ]    [  ]   [  ]   ( , )   [ ]    [     ]
   10   [               ]      [ ]    [  ]   [  ]   ( , )   [ ]    [     ]
   11   [               ]      [ ]    [  ]   [  ]   ( , )   [ ]    [     ]
   12   [               ]      [ ]    [  ]   [  ]   ( , )   [ ]    [     ]
   13   [               ]      [ ]    [  ]   [  ]   ( , )   [ ]    [     ]
   14   [               ]      [ ]    [  ]   [  ]   ( , )   [ ]    [     ]
                              ══════════ WBS Manager Form ══════════
                          SAILBOAT  End: 17-May-90   9:00am
```

Fig. 4.15. The WBS Manager Form screen.

Mast and Fore Mast. The WBS Manager Form provides space to specify numbering systems for up to fourteen task levels; these are what the fourteen rows shown in figure 4.15 represent. (If you don't use the WBS Manager Form screen, Time Line applies a default numbering system shown in figure 4.15.)

4. Enter the character sequence. The Character sequence field specifies how Time Line will identify the tasks in that task level. 0..9 indicates that Time Line will number tasks using the numbers from 0 to 9. A..HJ..NP..Y indicates that Time Line will letter tasks using the letters A through H, J through N, and P through Y. Skipping the letters I, O, and Z eliminates the possibility of confusing el with one, oh with zero, and zee with two.

5. Enter the Start with character. The Start with field specifies which number or letter in the character sequence Time Line should use to begin numbering. With a character sequence of 0..9, you probably want to begin numbering with 1. With a character sequence of A..HJ..NP..Y, you probably want to begin numbering with A.

6. Enter the minimum size of each part of the WBS Code. The Size Min field specifies how many numbers or characters Time Line should use to number or letter tasks. With a 0..9 character sequence, a 1 Start with setting, and a Size Min

equal to 3 (the defaults), Time Line numbers the first task in any given level as 001, the second as 002, the third as 003, and so forth. The subtasks under the summary task 001 would be numbered 001.001, 001.002, 001.003, and so on.

7. Enter the maximum size of each part of the WBS Code. The Max field specifies the maximize number of characters Time Line should use for creating WBS Codes on any level. A Max setting of 3, for example, means that Time Line wouldn't ever create numbers that use more than 3 characters.

8. Mark the Always Show field. The Always Show field specifies whether WBS characters show for the parts of a WBS Code that aren't needed. For example, a project such as the sailboat only uses three parts of the WBS Code because there are only three task levels. The Always show field controls whether the unused fourth, fifth, sixth and so on, parts also appear. If the Always Show field is set to Y for yes, all the higher level parts of the code must also be set to yes.

9. Specify the Fill character. The Fill character field indicates which characters Time Line should use for an unused task level for the part of a WBS Code that you've set to Always Show.

10. Specify the Separate by symbol. The Separate by field indicates which character Time Line should use to separate the parts of a WBS Code that number the tasks on a level. The default Separate by entry is a period which makes WBS Codes look like 001.001, 001.002, 001.003, and so forth. But you might decide to use another character—such as a hyphen or slash—to separate the parts of a WBS Code. You can use just about any character, except a character that's also used in the character sequence. The Separate by field is optional if the Max size and Min size fields are set to the same length, because you don't actually need the separate by character to tell where one part of a WBS code ends and another begins. (For example, if the first part is always three characters, you can simply count to the fourth character or number to see where the second part of the WBS Code begins.)

Erasing WBS Codes

To remove the WBS Codes currently entered for tasks, follow these steps:

1. Select the Erase menu option from the WBS Manager submenu. Time Line displays a message box that asks you to confirm you want to erase all the WBS Codes.

2. Select Proceed. Time Line next displays a message box like the one shown in figure 4.16 that asks whether you want to erase all the WBS Codes for all the tasks, for the current task and its subtasks, for the current task's subtasks, or for only the current task.

3. Mark the appropriate selection—Proceed or Cancel—and press Enter.

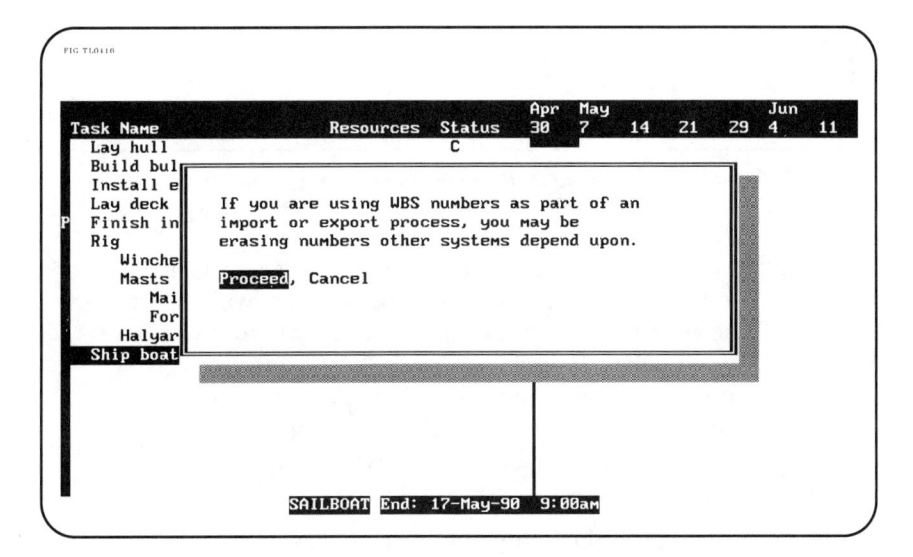

```
FIG TL0416
                                              Apr  May               Jun
Task Name                  Resources  Status  30   7    14   21  29  4    11
  Lay hull                              C
  Build bul
  Install e
  Lay deck     If you are using WBS numbers as part of an
P Finish in    import or export process, you may be
  Rig          erasing numbers other systems depend upon.
     Winche
     Masts     Proceed, Cancel
        Mai
        For
     Halyar
  Ship boat



                       SAILBOAT End: 17-May-90  9:00am
```

Fig. 4.16. The message box that confirms you want to erase WBS codes.

Checking WBS Codes

To check that each of your task's WBS Codes is correct according to the numbering scheme defined on the WBS Codes Form, follow these steps:

1. Select the Both Verify and Renumber or the Verify option from the WBS Manager submenu. Time Line then asks whether you want to check all the WBS Codes for all the tasks, for the current task and its subtasks, for the current task's subtasks, or for the just the current task using a message box like that shown in figure 4.17.

2. Mark the appropriate selection and press Enter.

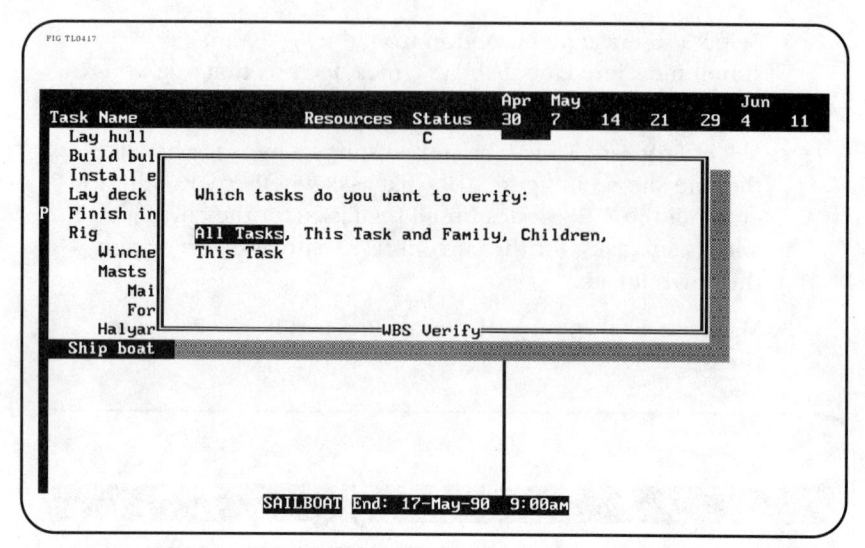

Fig. 4.17. The message box that confirms you want to verify WBS codes.

3. You have two options at this point:

    A. If you select both Verify and Renumber, when Time Line finds an incorrect WBS Code, the program will identify the code using a message box and ask whether you want to renumber the task with a new WBS code. Select No if you don't want to renumber, Yes if you do want to renumber, and Renumber all remaining if you want to renumber the identified task as well as any others that need it.

    B. If you select the Verify option, Time Line displays a message box indicating that there are tasks with incorrect WBS Codes. You may want to use the Renumber option, described later, to correct the situation.

    Note: There is a field called WBS Errors which the Verify option marks when it finds an incorrect WBS Code. Chapter 7, "Customizing Screens," describes how to use the Layout option to control which fields Time Line shows on the Gantt chart screen, including the WBS Code and WBS Errors fields.

Transferring the Contents of another Field to the WBS Code Field

To use what you've entered in the Task Name, Keyword, OBS Code, or Notes fields on the Task Form screen as the WBS Code, follow these steps:

1. Select the Transfer option from the WBS Manager submenu. Time Line then asks whether you want to transfer for all the tasks, for the current task and its subtasks, for the current task's subtasks, or for just the current task using a message box like that shown in figure 4.18.

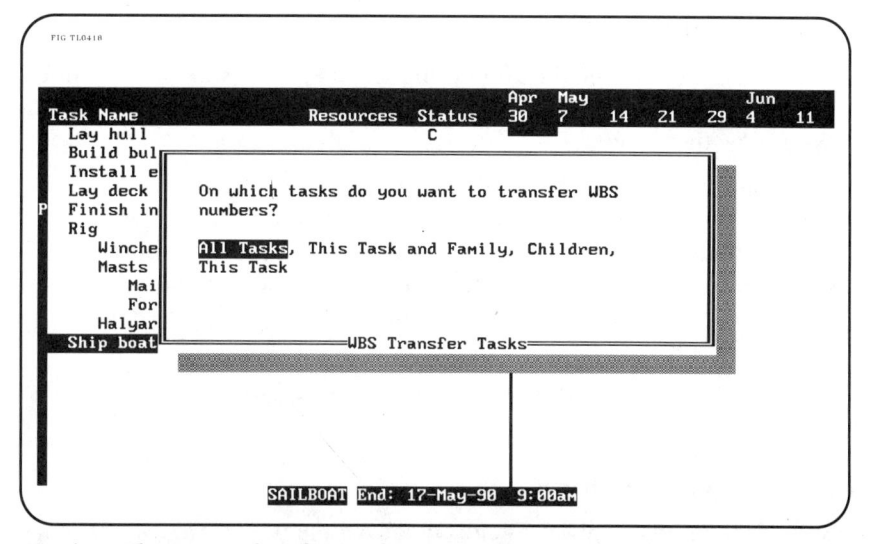

```
FIG TL0418
                                          Apr  May              Jun
Task Name              Resources  Status  30   7    14   21   29   11
     Lay hull                        C
     Build bul┌─────────────────────────────────────────────┐
     Install e│                                             │
     Lay deck │ On which tasks do you want to transfer WBS  │
   P Finish in│ numbers?                                    │
     Rig      │                                             │
     Winche   │ All Tasks, This Task and Family, Children,  │
     Masts    │ This Task                                   │
        Mai   │                                             │
        For   │                                             │
     Halyar   │                                             │
     Ship boat└═══════════════════WBS Transfer Tasks════════┘



                        SAILBOAT End: 17-May-90  9:00am
```

Fig. 4.18. *The message box that confirms you want to transfer WBS codes.*

2. Mark the appropriate selection and press Enter. Time Line then displays a second message box (not shown) that asks which field you want to use to create new WBS codes: Task Name, Key Word, OBS Code, Notes, or Aux 1, 2, or 3.

   Note: The AUX 1,2, and 3 fields are, in effect, extra fields that Time Line provides so you can collect information Time Line doesn't collect somewhere else. To use these fields as data entry fields, you would include them in a layout. Chapter 7 describes how to define layouts.

3. Mark the field you want to use to create WBS codes and press Enter. Time Line displays the a third message box (not shown) that asks how the transfer should be performed. You have two options:

   A. Mark the Extract up to space or / field if you want to move the contents of the field you identified in step 2 up to the first space or the first / symbol. For example, if the task name field contained *T1 lay hull*, only part of the field (T1) would be transferred.

B. Mark the Interchange to swap the contents of the WBS Code field with whatever you marked in step 3. (*Note:* if the field you identify in step 2 is empty, the Transfer option makes no changes to the WBS code field.)

Renumbering Tasks

If you add tasks or change the numbering scheme, you'll want to renumber all the tasks with the new WBS codes. To direct Time Line to renumber the tasks, follow these steps:

1. Select the Renumber option from the WBS Manager submenu. Time Line then asks whether you want to renumber all the tasks, for the current task and its subtasks, for the current task's subtasks, or for just the current task using a message box similar to those shown in figures 4.16, 4.17, and 4.18.

2. Mark the appropriate selection and press Enter.

Entering OBS Codes

OBS Codes is another optional field. OBS, which stands for *Organizational Breakdown Structure*, gives you up to thirty characters of space to further describe or classify a task. The basic idea is that you use the OBS Codes field to identify the department or division responsible for completing a task, but you can use the field in any way you want. You can also use the OBS Code field to sort or filter tasks as described in Chapter 7. Enter OBS Codes by accessing the Task Form, using the arrow keys to move to the OBS Code field, and then typing the OBS Code.

Linking Tasks to Another File

Sometimes what constitutes a task in one project is actually another project. The other project might even be defined as a separate project in Time Line. In the case of the sailboat, for example, the hull production department might treat the task Lay hull as a project in and of itself. Suppose for the sake of illustration that the hull production department sees the creation of a fiberglass hull as a separate project consisting of six steps:

1. Clean hull mold
2. Lay fiberglass cloth

3. Lay foam core

4. Lay fiberglass cloth

5. Remove hull from mold

6. Paint hull

When that's the case, you might want to define the Lay hull task in the overall sailboat project as being equal to the Lay hull project. Time Line allows you to do just this using a schedule link.

Other times what constitutes a task in one project is also a task in another project. Using the sailboat project example again, it might be that hull production views its April production plan as a project which consists of three tasks:

1. Lay hull for sailboat

2. Lay hull for power-boat

3. Build new mold for new motorsailer

When this is the case, you might want to define the Lay hull task in the sailboat project as being equal to the Lay hull for sailboat task in the April production plan project. Time Line allows you to do this using a task link.

Creating Schedule Links

To use define a task using a schedule link, follow these steps:

1. Select the task that should be linked.

2. Display the Task Form by pressing Ctrl-F2 or by activating the menu bar and selecting Schedule, Tasks, and Edit.

3. Move the cursor to the Link to File field. Press F2 when the cursor rests on the Link to File field. Time Line displays the Task Link Form box at the bottom of the screen (see fig. 4.19).

4. Move the cursor to the Directory field. Enter the complete pathname where the other project file resides in the Directory field. The other project is the one whose project schedule will become a task in the current project schedule. By default, Time Line fills the Directory field with the default data directory, C:\TL4\DATA. If you haven't stored project files in other directories, the default entry should be correct. To see a list of the other directories, press F2 while the

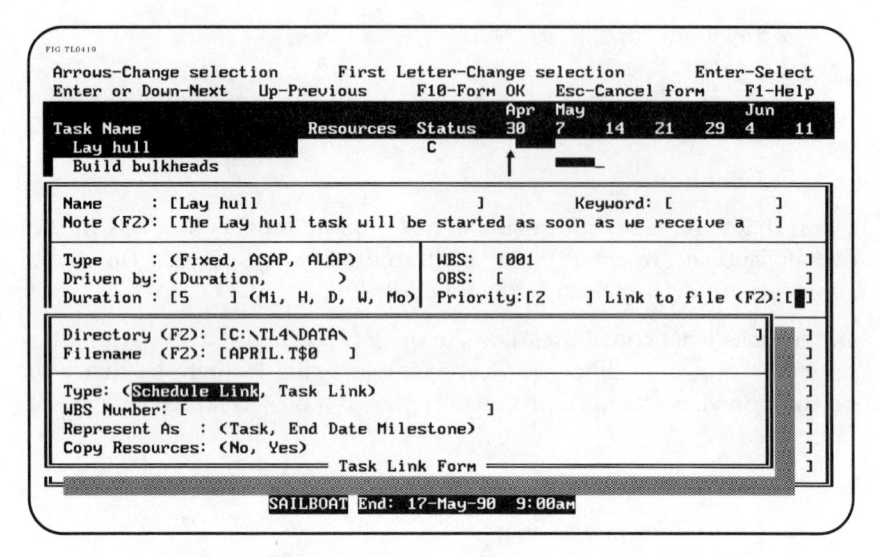

Part II: Advanced Project Management Techniques

```
FIG TL0419
 Arrows-Change selection      First Letter-Change selection        Enter-Select
 Enter or Down-Next   Up-Previous      F10-Form OK    Esc-Cancel form    F1-Help
                                              Apr  May                        Jun
 Task Name                       Resources  Status  30   7    14   21   29   4    11
    Lay hull                                  C
    Build bulkheads

   Name      : [Lay hull                       ]       Keyword: [              ]
   Note (F2): [The Lay hull task will be started as soon as we receive a       ]
   Type      : (Fixed, ASAP, ALAP)     WBS:  [001                              ]
   Driven by: (Duration,       )      OBS:  [                                  ]
   Duration  : [5   ] (Mi, H, D, W, Mo)  Priority:[2  ] Link to file (F2):[█]

   Directory (F2): [C:\TL4\DATA\                                       ]
   Filename  (F2): [APRIL.T$0  ]

   Type: (Schedule Link, Task Link)
   WBS Number: [                   ]
   Represent As  : (Task, End Date Milestone)
   Copy Resources: (No, Yes)
   ═══════════════════════════ Task Link Form ═══════════════════════════
           SAILBOAT  End: 17-May-90   9:00am
```

Fig. 4.19. A completed Task Link Form box that defines a schedule link.

cursor is on the Directory field and Time Line displays a Directory list box. In the Directory list box, use the arrow keys to select the directory, the - key to move to the higher level directory, and the + key to move to the lower level directory.

5. Move the cursor to the Filename field. Enter the file name of the other project file in the Filename field. The project file should use the file extension T$0 so Time Line fills that field for you. To see a list of the files with the T$0 extension in the specified directory, press F2 while the cursor is on the Filename field and Time Line displays the File list box. Use the arrow keys to select the file.

6. Move the cursor to the Type field. Type an S to indicate that this is a schedule link.

7. Move the cursor to the Represent As field. Type a T if the project should be shown as a task. Type an E if the project's completion date should be shown as a milestone.

8. (Optional) If you choose to show the project as a task, you can use the overall resource assignments for the other project as the resource assignments for the task. To do so, use the arrow keys to move the cursor to the Copy Resources field and then type Y for yes.

Note: Chapter 5, "Identifying and Allocating Resources and Costs," describes how you incorporate resources into your project management. You may want to refer there if you need help answering these questions.

Task Links

To define a task using a task link, follow these steps:

1. Look up the WBS Code of the subsidiary task you will link to the current project. (If you haven't defined a WBS Code for the subsidiary task, you'll need to do that first. Refer to the earlier chapter discussion on "Using Keywords, WBS Codes, and OBS Codes.")

2. Select the task that should be linked.

3. Display the Task Form screen by pressing Ctrl-F2 or by activating the menu bar and selecting Schedule, Tasks, and Edit.

4. Move the cursor to the Link to File field. Press F2 when the cursor rests on the Link to File field. Time Line displays the Task Link Form box at the bottom of the screen (see fig. 4.19).

5. Move the cursor to the Directory field and enter the directory. By default, Time Line fills the Directory field with C:\TL4\DATA. To see a list of the other directories, press F2 while the cursor is on the Directory field. Time Line displays a Directory list box. In the Directory list box, use the arrow keys to select the directory, the - key to move to the higher level directory, and the + key to move to the lower level directory.

6. Move the cursor to the Filename field and enter the file name of the other project file. The project file should use the file extension T$0 so Time Line fills that portion of the file name for you. To see a list of the files with the T$0 extension in the specified directory, press F2 while the cursor in on the Filename field. Time Line displays the File list box. Use the arrow keys to select the file.

7. Move the cursor to the Type field. Type an S to indicate that this is a schedule link.

Part II: Advanced Project Management Techniques

8. Move the cursor to the WBS Number field. Enter the WBS Code of the task in the other project to which the current task should be linked.

9. Move the cursor to the Represent As field. Type a T if the task should be shown as a task. Or type an E if the task's completion date should be shown as a milestone.

Note: The Copy Resources setting must be No for a Task Link so Time Line doesn't allow you to access the Copy Resources fields if the Task Link Type is Task.

Removing a Link

As long as a task is linked to a supporting task or project, Time Line updates the task information based on the underlying, supporting task every time you retrieve the project. You can, however, remove the link which means that Time Line no longer updates the task information for changes in the underlying, supporting task—and, instead, just uses the same task information from the last time it updated, or refreshed, the link.

To unlink a task from the supporting task or project, follow these steps:

1. Select the task that is linked.

2. Display the Task Form screen by activating the menu bar, and selecting Schedule, Tasks, and Edit; or by pressing Ctrl-F2.

3. Move the cursor to the Link to File box (which should be checked, indicating that the task is linked to another task or project).

4. Press the Del key to delete, or remove, the link.

5. Press F10 to save your changes to the task.

Using the Other Tasks Menu Options

Besides the Task menu options already discussed, there are several others that help you with the process of describing the tasks that make up a project. Copy makes a duplicate copy of the selected task, Notes lets you add up to a 10K textual description of a task, and Form displays the Task Form for the selected task.

Copying Tasks

Copy makes an almost exact duplicate of the selected task. If the selected task has subtasks, Copy duplicates the subtasks, too. The Copy operation doesn't copy the WBS Code or the dependencies of the original task, but that makes sense. WBS Codes are used to uniquely identify tasks so no two tasks should have the same WBS Code. Two similar tasks probably wouldn't have the same dependencies. To make a copy of a task, follow these steps:

1. Select the task to be duplicated.

2. Activate the menu bar and select Schedule Tasks Copy. Time Line displays the Task Form for the new task.

3. Make any changes to the definition of the task using the Task Form fields and then press F10 to complete the addition of the task. Time Line places the copy of the task immediately below the original task.

4. To move the copy task so it's located in the correct position, verify that the cursor marks the copy task. (If it doesn't, use the arrow keys to first mark the copy task.) Then press Shift-down-arrow to move the copy task down. Or press Shift-up-arrow to move the copy task up. Be sure to use the up- and down-arrow keys on the numeric keypad. (If your keypad has separate arrow keys, those will not work for moving a task.)

Documenting Tasks with Notes

The Notes menu option on the Tasks menu provides an alternative method of documenting tasks with notes: Simply select the task you want to describe, activate the menu bar, and then select Schedule Tasks Notes. Time Line displays the notepad box for the selected task. If you already created a notepad for the task, Time Line displays that note in the notepad box (see fig. 4.20). If you haven't already created a notepad for the task, Time Line displays an empty notepad box.

The notepads box works like a simple word processor: Position the cursor wherever you want to enter text and then type the characters you want to record. Most of the navigation keys to move the cursor. Table 4.1 summarizes the navigation keys you use and what they do.

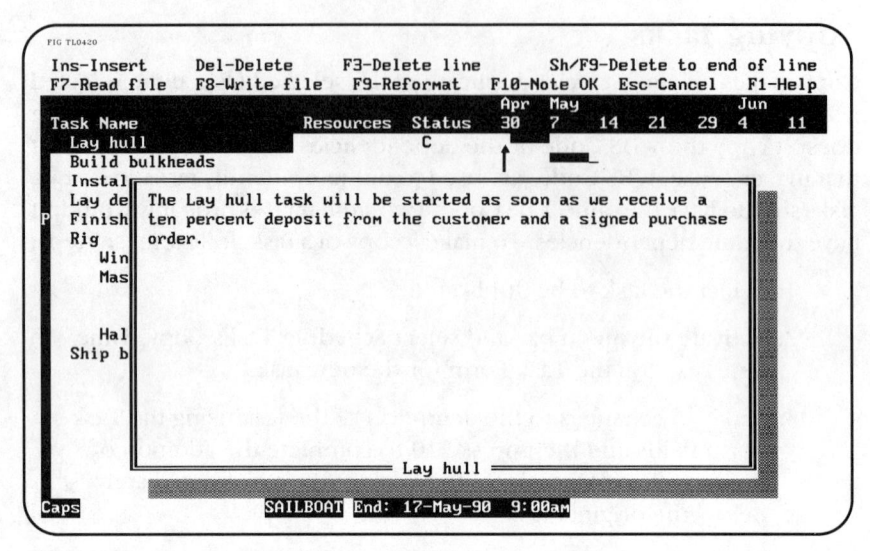

Part II: Advanced Project Management Techniques

```
FIG TL0420
 Ins-Insert      Del-Delete      F3-Delete line      Sh/F9-Delete to end of line
 F7-Read file    F8-Write file   F9-Reformat         F10-Note OK  Esc-Cancel    F1-Help
                                              Apr  May                    Jun
 Task Name                 Resources  Status  30   7    14   21   29   4    11
   Lay hull                           C
   Build bulkheads
   Instal┌──────────────────────────────────────────────────────┐
   Lay de│ The Lay hull task will be started as soon as we receive a │
P  Finish│ ten percent deposit from the customer and a signed purchase │
   Rig   │ order.                                                │
     Win │                                                       │
     Mas │                                                       │
         │                                                       │
         │                                                       │
     Hal │                                                       │
   Ship b│                                                       │
         │                                                       │
         │                                                       │
         └═══════════════════ Lay hull ═════════════════════════┘
 Caps                      SAILBOAT End: 17-May-90  9:00am
```

Fig. 4.20. The notepads box.

Table 4.1
Notepad Navigation Keys

Key	Action
Arrow keys	Moves cursor one character in the direction of the arrow
PgUp	Moves cursor one screen up
PgDn	Moves cursor one screen down
Home	Moves cursor to beginning of the line
Home Home	Moves cursor to beginning of the note
End	Moves cursor to the end of the line
End End	Moves cursor to the end of the note
Ctrl-$la	Moves cursor one word to the left
Ctrl-$ra	Moves cursor one word to the right

Time Line automatically moves the cursor and the words to the next line if the word you type won't fit on the current line. To insert characters in text you've already typed, move the cursor to the location you want to insert the text, press Ins, and then type the characters. To delete characters, move the cursor to the character you want to delete, and then press Del. To delete all the characters on a line the cursor is on, press F3. To delete all the characters on a line from where the cursor is to the end of the line, press Shift-F9. To reformat, or repeat the word wrap, press F9.

Note: There's no way within Time Line to delete all the text in a notepad or to delete the notepad itself. So to remove the text in a notepad, use the F3 key to remove the text, line by line.

You can save the text in a notepad to an ASCII file, and retrieve the text in ASCII file for use in a notepad. (ASCII is an acronym for *American Standard for Computer Information Interchange*.) By saving and retrieving text in ASCII files, you'll be able to pass notepad text between Time Line and any of the popular word processing programs such as WordPerfect, Microsoft Word, or WordStar. To save the text in an ASCII file, press F8. Time Line displays the File Save Form which you use to save the notepad text in a ASCII file. You can also retrieve text from an ASCII file to use as the text in a notepad by pressing F7. Time Line displays the File Access Form screen which you use retrieve an ASCII file for use as notepad text. (Chapter 3, "Getting Started with Time Line," describes how to use the File Save Form screen and File Access Form screen for projects, but they work the same way for ASCII text files.)

Form

The Form option on the Tasks menu displays the Task Form screen filled with the data from the currently selected task. Like the Edit option and pressing Ctrl-F2, the Form option is just another way of causing Time Line to display the Task Form so you can edit and update data.

More on Defining Projects

Most of the discussion thus far has centered on defining projects by defining their tasks and the dependencies between tasks. But there are two Time Line features you use to define project level information: the Option Form and the Journal. As you become more sophisticated in your project management with Time Line, you might want to use these features.

Using the Options Form

Time Line provides the Options Form screen to control and describe a project (see fig. 4.21). The information you enter and the settings you select with the Options Form are saved with the current project and used as the default options for the next project. The Option Form collects a lot of information, but the information really breaks down into nine general categories:

1. Project level information such as project name, description, and project manager
2. Setting the As-of date
3. Selecting the date display
4. Choosing the version of the Task Form screen you want to use
5. Selecting the recalculation method
6. Telling Time Line when future tasks should start
7. Deciding on Undo and Redo limits
8. Turning sound on and off
9. Controlling how PERT charts are drawn

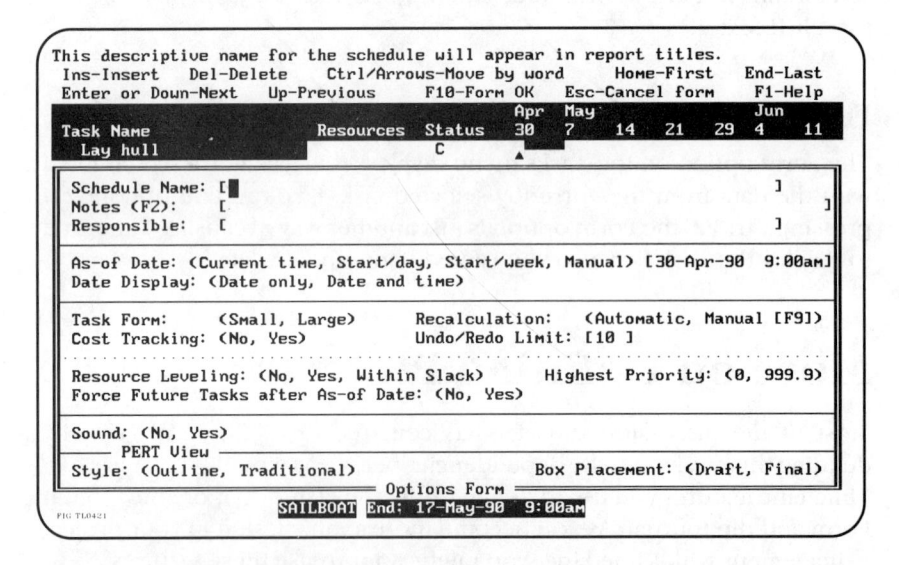

Fig. 4.21. The Options Form.

Collecting Project Level Information

The Options Form collects three pieces of project level information: Schedule Name, Notes, and Responsible. The Schedule Name field gives you up to 55 characters of space to enter a description of the project. The Notes field gives you up to 60 characters of space to further describe a project. You can also press F2 to open a notepad. (Refer to the earlier chapter discussion on "Documenting Tasks with Notes" for information on how the Time Line's notepads work.) The Responsible field gives you a place to record the project manager. Both Schedule Name and Responsible entries can be printed on project reports.

Setting the As-of Date

The As-of date divides the project calendar into the past and the future, which is important for two reasons: it determines where the As-of date line should be drawn on Gantt charts (refer to figure 4.6), and it tells Time Line when to schedule tasks that are supposed to start in the future.

Time Line provides four choices for As-of date settings: Current Time, Start/day, Start/week, and Manual. Current time means the As-of date equals the system date and time, and the As-of date changes in the same unit of time as the precision specified for the Calendar. Start/Day means the As-of date equals the beginning workhour of the current day. Time Line determines the beginning workhour by looking at the Workhours you specified for the calendar and the current day by looking at the system date. Start/Week means the As-of date equals the beginning day and workhour of the current week. Time Line determines the beginning day by looking at the Starting day you specified for the calendar, the beginning workhour by looking at the Workhours you specified for the calendar, and the current week by looking at the system date. Manual means that the As-of date equals the date you enter in the field following the As-of date selection. If you want to keep an unchanging copy of a project schedule as part of an audit trail, or archived version, set a Manual As-of date and enter the date as the historical As-of date. To select the appropriate As-of date, use the up- and down-arrow keys to move the cursor to the current As-of date selection. Then type the first letter of the option you want. Because both Start/Day and Start/Week begin with the letter S, S toggles between Start/Day and Start/Week.

Selecting the Date Display

By default, Time Line displays both the date and time when it gives the starts and finishes of tasks. If you always calibrate task durations in whole days, however, you probably don't need to show start times and finish times because tasks will always start at the beginning of a day and finish at the end of a day. To select the appropriate Date Display, use the up- and down-arrow keys to move the cursor to the current Date Display selection. Then type the letter D to toggle back and forth between the two display alternatives: Date only or Date and Time.

Choosing the Task Form Version

Time Line provides two versions of the Task Form screen: the large version and the small version. The large version is the default Task Form (refer to figure 4.1). You've already used the large version in both this and the previous chapter so I don't need to describe it. The small version simply amounts to an abbreviated version of the Task Form (see fig. 4.22). It omits the fields for collecting the WBS Code, OBS Code, Priority, and Link to File fields, and it omits the fields for collecting and reporting achievement and expenditure data. If you won't use these fields, set the Task Form size to small by using the up- and down-arrow keys to move the cursor until it marks the current Task Form size setting—probably large. Then type the first letter of the size you want: S for small or L for large.

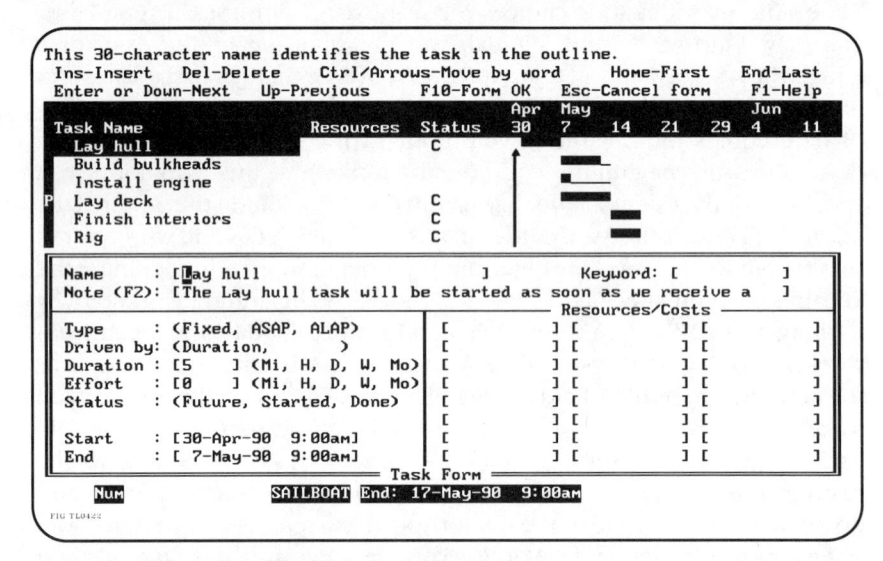

Fig. 4.22. The small version of the Task Form.

Choosing a Recalculation Method

Time Line can recalculate the schedule every time you make a change—called *automatic recalculation*—or only when you direct it to recalculate—called *manual recalculation*. Although automatic recalculation sounds more desirable, you probably don't need to recalculate the project schedule every time you make a change. Recalculation takes time even in small schedules. And you usually don't need to have the schedule recalculated until you've made all your changes. This is why the default setting for recalculation is Manual. If you want to use automatic recalculation instead of manual, use the up- and down arrow keys to move the cursor until it marks the Manual recalculation method and then type an A to select Automatic recalculation.

Deciding on Undo and Redo Limits

You already know about Undo and Redo and how you can use them to recover when you inadvertently make mistakes. By default, Time Line keeps track of the last ten changes to the project so you can undo and redo these. You can keep track of more changes or fewer changes by setting the Undo Redo Limit field to some other number. The smallest Undo Redo limit is 1, which would mean that you could undo or redo only the last change. The largest Undo Redo limit is 999, which means that you can undo or redo the last nine-hundred-and-ninety-nine changes—but don't set the Undo Redo limit higher than ten or fifteen. Time Line's Undo Redo feature uses memory and the higher the Undo Redo Limit setting, the more memory it uses.

Forcing Future Tasks After the As-of Date

The Force Future Tasks After the As-of Date field causes Time Line to schedule any task whose status is future after the As-of date and after the finish of any predecessor tasks. The default setting for the Force Future Tasks option is No, which means that Time Line won't automatically reschedule tasks into the future, although it will mark them for update when you choose Update from the Assist menu. (Chapter 7 describes the Assist Update menu option and how to use it.)

Turning Sound On and Off

Whenever Time Line displays a warning message, it beeps. You can turn off the beep by using the arrow keys to mark the Sound option and by then typing an N to indicate No. Even after you turn off the beep, Time Line still displays warning messages.

Controlling PERT Charts

The Options Form screen includes two settings for controlling how Time Line draws PERT Charts: Style and Quality. Style gives you two choices: Outline and Traditional. Outline, the default style, is illustrated in figure 4.5. Outline shows subtasks in smaller boxes inside a larger box which represents the summary task. The Traditional style also shows the subtasks in smaller boxes but instead of putting the smaller subtask boxes in a larger box, it indicates the start and the end of the summary task in smaller boxes (see fig. 4.23). To set the style, use the arrow keys to move the cursor to the current setting, and then type the first letter of the option you want: O for outline and T for traditional.

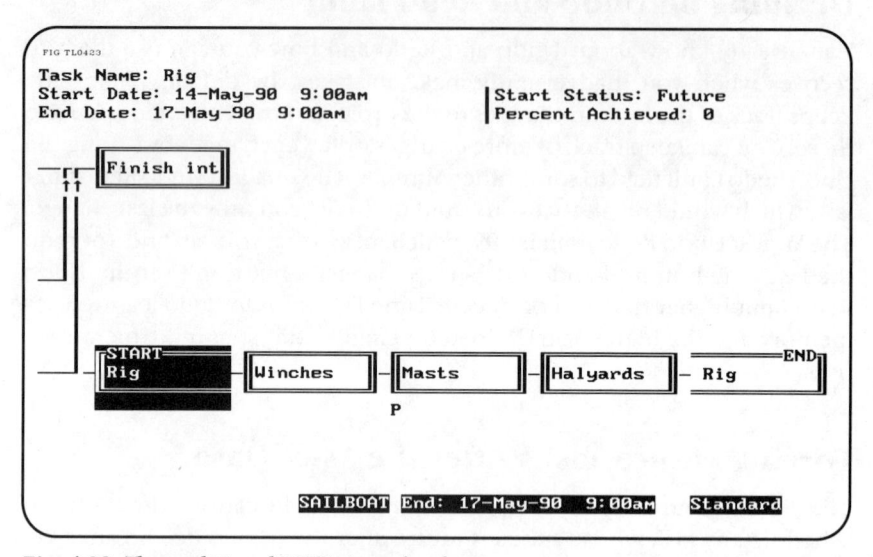

```
FIG TL0423
Task Name: Rig
Start Date: 14-May-90  9:00am         Start Status: Future
End Date:  17-May-90  9:00am          Percent Achieved: 0

        ┌─Finish int─┐

   ┌START═══╗  ┌────────┐  ┌──────┐  ┌─────────┐        ═END┐
   │  Rig   ╟──┤Winches ├──┤Masts ├──┤Halyards ├──  Rig     │
   └════════╝  └────────┘  └──────┘  └─────────┘            ┘
                               P

              SAILBOAT  End: 17-May-90  9:00am   Standard
```

Fig. 4.23. *The traditional PERT view of a chart.*

The Quality setting controls how much time Time Line spends to arrange the boxes that make up a PERT chart. The more time Time Line spends, the more compact and neatly arranged the PERT chart is. The less time Time Line spends, the less compact the Pert chart is. Draft is the default setting. Final simply directs Time Line to take more time so it arranges a more compact view of the project. To set the desired Quality, use the arrow keys to move the cursor to the current setting, and then type the first letter of the option you want: D for draft and F for final.

Using the Journal To Document the Project

Similar to using notes to document features of individual tasks, you can use notes to document the project. In the example of the sailboat project, you might use Project notes to document conversations with the sailboat buyer, to record minutes of project team meetings, or to write project status reports. To create project notes, you use the Journal option, which you access by pressing Alt-F2 or by activating the menu bar and selecting Schedule Journal. Time Line displays the empty Journal box initially because you haven't added any notes to the project.

Chapter 4: Managing Projects and Task Details

To add a project note, press Ins. Time Line displays the notepad box, which you use just as described earlier (see fig. 4.24). When a project note is complete, press F10. Time Line redisplays the Journal box, only this time listing the first line of the project note in the Journal box (see fig. 4.25). (For this reason, it's probably a good idea to use the first line of project notepads as a title or description of the note itself.) To leave the Journal box and return to the Project view, press F10.

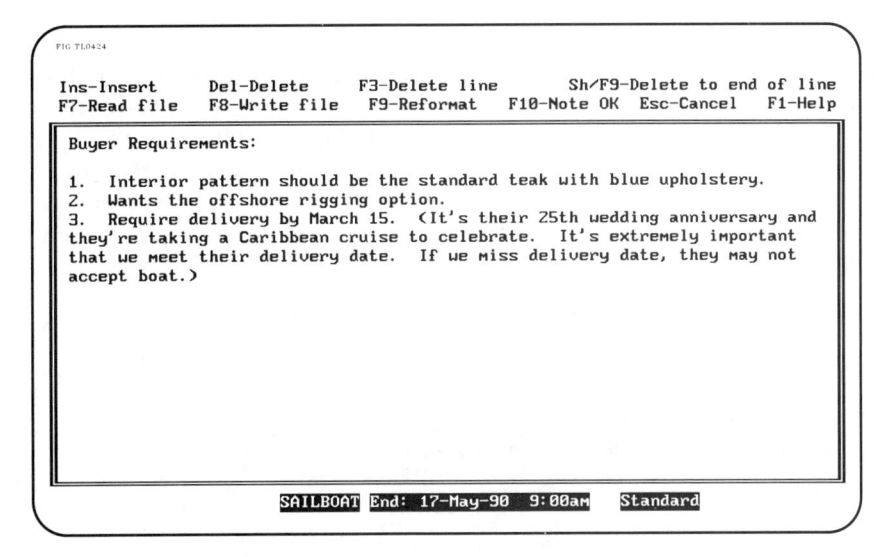

Fig. 4.24. The notepad box filled with an example project note.

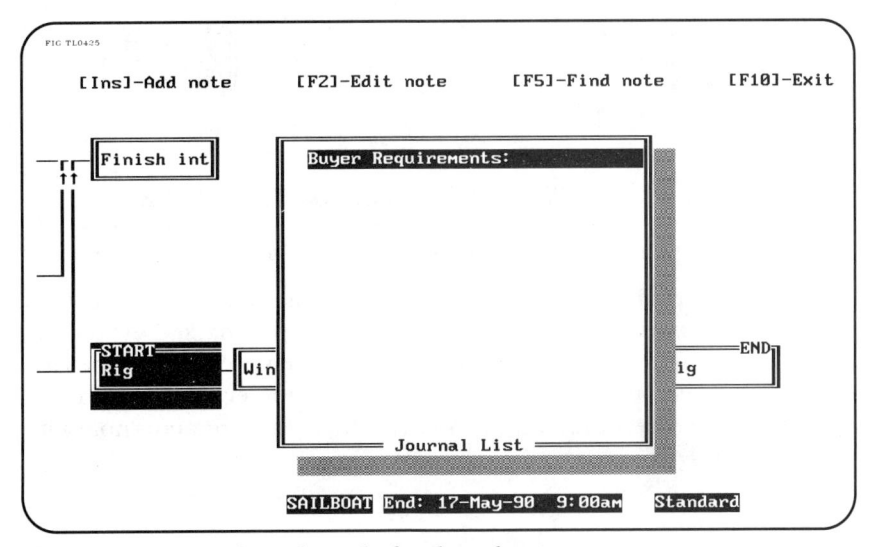

Fig. 4.25. The Journal List shows the first line of project notes.

Part II: Advanced Project Management Techniques

To edit a project note, access the Journal box, position the cursor on the note you want to modify, and then press F2. Time Line displays the notepad. Make the necessary changes, and then press F10 when you're done.

To delete a project note, access the Journal box, position the cursor on the note you want to delete, and then press Del. Time Line asks you to confirm you want to delete the note. Select Proceed to direct Time Line to make the deletion.

The Journal option also lets you organize the project notes in an outline fashion such as the one shown in figure 4.26. To indent the start of a note description, mark the note with the cursor and press Shift-right-arrow. To unindent, or outdent, a note description, mark the note with the cursor and press Shift-left-arrow. To move a note description up one line, mark the note with the cursor and press Shift-up-arrow. To move a note description down one line, mark the note with the cursor and press Shift-down-arrow.

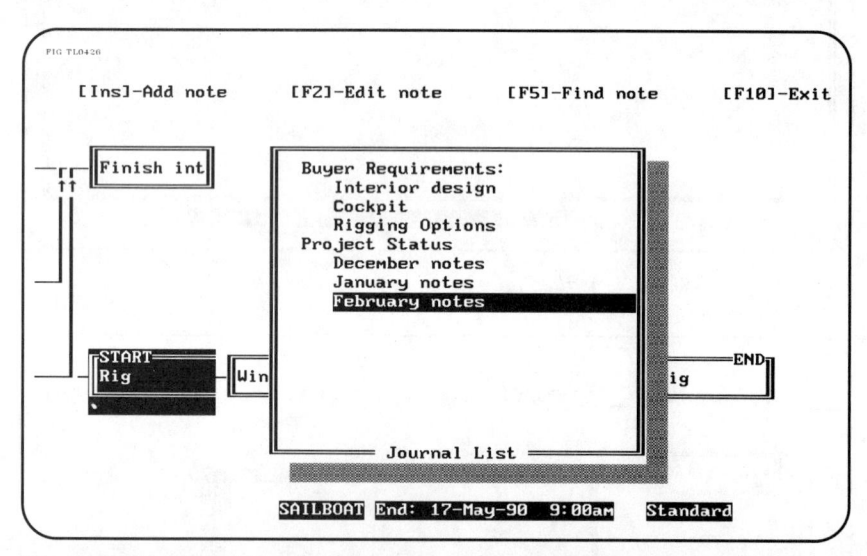

Fig. 4.26. The Journal box allows you to organize project notes in an outline.

If you organize project notes in an outline, you can use the – and + keys to condense and expand the outline. For example, if you marked the outline level, Buyer Requirements, with the cursor and then pressed –, Time Line hides the project notes indented under the Customer Correspondence note. To unhide the project notes, mark the Buyer Requirements note with the cursor and press +.

More on Defining Dependencies

Chapter 3, "Getting Started with Time Line," covers the basics of describing the task dependencies. But you can do more than what Chapter 3 describes. And, sooner or later, you're going to run into some of the common problems associated with task dependencies. This brief section describes how to use the Dependencies Form option to define partial dependencies, discusses how to review the task dependencies you've defined, and lists some common dependency errors you'll want to watch for.

Defining Partial Dependencies

Time Line calls task dependencies in which the successor task immediately follow the predecessor task *standard dependencies*. All the dependencies defined for the sailboat project in Chapter 3 were, for example, standard dependencies. But the condition where one task immediately follows another isn't always the case. Take the case of the sailboat project: the fiberglass hull constructed in the lay hull project might need to cure, or harden, before you begin any of the successor tasks that depend on Lay hull being complete—such as Build bulkheads or Install engine. Say it takes 24 hours for the hull to cure. In that case, the start of a successor task such as Build bulkheads or Install engine must lag the finish of the Lay hull task by 24 hours.

Or it may be that work on the Build bulkheads task or the Install engine task can actually begin before the predecessor task is complete. The mahogany plywood used for the bulkheads, for example, may be cut even as the Lay hull task is being completed. Or the diesel engine may be uncrated and tested even before the Lay hull task is completed. And so in these cases, the start of a successor task may lead, or precede, the completion of the predecessor task.

When the successor task lags or leads the predecessor task, Time Line calls the dependency a *partial dependency*. The steps you use to define the dependency vary from those used to define a standard dependency.

To define partial dependencies, you take the nine steps described below:

1. (Optional) Change the view of the project to a PERT chart. Activate the menu bar, select Views from the main menu, and then select PERT from the View submenu.

2. Use the arrow keys to highlight the predecessor task in a dependency and then press the Spacebar. Time Line marks the task with a P to indicate it will be the predecessor task in a dependency.

Part II: Advanced Project Management Techniques

3. Use the arrow keys to highlight the successor task in a dependency.

    Note: As an alternative to first marking the predecessor task in step 2, you can instead highlight the successor task by pressing the Spacebar twice so Time Line marks the task with an S to indicate it will be the successor task in a dependency. Then in step 3, you highlight the predecessor task.

4. Press Shift-F3 to display the Dependency Form. Or activate the main menu and then select Schedule, Dependencies, and then Form. Time Line displays the Dependency Form screen (see fig. 4.27).

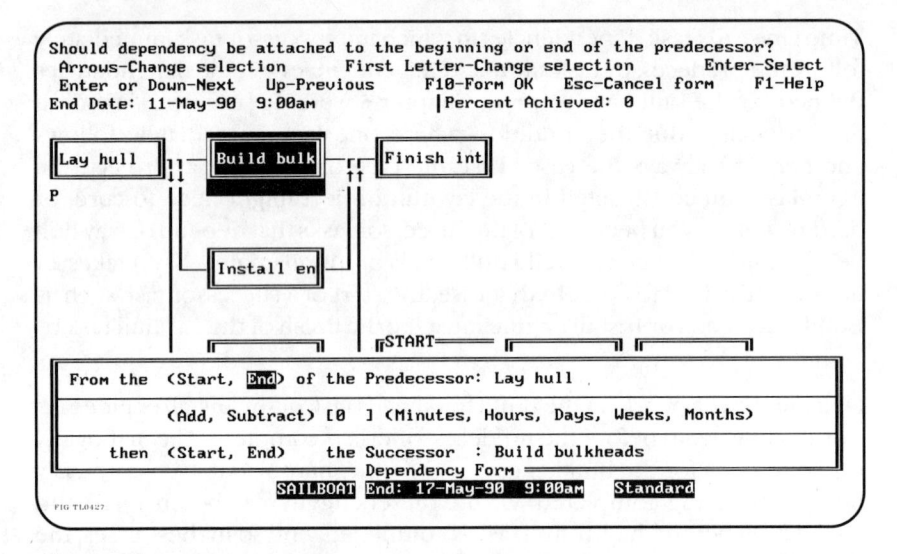

```
Should dependency be attached to the beginning or end of the predecessor?
 Arrows-Change selection      First Letter-Change selection       Enter-Select
 Enter or Down-Next   Up-Previous      F10-Form OK    Esc-Cancel form   F1-Help
 End Date: 11-May-90  9:00am          |Percent Achieved: 0

 |Lay hull |   |Build bulk|   |Finish int|
  P

                 |Install en|

                       ‖START‖
  From the  (Start, End) of the Predecessor: Lay hull
            (Add, Subtract) [0 ] (Minutes, Hours, Days, Weeks, Months)
       then (Start, End)    the Successor   : Build bulkheads
                             Dependency Form
                    SAILBOAT End: 17-May-90  9:00am    Standard
```

Fig. 4.27. The Dependency Form.

5. Move the cursor to the From the field and select whether the lag or lead should be calculated from the Start or the end of the predecessor task.

6. Move the cursor to the Add/Subtract field. Mark Add if the successor should lag the predecessor task, and mark Subtract if the successor should lead predecessor task. (Whether the lag or lead is based on the start or the end of the predecessor depends on the From the field.)

7. Move the cursor to the numeric field where you specify the actual lag or lead, and enter the lag or lead.

8. Move the cursor to the time unit settings which calibrate how the lag or lead time should be measured, and mark the correct time: Minutes, Hours, Days, Weeks, or Months.

9. Move the cursor to the Then field and select whether the lag or lead should be calculated to the Start of the successor task or to the End of the successor task.

Reviewing Task Dependencies

After you've defined dependencies, you need ways to review and verify your work. Three of the menu options on the Dependencies menu really amount to tools you can use for doing just this: Show, PERT, and List. I won't describe PERT here because all it does is draw a PERT chart, allowing you to review graphically task dependencies using a PERT chart. (In Chapter 3, in the section "Defining Dependencies," I suggested you do the same thing using the PERT option on the Views menu.)

Showing the Dependencies

The Show option highlights all the predecessor and successor tasks of the selected task. If you're working with PERT charts, Show doesn't really provide any additional value because PERT charts graphically depict task dependencies anyway. But on Gantt charts, Show gives you a quick way to identify dependent tasks. To use Show, follow these steps:

1. Move the cursor so it marks the task for which you want to identify predecessors and successors.

2. Activate the menu bar and select Schedule, Dependencies, and Show. Time Line highlights the predecessors and successors of the selected task.

Listing the Dependencies with the Dependency Box

The List option displays the Dependency box. The Dependency box lists the predecessor and successor tasks for the task the cursor marked when you selected the option. To see a Dependency box:

1. Move the cursor so it marks the task for which you want to identify predecessors and successors.

2. Activate the menu bar and select Schedule, Dependencies, and List. Time Line lists the selected task as well as any of its predecessors or successors (see fig. 4.28).

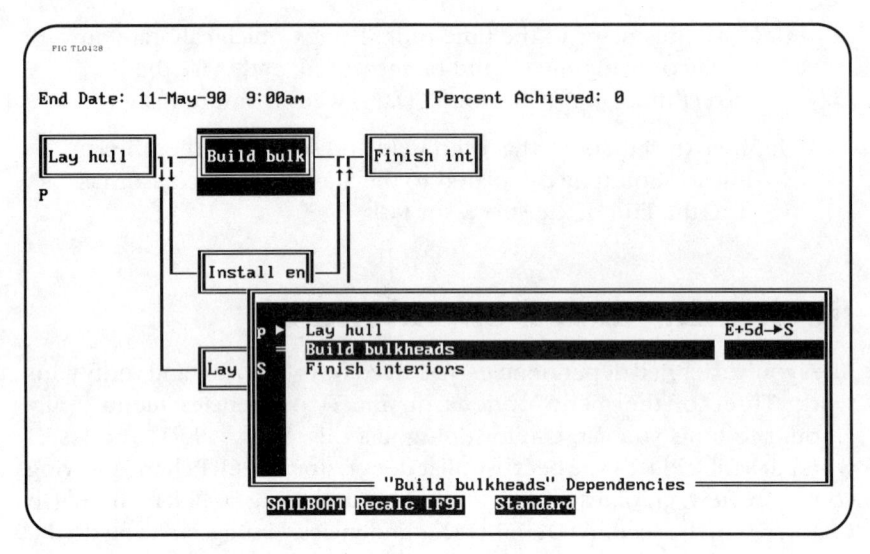

Part II: Advanced Project Management Techniques

Fig. 4.28. The Dependency List box.

To indicate which tasks are which, Time Line displays a one or two symbols along the left border of the Dependency List box:

Symbol	Description
=	Identifies the task for which dependencies are listed
P	Identifies a predecessor with a standard dependency
S	Identifies a successor with a standard dependency
p	Identifies a predecessor with a partial dependency
s	Identifies a successor with a partial dependency.
L	dentifies a task that is part of a dependency loop—an error I'll talk more about a little later
#	Identifies a predecessor task that controls when the task starts, or a successor task that is controlled the task finishes. (Time Line calls this sort of dependency a *controlling dependency*.)
>	Identifies a task on a critical path for either the project or for a successor fixed date task
?	Identifies that a task won't have its dependencies updates until you recalculate the project.

If a dependency is partial, on the right border of the screen Time Line displays an abbreviated description of the partial dependency. If you've reviewed the Dependency Form (refer to figure 4.27), the abbreviation should be pretty understandable. The abbreviation E+5d->S, for example, indicates that the end date of the predecessor must precede by five days the start date of the successor. And the abbreviation E-4h->S indicates that the end date of the predecessor must follow by four hours the start date of the successor task.

Correcting Dependencies from the Dependency Box

You will need to correct any dependency errors you discover after reviewing the Dependency box. But doing so isn't difficult. Just follow these steps:

1. Move the cursor to the predecessor or successor task that is part of the dependency you want to correct.

2. Press F2 to access the Dependency Form screen which you can use as described earlier to change a standard dependency into a partial dependency or to edit a partial dependency (for more information, see "Defining Partial Dependencies," earlier in this chapter).

3. To remove a dependency, press Del to unjoin the task.

Note: Time Line updates the Dependency box to reflect your changes, but you'll need to recalculate the project by pressing F9 to update the Gantt Chart or PERT Chart.

Understanding and Correcting Circular Dependencies

A *circular dependency* happens when a task directly or indirectly depends on itself. Time Line prevents the obvious circular dependencies such as a task A depending on task B which, in turn, depends on task A, or a subtask depending on its summary task. To illustrate this—and working through an example will help you correct circular dependencies in the future—mark the Lay hull task as a successor task by moving the cursor so it marks Lay hull and by pressing the Spacebar twice so Time Line marks Lay hull with an S for successor. Then move the cursor to the Build bulkheads task and press F3 to attempt joining Lay hull as a successor to Build bulkheads. What happens? Time Line doesn't let you join Lay hull to Build bulkheads as a successor task because Lay hull is already a predecessor task to Build bulkheads.

When the circular nature of the dependency isn't as obvious, however, Time Line doesn't prevent it. For example, mark Lay hull as a successor task. Then move the cursor to the Rig task and press F3 to attempt joining Lay hull as a successor to Rig. In this case, even though Lay hull is a predecessor to tasks that are predecessors for the Rig task, Time Line will join Lay hull to Rig as a successor task. You won't know about the circular dependency until you recalculate the project, but when you do that, Time Line alerts you to a circular dependency, called a *loop*, by displaying the words `calc error` at the bottom of the screen as soon as it identifies the circular dependency. Time Line can only identify a circular dependency when you recalculate the project.

Correcting When Recalculation Is Automatic

When the project recalculation is set to automatic, Time Line recalculates the project every time you make a change—either by adding a task or defining a dependency. Because of this, Time Line will immediately identify any circular dependency as soon as you create it. To correct the circular dependency, select Undo either by pressing Alt-F10 or by activating the menu bar and selecting Schedule 1-Undo.

Correcting When Recalculation Is Manual

When the project recalculation is set to manual, Time Line recalculates the project only when you press F9. So the only thing you know for sure is that sometime since the last recalculation, you created a circular dependency. As a first technique, attempt to undo the circular dependency by pressing Alt-F10 or by activating the menu bar, and selecting Schedule 1-Undo. You can Undo as many of the last changes as the Undo/Redo Limit setting on the Options Form screen. The default number is 10 so there's a good chance that you'll be able to undo your circular dependency. (If you frequently recalculate your project when defining dependencies, there's a greater chance you can use this approach.)

If you can't undo the circular dependency with Undo, redo all the changes. Then display a PERT chart view of the project by pressing Ctrl-F4, or by activating the menu bar and selecting Views PERT or selecting Schedule Dependencies PERT. Time Line will display a message box, alerting you that the project contains a loop. And the PERT chart it draws will use only the tasks that are part of the loop. Review the tasks in order, looking for the incorrect dependency.

Chapter Summary

This chapter expands the previous chapter's discussion of the tools that Time Line provides to help you with the first two components of project management: Organizing the pieces that make up a project, and showing the timing of those pieces, or tasks. The chapter gives you more information on adding tasks to a project, on describing the project itself, and on defining the task dependencies. The next two chapters, Chapters 5 and 6, cover the tools Time Line provides for the third and fourth components of project management: Identifying and allocating project resources, and monitoring project time, resources, and costs.

5

Identifying and Allocating Resources and Costs

Ordinarily, you are concerned with more than just the tasks that make up a project and the timing of the tasks; you are also concerned about which resources you need and how much money the project will require. What's more, the three things you use in any project—time, resources, and money—are often interdependent themselves: Taking more time may mean you require less people or equipment but that you spend more money, taking less time may mean you require more resources but also more money, and so forth. The point is that for many projects, it's also important to identify and allocate resources and costs. This chapter describes this important component of project management and the tools that Time Line provides to help you with it.

Expanding the Sailboat Project

The initial version of the sailboat project definition, which you might have created as part of following along with the examples in Chapter 3, consists of six tasks:

1. Lay hull
2. Build bulkheads
3. Install engine
4. Lay deck

5. Finish interiors

6. Rig

Figure 5.1 shows the Gantt chart originally created as part of describing the project which you might want to study for a moment because it will change as a result of allocating resources and identifying resources. Suppose for the sake of illustration that to build the sailboats your firm manufactures, you employ four people:

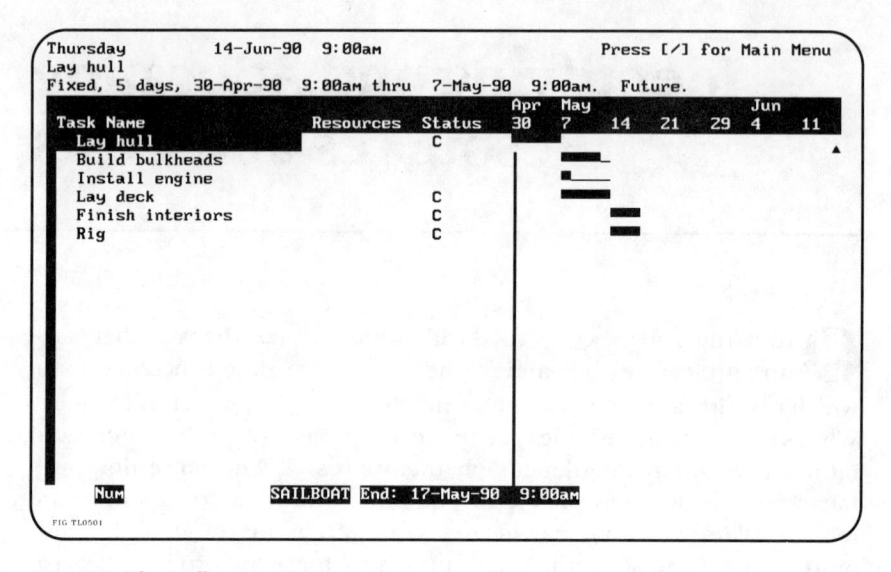

```
Thursday         14-Jun-90    9:00am                    Press [/] for Main Menu
Lay hull
Fixed, 5 days, 30-Apr-90  9:00am thru  7-May-90  9:00am.  Future.
                                          Apr  May                      Jun
   Task Name            Resources  Status  30   7    14   21   29    4    11
   Lay hull                          C
   Build bulkheads
   Install engine
   Lay deck                          C
   Finish interiors                  C
   Rig                               C




   Num              SAILBOAT End: 17-May-90  9:00am
FIG TL0501
```

Fig. 5.1. *The Sailboat project.*

1. Ellen Burg, a fiberglasser who works on laying fiberglass for hulls and decks

2. Everett Wood, a fiberglasser who also works on laying fiberglass for hulls and decks

3. Stan Arlington, a carpenter who builds bulkheads and finishes interiors

4. Mary Ville, a mechanic who installs the auxiliary diesel engines and the sailboat rigging

Also suppose there is a crane that is used to drop the engine into the hull, to lower the partially assembled bulkheads into the hull, and to set deck sections on the hull. To simplify things, let's assume that all of the other tools that the four people use are small hand tools that you don't need to schedule.

So as part of managing a project, you need to schedule the four people resources (Ellen, Everett, Stan, and Mary) and the single equipment resource (the crane). The reason is that completing any of the tasks requires that you have the necessary people and equipment.

Working with Resources

To include resources in your project management, you take three general steps:

1. Identify the resources
2. Allocate the resources
3. Adjust, or level, resource use so that the project doesn't schedule more of a resource than exists

None of this should sound difficult. It isn't. Essentially all you're saying is that, for example, you can't use have two people using the same crane at once. And you can't expect your people who lay fiberglass to be two places at once or doing two jobs at once.

Identifying Resources

The first step for including resources in to identify them. The earlier chapter section on expanding the sailboat project listed four people and one equipment resource:

1. Ellen Burg, a fiberglasser
2. Everett Wood, a fiberglasser
3. Stan Arlington, a carpenter
4. Mary Ville, a mechanic
5. A crane for the install engine, build bulkheads, and lay deck tasks.

To identify any of the resources, you take twelve steps:

1. Activate the menu bar and select Schedule Resources List. Time Line displays the empty Resource/Cost List box (see fig. 5.2).

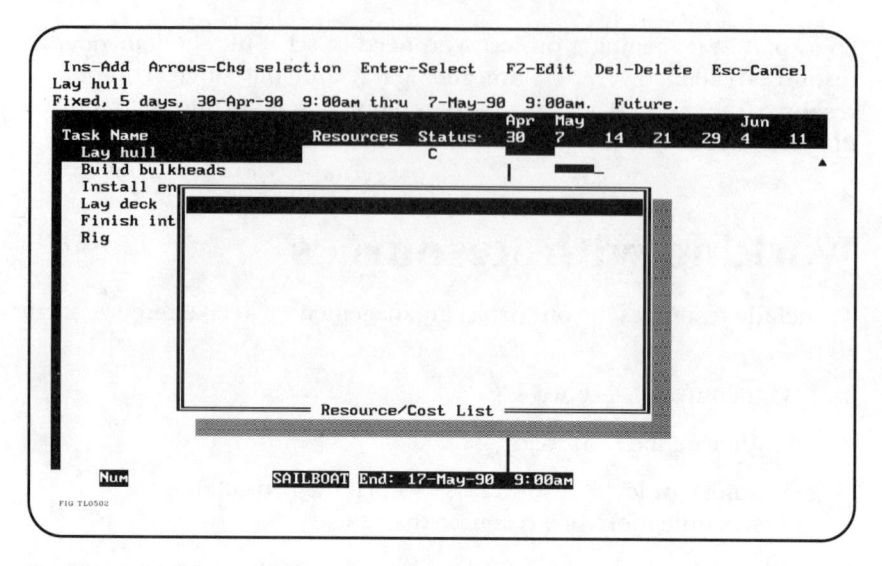

136 Part II: Advanced Project Management Techniques

```
    Ins-Add  Arrows-Chg selection  Enter-Select    F2-Edit   Del-Delete   Esc-Cancel
Lay hull
Fixed, 5 days, 30-Apr-90  9:00am thru  7-May-90  9:00am.  Future.
                                          Apr May                      Jun
Task Name              Resources  Status· 30   7    14   21   29   4      11
   Lay hull                         C
    Build bulkheads                        |
    Install en
    Lay deck
    Finish int
    Rig




                        = Resource/Cost List =


 Num           SAILBOAT End: 17-May-90  9:00am
```

Fig. 5.2. *The empty Resource/Cost List box.*

2. Press Ins. Time Line displays the Resource/Cost Form (see fig. 5.3).

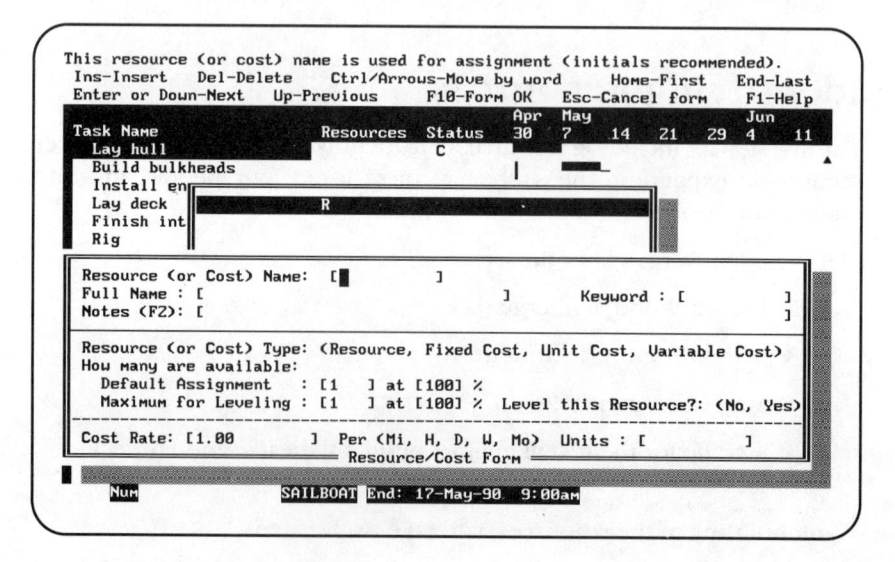

```
    This resource (or cost) name is used for assignment (initials recommended).
    Ins-Insert    Del-Delete    Ctrl/Arrows-Move by word     Home-First    End-Last
    Enter or Down-Next   Up-Previous     F10-Form OK    Esc-Cancel form     F1-Help
                                          Apr May                      Jun
Task Name              Resources  Status  30   7    14   21   29   4      11
   Lay hull                         C
    Build bulkheads                        |
    Install en
    Lay deck              R
    Finish int
    Rig

 Resource (or Cost) Name: [    ]
 Full Name : [             ]           Keyword : [        ]
 Notes (F2): [                                             ]

 Resource (or Cost) Type: (Resource, Fixed Cost, Unit Cost, Variable Cost)
 How many are available:
    Default Assignment  : [1   ] at [100] %
    Maximum for Leveling : [1   ] at [100] %  Level this Resource?: (No, Yes)

 Cost Rate: [1.00     ]  Per (Mi, H, D, W, Mo)  Units : [        ]
                        = Resource/Cost Form =

 Num           SAILBOAT End: 17-May-90  9:00am
```

Fig. 5.3. *The Resource Cost Form.*

3. Type the name of the resource in the Resource (or Cost) Name field. Resource names must be unique. (You've got only ten characters so you may want to abbreviate.) One other thing: With all due respect to the people's individuality and uniqueness, it's probably best to set up resources by type

Chapter 5: Identifying and Allocating Resources and Costs 137

of skill rather than by specific person. So rather than identify Ellen, Everett, Stan, and Mary as the resources, identify the resources as, say, *Fbrglssrs* (as abbreviation for fiberglassers which identifies Ellen and Everett), *Carpenter* (which identifies Stan), and *Mechanic* (which identifies Mary).

4. Move the cursor to the Full Name field and type the unabbreviated name of the resource. So fbrglssrs might be described as "Fiberglassers" or "Hull and Deck Fiberglassers".

5. (Optional) Move the cursor to the Keyword field, and type the keyword. The Keyword field provides 10 characters of space to further describe or classify a resource. You can also use the Keyword field to sort or filter resources as described in the Chapter 7.

6. (Optional) Move the cursor to the Notes field and type any additional description of the resource. You might want to use this field to record the names of the individuals who fall into the resource category such as "Ellen Burg and Everett Wood." You can also press F2 to access a notepad box which you can use as described in the previous chapter to create lengthy descriptions.

7. Move the cursor to the Resource (or Cost) Type field and type an R to indicate you're defining a resource.

8. Move the cursor to the Default Assignment field. Type the number of units of this resource and the percentage of the full workday the resource is available. Here are some examples: Two fiberglassers working full time would have the Default Assignment of 2 at 100%, one carpenter working three-quarter time would have the Default Assignment of 1 at 75%, one mechanic working full time would have the Default Assignment of 1 at 100%, and one crane available all day would have the Default Assignments of 1 at 100%, too.

    Note: Remember to allow time for holidays, vacation, meetings, and so forth. Rarely would a person be 100% available—especially over long projects.

9. Move the cursor to the Maximum for Leveling field. Type the number of units of this resource and the percentage of the full workday the resource might be scheduled, including overtime, if needed so the project isn't delayed. So if the fiberglassers agree to work an extra eight hours on Saturday when needed—as long as, of course, they get time and a

half—set the Maximum for Leveling as 2 at 120%. And if the carpenter will work full-time when needed, set the Maximum for Leveling as 1 at 100%.

10. Move the cursor to the Level this Resource field. *Resource leveling*, if you're not already familiar with the term, refers to adjusting the durations and completion dates of tasks when there aren't adequate resources to complete the tasks as originally scheduled. If you mark the Resource Leveling field to Yes, Time Line levels resources for this resource whenever you recalculate the schedule if the Option Form for the project indicates Resource Leveling as Yes or Within Slack. I'll talk more about resource leveling later in the chapter so for now, if you're not sure whether the answer should be yes or no, set the Resource Leveling field to Yes.

11. Move the cursor to the Cost Rate field. You will only use two of the cost rate fields—Cost Rate and Per—to show the cost of a resource. How you use these fields is probably pretty obvious: If fiberglassers cost you $12.00 per hour, enter 12 in the Cost Rate field, mark H for hours in the Per settings, and leave the Units field blank.

    Note: How precisely you want resource costs figured probably depends on how you'll use the cost data. If you're going to use the cost data in keeping rough track of a project's total costs, you can usually afford to be fairly general. After all, the costs of a project will usually be accounted for with a job cost accounting system. If you're attempting to use the costs data in Time Line to carefully monitor and track project costs, you'll need to be a good deal more precise. People resources should be counted at their full cost, which would include not only their hourly wage but also payroll taxes, benefits, and so forth. Equipment resources should also be counted at their full cost, which might include depreciation, insurance, and maintenance.

12. When the Resource/Cost Form is complete, press F10 to save the resource definition.

Figure 5.4 shows the completed Resource/Cost Form box for the fiberglassers resource. To identify the four resources you will use for the sailboat project, repeat steps 2 through 12 for each of the remaining three resources. When you complete identifying the last resource, the Resource/Cost List should look like the one shown in figure 5.5. To leave the Resource/Cost List, press Esc.

Chapter 5: Identifying and Allocating Resources and Costs 139

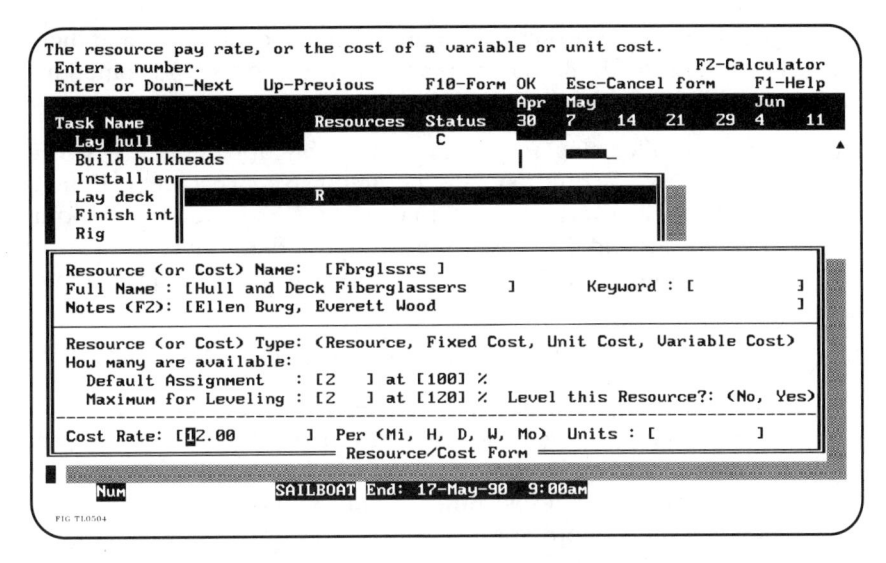

Fig. 5.4. The completed Resource/Cost Form.

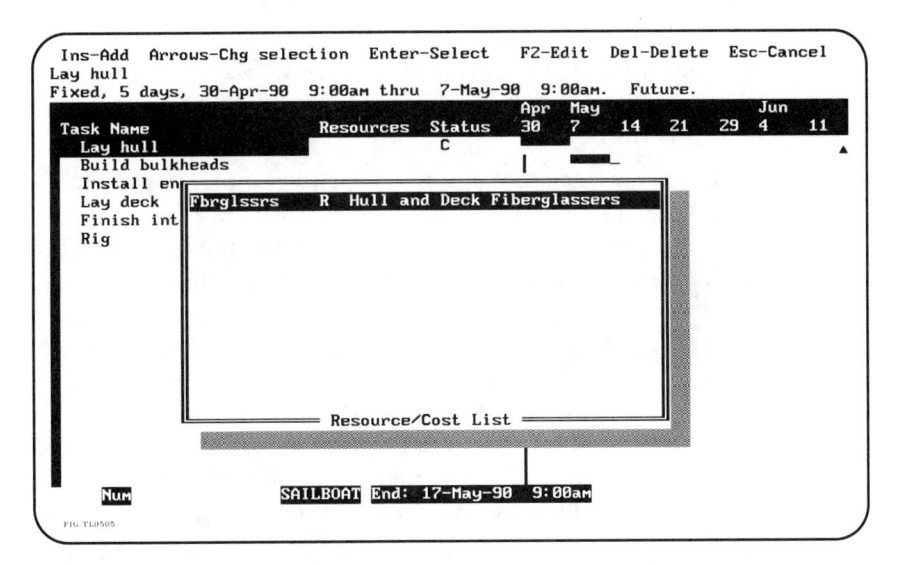

Fig. 5.5. The Resource/Cost List with the new resource.

Allocating Resources

Once you've identified the resources available for a project, you allocate the resources to the tasks that need them. There's nothing tricky about allocating equipment to tasks. Essentially all you're saying is that Ellen and

Everett will work full time on the lay hull task for one full week, and then Stan will work on the build bulkheads task for four days, and sometime during the same four days Mary will install the engine.

The reasons for allocating resources is probably apparent. It's worth mentioning, however, if only to prove the simplicity of what you're doing: You don't want to inadvertently plan to use Stan simultaneously on both the build bulkheads and the finish interiors. Or perhaps more likely, you won't want Stan and Mary to both be planning to use the crane on the same day.

To allocate resources, you follow the eight steps listed below:

1. Verify that Time Line is using the large version of the Task Form screen and the Cost Tracking version of the Resource Assignment Form screen for the project by activating the menu bar, and then selecting Schedule Options. Time Line displays the Options Form. The Cost Tracking setting should be set to Yes. If it isn't, use the arrow keys to mark Yes. The Task Form setting should be set as Large. If it isn't, use the arrow keys to mark Large. Press F10 to save your settings and leave the Option Form. (Refer to Chapter 4, "Managing Project and Task Details," for more information on the Options Form.)

2. Use the cursor to mark the task to which a resource is going to allocated, and then press Ctrl-F2 to display the Task Form for the task. Alternatively, you can also activate the menu bar, and then select Schedule Task Edit. Either way, Time Line displays the Task Form (see fig. 5.6).

3. Move the cursor to the first entry in the Resources/Costs portion of the Task Form. Once there, you can either type the resource name (such as *Fbrglssrs*); or you can press F2 to display the Resources/Costs List box, use the arrow keys to mark the resource, and press Enter. Next, press F2 so Time Line displays the Resource Assignment box (see fig. 5.7).

4. With the cursor positioned at the Assign resource field, type the number of the resource that you are assigning and the percent of time you're assigning the resource. Time Line fills the Assignment fields with the Default Assignment values from the Resource/Cost Form which you entered when you identified the resource. In the case of the fiberglassers, the Default Assignment was 2 at 100% These may be correct. But if, for example, Everett will be on vacation during the week of the Lay hull task, the resource assignment would instead be 1 at 100% because only Ellen will be available for work during the week.

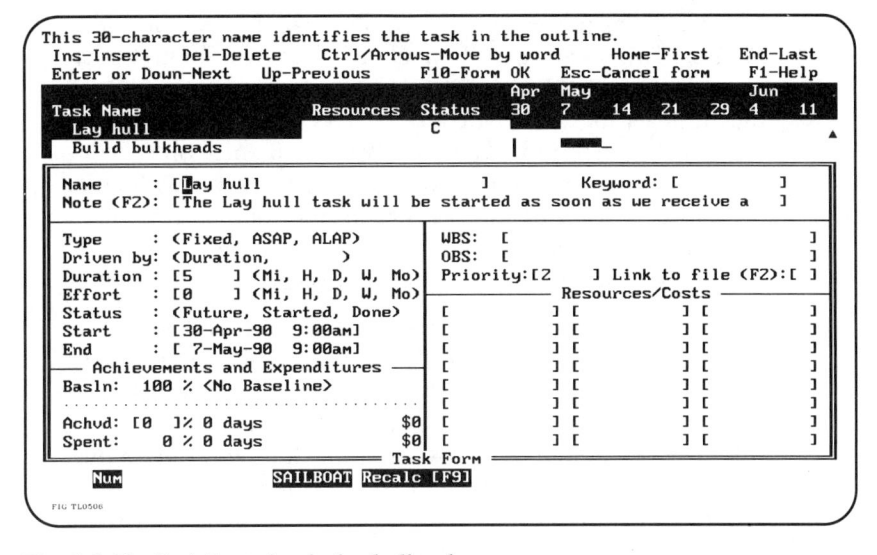

Chapter 5: Identifying and Allocating Resources and Costs

Fig. 5.6. The Task Form for the lay hull task.

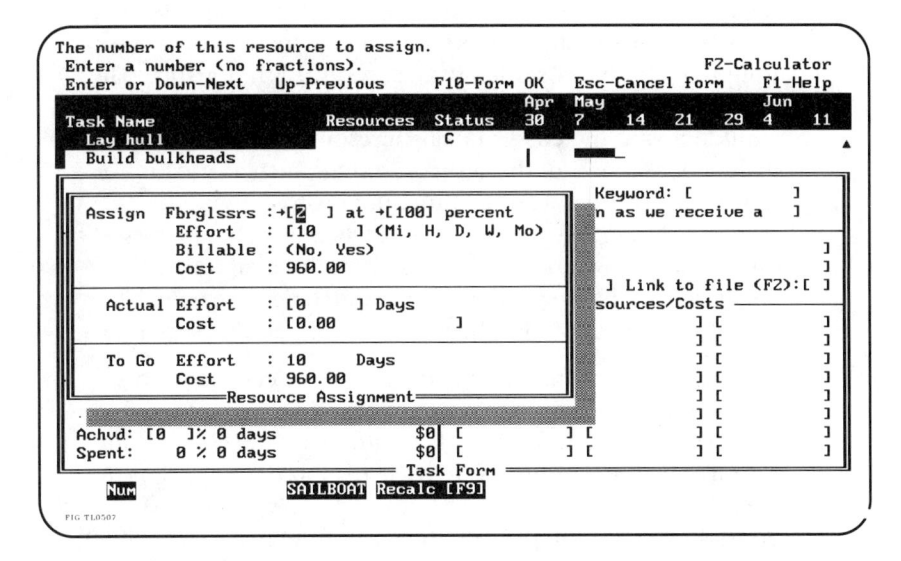

Fig. 5.7. The Resource Assignment Form box.

5. (Optional) As an alternative to entering the assignment as a percent, you may enter the assignment as an amount of time. (As soon as you assign a Resource, Time Line completes the Effort Field by using the duration and the default resource assignment, so you actually need to over-write a figure Time Line has already calculated. To do so, move the cursor to the Effort field, enter in the Effort field the number of time units, and then mark the type of units that calibrate the time: Mi for

minutes, H for hours, D for days, W for Weeks, and Mo for months. This means that if the fiberglassers will spend a total of 10 days, enter 10, press the down-arrow key to move the time unit settings, and type a D for days. You enter either the assignment percent or the effort. When you enter one, Time Line calculates the other for you. (By the way, you can't enter the Resource Assignment as a certain amount of effort if the task duration is effort driven. I'll talk more about effort-driven task durations a little later in this chapter.)

Note: On the Cost Tracking version of the Resource Assignment screen, Time Line provides several addition fields that let you account for the costs of using the resource for the project. If the Cost Tracking Setting for the project is Yes, you will see these fields. (The Cost Tracking Setting is one of the fields on the Options Form.) The next four steps describe how to fill or use these fields.

6. (Optional) Move the cursor to the Billable field. If the cost of the resource should appear on the project cost reports, type Y for yes. If it shouldn't, type N for no. (Why wouldn't you want to include a cost on a project report? I'm not sure. The user manual suggests that this would be the case when you wouldn't want the costs of using a resource to be billed, or included, as a part of the project—things such as vacation time or overhead. As an accountant, however, I would respectfully suggest that a project costs more than just its direct, more obvious costs. And so if you're assigning a resource, and have specified the resource costs reasonably accurately, you shouldn't have to exclude certain costs.)

7. (Optional) Review the Cost field. Time Line calculates this field for you, and so the program doesn't let you edit it. Time Line calculates the cost by multiplying the cost of the resource by the amount of time the resource is used. For the fiberglassers who cost $12 an hour and will work for 40 hours a piece on the project, the cost of the resource is $960, calculated as $12 times 2 fiberglassers times 40 hours. Review the Cost field because it lets you check your resource identification and assignment.

Note: The three remaining fields on the Resource Assignment box—Actual Effort, Cost, and To Go—fields help you monitor the actual resource costs. Chapter 6, "Monitoring Project Progress, Resources, and Costs" describes how and why you use these fields.

8. When you complete the Resource Assignment box, press F10 to save the assignment. Figure 5.8 shows the Resource Assignment box completed to allocating the fiberglassers to the Lay hull task. You would complete steps 2 through 8 for each of the resource allocations.

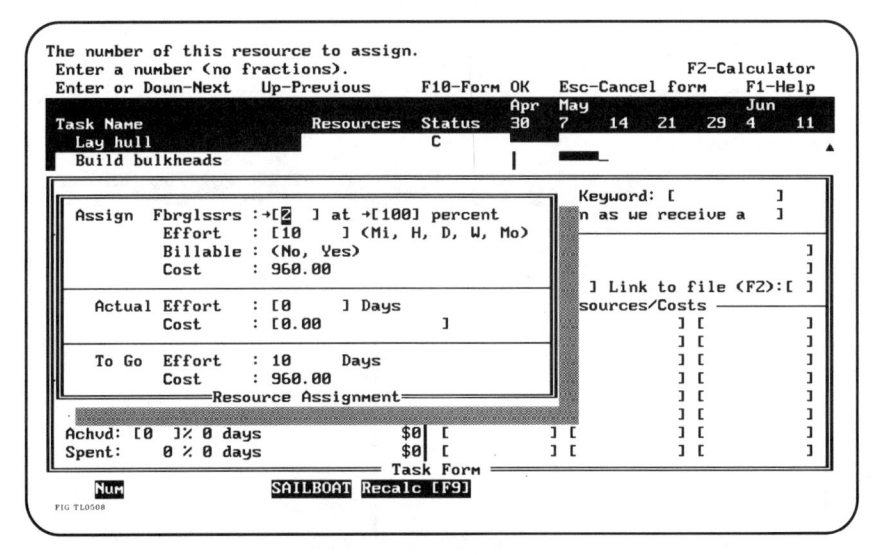

Fig. 5.8. The Resource Assignment box completed to allocate fiberglassers to the Lay hull task.

Reviewing Resource Allocations

The purpose in going to the trouble of allocating the resources is to verify that you aren't expecting more work from people than they can produce, that you aren't double-scheduling important pieces of equipment, and that, at an even more fundamental level, that you've got the necessary resources to complete the project. Accordingly, once you complete the process of allocating resources, you'll want to review your allocations. There are several relatively easy ways you can review the resource allocations.

Using a Gantt Chart To Display Allocations

When you complete the resource allocations, the Gantt chart screen fills the Resource column with the name of the first resource assigned. If more than one resource is assigned, the Gantt chart screen indicates this by displaying a + symbol after the name of the first resource. In figure 5.9, for example, the Build bulkheads and Install engine tasks show a resource—Carpenter in the case of Build bulkhead, and Mechanic in the case of the Install engine—and follow the resource with the + symbol. The + indicates that there is at least one other resource allocated to the task. In this case, there is only one other allocated task: the crane. If Time Line detects an overallocated resource, the program displays an R next to the resource name on the Gantt chart.

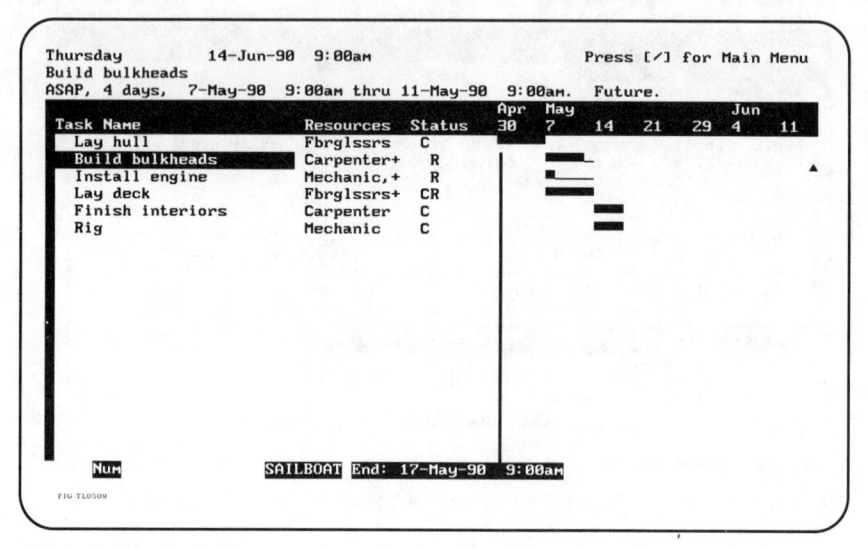

```
Thursday          14-Jun-90   9:00am                    Press [/] for Main Menu
Build bulkheads
ASAP, 4 days,  7-May-90   9:00am thru 11-May-90  9:00am.   Future.
                                             Apr   May              Jun
Task Name              Resources   Status    30    7     14    21   29   4    11
  Lay hull             Fbrglssrs     C
  Build bulkheads      Carpenter+    R
  Install engine       Mechanic,+    R
  Lay deck             Fbrglssrs+   CR
  Finish interiors     Carpenter     C
  Rig                  Mechanic      C




                   Num         SAILBOAT End: 17-May-90  9:00am
```

Fig. 5.9. The Gantt Chart screen shows the first resource allocated to a task and indicates if there are others.

Using a Histogram To Review Allocations

Another way you can review resource allocations is by using the Resource Histogram menu option. A Resource Histogram graphically shows with a bar chart the workloads of selected resources over the same period of time as the Gantt chart. You can show up to five resources at a time. Figure 5.10 shows a histogram for the fiberglassers resource. Time Line indicates the total resources available with a dashed horizontal line. The scheduled use of the resource is shown with the vertical bars. As long as the bars stay at or under the total resources available line, you know there isn't an overallocation. If the bars rise above the total resources available line, there is an overallocation.

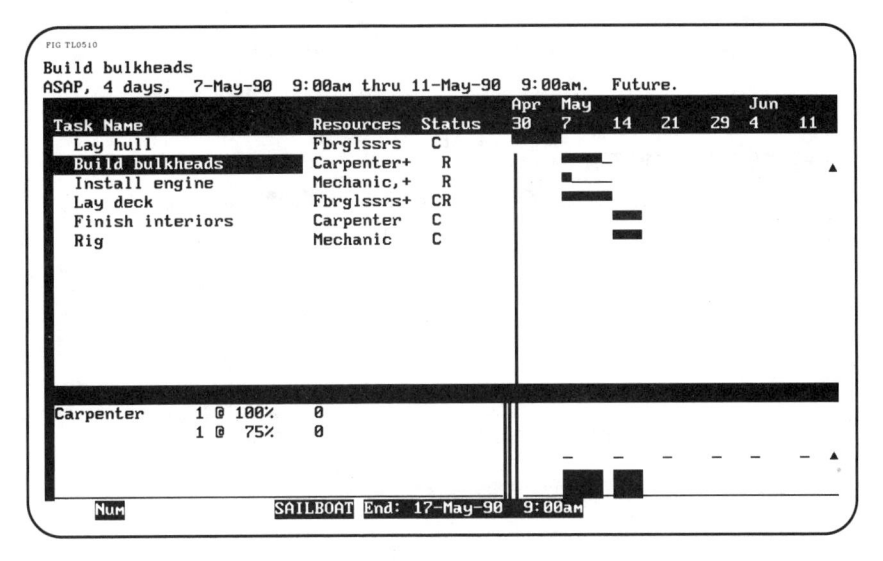

Chapter 5: Identifying and Allocating Resources and Costs 145

```
FIG TL0510
Build bulkheads
ASAP, 4 days,    7-May-90   9:00am thru 11-May-90   9:00am.   Future.
                                                  Apr  May              Jun
Task Name                   Resources  Status     30   7    14   21  29 4    11
     Lay hull               Fbrglssrs   C
     Build bulkheads        Carpenter+  R
     Install engine         Mechanic,+  R
     Lay deck               Fbrglssrs+  CR
     Finish interiors       Carpenter   C
     Rig                    Mechanic    C




Carpenter      1 @ 100%    0
               1 @  75%    0




Num              SAILBOAT End: 17-May-90  9:00am
```

Fig. 5.10. Time Line displays a Histogram at the bottom of the screen.

To display a histogram for a resource, follow these steps:

1. Activate the menu bar and select Schedule Resources Histogram. Time Line displays the Histogram Resources box (see fig. 5.11).

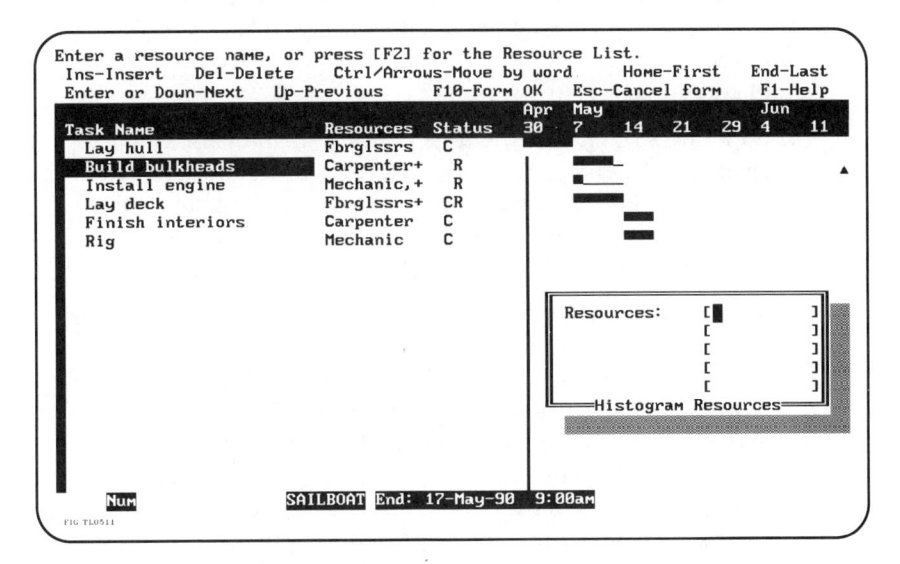

```
Enter a resource name, or press [F2] for the Resource List.
  Ins-Insert    Del-Delete     Ctrl/Arrows-Move by word    Home-First    End-Last
  Enter or Down-Next    Up-Previous    F10-Form OK   Esc-Cancel form    F1-Help
                                                  Apr  May              Jun
Task Name                   Resources  Status     30   7    14   21  29 4    11
     Lay hull               Fbrglssrs   C
     Build bulkheads        Carpenter+  R
     Install engine         Mechanic,+  R
     Lay deck               Fbrglssrs+  CR
     Finish interiors       Carpenter   C
     Rig                    Mechanic    C


                                        Resources:  [          ]
                                                    [          ]
                                                    [          ]
                                                    [          ]
                                        =Histogram Resources=


Num              SAILBOAT End: 17-May-90  9:00am
FIG TL0511
```

Fig. 5.11. The Histogram Resources box.

2. Press F2 to see a list of the resources for the project. Time Line displays the Resource/Cost List (see fig. 5.12).

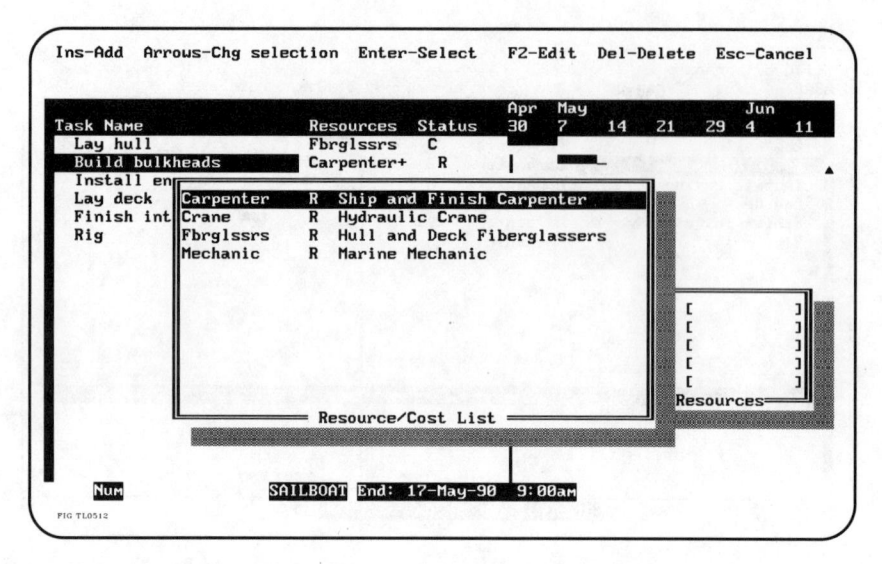

Part II: Advanced Project Management Techniques

```
Ins-Add  Arrows-Chg selection  Enter-Select   F2-Edit  Del-Delete  Esc-Cancel

                                             Apr  May                Jun
Task Name            Resources  Status       30   7    14   21   29  4    11
  Lay hull           Fbrglssrs    C
  Build bulkheads    Carpenter+   R           |   ▄▄▄▄▄
  Install en┌─────────────────────────────────────────────┐
  Lay deck  │Carpenter   R  Ship and Finish Carpenter     │
  Finish int│Crane       R  Hydraulic Crane               │
  Rig       │Fbrglssrs   R  Hull and Deck Fiberglassers   │
            │Mechanic    R  Marine Mechanic               │
            │                                      [    ] │
            │                                      [    ] │
            │                                      [    ] │
            │                                      [    ] │
            │                                      Resources
            │========== Resource/Cost List =========│

        NUM         SAILBOAT End: 17-May-90  9:00am
FIG TL0512
```

Fig. 5.12. The Resource/Cost List.

3. Use the cursor to mark the resource for which you want to display a histogram and then press Enter to fill the Histogram Resources box with the marked resource. Then press F10 to display the Histogram (see fig. 5.10). Time Line shows the resource usage as vertical bars and the total available resources as a horizontal dashed line. (*Note:* If later you want to redisplay the Resource List box so you can see histograms of additional resources, press F8.)

4. (Optional) To change the time period shown by the Gantt chart and the Histogram, press Tab to activate the calendar half of the Gantt chart screen. Then use the right- and left-arrow keys to move the time period into the future or into the past.

5. (Optional) In the Histogram portion of the screen, Time Line shows the maximum resource allocation allowed. In the case of the fiberglassers, for example, it shows 1 @ 100%. If you move the cursor, using the up- and down-arrow keys, so it marks a task that uses the carpenters resource, Time Line also displays the currently scheduled usage of the resource. (If you previously activated the calendar half of the Gantt chart screen, you will need to press Tab again to re-activate the Task list half of the Gantt chart screen.) Figure 5.13, where the Build bulkheads task is marked, shows that the actual allocation is 1 @ 75%.

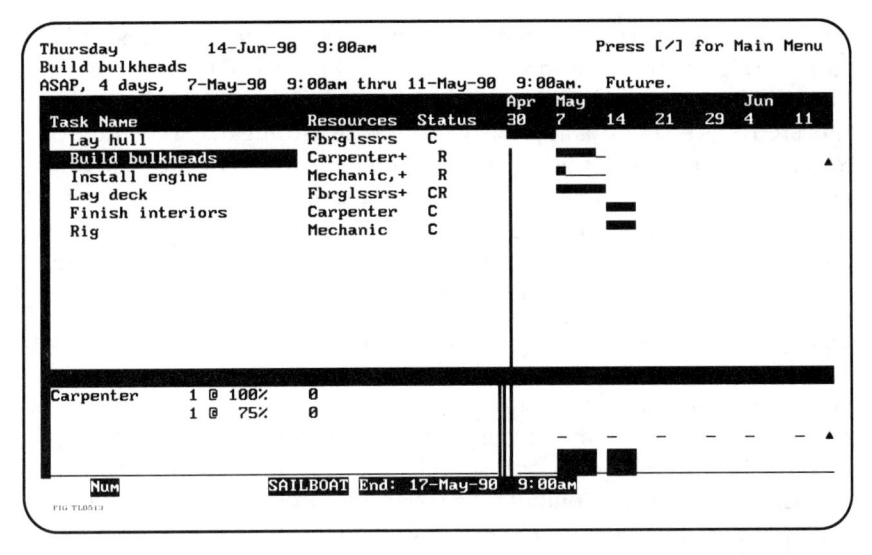

```
Thursday       14-Jun-90   9:00am              Press [/] for Main Menu
Build bulkheads
ASAP, 4 days,  7-May-90  9:00am thru 11-May-90  9:00am.  Future.
                                           Apr  May              Jun
Task Name                  Resources Status 30   7    14   21   29   4    11
  Lay hull                 Fbrglssrs   C
  Build bulkheads          Carpenter+  R
  Install engine           Mechanic,+  R
  Lay deck                 Fbrglssrs+ CR
  Finish interiors         Carpenter   C
  Rig                      Mechanic    C




Carpenter         1 @ 100%    0
                  1 @  75%    0


    Num              SAILBOAT End: 17-May-90  9:00am
```

Fig. 5.13. If a task using the resource is marked, Time Line shows that scheduled resource usage.

6. (Optional) To return to viewing only the Gantt Chart for the project, activate the menu bar and select Views Gantt. If, after you select Views Gantt, you later want to see the Histogram again, activate the menu bar and select Views Histogram.

Adjusting Resource Allocations

You may find that your allocations of resources require more time from a resource that is available. In that case, you need to perform resource leveling. Resource leveling simply means adjusting your resource allocations so that you're not overallocating a resource. Time Line provides two approaches for doing this: Manual and Automatic.

Manually Leveling Resources

You may choose to level resources manually. Manually leveling resources requires that you change aspects of the resource allocation using the Resource Assignment Form box, change aspects of a resource by using the Resource/Cost Form box, or change aspects of the task by using the Task Form screen. Changing who or what you use to accomplish a task, increasing the available quantity of a resource, and changing when a task is to be performed might all contribute to resource leveling.

Changing some part of your resource allocation usually represents the most straightforward approach and the first step to dealing with overallocation. You can either modify the resource used or the quantity allocated. Practically, this approach means you do things like substitute one resource for another or adjust the quantity allocated. In the case of the sailboat project, perhaps one of the fiberglassers might help reduce an overallocation of the carpenter's workload. Or perhaps work you scheduled as taking 2 days will really only take 1.5 days. To change any resource allocation, you use the Resource/Cost Form.

Changing the actual quantity of available resources represents another, more dramatic approach to dealing with overallocations. With this approach, you actually add resources to the resources list or increase the available quantity of some resource. Practically, this approach means you do things like hire more people, purchase additional equipment, or start having people and equipment work overtime. In the case of the sailboat project, this might mean you hire a third fiberglasser or purchase a second crane. To change the available quantity of a resource, you use the Resource/Cost Form screen.

Changing the tasks and task dependencies of a project represents the most severe approach for dealing with resource overallocation. Typically, at this level you've done all the resource leveling possible by changing either resource allocations or the available resources. At this stage, you're adjusting things like the order in which tasks are performed, the scope of the project, and the project completion date. You can also change the durations of tasks from being time-dependent to effort-dependent. To adjust the tasks that make up a project and their dependencies, you use the Task Form screen and the Dependencies Join and Dependencies Unjoin menu options.

Automatically Adjusting Allocations

Manually leveling resources represents one approach for dealing with resource overallocations. However, you can use the Time Line automatic resource leveling feature. To do so, you use the Options Form screen. The steps are as follows:

1. Activate the menu bar and select Schedule Options. Time Line displays the Options Form screen. (You can refer to figure 4.21 for an example of the Options Form screen.)

2. (Optional) Because resource leveling takes a significant amount of time—even for relatively small projects—you'll probably want to set the Recalculation to Manual. Move the cursor to the recalculation field, and type M to indicate that manual recalculation should be used.

3. Move the cursor to the Resource Leveling Field. Type Y to indicate that Time Line should level resources so there aren't resource overallocations. When the schedule is recalculated, Time Line moves tasks and the project completion date so that there aren't any resource over-allocations. Type W to indicate that Time Line should level resources by moving tasks that aren't on a critical path. Tasks that are on the critical path aren't delayed. (If Time Line delays a task as part of automatic resource leveling, it displays a lowercase r in the status column and a dotted line to the left of the task bar in the Gantt chart to show the amount of the delay.)

4. When the Options Form screen is complete, press F10 to leave the screen.

5. (Optional) If you set the schedule recalculation to manual, press F9 to recalculate the schedule. If you didn't set the recalculation to manual, the schedule automatically recalculates when you press F10 to leave the Options Form screen.

Using Effort-Driven Scheduling

In Chapters 3 and 4, task durations were expressed in elapsed time. With an elapsed-time duration, for example, a task takes a certain number of hours, days, or weeks. But task durations can also be expressed in resources required, which is called *effort-driven scheduling*. This simply means that a task requires a certain quantity of a resource to be completed rather than a certain period of elapsed time.

Although the difference between elapsed-time duration and resource-based durations may seem subtle, it's usually pretty easy to tell the difference: If you can speed up a task's completion by adding more of a resource, it can be considered a task with an effort-driven duration rather than an elapsed-time duration. (In the sailboat project, for example, you might be able to accelerate the Lay hull task's completion by hiring addition fiberglassers and the finish interior task's completion by hiring a second carpenter.)

Using effort-driven scheduling requires only that you express the durations of tasks as effort driven by using the Driven by and Effort fields on the Task Form. The steps are as follows:

1. Highlight the task you want to edit and then press Ctrl-F2. Or activate the menu bar and select Schedule Tasks Edit. Either way, Time Line displays the Task Form.

2. Mark the Driven by field as Effort. Then complete the Effort input fields—which includes both a field to input the number of resource time units and the type of time units—the same way you complete the Duration input fields. You might, for example, express a task duration as requiring 10 days of effort. Time Line then looks at the resources you've allocated, levels resources if necessary, and calculates the task completion date as whenever 10 days of effort has been expended. (Obviously, with effort-driven tasks, you need to assign at least one resource to the task in order for the scheduling calculations to make any sense.)

3. Press F10 to save your changes.

4. Press F9 to recalculate the project schedule—this time reflecting the fact that a task is effort-driven.

There are a couple other things you should know about effort-driven scheduling: First, only tasks with ASAP or ALAP types can be effort-driven. (If you specify a task's type as Fixed, it must be duration-driven.) A second thing you should know is that although Time Line assumes that the more resources you assign to an effort driven task, the more quickly it is completed, this is usually true only up to certain point. In the sailboat project, for example, you would quickly reach a point where even if you had, say, several hundred carpenters, you couldn't simply use more and more of them to accelerate the Finish interiors task. There are, after all, a limited number of people that can fit on a forty foot ketch. And even before you filled the boat up with carpenters, there would be productivity losses because the carpenters would start to get in each other's way. For this reason, you'll need to review the resulting task durations for reasonableness.

Working with Costs

Besides identifying and allocating the resources a project will use—and, as a result, indirectly calculating the costs of using these resources—there are also other costs related to a project.

Note: You may have a job costing system or a job costing module that is part of your company's accounting system. Chances are, your accounting system provides better project costing features than the ones you'll find in a project management package like Time Line. If you choose to use a different project costing package rather than the one provided with Time Line, you may want to skip this section.

In the example of the sailboat project, you might have the following costs associated with each of the six main steps:

1. Lay Hull

Chopper gun rental	$ 500
Fiberglass cloth and matting	2500
Resin and catalyst	2000
Lead for ballast in hull	500

2. Build bulkheads

Mahogany plywood	$1200
Mahogany 2x1s	500

3. Install Engine

40 horsepower diesel engine	$5000

4. Lay deck

Chopper gun rental	$ 500
Fiberglass cloth and matting	1500
Resin	1500

5. Finish Interiors

Upholstery and carpeting	$1000
Teak finishing	500
Kitchenette appliances	2000

6. Rig

Masts	$8000
Sails	8000
Other	8000

Total Costs	$43,000

In the case of the sailboat project, these other costs amount to a significant portion of the overall project cost. And so, for most projects, you'll also have costs that, like those for the sailboat project, should be identified and counted.

Identifying Costs

The steps for identifying costs roughly parallel those for identifying and allocating resources. To identify any of the resources, you take up to eleven steps:

1. Activate the menu bar and select Schedule Resources List. Time Line displays the empty Resource/Cost List box (refer to fig. 5.2). If you have had previously identified any resources or costs, they would be listed in this box.

2. Press Ins. Time Line displays the Resource/Cost Form box (refer to fig. 5.3).

3. Type the name of the Cost in the Resource (or Cost) Name field. Cost names must be unique. You can only use up to ten characters, so you may need to abbreviate.

4. (Optional) Move the cursor to the Full Name field and type the unabbreviated name of the cost. Engine, for example, might be described as "Volvo 40 horsepower diesel engine."

5. (Optional) Move the cursor to the Keyword field, and type the keyword. The Keyword field provides ten characters of space to further describe or classify a resource. You can also use the Keyword to sort or filter resources as described later in the chapter.

6. (Optional) Move the cursor to the Notes field and type any additional description of the cost. You might want to use this field to record the names of the vendor or to cross-reference the purchase order. As noted earlier, you can also press F2 to access a notepad box which you can use to create lengthy descriptions.

7. Move the cursor to the Resource (or Cost) Type field. There are three varieties of project costs: Fixed, Unit, and Variable. Type F to indicate you're defining a fixed cost and then skip ahead to step 11. Type U to indicate you're defining a unit cost. Type V to indicate you're defining a variable cost. In the case of the sailboat example, the engine might be expressed as fixed cost. Resin might be expressed as a unit cost of so many dollars per fifty gallon drum. And the chopper gun, a special tool you might rent by the day to lay the hull, would be accounted for as a variable cost because the total chopper gun rental cost would ultimately depend on the duration of the lay hull task.

8. If you defined the cost type as Variable, move the cursor to the Default Assignment field. Type the number of things causing the cost and the percentage of the full workday the variable cost will occur. This is a little difficult to see unless you have a concrete example. So, in the case of the chopper

gun, say you were renting one chopper gun and the costs would accrue all day long. The Default Assignment would be 1 and the percent would 100%. Or if you were renting 2 chopper guns and the costs would accrue only half the time, the default assignment would be 2 and the percent would be 50%.

9. If in step 7 you defined the cost type as Variable, move the cursor to the Cost Rate field. You will only use two of the cost rate fields—Cost Rate and Per—to show a variable cost. Enter the dollar cost in the cost rate field. Then move the cursor to the Per field and type the first letter of the time unit you used to denominate the cost. In the case of the chopper gun rental costing $100 a day, you would enter 100 in the cost rate field and mark D for days in the Per settings.

10. If in step 7 you defined the cost type as Unit, move the cursor to the Cost Rate field. You will use the Cost Rate and Unit fields to show a unit cost. Enter the dollar cost per unit in the cost rate field. Then move the cursor to the Units field and type out the units you want to use. By default, Time Line fills the Units field with the word Units, but you'll want to use something more descriptive. If the case of the Resin used for the sailboat, which comes in 50 gallon drums, you might type out *Barrel* or *drum*.

11. When the Resource/Cost Form is complete, press F10 to save the resource definition.

Figure 5.14 shows the completed Resource/Cost Form box for the fixed cost. Figure 5.15 shows the completed Resource/Cost Form box for a variable cost. Figure 5.16 shows the completed Resource/Cost Form box for a unit cost.

Budgeting For Costs

Accounting for, or allocating, project costs works similarly to allocating resources. Once you've identified the general cost categories for a project, you budget, or allocate, the costs by tasks. In the case of the sailboat project, completing the Install Engine task will, for example, require that you purchase an engine. And completing the rigging will require that you purchase sails and masts.

To budget for these sorts of costs, you follow the five steps listed below for each cost for which you want to budget:

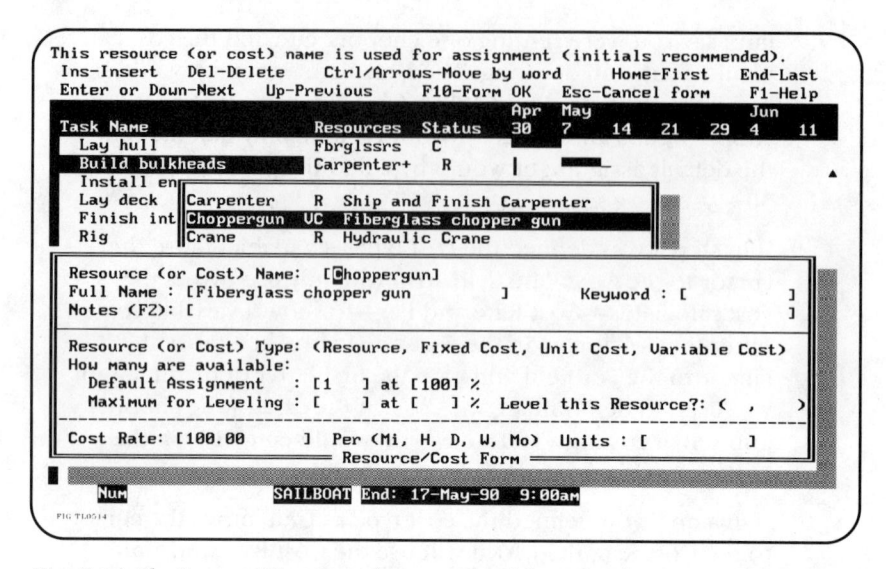

154 Part II: Advanced Project Management Techniques

Fig. 5.14. The Resource/Cost Form box completed for a fixed cost.

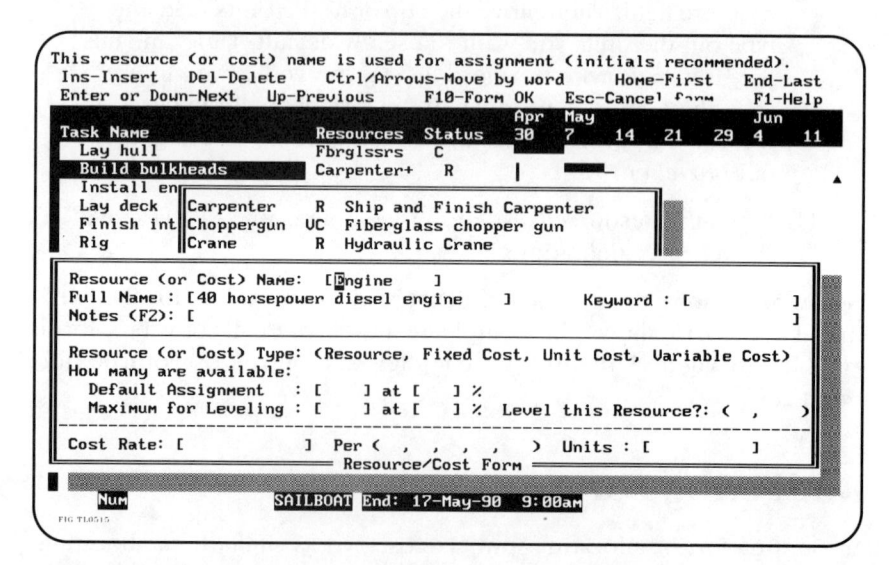

Fig. 5.15. The Resource/Cost Form box completed for a variable cost.

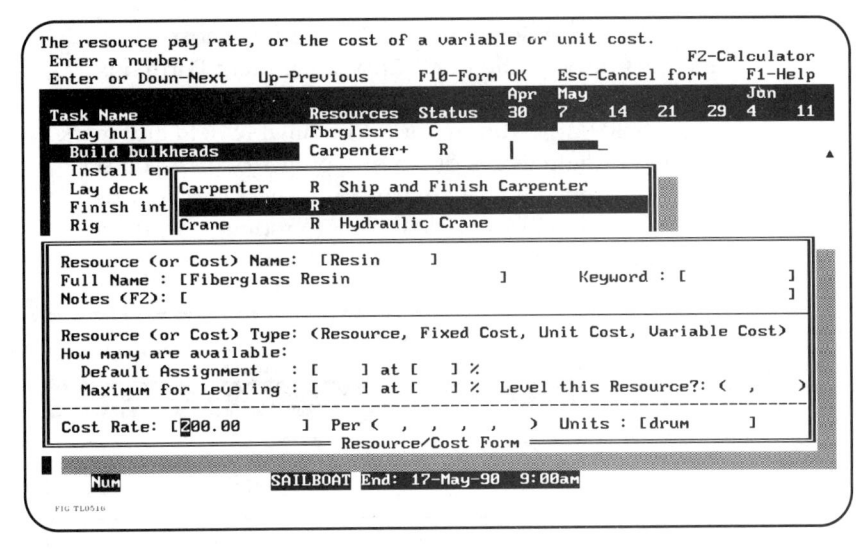

Chapter 5: Identifying and Allocating Resources and Costs 155

```
The resource pay rate, or the cost of a variable or unit cost.
  Enter a number.                                        F2-Calculator
  Enter or Down-Next   Up-Previous    F10-Form OK  Esc-Cancel form  F1-Help
                                              Apr May                Jun
Task Name                       Resources Status 30   7   14  21  29  4   11
  Lay hull                      Fbrglssrs   C
  Build bulkheads               Carpenter+  R    |
  Install en┌─────────────────────────────────────────────────┐
  Lay deck  │Carpenter   R  Ship and Finish Carpenter         │
  Finish int│            R                                    │
  Rig       │Crane       R  Hydraulic Crane                   │
┌───────────┴─────────────────────────────────────────────────┴──┐
│ Resource (or Cost) Name: [Resin          ]                     │
│ Full Name : [Fiberglass Resin            ]    Keyword : [    ] │
│ Notes (F2): [                                                ] │
│ Resource (or Cost) Type: (Resource, Fixed Cost, Unit Cost, Variable Cost)
│ How many are available:
│   Default Assignment   : [      ] at [    ] %
│   Maximum for Leveling : [      ] at [    ] %  Level this Resource?: ( , )
│ ─────────────────────────────────────────────────────────────
│ Cost Rate: [200.00     ] Per ( , , , , )  Units : [drum      ]
│                        ═══ Resource/Cost Form ═══
│
│  Num          SAILBOAT End: 17-May-90  9:00am
```

Fig. 5.16. The Resource/Cost Form completed for a unit cost.

1. Verify that Time Line is using the large version of the Task Form screen and the Cost Tracking version of the Resource Assignment Form screen for the project by activating the menu bar and then selecting Schedule Options. Time Line displays the Options Form. The Cost Tracking setting should be set as Yes. If it isn't, use the arrow keys to mark Yes. The Task Form setting should be set as Large. If it isn't, use the arrow keys to mark Large. Press F10 to save your settings and leave the Option Form. (Refer to Chapter 4, "Managing Project and Task Details," for more information on the Options Form.)

2. Use the cursor to mark the task to which a resource is going to be allocated, and then press Ctrl-F2 to display the Task Form for the task. Alternatively, you can also activate the menu bar and then select Schedule Task Edit. Time Line displays the Task Form.

3. Move the cursor to the first entry in the Resources/Costs portion of the Task Form. Once there, you can either type the Cost name such as "Engine" or you can press F2 to display the Resources/Costs List box, use the arrow keys to mark the cost, and press Enter.

4. Next, you have two options:

156 Part II: Advanced Project Management Techniques

A. If the cost you assigned in step 3 was a fixed cost, Time Line next displays the Fixed Cost Assignment Form box (see fig. 5.17). Enter the amount of the fixed cost in the Assign field. Move the cursor to the Billable field and mark the Billable field as Yes or No by typing Y or N. If you set Billable to Yes, this cost appears on project cost reports. (The Actual and To Go fields relate to monitoring actual costs and are discussed in the next chapter.)

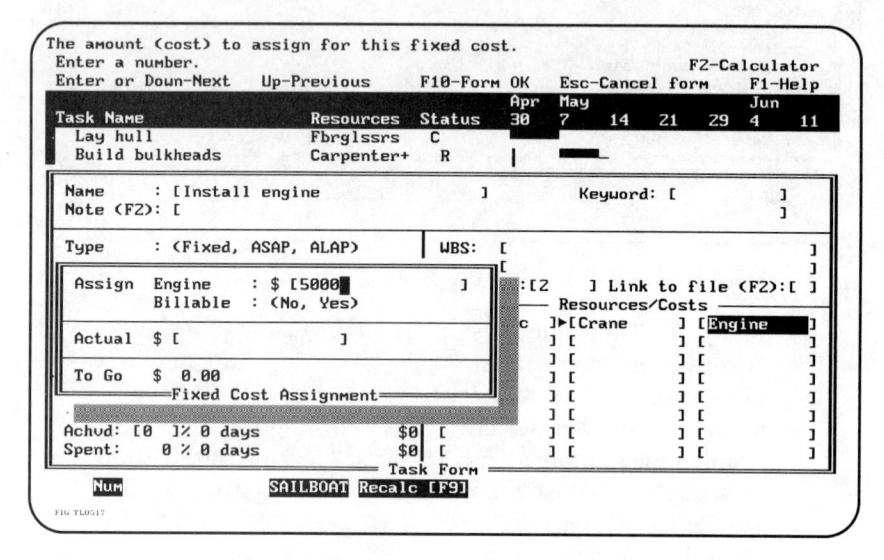

```
The amount (cost) to assign for this fixed cost.
Enter a number.                                              F2-Calculator
Enter or Down-Next    Up-Previous    F10-Form OK   Esc-Cancel form   F1-Help
                                           Apr  May                  Jun
Task Name                Resources  Status  30   7    14   21   29   4    11
  Lay hull               Fbrglssrs    C
  Build bulkheads        Carpenter+   R
┌──────────────────────────────────────────────────────────┐
│ Name       : [Install engine         ]    Keyword: [          ] │
│ Note (F2): [                                              ]     │
│                                                                 │
│ Type       : (Fixed, ASAP, ALAP)   │ WBS:  [               ]   │
│                                    │       [               ]   │
│ Assign  Engine    : $ [5000█     ] │:[2   ] Link to file (F2):[ ]│
│         Billable  : (No, Yes)      │──── Resources/Costs ────    │
│                                    │c  ]►[Crane     ] [Engine  ] │
│ Actual  $ [                    ]   │   ] [          ] [         ]│
│                                    │   ] [          ] [         ]│
│ To Go   $  0.00                    │   ] [          ] [         ]│
│═════════════Fixed Cost Assignment══│   ] [          ] [         ]│
│                                    │   ] [          ] [         ]│
│ Achvd: [0  ]% 0 days         $0  [ │   ] [          ] [         ]│
│ Spent:     0 % 0 days        $0  [ │   ] [          ] [         ]│
└────────────────────────────────────┴── Task Form ──────────────┘
 Num              SAILBOAT  Recalc [F9]
```

Fig. 5.17. The Fixed Cost Assignment box.

B. If the cost you assigned in step 3 was a unit cost, Time Line next displays the Unit Cost Assignment Form box (see fig. 5.18). Enter the number of units of the item that will be used or the actual dollars of the item that will be used. If you enter the number of units, Time Line calculates the cost by multiplying the number of units times the unit cost on the Resource/Cost Form box. Move the cursor to the Billable field and mark the Billable field as Yes or No by typing Y or N. If you set Billable to yes, this cost appears on project cost reports. (The Actual and To Go fields relate to monitoring actual costs and are discussed in the next chapter.)

Note: For variable costs, you don't need to complete an Assignment box because Time Line calculates the cost for you, using the variable cost and the duration of the task.

5. Press F10 to complete the Assignment Form box.

Chapter 5: Identifying and Allocating Resources and Costs **157**

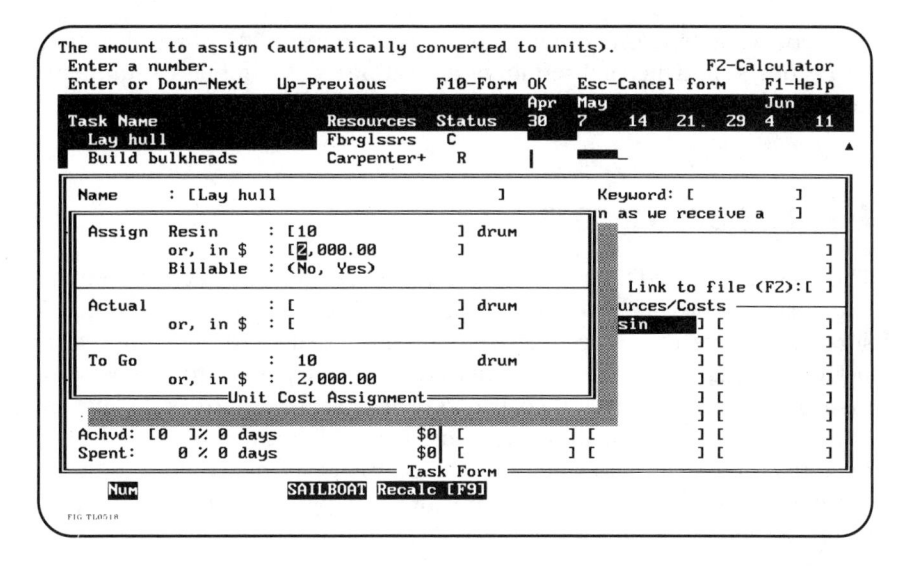

```
The amount to assign (automatically converted to units).
  Enter a number.                                         F2-Calculator
  Enter or Down-Next   Up-Previous   F10-Form OK   Esc-Cancel form   F1-Help
                                          Apr May                Jun
  Task Name              Resources Status  30   7    14   21   29   4    11
    Lay hull              Fbrglssrs   C
    Build bulkheads       Carpenter+  R      |     ▬▬▬▬
 ┌─────────────────────────────────────────────┐
 │ Name     : [Lay hull                      ]  Keyword: [            ]
 │                                             n as we receive a     ]
 │ Assign Resin    : [10          ] drum
 │        or, in $ : [2,000.00    ]                                  ]
 │        Billable : (No, Yes)                  Link to file (F2):[  ]
 │                                             urces/Costs
 │ Actual          : [            ] drum       sin          ] [      ]
 │        or, in $ : [            ]                         ] [      ]
 │ To Go           :  10            drum                    ] [      ]
 │        or, in $ :  2,000.00                              ] [      ]
 │════════════════Unit Cost Assignment═════════             ] [      ]
                                                           ] [      ]
  Achvd: [0  ]% 0 days           $0  [          ] [        ] [      ]
  Spent:     0 % 0 days          $0  [          ] [        ] [      ]
                                        Task Form
   Num                SAILBOAT Recalc [F9]
```

Fig. 5.18. The Unit Cost Assignment box.

Allocating Resources and Costs to Summary Tasks

Most of the time, you probably will want to allocate resources and costs to detail tasks. Be aware, however, that Time Line allows you also to allocate resources and costs to summary tasks. And you can assign resources and costs to a summary task even if the summary task's subtasks also have resources and costs assigned to them. There are, however, a few things you should understand about allocating to summary tasks.

The most important thing to remember is that Time Line evenly allocates the resource to the Summary task. This can be a benefit and the correct approach if the resource really is used by each of the summary task's subtasks. However, if only some of the subtasks use the resource, by allocating to the summary task you end up allocating the resource to other subtasks that don't really use the resource.

A second thing to consider when you allocate either resources or costs to summary tasks is that Time Line adds the allocations from the subtasks to the allocations to the summary task to get the total resource allocations or cost allocations for the summary task. Again, this will usually be exactly what you want, but don't double count a resource or cost by first allocating it to a subtask and then subsequently allocating it to the subtask's summary task.

Chapter Summary

This chapter covered the basics of identifying and allocating the resources and costs of a project. These are important concerns if you want to make sure you've got the people and equipment to successfully complete a project and that you've got the financial resources to pay for the project. But managing the resources and costs of a project requires more than just an initial set of estimates as to resource usage and financial costs. You'll also need to monitor the actual resources used and costs incurred—and those are two of the topics covered in the next chapter, "Monitoring Project Progress, Resources, and Costs."

6

Monitoring Project Progress, Resources, and Costs

▶ Even after you organize a project into its various pieces, showing the timing of tasks and their dependencies and identifying and allocates resources and costs, there's still another important component left: Comparing what was planned to what actually happens. Sometimes people view these comparisons as negative. The idea, however, is that if you're following your project plan in terms of time spent, resources used, or costs incurred, it means that you're moving towards successful completion of the project. If you're not following your project plan, it means that you're not moving toward successful completion of the project. And the earlier you're aware that something has going awry, the more time you have to fix the problem—hopefully while the problem is still small and the project damage minimal.

This chapter specifically addresses the mechanics of monitoring the actual time spent, resources used, and costs incurred and introduces the mechanics of comparing this actual data to whatever you planned. The chapter is broken into five sections: setting the baseline, monitoring progress time, monitoring resources, monitoring costs, and using the Assist/Update option. None of the material is difficult or complex—but it is essential to successful project management.

Setting the Baseline

The first step in monitoring a project is to set a standard, or *benchmark*, against which the actual project can be measured. Usually the standard is the original project schedule, resource allocations, and budgeted costs.

The basic idea is that as work on the project progresses, you can compare the actual progress to the planned progress. Within Time Line, the way you set the standard is to create a baseline. The *baseline* is simply a record of the original task start and finish dates, resource allocations, and budgeted costs. In effect, setting the baseline schedule directs Time Line to memorize your original project plans.

To set the baseline for the project schedule currently displayed, follow these steps:

1. Verify that you've identified all the project tasks, made all the resource allocations, and entered any budgeted costs.

2. Recalculate the project schedule by pressing F9.

3. Activate the menu bar and then select Schedule Baseline to direct Time Line to keep a separate, distinct copy of the original project plans.

4. To save the baseline schedule, save the project by activating the menu bar and selecting File Save Replace.

If you've previously set the baseline—either intentionally or unintentionally—and now want to reset the baseline, say because now you understand why it's important and what it's used for, you take the first three steps listed above. However, because you've already set the baseline, Time Line displays the message box shown in figure 6.1 which indicates you've already set a baseline schedule for the displayed project.

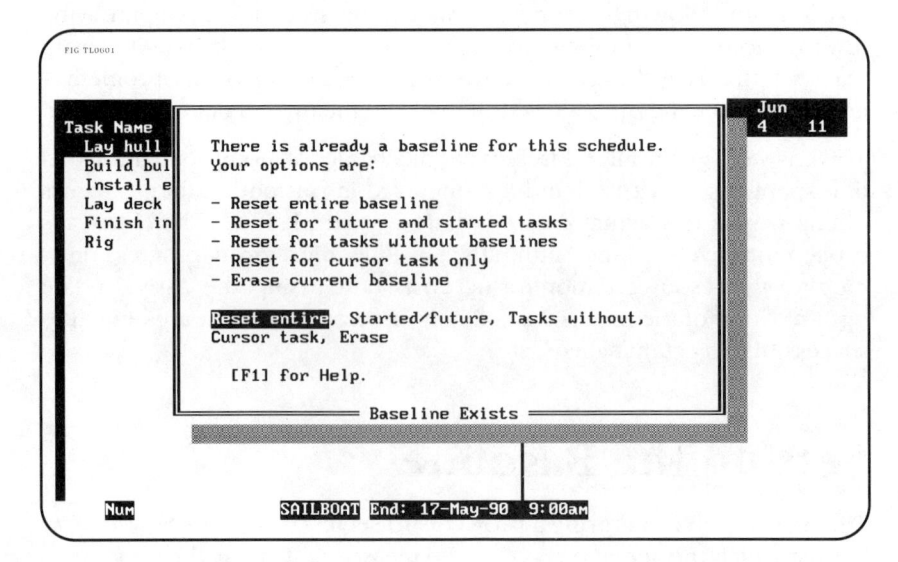

Fig. 6.1. *The message box indicating you've already set a baseline schedule for the displayed project.*

As figure 6.1 shows, Time Line gives you five options when you reselect Baseline for a project that already has a base schedule: Reset Entire, Started/Future, Tasks Without, Cursor Task, and Erase. To select one of these five options, use the arrow keys to highlight the option and then press Enter.

To replace the previous baseline schedule with the current schedule, select the Reset Entire option.

To set a baseline only for tasks that have not yet finished, select the Started/Future option.

To set baseline information for tasks that exist in the current schedule but don't exist in the baseline schedule, select Tasks Without.

To set a new baseline only for the task marked on the current schedule by the cursor, select Curser Task.

To remove the baseline schedule, select Erase.

After you've set the baseline, you'll probably want to compare the actual schedule to the baseline schedule. To do so, you'll need to use a different layout of the Gantt chart. It will show both the baseline and the current project schedule data. To use a different layout which shows the baseline schedule, follow these steps:

1. Activate the menu bar and select Schedule Layout. Time Line displays the Layouts box (see fig. 6.2).

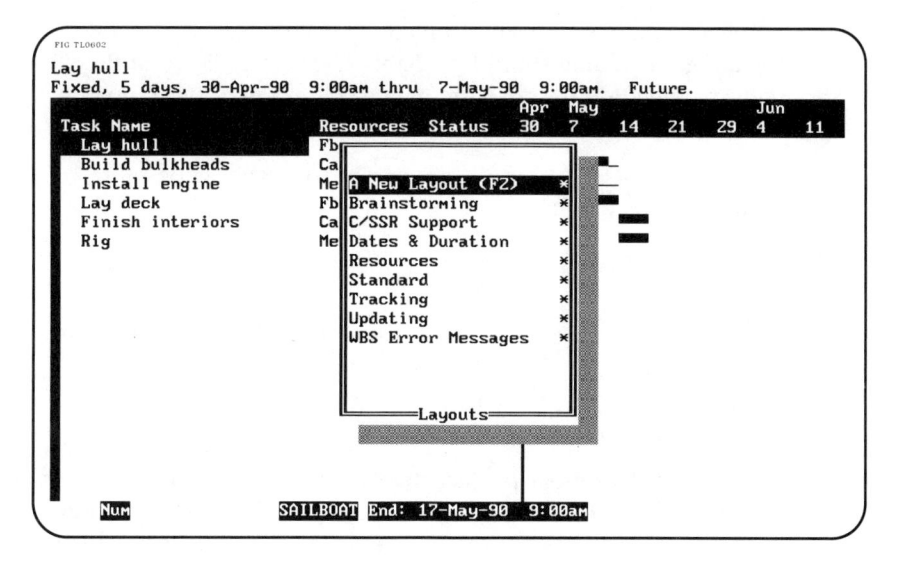

Fig. 6.2. The Layouts box.

Part II: Advanced Project Management Techniques

2. Use the arrow keys to move the cursor so it marks the first option listed (A New Layout), and then press F2. Time Line displays the Layout Form which you can use to create custom forms (see fig. 6.3). Chapter 7 describes in detail how to use the Layout Form so I'll only cover the parts of the screen you need here.

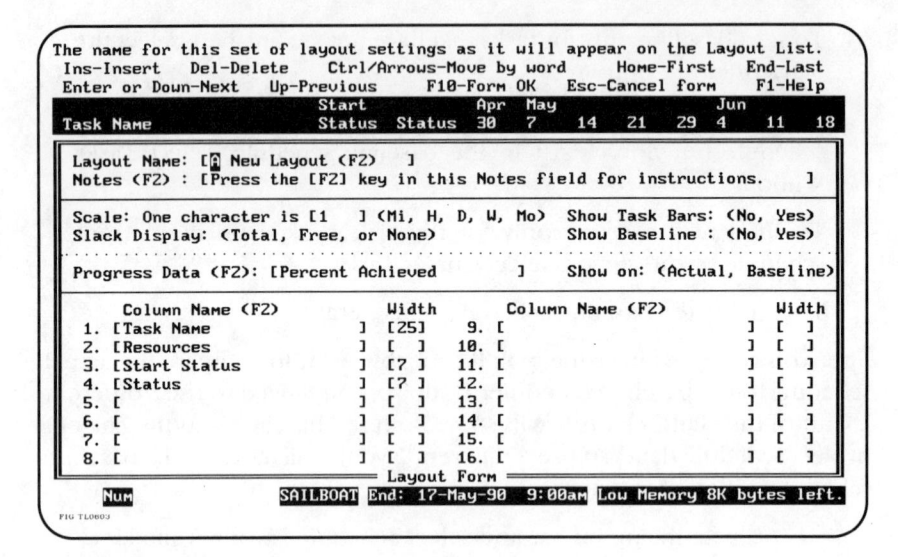

```
The name for this set of layout settings as it will appear on the Layout List.
  Ins-Insert     Del-Delete      Ctrl/Arrows-Move by word      Home-First    End-Last
  Enter or Down-Next    Up-Previous     F10-Form OK    Esc-Cancel form    F1-Help
                             Start           Apr  May                 Jun
  Task Name                  Status Status   30   7    14   21   29   4    11   18

  Layout Name: [A New Layout (F2)    ]
  Notes (F2) : [Press the [F2] key in this Notes field for instructions.       ]

  Scale: One character is [1   ] (Mi, H, D, W, Mo)   Show Task Bars: (No, Yes)
  Slack Display: (Total, Free, or None)              Show Baseline : (No, Yes)

  Progress Data (F2): [Percent Achieved      ]       Show on: (Actual, Baseline)

       Column Name (F2)            Width      Column Name (F2)           Width
  1. [Task Name             ]     [25]    9. [                     ]     [   ]
  2. [Resources             ]     [  ]   10. [                     ]     [   ]
  3. [Start Status          ]     [7 ]   11. [                     ]     [   ]
  4. [Status                ]     [7 ]   12. [                     ]     [   ]
  5. [                      ]     [  ]   13. [                     ]     [   ]
  6. [                      ]     [  ]   14. [                     ]     [   ]
  7. [                      ]     [  ]   15. [                     ]     [   ]
  8. [                      ]     [  ]   16. [                     ]     [   ]
                                 ====== Layout Form ======
       Num                  SAILBOAT End: 17-May-90  9:00am Low Memory 8K bytes left.
```

Fig. 6.3. *The Layout Form.*

3. Type a name that describes the customized view you're creating. The name should probably refer to the fact that the view will include the baseline data so names like "Baseline vs Current" and "Baseline" are fine.

4. Use the arrow keys to move the cursor to the Show Baseline field and type a Y for yes.

5. Press F10 to save your changes. Time Line again displays the Layouts box.

6. When the newly created Layout is highlighted, press Enter to return to the Gantt chart view of the worksheet. (If the Gantt chart view isn't the one currently displayed, you can display it by activating the menu bar and selecting Views Gantt.)

Figure 6.4 shows the sailboat project displayed using a layout that also shows the baseline data. Even as the current schedule changes, the baseline schedule will remain constant—which means that you'll easily be able to visually compare the current schedule to the original schedule. Time Line shows the baseline schedule tasks show as a series of circles, or lowercase "o"s. The current schedule tasks show as a vertical bar.

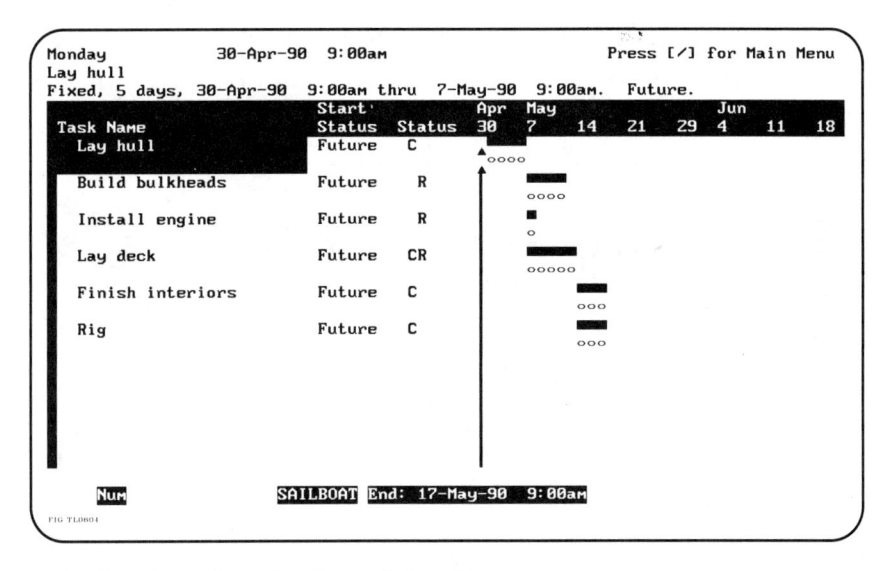

```
Monday            30-Apr-90   9:00am                       Press [/] for Main Menu
Lay hull
Fixed, 5 days, 30-Apr-90   9:00am thru  7-May-90  9:00am.  Future.
                            Start·              Apr   May              Jun
Task Name                   Status  Status      30    7    14    21    29   4    11    18
Lay hull                    Future  C           ▲
                                                 oooo
Build bulkheads             Future  R             ▬▬
                                                  oooo
Install engine              Future  R             ▪
                                                   o
Lay deck                    Future  CR             ▬▬▬
                                                   ooooo
Finish interiors            Future  C                  ▬▬
                                                       ooo
Rig                         Future  C                  ▬
                                                       ooo




    Num            SAILBOAT End: 17-May-90   9:00am
FIG TL0601
```

Fig. 6.4. A Gantt chart that shows the baseline.

Monitoring Actual Project Time

As part of defining a project's tasks, you either enter planned task start and completion dates or you accept the values that Time Line calculates using the completion dates of predecessor tasks and the task durations. When you start work on a task or complete a task, you can record these actual dates—which gives Time Line the necessary data to show planned versus actual times.

To record when work actually starts on a task, you follow these steps:

1. Verify that Time Line is using the large version of the Task Form screen and the Cost Tracking version of the Resource Assignment Form screen for the project by activating the menu bar, and then selecting Schedule Options. Time Line displays the Options Form. The Cost Tracking setting should be set to Yes. If it isn't, use the arrow keys to mark Yes. The Task Form setting should be set to Large. If it isn't, use the arrow keys to mark Large. To save your settings changes and leave the Options Form, press F10. (Refer to Chapter 4, "Managing Project and Task Details," for more information on the Options Form.)

Part II: Advanced Project Management Techniques

2. Move the cursor so it highlights the task for which you want to record the start of work.

3. Access the Task Form either by pressing Ctrl-F2 or by activating the menu bar and selecting Schedule Tasks Edit.

Figure 6.5 shows the larger version of the Task Form screen filled with the lay hull task data.

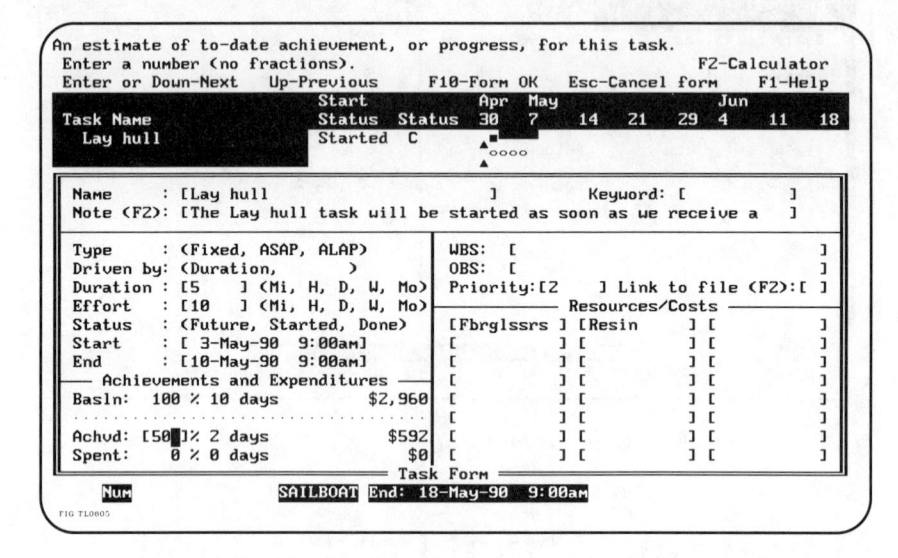

```
An estimate of to-date achievement, or progress, for this task.
  Enter a number (no fractions).                         F2-Calculator
  Enter or Down-Next    Up-Previous    F10-Form OK  Esc-Cancel form   F1-Help
                          Start             Apr  May                Jun
  Task Name               Status Status     30   7    14   21   29  4    11   18
  Lay hull                Started  C
                                          ▲▪
                                           ◦◦◦◦
                                          ▲
 ┌──────────────────────────────────────────────────────────────────────────┐
 │ Name       : [Lay hull                    ]      Keyword: [           ]  │
 │ Note (F2): [The Lay hull task will be started as soon as we receive a ]  │
 │                                                                          │
 │ Type       : (Fixed, ASAP, ALAP)       WBS: [                         ]  │
 │ Driven by: (Duration,       )          OBS: [                         ]  │
 │ Duration : [5    ] (Mi, H, D, W, Mo)   Priority:[2   ] Link to file (F2):[ ] │
 │ Effort    : [10   ] (Mi, H, D, W, Mo)  ─────── Resources/Costs ──────    │
 │ Status    : (Future, Started, Done)    [Fbrglssrs ] [Resin    ] [    ]   │
 │ Start     : [ 3-May-90  9:00am]        [         ] [         ] [    ]    │
 │ End       : [10-May-90  9:00am]        [         ] [         ] [    ]    │
 │ ── Achievements and Expenditures ──    [         ] [         ] [    ]    │
 │ BasIn:     100 % 10 days       $2,960  [         ] [         ] [    ]    │
 │ ........................................[         ] [         ] [    ]   │
 │ Achvd: [50 ]% 2 days            $592   [         ] [         ] [    ]    │
 │ Spent:    0 % 0 days              $0   [         ] [         ] [    ]    │
 │                                    Task Form                             │
 │ Num              SAILBOAT End: 18-May-90  9:00am                         │
 └──────────────────────────────────────────────────────────────────────────┘
 FIG TL0605
```

Fig. 6.5. *The Task Form filled with the lay hull task data.*

4. Move the cursor to the Status field and type S for Started.

5. Move the cursor to the Start Date field and type in the actual start date.

6. Move the cursor to the Achvd field and enter the percent of the task that's already been completed. For example, if the half the work on the task has been completed. enter 50.

7. When the Status, Start Date, and Achvd fields are correct, press F10 to save your changes and return to the Task Form screen.

8. Press F10 to return to the project schedule screen.

9. Press F9 to recalculate the project schedule.

Figure 6.6 shows the recalculated project schedule after the status was updated to started and the actual start date and the achieved percent figures were entered. By comparing the baseline task bar for Lay Hull to the current schedule for the Lay Hull, you can tell the task start and completion dates slightly slipped. Within the current schedule, Time Line shows the completed portion of a task with a broken vertical bar or a series of square symbols.

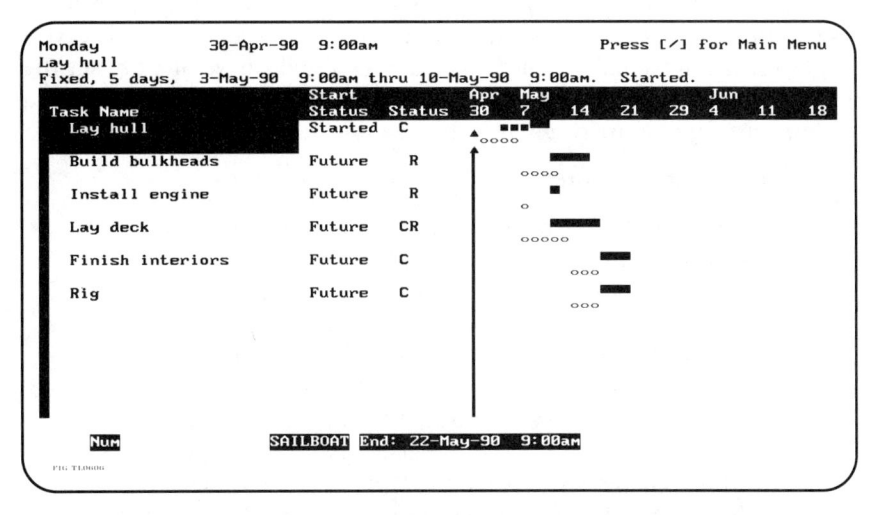

```
Monday              30-Apr-90   9:00am                    Press [/] for Main Menu
Lay hull
Fixed, 5 days,  3-May-90   9:00am thru 10-May-90   9:00am.  Started.
                            Start              Apr    May              Jun
Task Name           Status  Status   30    7    14    21    29    4    11    18
Lay hull            Started    C       ■■■
                                      ○○○○
Build bulkheads     Future     R                ■■
                                        ○○○○
Install engine      Future     R              ■
                                            ○
Lay deck            Future     CR                   ■■
                                              ○○○○○
Finish interiors    Future     C                         ■
                                                    ○○○
Rig                 Future     C                         ■
                                                    ○○○

Num                      SAILBOAT End: 22-May-90    9:00am
```

Fig. 6.6. The updated sailboat project schedule viewed in a Gantt chart after the lay hull task is started.

When you complete work on a task, you also need to record this. To record when work finishes on a task, you follow these steps:

1. Move the cursor so it highlights the task for which you want to record the completion of work.

2. Access the Task Form either by pressing Ctrl-F2 or by activating the menu bar and selecting Schedule Tasks Edit.

3. Move the cursor to the Status field and type D for Done.

4. If you haven't previously done so, move the cursor to the Start Date field and type in the actual start date.

5. Move the cursor to the End Date field and type in the actual end date.

6. When the Status, Start Date, and End Date fields are correct, press F10 to save your changes and return to the project schedule screen.

7. Press F9 to recalculate the project schedule.

Monitoring the Actual Resource Usage

If you allocated resources, you'll also want to monitor actual resource usage and compare it to the original resource allocations. (Before you begin recording actual resource usage, you should have already set the baseline schedule as described earlier in this chapter so that you have a permanent copy of the original resource allocations.)

To record use of a resource, you follow these steps:

1. Verify that Time Line is using the large version of the Task Form screen and the Cost Tracking version of the Resource Assignment Form screen for the project by activating the menu bar and then selecting Schedule Options. Time Line displays the Option Form. The Cost Tracking setting should be set to Yes. If it isn't, use the arrow keys to mark Yes. The Task Form setting should be set to Large. If it isn't, use the arrow keys to mark Large. If necessary, press F10 to save your settings changes and leave the Options Form. (Refer to Chapter 4, "Managing Project and Task Details," for more information on the Options Form.)

2. Move the cursor so it highlights the task for which you want to record the resource usage.

3. Access the Task Form either by pressing Ctrl-F2 or by activating the menu bar and selecting Schedule Tasks Edit.

4. Move the cursor to the Resource for which you want to record actual usage.

5. Press F2 to access the Resource/Cost Assignment Form screen.

6. Move the cursor to Actual Effort field and enter the units of the resource that has been used. After you enter the Actual amount, Time Line recalculates the To Go Effort amount by subtracting the Actual Effort amount from the Total Effort amount. If the To Go Effort amount isn't correct, you'll need to edit the Total Effort field so the (Total Effort - Actual Effort) calculation produces the correct To Go Effort. Figure 6.7 shows the Resource Assignment Form screen completed to show resource usage.

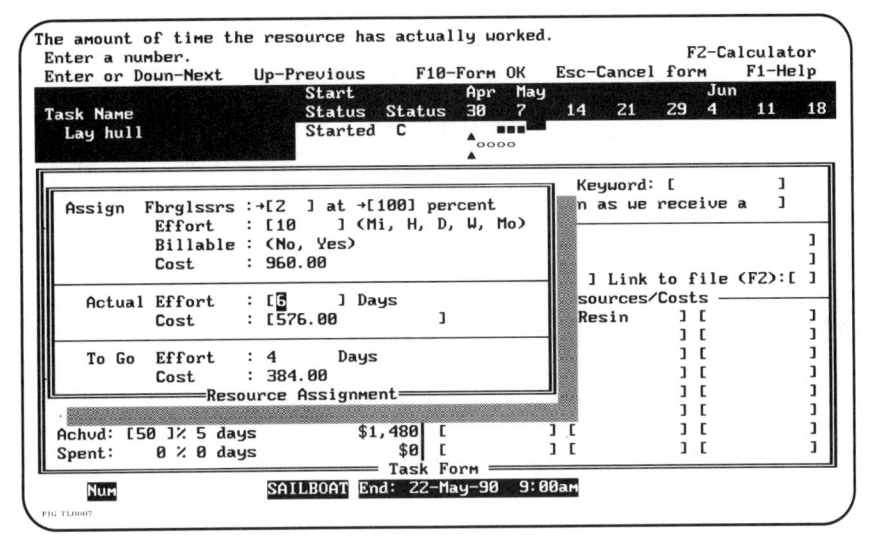

```
The amount of time the resource has actually worked.
  Enter a number.                                       F2-Calculator
  Enter or Down-Next   Up-Previous    F10-Form OK  Esc-Cancel form   F1-Help
                      Start              Apr  May              Jun
 Task Name            Status  Status     30   7    14   21   29  4    11    18
 Lay hull             Started   C          ▲  ■■■
                                             ○○○○
                                           ▲
 ┌─────────────────────────────────────────────┐ Keyword: [        ]
 │ Assign  Fbrglssrs :→[2  ] at →[100] percent │ n as we receive a ]
 │         Effort    : [10 ] (Mi, H, D, W, Mo) │                   ]
 │         Billable  : (No, Yes)               │                   ]
 │         Cost      : 960.00                  │ ] Link to file (F2):[ ]
 │                                             │ sources/Costs ─────
 │ Actual  Effort    : [6  ] Days              │ Resin    ] [        ]
 │         Cost      : [576.00      ]          │          ] [        ]
 │                                             │          ] [        ]
 │ To Go   Effort    : 4   Days                │          ] [        ]
 │         Cost      : 384.00                  │          ] [        ]
 │         ════════Resource Assignment═════════│          ] [        ]
 .                                                        ] [        ]
 Achvd: [50 ]% 5 days         $1,480 [       ] [          ] [        ]
 Spent:      0 % 0 days         $0   [       ] [          ] [        ]
                                       ══════ Task Form ══════
   Num              SAILBOAT End: 22-May-90  9:00am
```

Fig. 6.7. The Resource Assignment Form completed to show resource usage.

7. When the Actual Effort and To Go Effort fields are correct, press F10 to save your changes and return to the Task Form screen. On the Task Form screen, Time Line updates the Spent fields in the lower left corner to show the resource usage (see fig. 6.8).

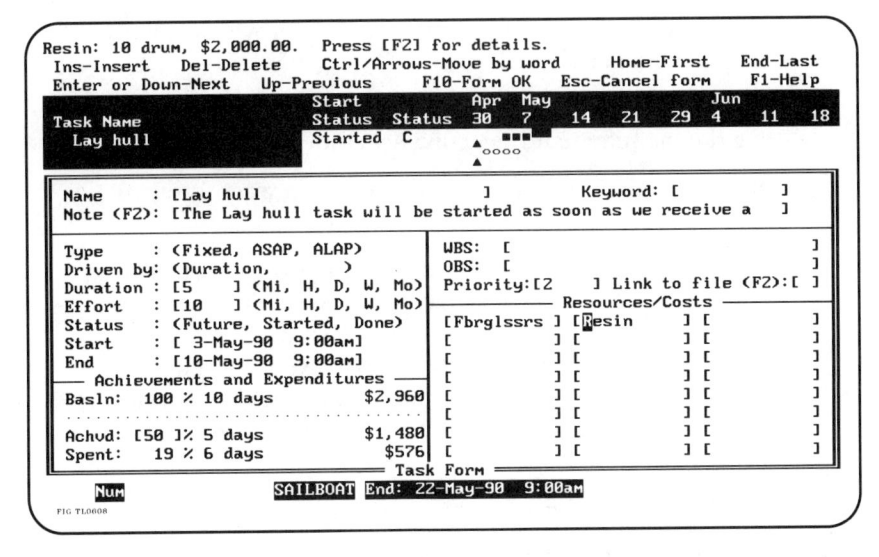

```
Resin: 10 drum, $2,000.00.  Press [F2] for details.
 Ins-Insert   Del-Delete   Ctrl/Arrows-Move by word   Home-First   End-Last
 Enter or Down-Next   Up-Previous    F10-Form OK  Esc-Cancel form   F1-Help
                      Start              Apr  May              Jun
 Task Name            Status  Status     30   7    14   21   29  4    11    18
 Lay hull             Started   C          ▲  ■■■
                                             ○○○○
                                           ▲
 Name     : [Lay hull              ]              Keyword: [          ]
 Note (F2): [The Lay hull task will be started as soon as we receive a ]
 Type     : (Fixed, ASAP, ALAP)          WBS: [                        ]
 Driven by: (Duration,     )             OBS: [                        ]
 Duration : [5   ] (Mi, H, D, W, Mo)   Priority:[2  ] Link to file (F2):[ ]
 Effort   : [10  ] (Mi, H, D, W, Mo)   ────── Resources/Costs ──────
 Status   : (Future, Started, Done)    [Fbrglssrs] [Resin    ] [       ]
 Start    : [ 3-May-90  9:00am]        [         ] [         ] [       ]
 End      : [10-May-90  9:00am]        [         ] [         ] [       ]
  ── Achievements and Expenditures ──  [         ] [         ] [       ]
 BasIn:  100 % 10 days         $2,960  [         ] [         ] [       ]
 ..........................            [         ] [         ] [       ]
 Achvd: [50 ]% 5 days          $1,480  [         ] [         ] [       ]
 Spent:    19 % 6 days           $576  [         ] [         ] [       ]
                                       ══════ Task Form ══════
   Num              SAILBOAT End: 22-May-90  9:00am
```

Fig. 6.8. Time Line shows the actual resources used on in the lower left corner of the Task Form.

8. Press F10 to return to the project schedule screen.

9. Press F9 to recalculate the project schedule.

Although the actual resources used doesn't show on the Gantt Chart view, it does show on several of the reports that Time Line generates. In addition, Chapter 7, "Customizing Time Line Screens," describes how to direct Time Line to display this data on project schedule screens.

Monitoring the Actual Costs

If you budgeted costs, you'll also want to monitor the actual spending and compare it to your original budgeted costs. The steps for doing this parallel those for recording actual resource usage. (Again, you should have already set the baseline schedule so that you have a permanent copy of your original budgeted costs.)

To record a cost, you follow these steps:

1. Verify that Time Line is using the large version of the Task Form screen and the Cost Tracking version of the Resource Assignment Form if you haven't already done this. (If you need help refer to the first step listed for monitoring actual resource usage.)

2. Move the cursor so it highlights the task for which you want to record the cost.

3. Access the Task Form either by pressing Ctrl-F2 or by activating the menu bar and selecting Schedule Tasks Edit.

4. Move the cursor to the Cost for which you want to record actual usage.

5. Press F2 to access the Cost Assignment Form screen. The type of Cost assignment screen that is displayed will depend on the type of cost. For example, a unit cost will result in the Unit Cost Assignment Form being displayed. A fixed cost will result in the Fixed Cost Assignment Form being displayed. A variable cost will result in the Variable Cost Assignment Form being displayed.

6. You then have a few options:

    A. (Optional) If the cost is a unit cost, either move the cursor to Actual Units field and enter the units of the item that have been used or move the cursor to the Actual $ field and enter the dollars of the item that have been used.

If you enter the actual units, Time Line calculates the dollar cost by multiplying the actual units by the default unit cost. If you enter the cost by specifying the dollars of cost, Time Line calculates the actual units by dividing the costs by the default unit costs.

After you enter the cost data, Time Line recalculates the To Go Cost amount by subtracting the Actual cost amount from the Total cost amount. If the To Go Cost amount isn't correct, you'll need to edit the Total Cost field so the (Total Cost - Actual Cost) calculation produces the correct To Go Cost. Figure 6.9 shows the Unit Cost Assignment Form.

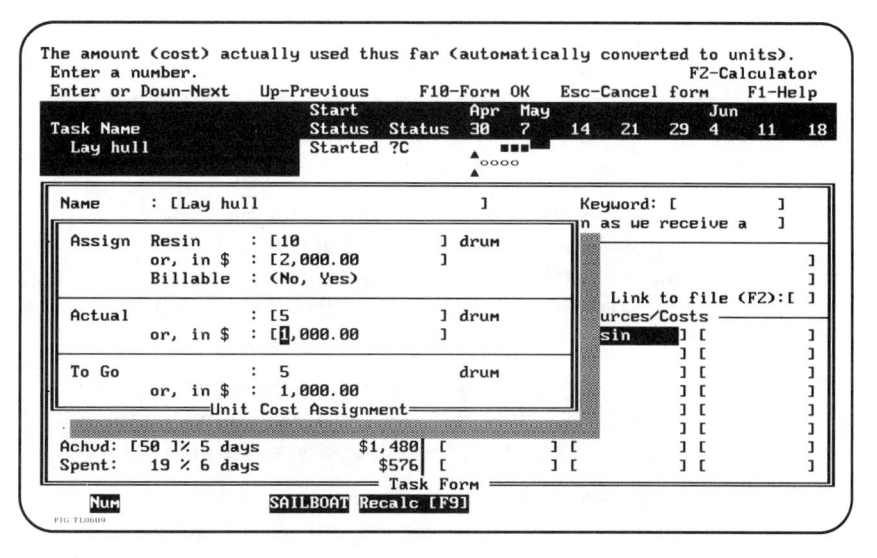

Fig. 6.9. The Unit Cost Assignment Form completed to account for actual unit costs.

B. (Optional) If the cost is a fixed cost, move the cursor to Actual cost field and enter the actual cost in dollars. After you enter the Actual cost amount, Time Line recalculates the To Go Cost amount by subtracting the Actual cost amount from the Total cost amount. If the To Go Cost amount isn't correct, you'll need to edit the Total Cost field so the (Total Cost - Actual Cost) calculation produces the correct To Go Cost. Figure 6.10 shows the completed Fixed Cost Assignment Form.

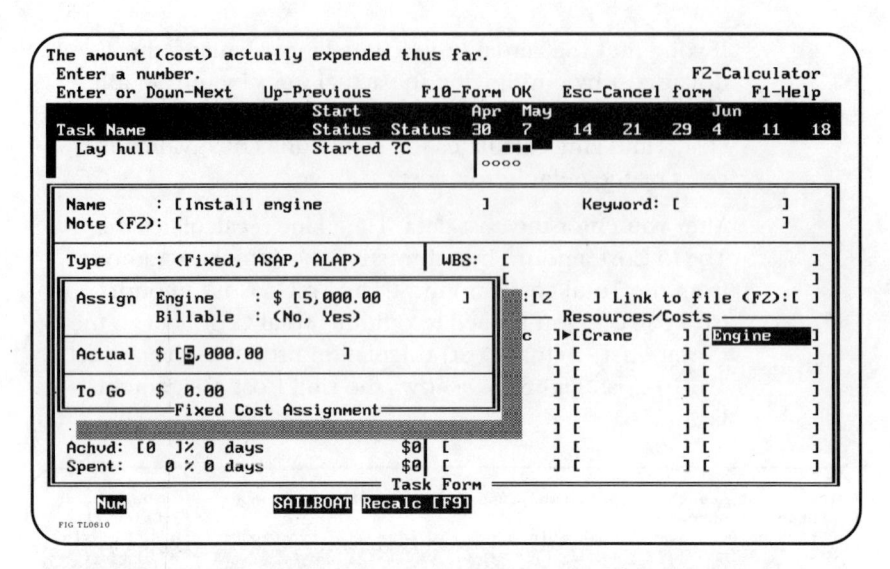

Part II: Advanced Project Management Techniques

Fig. 6.10. The Fixed Assignment Form screen completed to account for actual fixed costs.

      C. (Optional) If the cost is a variable cost, either move the cursor to Actual Time field and enter the time units of the item that have been used, or move the cursor to the Actual Cost field and enter the dollar cost of using the item.

      If you enter the cost by recording the actual time units, Time Line calculates the dollar cost by multiplying the time units by the default variable cost per unit.

      After you enter the Actual cost amount, Time Line recalculates the To Go Cost amount by subtracting the Actual cost amount from the Total cost amount. If the To Go Cost amount isn't correct, you'll need to edit the Total Cost field so the (Total Cost - Actual Cost) calculation produces the correct To Go Cost. Figure 6.11 shows the completed Variable Cost Assignment Form.

7. When the Actual and To Go fields are correct, press F10 to save your changes and return to the Task Form. Time Line updates the Spent fields in the lower left corner of the Task Form screen to show the resource usage.

8. Press F10 to return to the project schedule screen.

9. Press F9 to recalculate the project schedule.

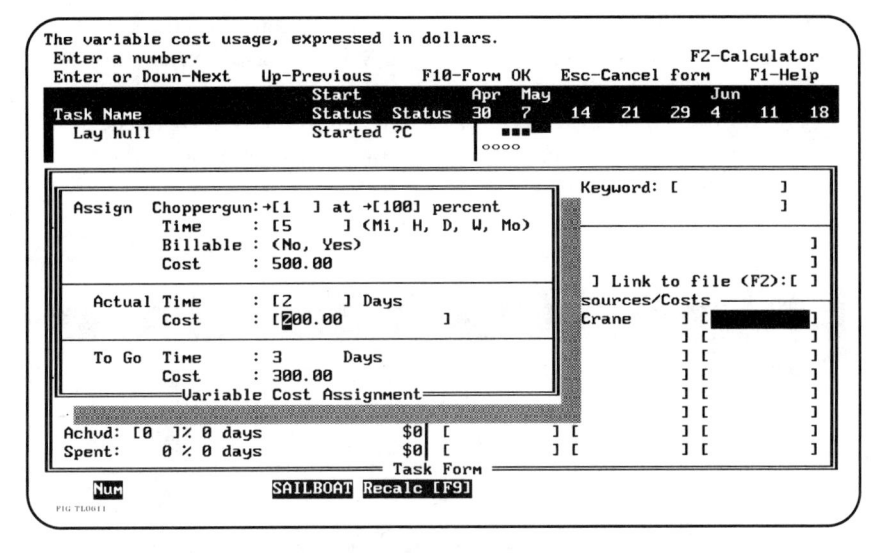

```
The variable cost usage, expressed in dollars.
  Enter a number.                                             F2-Calculator
  Enter or Down-Next    Up-Previous      F10-Form OK    Esc-Cancel form    F1-Help
                        Start                     Apr  May              Jun
Task Name               Status  Status    30   7   14   21   29   4    11   18
  Lay hull                      Started ?C        ■■■
                                                  oooo
                                                          Keyword: [           ]
    Assign   Choppergun: →[1  ] at →[100] percent                               ]
             Time     : [5   ] (Mi, H, D, W, Mo)
             Billable : (No, Yes)                                              ]
             Cost     : 500.00                                                 ]
                                                       ] Link to file (F2):[ ]
    Actual Time       : [2   ] Days                   sources/Costs
           Cost       : [200.00        ]              Crane     ] [          ]
                                                                ] [          ]
    To Go  Time       : 3     Days                              ] [          ]
           Cost       : 300.00                                  ] [          ]
                     Variable Cost Assignment                   ] [          ]
                                                                ] [          ]
Achvd: [0   ]% 0 days              $0| [            ] [         ] [          ]
Spent:      0 % 0 days             $0| [            ] [         ] [          ]
                                   Task Form
   Num                    SAILBOAT Recalc [F9]
```

Fig. 6.11. The Variable Cost Assignment Form screen completed to account for actual variable costs.

Just as is the case with resource usage, the actual costs incurred don't show on the Gantt Chart view. They do, however, show on several of the reports that Time Line generates. Chapter 7 describes how to direct Time Line to display this data on project schedule screens.

Using the Assist Update Option

Time Line provides a special menu option that lets you more easily record the actual start and completion dates of project tasks, resources used, and costs incurred: the Assist menu's Update option. The Assist menu's Update option identifies the tasks whose planned start dates precede the current date. It then walks you through the same basic steps described earlier in the chapter for recording actual start and completion dates, resource usage, and costs. Before you use the Assist Update option, you first should understand the basic process for updating the project—this is the material covered in the earlier sections of this chapter. Once you understand this information, you can use the Assist Update option to speed things up.

To use the Assist Update option on the current schedule, follow these steps:

1. Activate the menu bar and select Assist and then Update.
   Time Line compares the planned start and end dates for each task with the As-of Date.

Part II: Advanced Project Management Techniques

For each task whose planned start or end date precedes the As-of Date, Time Line displays the Status Assistant box (see fig. 6.12). The Status Assistant box identifies a task and whether, based on a comparison of the As-of Date with the planned start and end dates, it should have been started or finished.

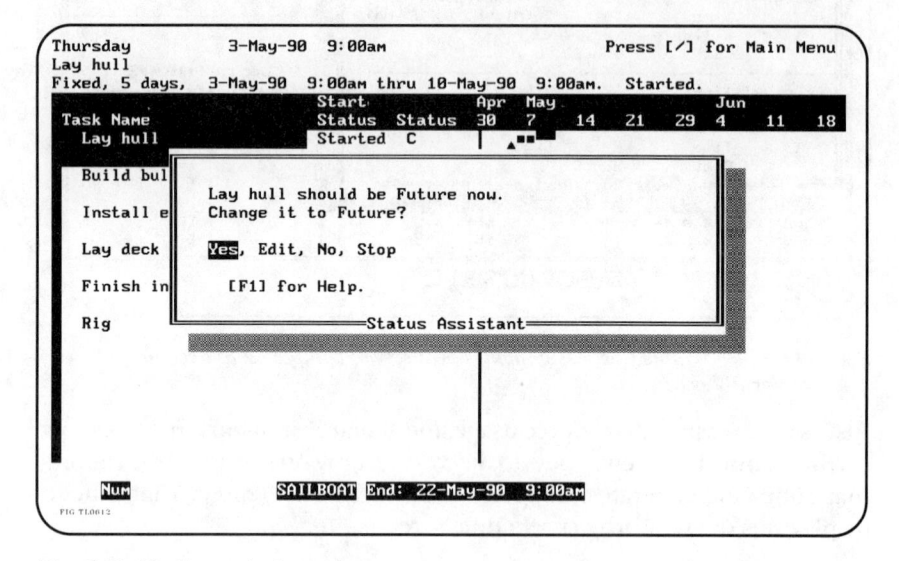

```
Thursday         3-May-90  9:00am                    Press [/] for Main Menu
Lay hull
Fixed, 5 days,   3-May-90  9:00am thru 10-May-90  9:00am.  Started.
                         Start.              Apr   May              Jun
Task Name                Status Status  30    7    14   21   29   4    11   18
Lay hull                 Started   C         ▲■■
    Build bul┌─────────────────────────────────────────────────────┐
    Install e│  Lay hull should be Future now.                     │
             │  Change it to Future?                               │
    Lay deck │                                                     │
             │  Yes, Edit, No, Stop                                │
    Finish in│                                                     │
             │     [F1] for Help.                                  │
    Rig      │                                                     │
             └══════════════════════Status Assistant═══════════════┘


       Num               SAILBOAT End: 22-May-90  9:00am
FIG TL0612
```

Fig. 6.12. The Status Assistant box.

2. Complete the Status Assistant box by highlighting one of the four possible choices: Yes, Edit, No, or Stop.

    Select Yes to update the task's status to Done if the planned end date precedes the As-of Date or to update the task's status to Started if the planned start date precedes the As-of Date. Time Line updates the task's status to either Done or Started as appropriate.

    Select Edit to leave the task's status unchanged and to display the Task Form for the indicated task.

    Select No to bypass the indicated task without making any changes and move to the next task whose planned start or end date precedes the As-of Date.

    Select Stop to bypass the indicated task without making any changes and then to terminate the Assist Update process.

3. (Optional) If a task is marked as Done (either manually by you or by using the Assist Update option) and the actual

Chapter 6: Monitoring Project Progress, Resources, and Costs

effort for the resource and cost assignments doesn't equal the total estimated effort, Time Line displays the Actuals Don't Match Estimated box (see fig. 6.13).

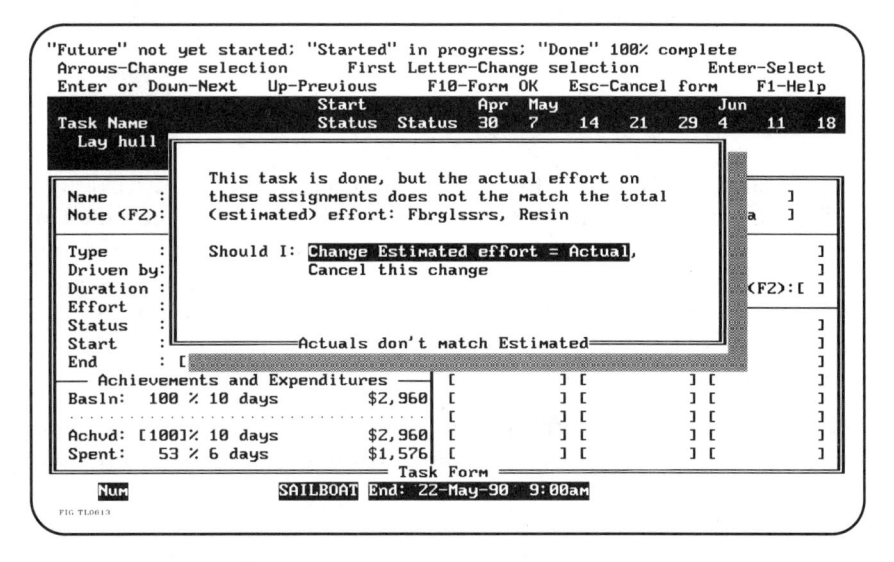

```
"Future" not yet started; "Started" in progress; "Done" 100% complete
Arrows-Change selection    First Letter-Change selection    Enter-Select
Enter or Down-Next    Up-Previous    F10-Form OK    Esc-Cancel form    F1-Help
                      Start         Apr  May              Jun
Task Name             Status Status 30   7   14   21  29  4   11  18
  Lay hull
          ┌──────────────────────────────────────────────┐
  Name    │ This task is done, but the actual effort on  │        ]
  Note(F2)│ these assignments does not the match the total│     a  ]
          │ (estimated) effort: Fbrglssrs, Resin          │
  Type    │ Should I: Change Estimated effort = Actual,   │        ]
  Driven by│          Cancel this change                  │        ]
  Duration │                                              │  (F2):[ ]
  Effort   │                                              │
  Status   │                                              │        ]
  Start    │════════Actuals don't match Estimated═════════│        ]
  End    :[                                                         ]
  ── Achievements and Expenditures ──  [       ] [        ] [      ]
  BasIn:   100 % 10 days    $2,960   [         ] [        ] [      ]
  ..........................          [         ] [        ] [      ]
  Achvd: [100]% 10 days     $2,960   [         ] [        ] [      ]
  Spent:   53 % 6 days      $1,576   [         ] [        ] [      ]
                        ═══════ Task Form ═══════
  Num             SAILBOAT End: 22-May-90  9:00am
FIG TL0613
```

Fig. 6.13. The Actuals Don't Match Estimated box.

Time Line identifies the resources and costs for which the actual figures don't match, or equal, the estimate figures. You get two choices: You can change the estimated effort you originally recorded to whatever the actual effort current shows, or you can cancel the change in status.

Note: If you haven't recorded any actual amounts yet, select Cancel this change. You'll then need to record the actual amounts and update the status as part of step 4.

4. (Optional) If you select either Yes or Edit on the Status Assistant box, Time Line displays the Task Form so you can enter actual resource usage and costs incurred. Complete the Task Form so as to record task progress, resources used, and costs spent. (For information on recording this data, refer to the earlier chapter sections, "Monitoring Actual Resource Usage" and "Monitoring the Actual Costs.")

You end up repeating step 2 and, optionally, steps 3 and 4, for each of the tasks in the project schedule whose planned start date or end date falls after the As-of Date. But that's all there is to it. In effect, the Assist Update option really gives you a way of identifying the tasks for which you should be recording progress. The main thing you need to be cognizant of, however, is that the identification is made by comparing the planned start and end dates to the As-of Date. So if your progress is ahead of schedule or your spending is ahead of schedule, you'll need to identify this other progress or spending some other way.

Chapter Summary

This chapter covers the steps for tracking project progress, resource usage, and costs—the fourth component of project management as identified in Chapter 1, "A Primer on Project Management." This chapter described how to monitor and record actual project progress, resource usage, and spending. It also described how the Time Line Assist Update option makes the whole process easier. This chapter also concludes the second section of *Using Time Line*, "Advanced Project Management Techniques."

There is, however, still more to using Time Line: The next section of the book covers the mechanics of managing the system you'll use to run Time Line.

Part III

Managing the System

Includes

Customizing Gantt, PERT, and Tree Chart Screens

Printing Reports

Working with the Time Line Files

Using the Time Line Files

Using Time Line Utilities and Macro Features

Protecting against System Disasters

Customizing Gantt, PERT, and Tree Chart Screens

This first chapter of Part III of *Using Time Line* tells you how to customize the screens that Time Line displays. To do this, you use three options on the Schedule menu: Sort, Filter, and Layout. None of these three options is difficult to use, but each gives you flexibility over how the screens showing project information are displayed. You can probably use these three options to make many of the screens more closely fit your requirements.

Using the Sort Option

The Sort option lets you choose how the tasks and subtasks for a project are ordered, or arranged. You choose the order by specifying the key or keys you want to use and then sorting the tasks and subtasks using the keys. Keys simply represent the field you use to order or arrange. For instance, you might use the planned starting date as a key. Or you might use the actual finish date. The choice is yours: You simply pick the key that makes most sense and then sort the tasks and subtasks by using the key.

Picking a Sort Key

Time Line lets you specify three types of keys; the primary key, the secondary key, and the other keys. The mechanics of specifying any of these three keys is roughly the same, but I'll list the steps for each anyway.

To specify a primary key, you follow these steps:

1. Activate the menu bar, select Schedule and then select Sort. Time Line displays the Sort menu shown in figure 7.1.

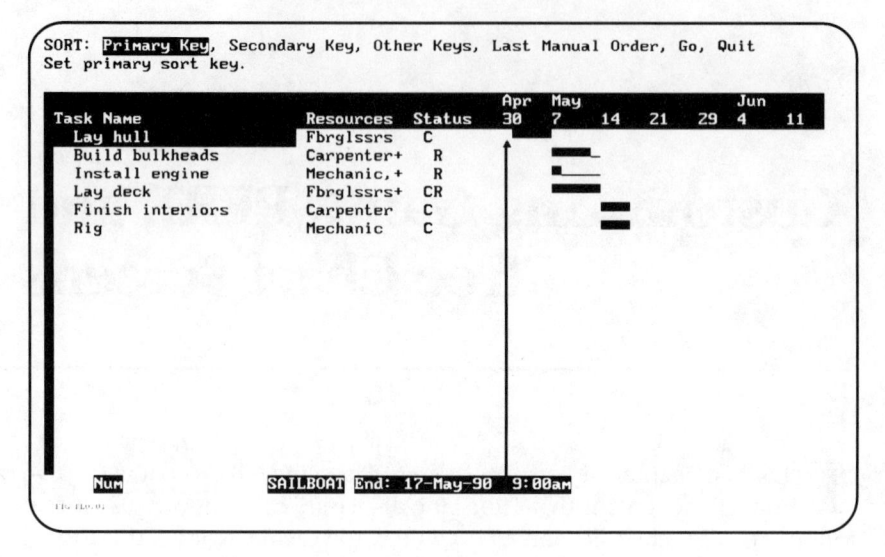

```
SORT: Primary Key, Secondary Key, Other Keys, Last Manual Order, Go, Quit
Set primary sort key.

                                               Apr  May              Jun
Task Name              Resources  Status       30   7    14   21  29 4    11
    Lay hull           Fbrglssrs    C
    Build bulkheads    Carpenter+   R
    Install engine     Mechanic,+   R
    Lay deck           Fbrglssrs+   CR
    Finish interiors   Carpenter    C
    Rig                Mechanic     C




     Num                SAILBOAT End: 17-May-90  9:00am
```

Fig. 7.1. *The Sort menu.*

2. Select the Primary key option from the Sort menu. Time Line displays the Ascending-Descending menu which you use to specify how Time Line should use the key (see fig. 7.2). Ascending means 1 comes before 2 and A comes before B. Descending means just the opposite. For example, a 2 would come before a 1, and B would come before A.

3. Mark the sort order you want—ascending or descending—and then press Enter. Time Line displays the Column list on the right side of the screen box (see fig. 7.3). The Column list box shows only a few of the fields that Time Line collects for each task and subtask at a time. You can, however, use the arrow keys and the page up and page down keys to see the next screenful of the list.

4. Mark the actual sort field you want to use and then press Enter.

Time Line uses a secondary sort key to arrange tasks or subtasks that have the same value for the primary key. To specify a secondary key, you follow the same basic steps:

1. Activate the menu bar, select Schedule and then select Sort. Time Line displays the Sort menu.

Chapter 7: Customizing Gantt, PERT, and Tree Chart Screens 179

```
DIRECTION: Ascending, Descending
Sort from: A-to-Z, low-to-high (numbers), etc.
```

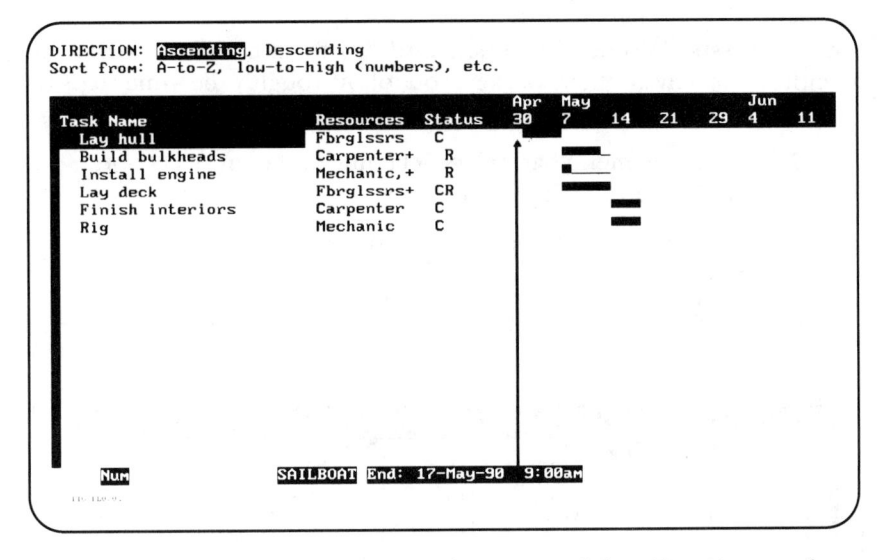

Fig. 7.2. The Ascending-Descending menu lets you specify how Time Line uses the key.

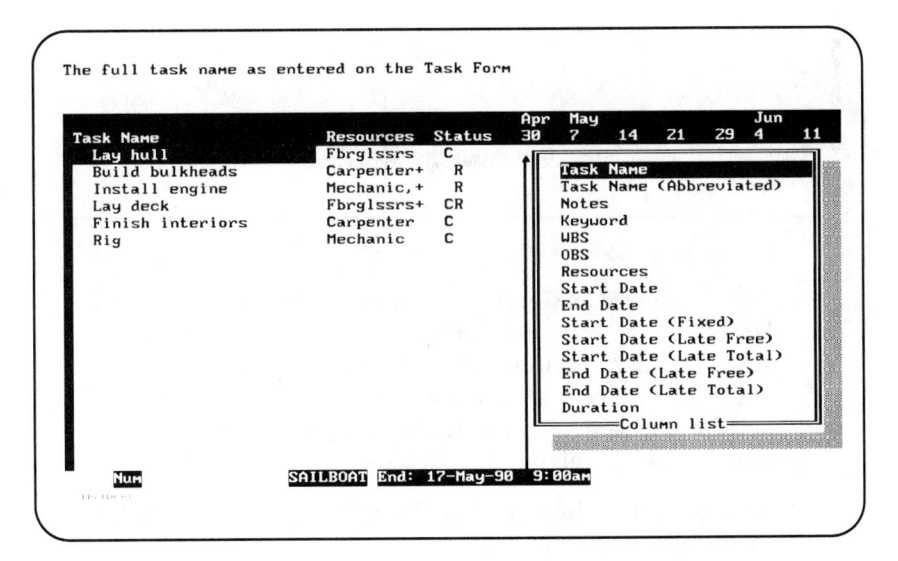

Fig. 7.3. The Column list box.

    2. Select the Secondary key option from the Sort menu. Time Line displays the Ascending-Descending menu.

    3. Mark the sort order you want—ascending or descending—and then press Enter.

    4. Mark the sort field you want to use and then press Enter.

Part III: Managing the System

You can also specify other sort keys: a third, fourth, fifth, and so on through a ninth. To specify another sort key, you follow roughly the same steps as you did for setting a primary or secondary sort key:

1. Activate the menu bar, select Schedule and then select Sort. Time Line displays the Sort menu.

2. Select the Other key option. Time Line displays the Other keys menu (see fig. 7.4).

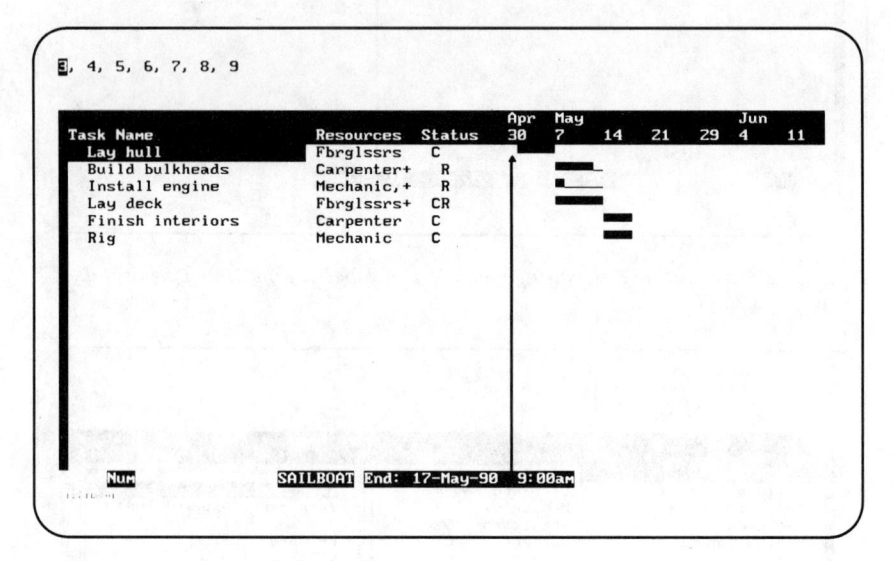

```
3, 4, 5, 6, 7, 8, 9

                                            Apr  May                  Jun
Task Name              Resources   Status   30   7    14   21   29   4    11
   Lay hull            Fbrglssrs   C
   Build bulkheads     Carpenter+  R
   Install engine      Mechanic,+  R
   Lay deck            Fbrglssrs+  CR
   Finish interiors    Carpenter   C
   Rig                 Mechanic    C




     Num              SAILBOAT End: 17-May-90  9:00am
```

Fig. 7.4. The Out keys menu.

3. Pick the other key you want to specify 3 indicates the third key effects the ordering when the primary and secondary keys are the same. 4 indicates the fourth key and would only effect the ordering when the primary, secondary, and third keys are the same. Time Line also lets you specify a fifth, sixth, seventh, eighth, and ninth key.

   After you select the other key, Time Line displays the Ascending-Descending menu

4. Mark the sort order you want—ascending or descending—and then press Enter. Time Line displays the Column list box.

5. Mark the sort field you want to use and then press Enter.

Sorting the Tasks

The two options not described above—Go and Last Manual Order—perform the actual sorting. After you've specified the keys you want to Time Line to use, you use Go to initiate the sort operation. The steps are as follows:

1. Activate the menu bar, select Schedule and then select Sort. Time Line displays the Sort menu.
2. Select Go and Time Line rearranges the tasks according to your keys.

If, after a number of sorts, you want to return to the original order in which you entered the tasks, you use the Last Manual Order option. The steps for doing this are as follows:

1. Activate the menu bar, select Schedule and then select Sort. Time Line displays the Sort menu.
2. Select Last Manual Order. Time Line rearranges the tasks so they are in the same order they were before you began sorting.

(*Note:* Typically, Time Line returns the tasks to the same order they were in when you originally created the project schedule. However, whenever you move tasks, Time Line asks whether you want the last manual order overwritten as the current manual order. If you answer Yes, Time Line considers the task arrangement after you complete the move to be the original order. Accordingly, it is this order to which the task arrangement will be returned if later you use the Last Manual Order option.)

One final thing about sorting: Keep in mind that sorting doesn't change the relationships between tasks. Task dependencies don't change. And task-subtask relationships don't change. As you might expect, then, you can't use sorting to change task dependencies, nor can you use sorting to move a subtask out from under the summary task to which it belongs.

Using the Filter Option

With larger projects—say those with more than one hundred tasks—you'll often find yourself searching through a project for tasks and subtasks with a certain characteristic. If you're concerned about project delays, for example, you might be paying particular attention to tasks on the critical

Part III: Managing the System

path. If you're monitoring actual progress, resource usage, and costs, you might be continually searching for all the tasks that need updating. And your specific situation, of course, you'll have other similar requirements to look through a project for certain sets or categories of tasks.

The Filters option displays a menu of choices that let you selectively include tasks and subtasks and that let you identify using color or different intensities tasks and subtasks that have certain characteristics (see fig. 7.5). Although this discussion focuses on how to use the filters option to customize your screen, you can also use it to affect the data that appears on Time Line reports, too. (This is explained fully in the next chapter.)

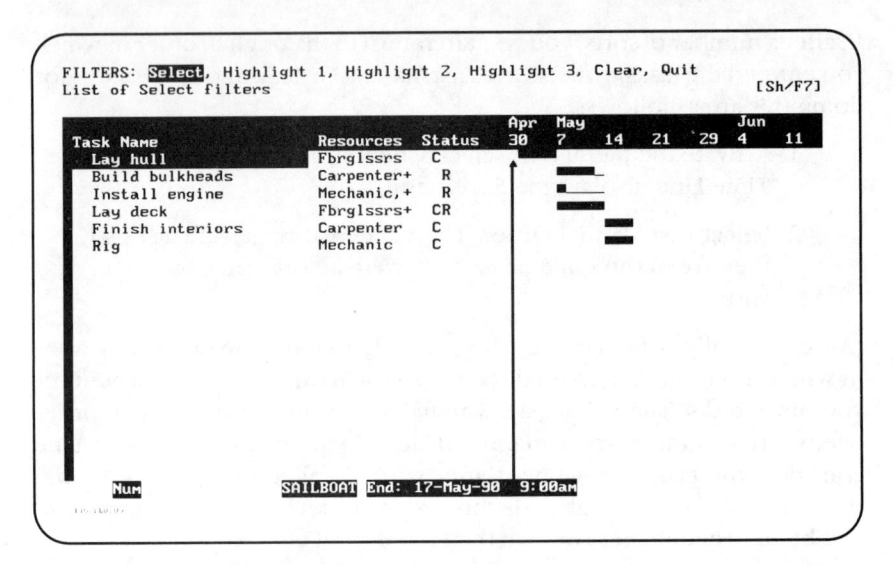

```
FILTERS: Select, Highlight 1, Highlight 2, Highlight 3, Clear, Quit
List of Select filters                                          [Sh/F7]
                                        Apr  May              Jun
Task Name              Resources Status 30   7    14   21  29 4    11
  Lay hull             Fbrglssrs   C
  Build bulkheads      Carpenter+  R
  Install engine       Mechanic,+  R
  Lay deck             Fbrglssrs+  CR
  Finish interiors     Carpenter   C
  Rig                  Mechanic    C




      Num              SAILBOAT End: 17-May-90  9:00am
```

Fig. 7.5. The Filters option displays a menu that lets you selectively include and highlight certain tasks and subtasks.

Selecting Tasks and Subtasks with a Filter

To select all the tasks and subtasks in a project that meet certain criteria, you use the Select option. The steps are as follows:

1. Activate the menu bar, select Schedule, Filters, and then Select. Time Line displays the Select Filter box (see fig. 7.6).

2. Use the arrow keys to mark one of the predefined filters that come with Time Line.

    Critical Path is a filter that selects only those tasks and subtasks that fall on the project's critical path.

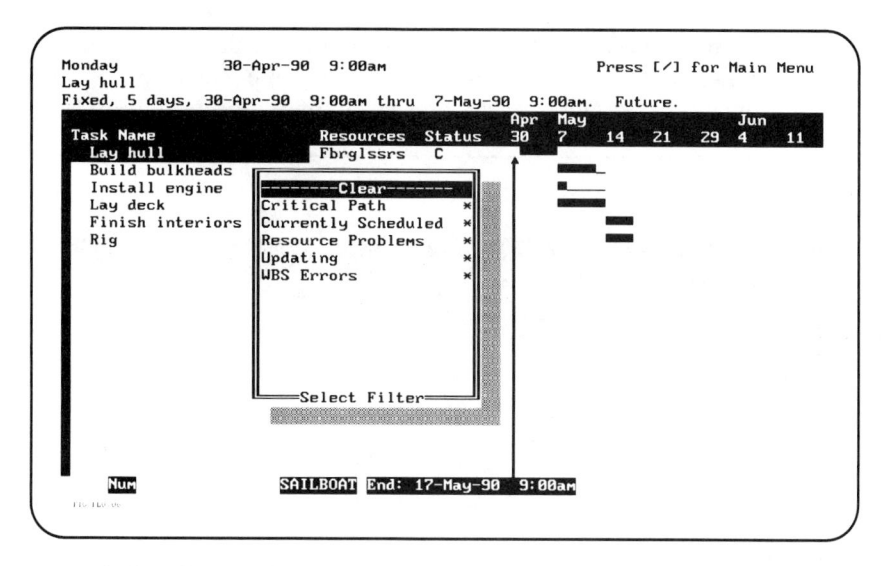

Chapter 7: Customizing Gantt, PERT, and Tree Chart Screens **183**

```
Monday          30-Apr-90   9:00am                 Press [/] for Main Menu
Lay hull
Fixed, 5 days, 30-Apr-90  9:00am thru  7-May-90  9:00am.  Future.
                                                Apr  May            Jun
   Task Name              Resources  Status      30   7   14  21  29  4   11
       Lay hull           Fbrglssrs    C
       Build bulkheads   ┌──────Clear──────┐
       Install engine    │Critical Path    *│
       Lay deck          │Currently Scheduled *│
       Finish interiors  │Resource Problems *│
       Rig               │Updating         *│
                         │WBS Errors       *│
                         │                 │
                         │                 │
                         │                 │
                         │                 │
                         └═Select Filter═══┘

       Num            SAILBOAT End: 17-May-90  9:00am
```

Fig. 7.6. *The Select Filter box.*

    Currently Scheduled is a filter that selects only those tasks that have a status of either future or started.

    Resource Problems is a filter that selects those tasks with resource conflicts. (Refer to Chapter 5, "Identifying and Allocating Resources and Costs," for more information on resource conflicts.)

    Updating is a filter that selects those tasks that probably need to be updated. (Refer to Chapter 6, "Monitoring Project Progress, Resources and Costs," for more information on the updating process.)

    WBS Errors selects the tasks that the WBS Manager's Verify option thinks are incorrect (Refer to Chapter 4, "Managing Project and Task Benefits," for more information on the WBS Manager and WBS Errors.)

Note: Later on, I'll explain how you can create your own filters from scratch, but for now we'll just use the ones that come prepackaged with Time Line. By the way, the asterisk character indicates those that come prepackaged with Time Line.

3. When the filter you want to use is highlighted, press Enter. Time Line then displays only those tasks that match the filter. If a summary task doesn't match the filter, but one of the

summary task's subtasks does, Time Line includes the summary task. When a filter is in effect, Time Line displays the word `Filtered` at the bottom of the screen (see fig. 7.7).

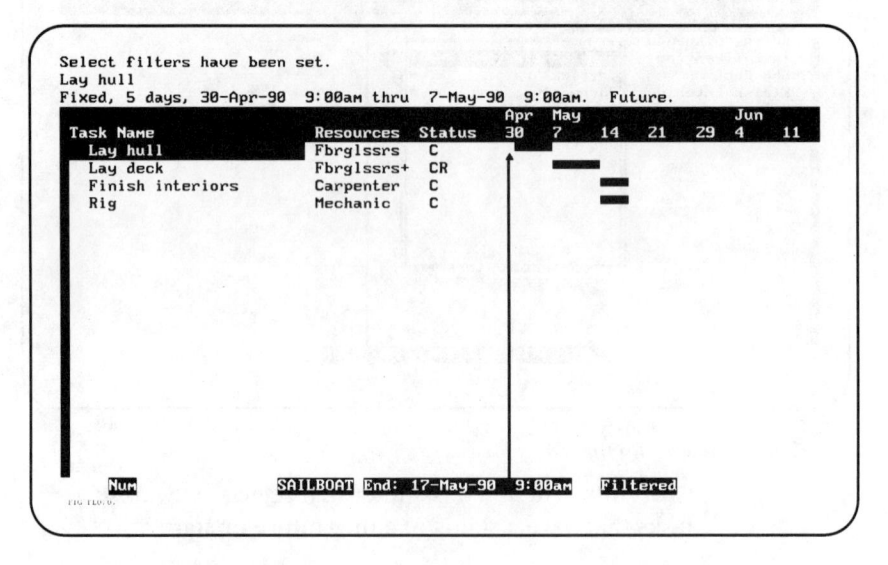

```
Select filters have been set.
Lay hull
Fixed, 5 days, 30-Apr-90  9:00am thru  7-May-90  9:00am.  Future.
                                          Apr  May                Jun
Task Name              Resources   Status  30   7    14   21  29  4    11
  Lay hull             Fbrglssrs   C
  Lay deck             Fbrglssrs+  CR
  Finish interiors     Carpenter   C
  Rig                  Mechanic    C




      Num              SAILBOAT End: 17-May-90  9:00am    Filtered
```

Fig. 7.7. *Time Line displays the word* **Filtered***, in the lower right corner of the screen to show when tasks are being filtered.*

4. (Optional) To remove the filter, first activate the menu bar. Then select Schedule Filter Clear; or select Schedule Filter Select and from the Filter List screen, select the Clear option.

Highlighting Tasks and Subtasks with a Filter

In a way, highlighting is similar to selecting. Using a filter, Time Line identifies all the tasks and subtasks in the project with certain characteristics. On a color monitor, Time Line displays the highlighted tasks in a different color. On a monochrome monitor, Time Line displays the highlighted tasks with bold intensity.

To highlight the tasks and subtasks in a project that meet certain criteria, you use the Select option. The steps are as follows:

1. Activate the menu bar, select Schedule Filters and then either Highlight 1, Highlight 2, or Highlight 3. Time Line displays the Highlight Filter box as shown in figure 7.8.

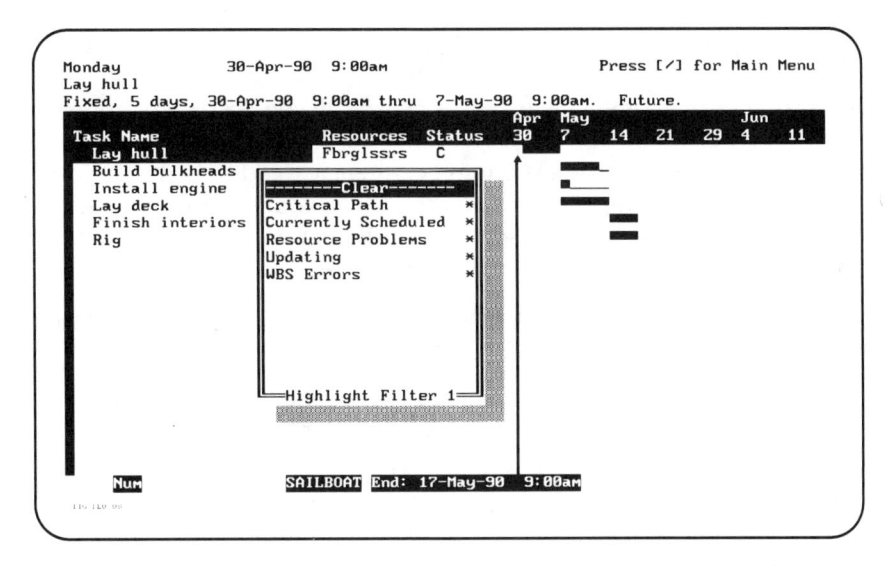

Chapter 7: Customizing Gantt, PERT, and Tree Chart Screens 185

```
Monday          30-Apr-90   9:00am                Press [/] for Main Menu
Lay hull
Fixed, 5 days, 30-Apr-90  9:00am thru  7-May-90  9:00am.  Future.
                                          Apr  May              Jun
Task Name            Resources Status     30   7    14   21  29  4    11
    Lay hull          Fbrglssrs   C
    Build bulkheads  ┌────────Clear────────┐
    Install engine   │Critical Path       *│
    Lay deck         │Currently Scheduled *│
    Finish interiors │Resource Problems   *│
    Rig              │Updating            *│
                     │WBS Errors          *│
                     │                     │
                     │                     │
                     │                     │
                     └═Highlight Filter 1══┘

    Num              SAILBOAT End: 17-May-90  9:00am
```

Fig. 7.8. The Highlight Filter box.

   2. In answer to the Select option, use the arrow keys to mark one of the predefined filters that come with Time Line. (The highlight filters correspond to the identically titled regular filters described earlier in the chapter.)

   3. When the filter you want to use is highlighted, press Enter. Time Line then highlights the tasks that match the Filter. *Note:* Unlike the Select option, if a summary task doesn't match the filter, but one of the summary task's subtasks does, Time Line doesn't include the summary task.

   4. (Optional) If you specify more than one highlight filter by successively using the Highlight 1, Highlight 2, and Highlight 3 commands, you can flip between the different highlight filters without having to select repeatedly the filter on the Filter List box. To do so, use function key combinations: F7 displays the highlight filter 1, Ctrl-F7 displays the highlight filter 2, and Alt-F7 displays the highlight filter 3.

   5. (Optional) To remove the filter, first activate the menu bar. Then select Schedule Filter Clear; or select Schedule Filter Highlight 1, Highlight 2, or Highlight 3, and from the Filter List box, select the Clear option.

Creating Your Own Filters

The five filters that Time Line provides may be all you ever need, but you can add others. You can even modify these if you want. This means, of course, that you've got the option of creating custom filters that let you selectively include or highlight tasks according to your priorities or needs. For example, you might want to see all the tasks that start or end in a certain month. Or you might want to see all the tasks that use a certain resource.

It isn't difficult to create custom filters. To do so, you simply follow these steps:

1. Activate the menu bar, and then select Schedule Filters and Select. Time Line displays the Select Filter box (see fig. 7.8).

2. If you want the filter to be available only for the project currently displayed, press Ins. If you want the filter to be available for all projects, press Shift-Ins. Time Line display the Filter Form screen (see fig. 7.9). You'll use the Filter Form screen to create a custom filter.

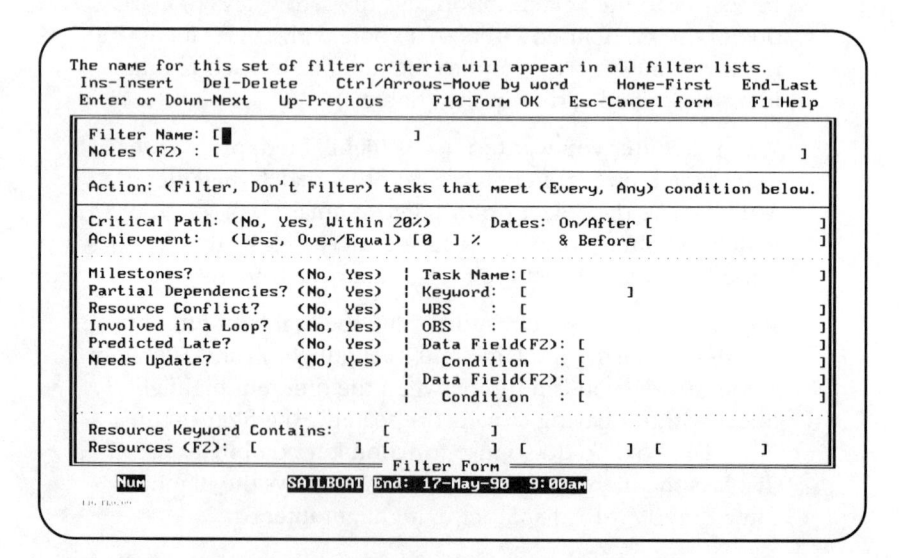

```
The name for this set of filter criteria will appear in all filter lists.
  Ins-Insert   Del-Delete    Ctrl/Arrows-Move by word    Home-First    End-Last
  Enter or Down-Next    Up-Previous      F10-Form OK    Esc-Cancel form    F1-Help

   Filter Name: [                    ]
   Notes (F2) : [                                                              ]
  .............................................................................
   Action: (Filter, Don't Filter) tasks that meet (Every, Any) condition below.
  .............................................................................
   Critical Path: (No, Yes, Within 20%)     Dates: On/After [            ]
   Achievement:    (Less, Over/Equal) [0  ] %         & Before [            ]
  .............................................................................
   Milestones?                  (No, Yes)  | Task Name:[                      ]
   Partial Dependencies? (No, Yes)         | Keyword:  [            ]
   Resource Conflict?    (No, Yes)         | WBS     : [                      ]
   Involved in a Loop?   (No, Yes)         | OBS     : [                      ]
   Predicted Late?       (No, Yes)         | Data Field(F2): [                ]
   Needs Update?         (No, Yes)         |   Condition   : [                ]
                                           | Data Field(F2): [                ]
                                           |   Condition   : [                ]
  .............................................................................
   Resource Keyword Contains:      [                    ]
   Resources (F2): [          ] [          ] [          ] [          ]
  ================================ Filter Form ================================
     Num              SAILBOAT  End: 17-May-90  9:00am
```

Fig. 7.9. The Filter Form.

3. With the cursor at the Filter Name field, enter the name you want Time Line to display on the Filter List box to identify this filter.

Chapter 7: Customizing Gantt, PERT, and Tree Chart Screens

4. (Optional) Move the cursor to the Notes field and type a description of the filter. You can press F2 to create a larger Notes text file so you have more space to describe or document the filter if you want. (Chapters 3 and 4 describe this basic feature in more detail.)

5. Move the cursor to the Filter-Don't Filter field. Mark Filter if you want to select or highlight tasks that meet the characteristics you'll describe. Mark Don't Filter if you want to select or highlight the tasks that don't meet the characteristics you'll describe.

6. Move the cursor the Every-Any field. Mark Every if you want to select or highlight tasks based on all the characteristics, or conditions, listed on the Filter Form. Mark Any if you want to select or highlight tasks based on any one of the characteristics, or conditions, listed on the Filter Form.

7. (Optional) Move the cursor to the Critical Path field. Mark No if you want to specify the condition that a task fall on the critical path, mark Yes if you want to specify the condition that a task not fall on the critical path, and mark within 20% if you want to specify, as the condition that a task's total slack equal twenty percent or less of its total duration.

8. (Optional) Move the cursor to the Achievement field. You can use the Achievement field to specify a task's achieved percent as a select or highlight condition. To set the condition as those tasks with less than a certain percentage of completion, mark the Less field and enter the percentage in the % field. To set the condition as those tasks with equal to or greater than a certain percentage of completion, mark the Over/Equal field and enter the percentage in the % field.

9. (Optional) Move the cursor to the Dates field. You can use the Dates fields to use a task's start date as a select and highlight condition. Enter in the On/After field the date (and optionally, the time) that a task should follow. In the Before field, enter the date and time that a task should precede.

You can use any of the valid date and time formats to enter the date and time as well as a few special keywords such as *today*, *tomorrow*, and *yesterday*. To see a list of the date and time formats and the special keywords, press F1 to access Help when the cursor is on the Dates field.

10. (Optional) Move the cursor to any of the No-Yes switches in the lower left corner of the Filter Form. You can choose whether a task is milestone, part of a partial dependency, subject to a resource conflict, involved in a dependency loop, predicted to start later then originally scheduled, or probably needs to be updated. Mark No if you don't want to use the condition and Yes if you do want to use the condition.

11. (Optional) Move the cursor to the Task Name field. Enter the task name or the phrase or letters used in a task name that you want to use as a condition. To select or highlight based on the complete task name, enter the full name.

    To select or highlight based on the phrase or letters used, you use three wildcard characters: the periods (.$th.). The question mark (?) and the tilde (~). You can use the question mark to represent any single character. So the entry "A?AP" would select or highlight both ASAP and ALAP. You can use the periods to represent a series of characters. So the entry "Lay.." would select or highlight both Lay hull and Lay deck. And the entry "..Lay.." would select or highlight any task that uses the word "lay".

    For purposes of making the text comparisons, Time Line ignores the case of the letters so, for example, Lay is the same as LAY. To select or highlight based on the task name not being equal to something, you use the tilde character (~). For example, to set the condition to find entries *not using* the phrase "Lay," you would enter the following line:

    ~..Lay..

    Additionally, to find entries not equal to ASAP, you enter

    ~ASAP

12. (Optional) Move the cursor to the Keyword field. Enter the keyword or the phrase or letters you want to use as a condition. For the task name field, you can use the three wildcard characters—question mark, periods, and tilde—in your entry.

13. (Optional) Move the cursor to the WBS field. Enter the WBS Code or the portion of the code you want to use as a condition. For the task name and Keyword fields, you can use the three wildcard characters in your entry.

14. (Optional) Move the cursor to the OBS field. Enter the OBS code of the portion of the code you want to use as a condition. Here, you can use the three wildcard characters.

Chapter 7: Customizing Gantt, PERT, and Tree Chart Screens 189

15. (Optional) Move the cursor to either of the Data Fields, press F2 to see a list of the fields that Time Line stores for a task, highlight the field you want to use in your condition, and then press Enter. Move the cursor to the Condition field and enter the value, word, or character string you want to use as the condition. For textual data fields, you can use the same three wildcard characters as are available for the task name, Keyword, WBS code and OBS code fields. If you choose to use a numeric data field such as cost or duration, you can't use the three wildcard characters, but you can use one of six Boolean operators: < , <= , > , >= , = , <>.

    < is the less-than symbol, so if you select Durations as the condition field and want to specify the condition as "all the tasks with the duration less than 10", you could enter the condition as <10. The remaining six symbols work the same way. <= is the less-than-or-equal-to symbol. > is the greater-than symbol. >= is the greater-than-or-equal-to symbol. = is the equal sign. <> is the not-equal-to symbol.

    You can specify the same field in both Data fields. So, for example, you could select all the tasks with duration between 5 and 10 by entering specifying the first data field as duration and its condition as >=5, and then specifying the second data field as duration and its condition as <=10.

16. (Optional) Move the cursor to the Resource Keyword Contains field. If you want to select or highlight based on what a task's resources show in the Keyword field on the Resource Form screen, enter the word or character string that you want to use as the condition in this field. (Chapter 5, "Identifying and Allocating Resources," describes the Resource Form and the Keyword field that appears on the screen.)

17. (Optional) Move the cursor to the Resources fields. If you want to select or highlight based on the resources or costs that a task shows, enter the resource and cost names. If you press F2, Time Line will display a list of the resource and cost names.

    Note: Remember that if you set the condition as Every in step 6, Time Line will only select or highlight those tasks that use the resources or costs you specify as well as every other condition you defined.

18. When the Filter Form is complete, press F10 to save your work. Time Line redisplays the Select Filter box. Press Esc to remove the box and return to the project screen.

Editing and Deleting Filters

You can edit and delete an existing filter. To do so, you follow the same 18 steps described for creating a filter from scratch—except that instead of pressing Ins or Shift-Ins in step 2, you highlight the filter you want to modify and then press F2.

To delete a filter, you activate the menu bar, select Schedule Filter Select, mark the filter you want to delete, and then press Del. Time Line asks whether you're sure you want to delete the filter, and if you do, select **Proceed** and press Enter.

Using the Layout Option

As this point, you know that Time Line collects up to several dozen pieces—actually over a hundred if you use every available field—of information about each task in a project. You also know that Time Line displays some of this information—the name, the first resource allocated, and the status—on the left half of the Gantt chart screen (see fig. 7.10).

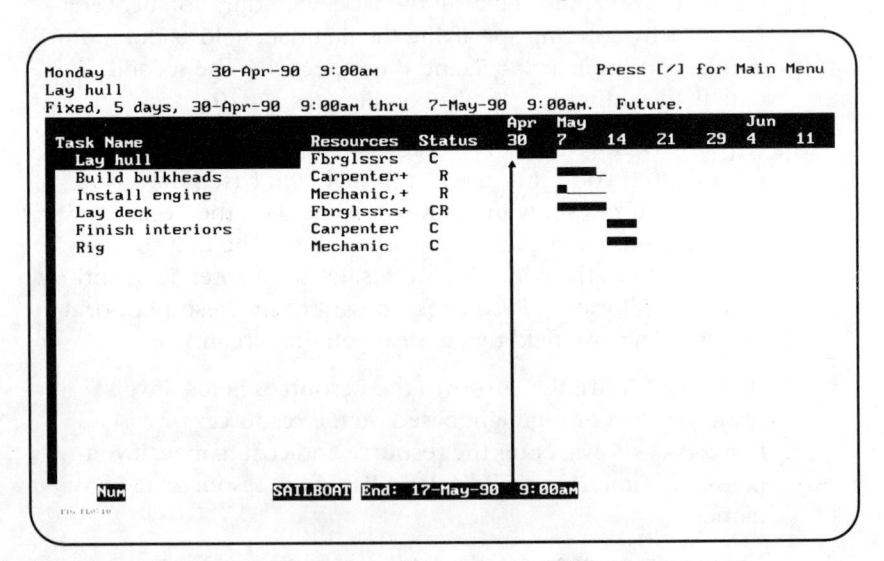

```
Monday          30-Apr-90   9:00am                Press [/] for Main Menu
Lay hull
Fixed, 5 days, 30-Apr-90  9:00am thru  7-May-90  9:00am.  Future.
                                        Apr  May                Jun
Task Name              Resources  Status 30   7   14   21   29  4    11
  Lay hull             Fbrglssrs  C
  Build bulkheads      Carpenter+ R
  Install engine       Mechanic,+ R
  Lay deck             Fbrglssrs+ CR
  Finish interiors     Carpenter  C
  Rig                  Mechanic   C




 Num                  SAILBOAT End: 17-May-90  9:00am
```

Fig. 7.10. The standard layout of the Gantt chart screen.

You can direct Time Line to display other pieces of information on the Gantt chart screen, as well. You also can control how Time Line calibrates the time scale that appears on the right half of the Gantt chart screen. You do all this with the Layout option in the Schedule menu. The Layout option lists several additional predefined layouts that you can use in place of the standard Gantt layout shown in figure 7.10, the standard PERT layout shown in figure 7.11, and the standard Tree layout shown in figure 7.12. The Layout option also lets you create customized layouts so you can view Gantt charts and PERT charts that perfectly match your requirements. (You can also use the Layout option to create customized Gantt chart and PERT chart reports. I'll talk more about this in Chapter 8, "Printing Reports.")

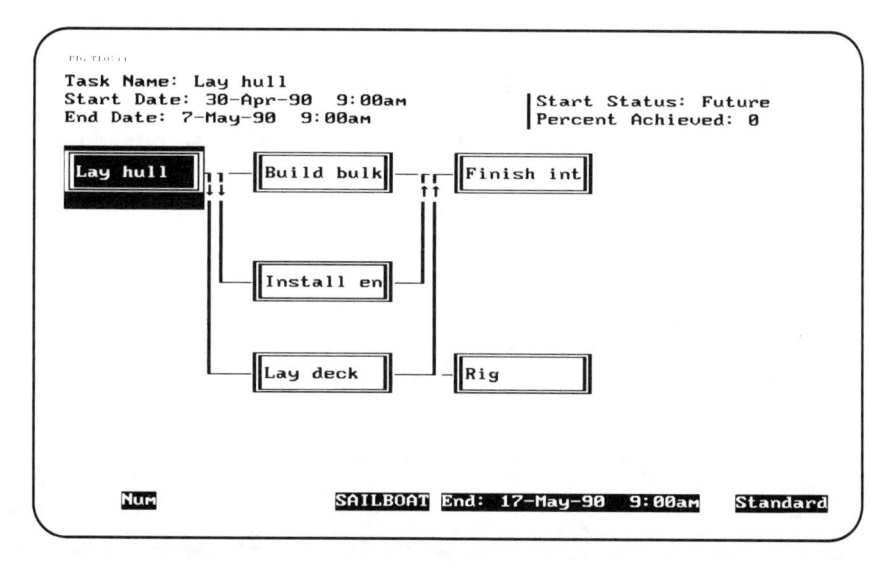

Fig. 7.11. The standard layout of the PERT chart screen.

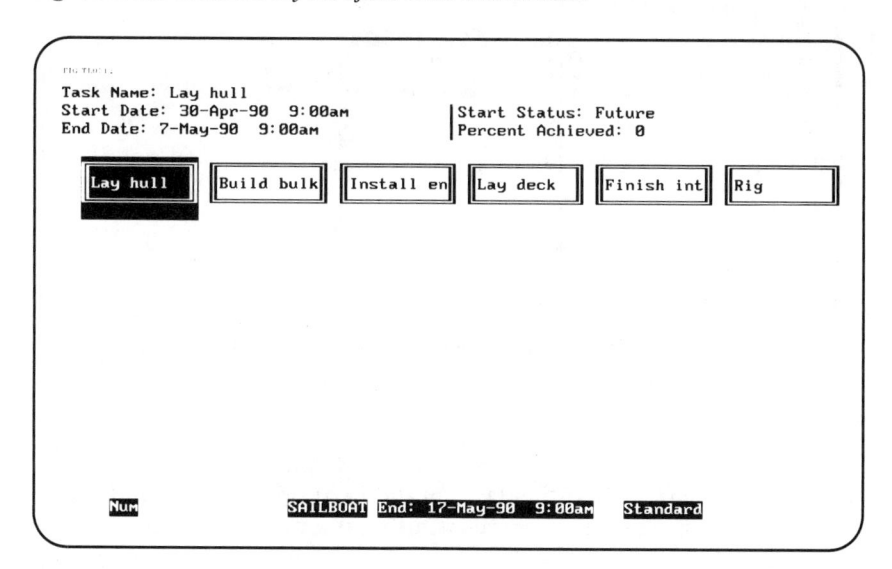

Fig. 7.12. The standard layout of the Tree chart screen.

Part III: Managing the System

Note: As a reminder, remember that you can enter data into fields that Time Line doesn't calculate for you right in the left half of the Gantt chart screen by moving the cursor to the field and pressing F2. So not only do the other layouts let you see different views of the Gantt chart, but they sometimes also provide convenient methods for collecting or entering certain sets of task data.

Using a Predefined Layout

As mentioned earlier, Time Line provides several additional predefined layouts that you can use to see different versions of the Gantt chart and the PERT and Tree chart. To use any of these, you follow the steps listed below:

1. Activate the menu bar and select Schedule and then select Layout. Time Line displays the Layout list box shown in figure 7.13 if a Gantt chart was displayed when you activated the menu bar, and it displays the Layout list box, shown in figure 7.14, if a PERT or Tree chart was displayed when you activated the menu bar.

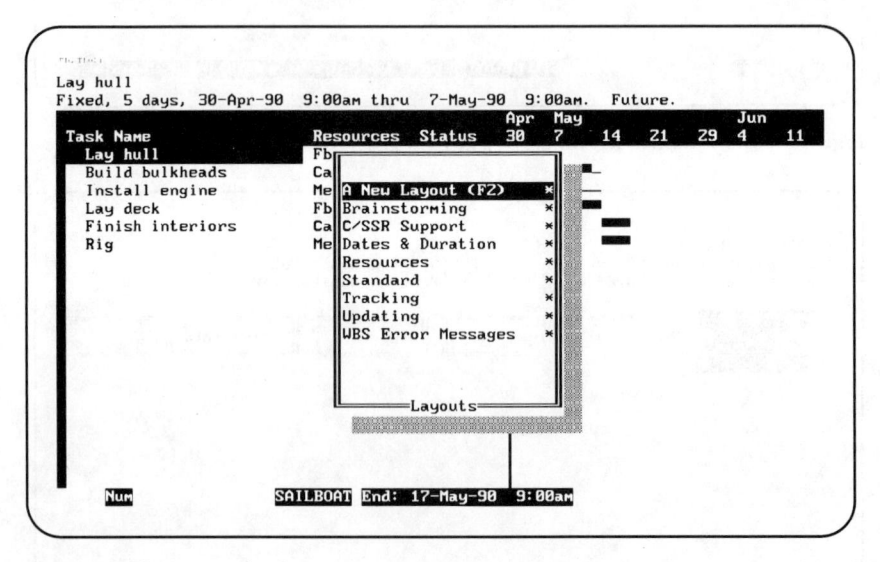

```
TL TIME
Lay hull
Fixed, 5 days, 30-Apr-90  9:00am thru  7-May-90  9:00am.  Future.
                                          Apr  May              Jun
Task Name           Resources  Status      30   7    14   21   29   4    11
  Lay hull              Fb
  Build bulkheads       Ca
  Install engine        Me  ┌A New Layout (F2)      ┐
  Lay deck              Fb  │Brainstorming          │
  Finish interiors      Ca  │C/SSR Support          │
  Rig                   Me  │Dates & Duration       │
                            │Resources              │
                            │Standard               │
                            │Tracking               │
                            │Updating               │
                            │WBS Error Messages     │
                            │                       │
                            └═════════Layouts═══════┘

   Num             SAILBOAT End: 17-May-90  9:00am
```

Fig. 7.13. *The Layout list box.*

2. Pick one of the existing layouts and then press Enter. Time Line redisplays the Gantt chart using the new layout you selected.

Chapter 7: Customizing Gantt, PERT, and Tree Chart Screens 193

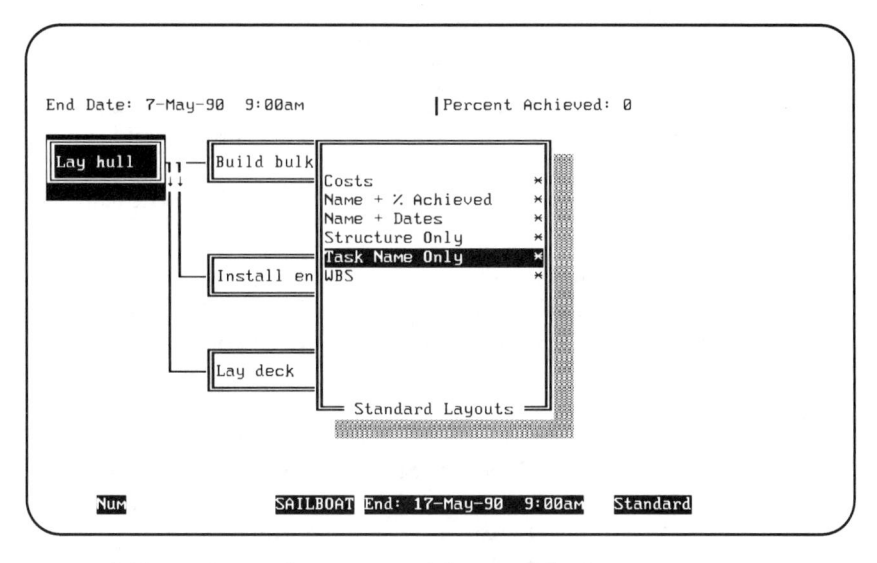

```
End Date: 7-May-90  9:00am        |Percent Achieved: 0

 ┌──────┐    ┌──────────┐
 │Lay hull│──┤Build bulk│
 └──────┘    └──────────┘ Costs            *
                          Name + % Achieved *
                          Name + Dates     *
                          Structure Only   *
             ┌──────────┐ Task Name Only   *
             │Install en│ WBS              *
             └──────────┘

             ┌──────────┐
             │Lay deck  │
             └──────────┘
                          Standard Layouts

  Num        SAILBOAT End: 17-May-90  9:00am   Standard
```

Fig. 7.14. The PERT/Tree chart version of the Layout list box.

3. (Optional) To return to the original Gantt layout, reactivate the menu bar, select Schedule Layout, and then pick the Standard Layout option. To return to the original PERT or Tree chart layout, reactivate the menu bar, select schedule layouts, and then pick the Task Name Only option. Either way Time Line redisplays the chart using the original layout.

In all, Time Line provides eight predefined Gantt layouts and five predefined PERT/Tree chart layouts in addition to the standard formats. Each contains different information as indicated in table 7.1. If you have questions about any of the fields listed in table 7.1, refer to Chapter 4, "Managing Project and Task Details."

Note: The more information a Gantt chart layout includes the less room there is for the time scale. Two of the predefined Gantt chart layouts, C/SSR Support and Tracking, don't even show the time scale because there isn't room because of all the other information shown for tasks.

Table 7.1
Descriptions of the Predefined Gantt, PERT, and Tree Chart Formats

Layout Name	Fields Displayed	Description
GANTT CHART LAYOUTS:		
Baseline	Task name Start Status Status	Shows both current and baseline information

Table 7.1 Continued

Table 7.1–*continued*

Layout Name	Fields Displayed	Description
Brainstorming	Task name notes	Lets you add and see notes for several tasks, all on the same screen
C/SSR Support	WBS Code Task Name Elapsed Baseline Spending Achieved Baseline Spending Actual Dollars Spent Variance between Achieved and Actual	Compares what you've spent with what you planned to spend. (*Note:* This doesn't show the time scale because there isn't room with all the other data displayed.)
Dates & Durations	Task name Start Date Duration End Date	Shows timing of tasks with greater precision than the timescale does
Resources	Task name Resources Status Sched Delay	Similar to Standard layout except that this also shows any schedule delay which may be stemming from resource conflicts
Standard	Task name Resources Status	This is the default Gantt chart view
Tracking	Task name Percent Achieved Current Total Dollars Dollars Spent Dollars to Go Projected Cost Baseline Total Dollars	Shows what you've spent and what you will spend. (*Note:* Like the C/SSR Support layout, this doesn't show the time scale because there isn't room with all the other data displayed.)

Layout Name	Fields Displayed	Description
Updating	Task name Start date Duration End date Percent Achieved Start date variance	Lists the fields you would usually update as part of monitoring the actual progress of a project
WBS Errors	Task name Parent WBS Code WBS Errors	Helps you correct errors in the WBS codes that the WBS Manager's Verify option finds

PERT/TREE CHART LAYOUTS

Layout Name	Fields Displayed	Description
Costs	Task Name Total Dollars Spend Dollars Achieved Dollars To Go Dollars	Adds cost information to a standard PERT and Tree chart
Name + Achieved	Task Name Achieved Percents	Adds the percent of completion to a standard PERT and Tree chart
Name + Dates	Task Name Start Date End Date	Add task start and end dates to a standard PERT and Tree chart.
Structure Only	No data fields show on a "Structure Only" PERT or Tree chart	Sometimes useful for looking at overall project organization
WBS	WBS Code Predecessor WBS Code Successor WBS Code	Adds WBS Codes to standard PERT and Tree chart

Creating a Custom Gantt Chart or PERT/Tree Layout

Just as you can create custom filters, you can also create custom Gantt chart and PERT/Tree chart layouts. This means that you can select which information a project chart view shows. For a Gantt chart, you can also control certain aspects of how the time scale works.

The steps for creating a custom Gantt layout are as follows:

1. Activate the menu bar, select **Schedule** and then select **Layout**. Time Line displays the Layout list box.

2. If you want the layout to be available only for the project currently displayed, press Ins. If you want the filter to be available for all projects, press Shift-Ins. Time Line displays the Gantt Chart Layout Form (see fig. 7.15).

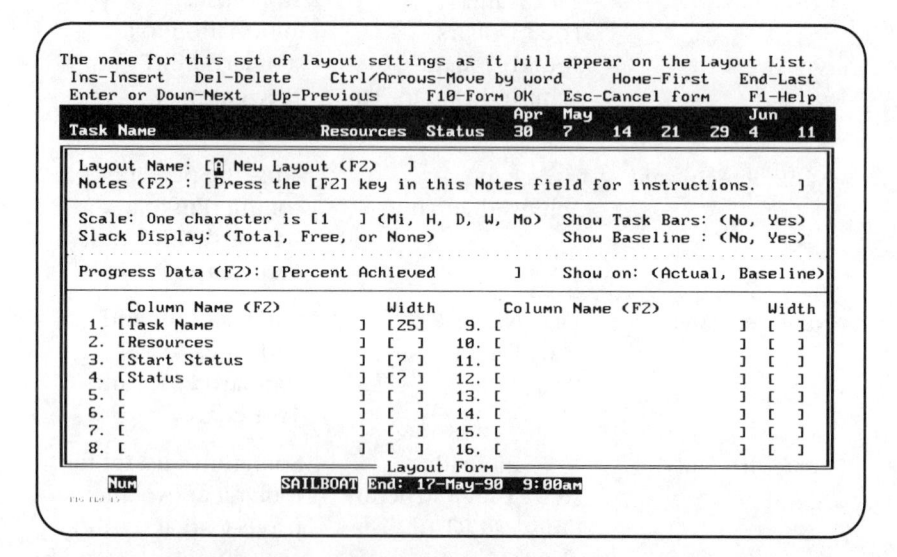

```
The name for this set of layout settings as it will appear on the Layout List.
Ins-Insert    Del-Delete    Ctrl/Arrows-Move by word    Home-First    End-Last
Enter or Down-Next    Up-Previous    F10-Form OK    Esc-Cancel form    F1-Help
                                          Apr  May                   Jun
Task Name                    Resources  Status  30   7    14   21   29  4    11

  Layout Name: [  New Layout (F2)    ]
  Notes (F2) : [Press the [F2] key in this Notes field for instructions.    ]

  Scale: One character is [1   ] (Mi, H, D, W, Mo)   Show Task Bars: (No, Yes)
  Slack Display: (Total, Free, or None)              Show Baseline : (No, Yes)

  Progress Data (F2): [Percent Achieved    ]   Show on: (Actual, Baseline)

      Column Name (F2)         Width        Column Name (F2)         Width
  1. [Task Name            ]  [25]     9. [                      ]  [   ]
  2. [Resources            ]  [  ]    10. [                      ]  [   ]
  3. [Start Status         ]  [ 7]    11. [                      ]  [   ]
  4. [Status               ]  [ 7]    12. [                      ]  [   ]
  5. [                     ]  [  ]    13. [                      ]  [   ]
  6. [                     ]  [  ]    14. [                      ]  [   ]
  7. [                     ]  [  ]    15. [                      ]  [   ]
  8. [                     ]  [  ]    16. [                      ]  [   ]
                                    Layout Form
   Num                SAILBOAT End: 17-May-90  9:00am
```

Fig. 7.15. The Gantt Chart Layout Form screen.

3. With the cursor at the Layout Name field, enter the name you want Time Line to display on the Layout list box to identify this layout.

4. (Optional) Move the cursor to the Notes field and type a description of the layout. You can press F2 to create a larger Notes text file so you have more space to describe or document the layout if you want.

Chapter 7: Customizing Gantt, PERT, and Tree Chart Screens

5. Move the cursor to the Scale field. Enter the number of characters you want to represent the timescale time units such as minutes, hours, days, weeks, or months. Then move the cursor to the fields that indicate these various time scale time units and highlight the time unit you want to use.

6. Move the cursor to the Show Task Bars field. Mark No if you don't want the task bars to show on the Gantt Chart screens for this layout. (This has the effect of creating a Gantt chart layout that shows only columns of data and no task bars.) Mark Yes if you do want the task bars to show.

7. Move the cursor to the Slack Display field. Mark Total if you want the Gantt chart to show (with thin lines attached to the task bars) the amount of time a task can be delayed without delaying a successor task with a fixed start date or the project's completion date. Mark Total Free if you want the Gantt chart to show the amount of time a task can be delayed without delaying another task. Mark None if you don't want the Gantt chart to indicate slack.

8. Move the cursor to the Show Baseline field. Mark Yes if you want Time Line to display the baseline project schedule information on the line below the current project schedule information. Mark No if you don't. (*Note:* You need to have first created a baseline project schedule. Refer to Chapter 6, "Monitoring Project Progress, Resources, and Costs" for help on setting the baseline schedule.)

9. Move the cursor to the Progress Data field. The Progress field lets you choose the method that Time Line uses to calculate progress on a task so that it can show the progress on the task bars. Press F2 to see a list box that gives the available progress calculation methods. Highlight the method you want to use and then press Enter.

10. Move the cursor to the Show on field. If the Show Baseline field is set to Yes, you can use either the baseline or the current schedule's task bar to show the progress on the task. Mark Actual if you want to use the Current schedule's task bars; mark Baseline if you want to use the baseline schedule's task bars.

11. For each data field you want to display on the Gantt chart screen, you'll need to indicate the field's name and allocate a certain number of characters for the column that will contain the data. The data field you want to see in the first, or

leftmost, column should be entered in Column 1. Press F2 to see a list of the data fields you can use. Only a portion of the available fields appears in the list box at any one time so you'll want to use the arrow keys and the PgUp and PgDn keys to see different portions of the list. Highlight the field you want to appear in the column and then press Enter.

12. Move the cursor to the Width field for the Column field you have just defined. Enter the number of characters you want Time Line to use for the column. A Column width can be as large as 80 characters. You can specify a 0 width if you don't want the field to show on the screen. If Time Line needs more space than your column width provides to display the data, it uses the plus symbol (+) or the asterisk (*) to indicate that the column width isn't large enough. A plus symbol is used for text fields. An asterisk symbol is used for numeric fields.

13. Repeat steps 11 and 12 for each of the data fields you want to appear on the Gantt chart. Enter the fields in the order you want them to appear from left to right.

To define a custom layout for a PERT or Tree chart, you follow a similar sequence of steps, although the Layout Form used to define PERT and Tree charts doesn't have as many options.

The steps for creating a custom PERT or Tree layout are as follows:

1. With a PERT or Tree chart displayed, activate the menu bar, select Schedule and then select Layout. Time Line displays the Layout list box (refer to fig. 7.14).

2. If you want the layout to be available only for the project currently displayed, press Ins. If you want the filter to be available for all projects, press Shift-Ins. Time Line display the PERT/Tree Layout Form (see fig. 7.16).

3. With the cursor at the Layout Name field, enter the name you want Time Line to display on the Layout list box to identify this layout.

4. (Optional) Move the cursor to the Notes field and type a description of the layout. You can press F2 to create a larger Notes text file so you have more space to describe or document the layout if you want.

5. Move the cursor to the Box Outline field. To direct Time Line to draw boxes around the tasks, mark Yes. If you don't want Time Line to draw boxes around the tasks, mark No.

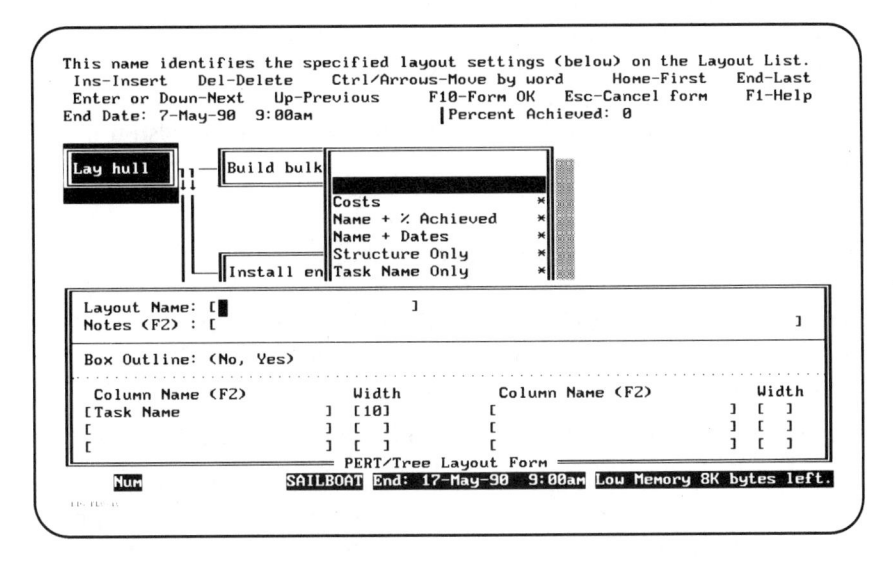

Chapter 7: Customizing Gantt, PERT, and Tree Chart Screens 199

Fig. 7.16. The PERT/Tree Layout Form.

6. For each data field you want to display in boxes on the PERT or Tree chart, you'll need to indicate the field's name and allocate a certain number of characters for the column's width. The data field you want to see in the first, or leftmost, column should be entered in Column 1. Press F2 to see a list of the data fields you can use. Use the arrow keys and the PgUp and PgDn keys to see different portions of the list. Highlight the field you want to appear in the column, and then press Enter.

7. Move the cursor to the Width field for the Column field you have just defined. Enter the number of characters you want Time Line to use for the column. If Time Line needs more space than your column width provides to display the data, it uses the plus symbol (+) or the asterisk (*) to indicate that the column width isn't large enough. A plus symbol is used for text fields. An asterisk symbol is used for numeric fields.

8. Repeat steps 6 and 7 for each of the data fields you want to appear on the PERT or Tree chart.

As you define custom layouts, there are a couple of special data fields you should know about because they make the whole process of creating custom layouts easier: the Spaces field and the Aux fields like Aux 1, Aux 2, Aux 3, and so on. Spaces is a field that always shows a blank for every task. Spaces lets you put spaces between the Gantt chart columns so the data in one column doesn't butt up against another column. The Aux fields are simply unused data fields. Time Line doesn't use them in any of its calculations. Instead, they are simply there for you to store additional information that doesn't fit neatly somewhere else. You can also use the Aux fields to sort and filter.

Editing and Deleting Layouts

You can edit and delete an existing layout. To do so, access the Layout List box that shows the layout by activating the menu bar and selecting Schedule Layout. Then highlight the layout you want to modify, and press F2.

Time Line displays the Layout you use to make the changes.

Deleting a layout is also very easy. To delete a layout, you activate the menu bar, select Schedule Layout, mark the layout you want to delete, and press Del. Time Line asks you whether you're sure you want to delete the layout, and if you do, you highlight Proceed and press Enter.

Chapter Summary

This chapter describes how you can use three options on the Schedule menu: Sort, Filter, and Layout—to affect the Gantt, PERT and Tree chart screens. With these options, you can affect the way tasks are arranged, the tasks that appear, and even the task information that appears. All this means that you should now be able to customize the Time Line screens so that they more closely match your requirements.

8

Printing Reports

The reports that Time Line produces deliver many benefits. You can show project participants—and anyone else who is interested—the various pieces that make up a project. You can show the progress of the project. You can account for and report on the actual and planned costs of the project. You can also monitor the resources needed and used by the project. In effect, the Time Line reports expand the benefits of the Time Line project management system because they package the benefits of the system in a format—printed reports—that can be faxed or mailed to remote locations, reviewed in project status meetings, and pinned up on office and conference room walls.

This chapter describes the basic steps for printing each of the thirteen reports that are available in Time Line. The chapter also provides examples of the standard reports and describes how to customize the standard reports.

Using Time Line's Text Reports

Time Line provides eleven text reports that you print by using the Reports menu. Table 8.1 lists the reports and provides brief descriptions of each. The reports are text reports because they only use letters, numbers, and keyboard symbols. Time Line also prints graphics reports (described later in this chapter). These reports can include special graphics features such as lines, bars, and shading.

**Table 8.1
A List of Time Line Text Reports**

Report Name	Report Description	Application
Assignment	Identifies resource assignments either by task or by resource	Useful for seeing what it takes in the way of resources to complete a particular task and for seeing where a resource is used
Cross Tab	Cross tabulates a piece of project data and then produces a report, using the results	Useful for looking at individual pieces of project data from two perspectives such as "total costs by task and by week" or "actual resource usage by resource and by task"
Detail	Delivers a collection of task level information including things like task notes, predecessors, and successors	Because you specify which task level information you want on the report, the Detail Report provides a convenient way to see on one report a great deal of specific task level information
Gantt Chart	Shows the tasks that make up a project in a bar chart	Useful for showing the timing of tasks and of the project and for monitoring actual progress if you set a baseline
Histogram	Shows the planned usage of project resources	Useful for determining whether a resource is overallocated or underallocated
PERT Chart	Shows the tasks that make up a project as boxes and draws lines between these boxes to show the dependencies between tasks	Useful for reviewing the order in which tasks must occur, the project's critical path, and task dependencies

Report Name	Report Description	Application
Resource	Show where and how a resource will be used or was used	Useful for tracking planned and actual resource usage
Status	Identifies the tasks on which work should be progressing on a certain day, week, or month and the tasks that require that resource on a certain day, week or month	Useful for monitoring planned progress and resource use
Tasks	Shows the task information that appears on a Gantt Chart	Useful for reviewing task level information. Using the Layout option (described in Chapter 7), you can also include any task level data you want on the report
Tree	Shows the tasks that make up a project as a series of boxes in roughly the same order as the tasks start and end with subtasks shown under their summary tasks	Useful for focusing on the breakdown of tasks into subtasks

A Few Words about Strips

One final thing you need to know about before you begin printing reports is strips. (There's nothing tricky about this strips business but if I explain it here, I'll save you five minutes of confusion the first time you print a report.)

When printing a report, Time Line usually takes more than a single page. The reason, of course, is that the task bars and boxes take up quite a bit of space. Even a small project like the sailboat example won't fit onto a single page if you use a standard Gantt, PERT, or Tree chart layout. Accordingly, Time Line prints out a chart by using individual pieces of paper like building blocks. A large project, for example, might require several horizontal building blocks as well as several vertical building blocks. Figure 8.1 illustrates this basic approach. Each rectangle in figure 8.1 represents an 8 1/2-inch-by-11-inch sheet of paper.

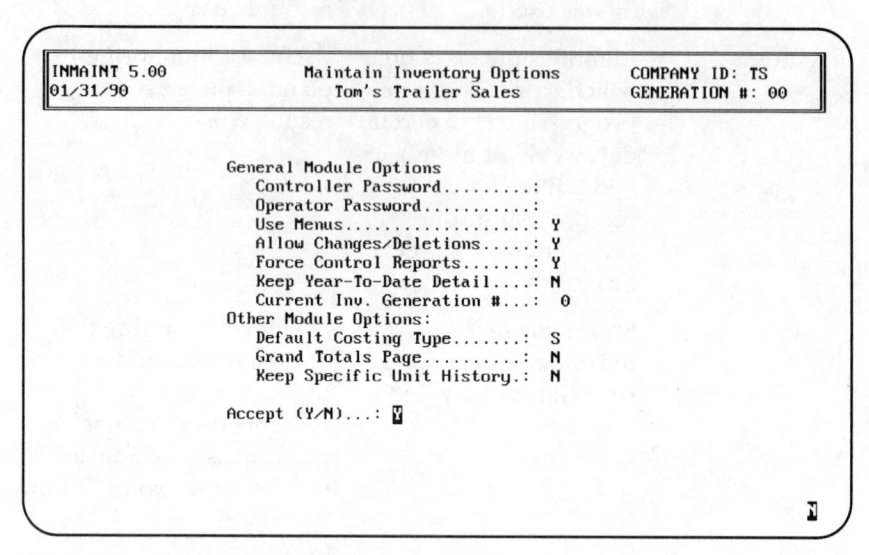

```
INMAINT 5.00            Maintain Inventory Options      COMPANY ID: TS
01/31/90                   Tom's Trailer Sales          GENERATION #: 00



                    General Module Options
                        Controller Password.........:
                        Operator Password..........:
                        Use Menus..................: Y
                        Allow Changes/Deletions....: Y
                        Force Control Reports......: Y
                        Keep Year-To-Date Detail...: N
                        Current Inv. Generation #..:  0
                    Other Module Options:
                        Default Costing Type.......: S
                        Grand Totals Page..........: N
                        Keep Specific Unit History.: N

                    Accept (Y/N)...: Y
```

Fig. 8.1. Time Line prints large charts using several pages of paper.

To help you arrange the pages that make up a chart, Time Line calls each vertical column of page blocks a *strip*, and the program numbers the page blocks that belong in a strip to make it easier to piece them together. In figure 8.1, for example, pages 1, 6, and 11 would be labeled "Strip 1"; pages 2, 7, and 12 would be labeled "Strip 2"; and so on.

Note: Strips apply to both textual and graphics reports.

Controlling Printing with the Form Option

Before you begin printing text reports, you'll need to specify some of the printing details. These details include things like:

1. Whether you want the report sent to your printer—the usual case—or you instead want the report created on your disk so you can print it with another program,

2. What the report's page margins should look like,

3. What information should go on the top of the report as a header.

> You don't have to change the Report Form settings. The default settings will usually do just fine. Accordingly, don't get bogged down with this topic if you find it confusing. Rather, just skip it. *Tip*

To specify these details, you use the Report menu's Form option. To use this option, you take the following steps:

1. Activate the menu bar, select Reports, and then select Form. Time Line displays the Report Form screen (see fig. 8.2).

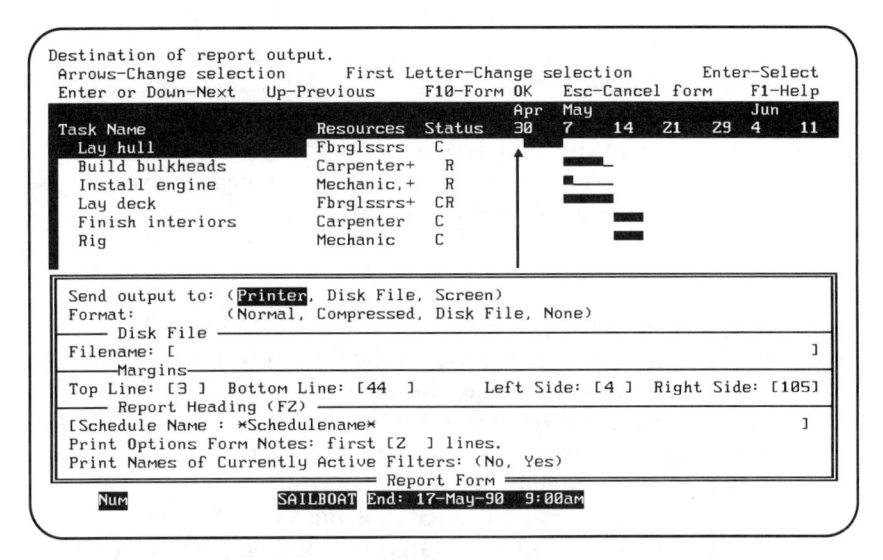

```
Destination of report output.
  Arrows-Change selection      First Letter-Change selection        Enter-Select
  Enter or Down-Next    Up-Previous      F10-Form OK    Esc-Cancel form    F1-Help
                                          Apr  May                      Jun
Task Name                  Resources  Status  30   7    14   21   29   4    11
  Lay hull                 Fbrglssrs    C
  Build bulkheads          Carpenter+   R
  Install engine           Mechanic,+   R
  Lay deck                 Fbrglssrs+   CR
  Finish interiors         Carpenter    C
  Rig                      Mechanic     C

Send output to: (Printer, Disk File, Screen)
Format:         (Normal, Compressed, Disk File, None)
 ── Disk File ──
Filename: [                                                                    ]
 ──Margins──
Top Line: [3 ]  Bottom Line: [44 ]       Left Side: [4 ]  Right Side: [105]
 ── Report Heading (FZ) ──
[Schedule Name : *Schedulename*                                                ]
Print Options Form Notes: first [Z ] lines.
Print Names of Currently Active Filters: (No, Yes)
════════════════════════════ Report Form ════════════════════════════
  Num            SAILBOAT End: 17-May-90  9:00am
```

Fig. 8.2. The Report Form.

2. With the cursor positioned at the Send Output To field, indicate whether you want the report to print on your printer, to be stored on your disk as a text file that you'll print with some other program, or to be displayed on the screen.

3. Move the cursor to the Format field. The format field controls whether reports are printed in regular 10 characters per inch type or in compressed 15 characters per inch type. Mark Normal to indicate 10 characters per inch; mark Compressed to indicate 15 characters per inch. If you marked the Send Output to field as Disk File in step 1, set the Format to Disk File. If you marked the Send Output to field as screen in step 1, set the Format to Screen.

4. (Optional) Time Line will, by default, use the name REPORT.TXT for report disk files it creates and stores in the default directory—usually C:\TL4. You can, however, tell Time Line to use some other name for the text file it will create. You can also specify the disk and directory where the disk file that's created should be stored. For example, you could specify that the report be named GANTT_Q1.DOC and stored in the C drive directory, PROJECT, by entering the Filename as C:\PROJECT\GANTT_Q1.DOC.

Note: If you send one report to the disk and then attempt to send another report to the disk without changing the Filename setting on the Report screen, Time Line asks as a safety precaution that you confirm that you want to overwrite the first disk file you created. If you confirm you want to proceed, Time Line, in effect, wipes out the first disk file and replaces it with the second disk file. Accordingly, if you're creating multiple report disk files, you'll usually want to name each one.

5. (Optional) To set the top and bottom of the page print margins, move the cursor to the Margins fields and enter in the Top Line field the number of the line on which you want printing to begin; then enter in the Bottom Line field the number of the line on which you want printing to stop. This may sound complicated, but it's not. Your printer most probably prints 10 lines per inch, so if you're using 8 1/2-inch-by-11-inch paper, the page is 66 lines long. To set a one-inch margin at the top of the page, set the Top Line to 7 (this leaves lines 1 through 6 empty, resulting in a one-inch space at the top of the page). Similarly, to set a one-inch margin at the bottom of the page, set the Bottom Line to 60 (this leaves lines 61 through 66 empty, also resulting in a one-inch space at the bottom of the page).

6. (Optional) To set the left and right print margins, move the cursor to the Margins fields and enter in the Left Side field the first character position at which you want printing to begin; then in the Right Side field, enter the character position at which you want printing to stop. Again, this sounds a little complicated, but it's not. If you set the Format field to Normal in step 3, Time Line prints ten characters to the inch, and if the page is 8 1/2-inches wide, the page is eighty-five characters wide. To set a one-inch margin on the left edge of the page, set the Left Side to 11 (this leaves

character positions 1 through 10 empty, resulting in a one-inch margin on the left edge of the paper). Similarly, to set a one-inch margin on the right edge of the page, set the Right Side to 75 (this leaves character positions 76 through 85 empty, resulting in a one-inch space at the bottom of the page).

7. (Optional) You can use the Report Heading field, Schedule Name, to control information Time Line prints at the top of text reports. You can enter the exact text you want to appear, such as *October Gantt Chart Report*. And if you want to put more than one line of text at the top of the report, you can press F2 to open small notepad into which you can type several lines of text which will then appear at the top of each report.

   You can also use keywords that Time Line recognizes and interprets as part of the text you enter. The keyword *Date*, for example, places the current system date in the header. And the keyword *Schedulefile* results in the Schedule filename being included. To identify keywords, you enclose them between two asterisks, for example, *Date* or *Schedulefile*. You can include more than one keyword in the Report Heading's Schedule Name field. You can also direct Time Line to left-justify and right-justify the keywords by tagging (l) for left or (r) for right onto the end of the keyword. For example, *Date(l)* would print the current system date at the left edge of the report page, and *Schedule(r)* would print the schedule filename at the right edge of the paper. Table 8.2 provides a complete list of the keywords you can use for in the Report Heading field.

8. (Optional) Move the cursor to the Print Options Form Notes field. If you want to see whatever notes were entered on the Options Form, enter some number other than zero here. If you only used one line for notes on the Options Form and want to see those notes, you can enter a 1. If you used more than one line, enter the number of lines you want to see.

9. (Optional) Move the cursor to the Print Names of Currently Active Filters field. If you want Time Line to identify the filters which determined the tasks that print on a report, mark Yes. If you aren't using filters or don't want to see them on the report, mark No.

Table 8.2
A List of Report Heading Keywords

Keyword	Description
Asof	Gives the project as-of date—usually the same thing as the current system date
Calc	Shows the current calculation status such as "needs recalc," "calc error," "CPM" (which indicates a critical path method based calculation), or "Resource leveled" (which indicates a resource leveling based calculation)
Calculation	Works like the Calc keyword
Date	Gives the current system date
Dateandtime	Gives the current system date and time
Directory	Identifies the disk and directory where the project files are stored
Dt	Works like the Dateandtime keyword
Pjdir	Works like the Directory keyword
Projectdir	Works like the Directory and Pjdir keywords
Recalc	Indicates whether the project schedule has been re-calculated since the last change to the schedule
Resp	Gives the contents of the responsible field from the Options Form. (Refer to Chapter 4 for information on the Options Form.)
Responsible	Works like the Resp keyword
Schedule	Shows the project schedule filename
Schedulefile	Works like the Schedule keyword
Schedulename	Shows the project schedule name as entered in the schedule name field on the Options Form. (Refer to Chapter 4 for information on the Options Form.)
Schfile	Works like the Schedulefile keyword
Schname	Works like the Schedulename keyword
Today	Works like the Dateandtime keyword
User	Gives the username defined during the installation of the individual printing the report
Username	Works like the User keyword

Printing a Text Report

The steps for printing any of the text reports is essentially the same. There are three basic steps. First, activate the menu bar and then select Reports. Next, select the Report you want to print from the Reports menu. Figure 8.3 shows the Reports menu. When you select the Report option from the Report menu, Time Line displays a Report Form screen that you use to control the specifics of the particular report you're requesting. You complete this form and press F10. Figure 8.4 shows an example of the Gantt chart Report Form screen. (The Report Form, however, varies depending on the report you're printing.)

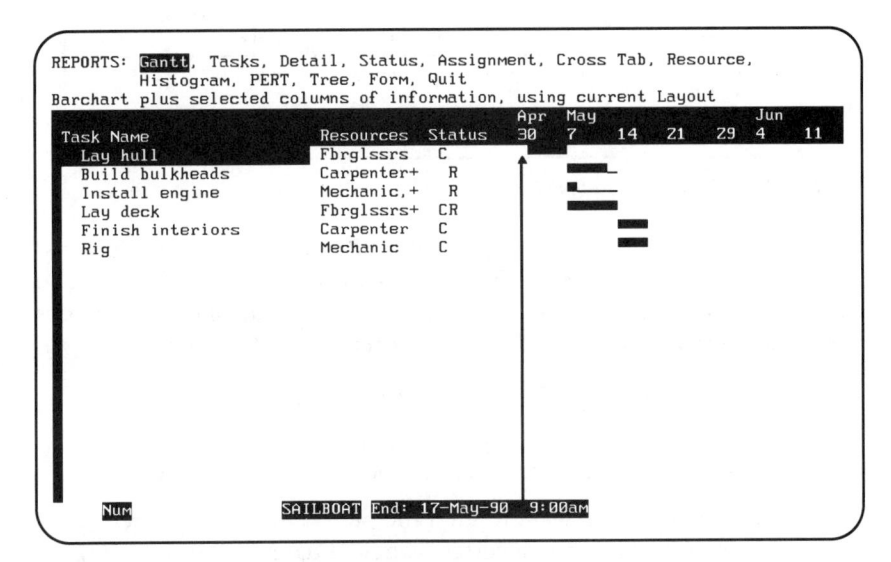

```
REPORTS: Gantt, Tasks, Detail, Status, Assignment, Cross Tab, Resource,
         Histogram, PERT, Tree, Form, Quit
Barchart plus selected columns of information, using current Layout
                                          Apr  May              Jun
Task Name              Resources Status   30   7    14   21  29 4    11
  Lay hull             Fbrglssrs    C
  Build bulkheads      Carpenter+   R
  Install engine       Mechanic,+   R
  Lay deck             Fbrglssrs+  CR
  Finish interiors     Carpenter    C
  Rig                  Mechanic     C




 Num              SAILBOAT End: 17-May-90  9:00am
```

Fig. 8.3. The Reports menu lists the ten text reports that Time Line provides.

Printing a Gantt Chart

The Bulk of the Gantt Chart report resembles the actual Gantt Chart screen. At the top of the report, the heading appears using certain data you might have entered using the Form option on the Reports menu. (Refer to the earlier chapter section, "Controlling Printing with the Form Option," for more information.) The report shows tasks along the left edge and task bars along the right edge. At the bottom of the report, Time Line prints a legend of the symbols used in the report.

Note: Time Line applies the current Sort, Filter, and Layout settings when it prints the Gantt Chart. This means you can control the arrangement of the tasks, the tasks that appear, and the individual task information that

Part III: Managing the System

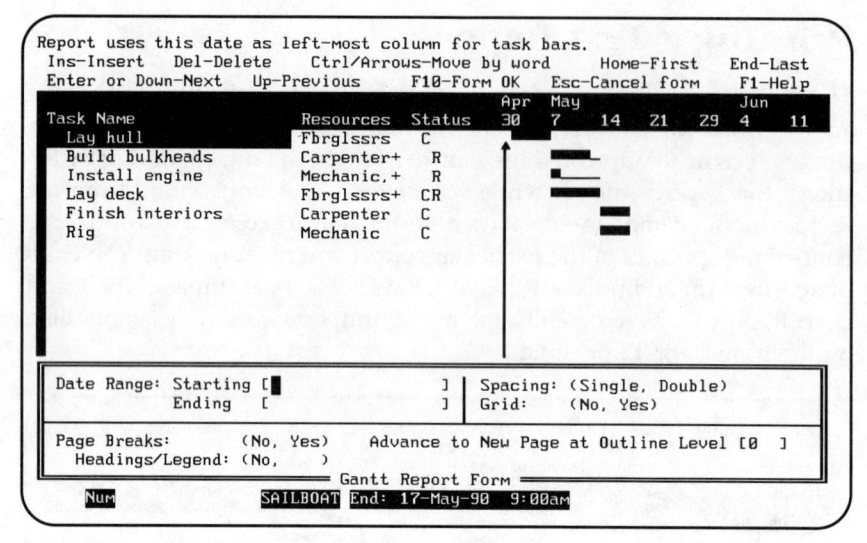

```
Report uses this date as left-most column for task bars.
 Ins-Insert   Del-Delete    Ctrl/Arrows-Move by word      Home-First     End-Last
 Enter or Down-Next    Up-Previous       F10-Form OK    Esc-Cancel form    F1-Help
                                                    Apr May              Jun
 Task Name               Resources   Status       30   7   14   21   29   4    11
   Lay hull              Fbrglssrs      C
   Build bulkheads       Carpenter+     R
   Install engine        Mechanic,+     R
   Lay deck              Fbrglssrs+    CR
   Finish interiors      Carpenter      C
   Rig                   Mechanic       C


 Date Range: Starting [           ]    Spacing:   (Single, Double)
             Ending   [           ]    Grid:      (No, Yes)

 Page Breaks:       (No, Yes)    Advance to New Page at Outline Level [0  ]
 Headings/Legend: (No,  )
 ═══════════════════════════════════ Gantt Report Form ═══════════
  Num                   SAILBOAT End: 17-May-90  9:00am
```

Fig. 8.4. The Gantt Chart Report Form.

appears. Chapter 7, "Customizing Gantt, PERT, and Tree Chart Screens" explains how to use the Sort, Filter, and Layout options with an eye to controlling the appearance of Charts on the screen. But all the techniques described there also work for Gantt Chart reports.

To print a Gantt Chart, you take the following steps:

1. Activate the menu bar and select Reports Gantt. Time Line displays the Gantt Chart Report Form as shown in figure 8.4.

2. (Optional) If you want to limit the period of time reported on the Gantt chart to a certain range of dates, enter a starting and ending date in the date range fields. To enter the starting and ending dates, you can use any of the valid date formats. There are a couple of other things you should know about the Date Range entries: (1) The entire schedule prints if you don't enter a start or end date which means that it's as if you entered the start date as the first task's start date and the ending date as the last task's end date; and (2) The Date Range doesn't affect the task names printed on the Gantt Chart report, which means that if you use the Date Range there may be tasks for which task bars don't show.

3. (Optional) Move the cursor to the Spacing field. Mark Single to print a single-spaced report and mark Double to print a double-spaced report.

4. (Optional) Move the cursor to the Grid field. Mark Yes if you want Time Line to print a grid of vertical lines made up of dots, or period symbols, to make it easier to tell precisely when tasks start and end.

5. (Optional) Move the cursor to the Page Breaks field. Mark Yes if you want to control how Time Line breaks, or advances, to the next page. If you set the Page Breaks field to Yes, Time Line lets you force page breaks at specified outline levels (see step 6) and Time Line skips over the perforation between pages of continuous form paper.

6. (Optional) If you set the Page Breaks field to Yes, Time Line allows you to move the cursor to the Advance to New Page at Outline Level field. With this field set to 0, Time Line breaks to a new page only when the current page is full. With this field set to 1, Time Line breaks to a new page at every first, or main, level task. With this field set to 2, Time Line breaks to a new page at every second level task. (Second level tasks are those that are subtasks to the first level tasks.) Similarly, a setting of 3 means the page break occurs at every third level task, a setting of 4 indicates the page break occurs at every fourth level task, and so forth.

7. (Optional) If you set the Page Breaks field to Yes, Time Line allows you to move the cursor to the Headings/Legend field. Mark Yes if you want the report title, the report date, and a legend of symbols used printed on each page.

    Note: If you're going to be pasting or taping together the pages that make up a complete Gantt chart, don't set the Page Breaks field to Yes. The dual reasons for this relate to steps 4 and 6: You don't want page breaks—even at the perforations—and you only want the report title date and legend printed once.

8. Once you complete the Gantt Chart Report Form screen, press F10 to initiate printing of the report. Figure 8.5 shows an example of a Gantt Chart Text Report using the familiar sailboat project.

Printing the Tasks Report

The Tasks Report simply lists the task information shown on the Gantt Chart screen. At the top of the report, the heading appears using data you may have entered with the Form option of the Reports menu (described

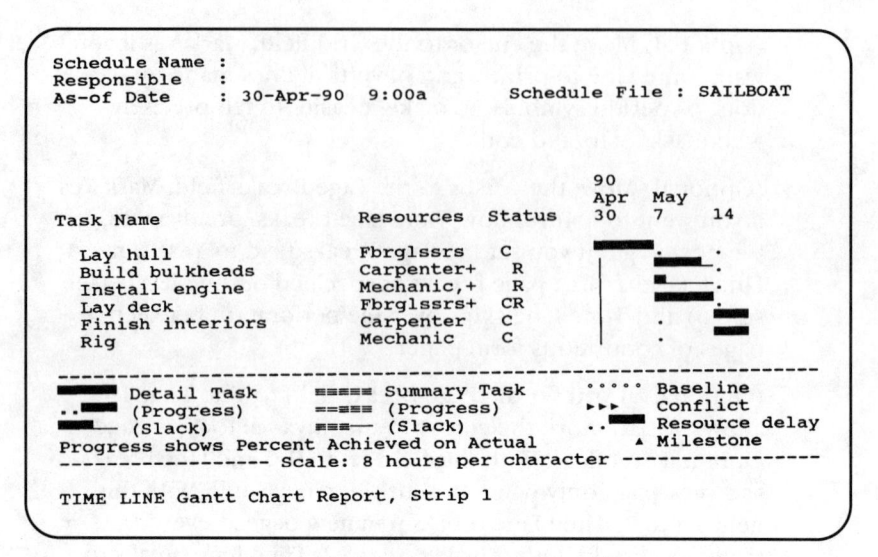

```
Schedule Name  :
Responsible    :
As-of Date     : 30-Apr-90  9:00a        Schedule File : SAILBOAT


                                             90
                                             Apr    May
Task Name                Resources  Status   30     7     14
    Lay hull             Fbrglssrs    C      ██▬    .
    Build bulkheads      Carpenter+   R         .██▬───
    Install engine       Mechanic,+   R         ▬──██
    Lay deck             Fbrglssrs+   CR          ▬──██
    Finish interiors     Carpenter    C               .██
    Rig                  Mechanic     C               .██
-----------------------------------------------------------------
        ██▬  Detail Task      ═════ Summary Task    ····· Baseline
        ··██ (Progress)       ═══   (Progress)      ►►►   Conflict
        ──   (Slack)          ═══   (Slack)         ··    Resource delay
     Progress shows Percent Achieved on Actual      ▲     Milestone
     ------------------ Scale: 8 hours per character -----------------
     TIME LINE Gantt Chart Report, Strip 1
```

Fig. 8.5. An example of the Gantt Chart text report.

earlier in this chapter). The Bulk of the Tasks report resembles the left half of the actual Gantt Chart screen and shows tasks names, resources used, and task status. As is the case with the Gantt Chart, Time Line applies the current Sort, Filter, and Layout when it prints the Tasks report. This means you can control the arrangement of the tasks, the tasks that appear, and the individual task information that appears. Chapter 7, "Customizing Gantt, PERT, and Tree Chart Screens" explains how to use the Sort, Filter, and Layout options. The techniques described there also work for Tasks reports.

To print a Task Report, you take the following steps:

1. Activate the menu bar and select Reports and then Tasks.
   Time Line displays the Page Control Form (see fig. 8.6.)

Tip You can press F10 when the Page Control Form appears to accept the default settings.

2. (Optional) With the cursor on the Page Breaks field, mark Yes if you want to control how Time Line advances to the next page. If you set the Page Breaks field to Yes, Time Line lets you force page breaks at specified outline levels (see step 3), and it prints page numbers.

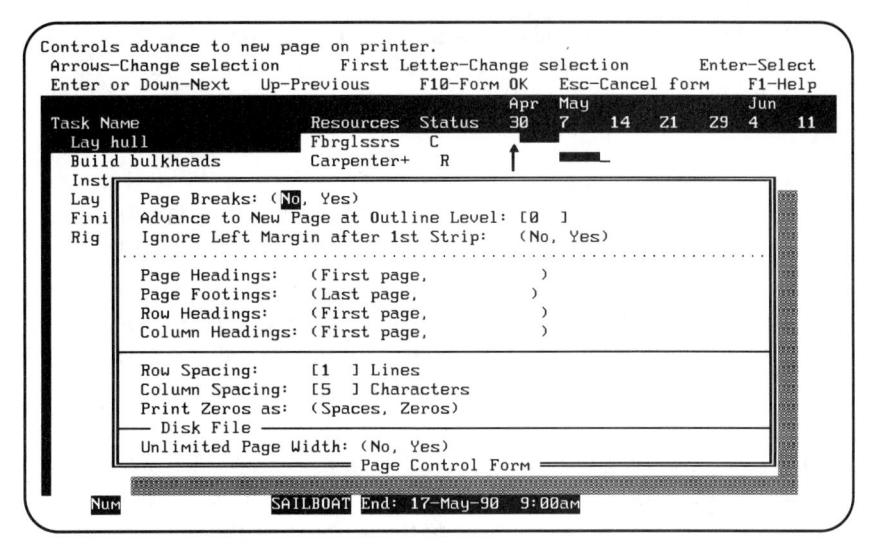

Fig. 8.6. The Page Control Form.

3. (Optional) If you set the Page Breaks field to Yes, Time Line allows you to move the cursor to the Advance to New Page at Outline Level field. With this field set to 0, Time Line breaks to a new page only when the current page is full. With this field set to 1, Time Line breaks to a new page at every first, or main, level task. With this field set to 2, Time Line breaks to a new page at every second level task. (Second level tasks are those that are subtasks to the first level tasks.) Similarly, a setting of 3 means the page break occurs at every third level task and so forth.

4. (Optional) If you're going to tape the pages of the Tasks Report together, end to end, you can set the Ignore Left Margin After 1st Strip field to Yes so Time Line doesn't use a left margin on pages in strips 2, 3, 4, and so on.

5. (Optional) If you set the Page Breaks field to Yes, Time Line allows you to specify whether you want Page and Row headings to appear on just the first page or on every page and the Page and Row Footings to appear on just the last page or on every page.

6. (Optional) Move the cursor to the Row Spacing field. Enter a 1 to print a single-spaced report, a 2 to print a double-spaced report, a 3 to print a triple-spaced report, and so on.

7. (Optional) Move the cursor to the Column Spacing field. Enter the number of spaces you want Time Line to put between columns of data. You can enter a number from 1 to 77.

8. (Optional) Move the cursor to the Print Zeros as field. If when a cost amount is zero, you want Time Line to print the zero, mark Yes. If you instead want Time Line to leave the field blank, mark Spaces.

9. (Optional) Move the cursor to the Unlimited Page Width field. Mark Yes if you're going to create a disk file that you plan to print later, using one of the sideways printing programs.

10. Once you complete the Page Control Form screen, press F10 to initiate printing of the report. Figure 8.7 shows an example of a Tasks Report using the sailboat project.

```
Schedule Name :
Responsible   :
As-of Date    : 30-Apr-90  9:00a        Schedule File : SAILBOAT




Task Name                       Resources       Status
------------------------        ----------      --------
Lay hull                        Fbrglssrs         C
Build bulkheads                 Carpenter,        R
Install engine                  Mechanic,         R
Lay deck                        Fbrglssrs,       CR
Finish interiors                Carpenter         C
Rig                             Mechanic          C

TIME LINE Task Report
```

Fig. 8.7. An example of the Tasks Report.

Printing a Detail Report

The Detail report lists the task information you indicate on the Detail Report Form. At the top of the report, the heading appears. Two columns of up to five rows each give the data you requested on the Detail Report

Form. As is the case with several of the other reports, Time Line applies the current Sort, Filter, and Layout settings when it prints this report, too. (Refer to Chapter 7 for more information on Sort, Filter, and Layout options.)

To print a Detail report, you take the following steps:

1. Activate the menu bar and select Reports and Detail. Time Line displays the Detail Report Form shown in figure 8.8.

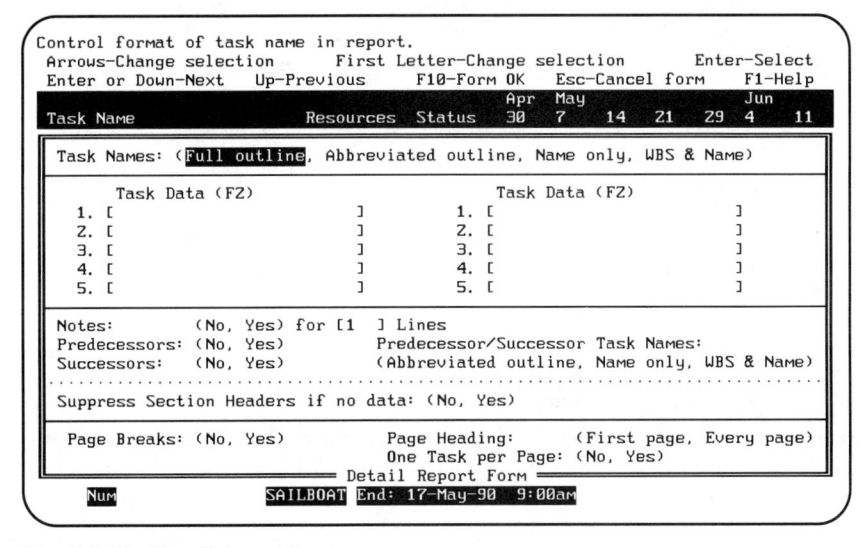

```
Control format of task name in report.
 Arrows-Change selection      First Letter-Change selection       Enter-Select
 Enter or Down-Next    Up-Previous    F10-Form OK   Esc-Cancel form    F1-Help
                                             Apr  May              Jun
 Task Name                    Resources Status 30   7   14  21  29  4   11
 ┌──────────────────────────────────────────────────────────────────────────┐
 │ Task Names: (Full outline, Abbreviated outline, Name only, WBS & Name)   │
 │                                                                          │
 │      Task Data (F2)                       Task Data (F2)                 │
 │  1. [               ]                 1. [                    ]          │
 │  2. [               ]                 2. [                    ]          │
 │  3. [               ]                 3. [                    ]          │
 │  4. [               ]                 4. [                    ]          │
 │  5. [               ]                 5. [                    ]          │
 │                                                                          │
 │ Notes:         (No, Yes) for [1 ] Lines                                  │
 │ Predecessors:  (No, Yes)      Predecessor/Successor Task Names:          │
 │ Successors:    (No, Yes)         (Abbreviated outline, Name only, WBS & Name)│
 │..........................................................................│
 │ Suppress Section Headers if no data: (No, Yes)                           │
 │                                                                          │
 │ Page Breaks: (No, Yes)        Page Heading:    (First page, Every page)  │
 │                               One Task per Page: (No, Yes)               │
 │════════════════════════════ Detail Report Form ═════════════════════════ │
 │  Num              SAILBOAT End: 17-May-90  9:00am                        │
 └──────────────────────────────────────────────────────────────────────────┘
```

Fig. 8.8. The Detail Report Form.

2. (Optional) With the cursor on the Task Name field, mark Full Outline or Abbreviate Outline if you want the summary tasks above a subtask printed. If you don't care about the summary tasks above a subtask, mark Name only or WBS and Name. Full Outline prints each the summary tasks above a subtask on its own line.

A full outline, for example, might show the Rig main mast task like this:

Rig
    Masts
        Main Mast

Abbreviated Outline abbreviates the summary task names, separates the abbreviations with slashes, and prints the abbreviations on the same line as the subtask.

An abbreviated outline might show the Rig main mast task like this:

Rg/Msts - Main Mast

3. (Optional) You can select up to ten pieces of task data to be printed for each task. Time Line arranges two five-row columns of data accordingly to the way you fill the Task Data fields. To fill a Task Data field, move the cursor to the appropriate field and press F2. Time Line displays a box that lists each of the data fields, or pieces of information, Time Line collects or calculates for a task. Use the arrow keys to highlight the data field you want. (Only a portion of the list of task data fields appears in the list box at a time, so you need to use the PgUp and PgDn keys to display different portions of the list.)

Note: If, after entering the task data fields, you want to move a task data field ahead of the one that appears before it, highlight the data field you want to move forward and press Shift-up-arrow. If you want to move a task data field behind the one that follows it, highlight the data field you want to move backwards and press Shift-down-arrow.

Tip Remember to include as one of the Task data fields the task name, abbreviated name, or WBS Code, so you have some way to identify tasks.

4. (Optional) Move the cursor to the Notes field. If you want to see the notes attached to the task, mark Yes. If you do mark Yes, you can also indicate how many lines of the note you want to print. Leaving the Lines field blank causes Time Line to print all the lines of the note. (Chapter 4, "Managing Project and Task Details," describes how to create task note text files which might end up being many lines long.) If you don't want to print notes, mark No.

5. (Optional) Move the cursor to the Predecessors field. Mark Yes if you want Time Line to identify and describe a task's predecessors. Mark No if you don't.

6. (Optional) Move the cursor to the Successors field. Mark Yes if you want Time Line to identify and describe a task's successors. Mark No if you don't.

7. (Optional) If you marked either the Predecessors or Successors fields as Yes in steps 5 or 6, you need to show Time Line how to print this information. Move the cursor to the Predecessor/Successor Task Names field. Mark Abbreviated Outline if you want to see predecessor and successor tasks identified using the abbreviated outline format described in step 1. Mark Name Only if you want to see the name of only the predecessor or successor task. Mark WBS & Name if you want to see the WBS Code and the Name of the predecessor or successor task.

8. (Optional) Move the cursor to the Suppress Section Headers field. Mark Yes if you want Time Line to skip printing the descriptions for sections of the report that show no data. For example, if you don't want Time Line to print the description Notes when there aren't any notes or you don't want Time Line to print the description Successors when there aren't any successor tasks, mark Yes.

9. (Optional) Move the cursor on the Page Breaks field. Mark Yes if you want Time Line to advance when it gets to the end of the page and to skip over the perforation at the bottom of continuous form paper. Mark No if you don't want Time Line to break when it gets to the end of the page (for example, when you're pasting or taping together the page blocks of the report).

10. (Optional) Move the cursor to the Page Heading field. Mark Yes if you want a report heading that includes the project level information, any filters used, and the report title printed on every page of the report. Mark No if you don't want this information printed.

11. (Optional) If you set the Page Breaks field to Yes, Time Line allows you to specify whether you want each page to appear on its own page. If you do, move the cursor to the One Task Per Page field and mark Yes if you do.

12. Once you complete the Detail Report Form screen, press F10 to initiate printing of the report. Figure 8.9 shows a page from an example Detail Report.

```
Schedule Name   :
Responsible     :
As-of Date      : 30-Apr-90  9:00a      Schedule File : SAILBOAT


Task Name
---------
    Lay hull
Notes
-----
The Lay hull task will be started as soon as we receive a
Task Name: Lay hull
WBS:
Start Date: 30-Apr-90  9:00am
End Date: 7-May-90  9:00am
Duration: 5.0 days
Successors
----------
    - Install engine (E→S)
    - Build bulkheads (E→S)
    - Lay deck (E→S)
------------------------------------------------------------------------
Task Name
---------
    Build bulkheads
Task Name: Build bulkheads
WBS:
Start Date: 7-May-90  9:00am
End Date: 11-May-90  9:00am
Duration: 4.0 days


TIME LINE Detail Report Page 1
```

Fig. 8.9. *An example of the Detail Report.*

Printing a Status Report

There are two varieties of Time Line status reports: Task-focused and resource-focused. The Task-focused status report identifies the tasks on which work should be progressing on a certain day, week, or month. The resource-focused status report shows for each resource the tasks that require that resource on a certain day, week, or month. In a fashion similar to the detail report described earlier, Time Line gives you flexibility in determining which information appears on the status.

To print a Status Report, you take the following steps:

1. Activate the menu bar and select Reports and then Status. Time Line displays the Status Report Form screen (see fig. 8.10) which you use to determine what the Status Report ends up looking like.

2. With the cursor on the Group by field, mark Task if you want a report that is arranged by tasks. Alternatively, mark Resource if you want a report that is arranged by resources.

3. If you set the Group by field to Resources, move the cursor to the Show field. Then mark Resources if you want the report to list only resources and mark Costs & Resources if you want the report to list costs along with the resources.

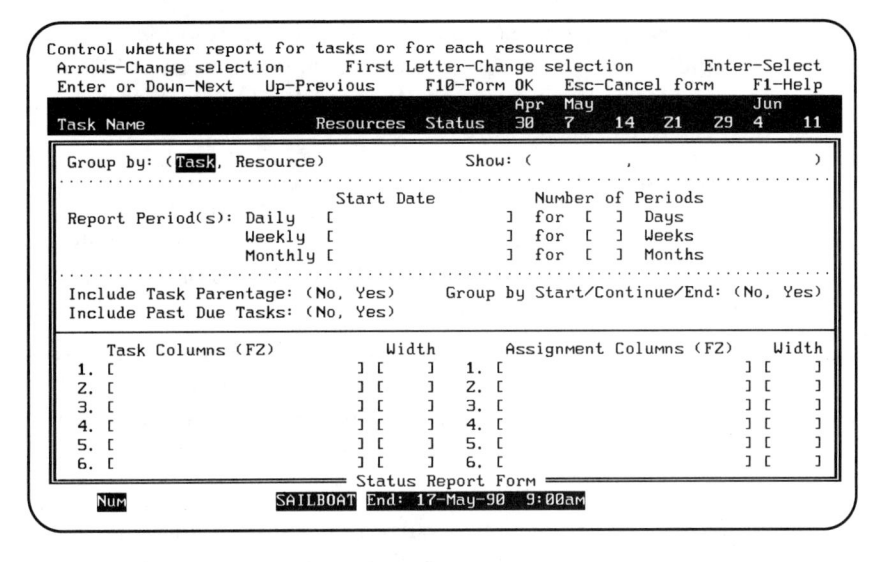

```
Control whether report for tasks or for each resource
Arrows-Change selection      First Letter-Change selection      Enter-Select
Enter or Down-Next    Up-Previous    F10-Form OK    Esc-Cancel form    F1-Help
                                                    Apr   May              Jun
Task Name                      Resources  Status    30    7    14   21   29  4    11
  ┌─────────────────────────────────────────────────────────────────────────────┐
  │ Group by: (Task, Resource)         Show: (           ,                    ) │
  │.............................................................................│
  │                      Start Date         Number of Periods                   │
  │ Report Period(s): Daily   [         ]  for [   ]  Days                      │
  │                   Weekly  [         ]  for [   ]  Weeks                     │
  │                   Monthly [         ]  for [   ]  Months                    │
  │.............................................................................│
  │ Include Task Parentage: (No, Yes)   Group by Start/Continue/End: (No, Yes)  │
  │ Include Past Due Tasks: (No, Yes)                                           │
  │     Task Columns (F2)         Width        Assignment Columns (F2)    Width │
  │  1. [                ]     [        ]   1. [                    ]   [     ] │
  │  2. [                ]     [        ]   2. [                    ]   [     ] │
  │  3. [                ]     [        ]   3. [                    ]   [     ] │
  │  4. [                ]     [        ]   4. [                    ]   [     ] │
  │  5. [                ]     [        ]   5. [                    ]   [     ] │
  │  6. [                ]     [        ]   6. [                    ]   [     ] │
  │══════════════════════════ Status Report Form ═══════════════════════════════│
  │ Num              SAILBOAT End: 17-May-90  9:00am                            │
  └─────────────────────────────────────────────────────────────────────────────┘
```

Fig. 8.10. The Status Report Form screen.

4. Move the cursor to the Report Period(s) fields. The report periods fields control for which periods Time Line prints status reports. Time Line actually prints a status report for each report period you identify. Time Line prints Daily, Weekly, and Monthly status reports.

To print daily status reports, enter the first day for which you want to see a daily status report in the Start Date field. Then move the cursor to the Number of Periods field and enter the number of days for which you want to see the daily status report.

To print weekly status reports, enter in the Start Date field the first day of the week for which you want to see a weekly status report. Then move the cursor to the Number of Periods field and enter the number of weeks including the week that begins on the start date for which you want to see the weekly status report.

To print monthly status reports, enter in the Start Date field the first day of the month for which you want to see a monthly status report. Then move the cursor to the Number of Periods field and enter the number of months including the month that begins on the start date for which you want to see the monthly status report.

Note: Time Line allows you to use several words in the Start date field including *today*, *tomorrow*, and *yesterday*, which means you don't have to actually enter the date. Instead, you can use one of these words.

5. If the status report is grouped by tasks, move the cursor to the Include Task Parentage field. Mark No if you want to print only detail tasks and summary tasks with whose detail tasks have been hidden. Mark Yes if you want to print all the tasks that show on the screen.

6. Move the cursor to the Include Past Due Tasks field. Mark Yes if you want to include tasks on the status report whose actual end date precedes the start date of the status report. Mark No if you don't want to include these tasks.

7. Move the cursor to the Group by Start/Continue/End field. Mark No if you want tasks arranged, or grouped, the same way they are on the screen. Mark Yes if you want to group tasks according to whether they started during the period of time the status report covers, whether they started before and will finish after the period of time the status report covers, or whether they end during the period of time the status report covers.

Note: If the Include Past Due Tasks field is set to yes, setting the Group by field to Yes also results in a fourth grouping—one for the tasks that ended before the period of time the status report covers.

8. You then have two options:

    A. If the status report is grouped by tasks, you can select up to six pieces of task data to be printed for each task. To fill a Task Data field, move the cursor to the appropriate field and press F2. Time Line displays a box which lists each of the data fields Time Line collects or calculates for a task. Use the arrow keys to highlight the data field you want and then press Enter. Time Line next fills the Width column behind the Task Data field with the width of the actual data field, but you can change this to some smaller number if you don't want to see the entire field's contents. If you end up truncating, or cutting off, a portion of the field on the actual status report, Time Line indicates this condition by displaying the plus symbol (+) for truncated text fields or the asterisk symbol (*) for numeric fields.

Note: If after entering the task data fields, you want to move a task data field ahead of the one that appears before it, highlight the data field you want to move forward and press Shift-up-arrow. If you want to move a task data field behind the one that follows it, highlight the data field you move to move backwards and press Shift-down-arrow. (You need to use the arrow keys on the numeric keypad for this.)

Tip

As with other reports, you need to include enough information about tasks to identify them on the daily status report. For this reason, include the task name, abbreviated name, or WBS Code.

B. If the status report is grouped by resources, you can select up to six pieces of resource data to be printed for each task. To fill a Resource Data field, move the cursor to the appropriate field and press F2. Time Line displays a box listing each of the data fields Time Line collects or calculates for a resource. Use the arrow keys to highlight the data field you want and then press Enter. Time Line next fills the Width column behind the Resource Data field with the width of the actual data field, but you can change this to some smaller number if you don't want to see the entire contents of the field. However, if you end up truncating, or cutting off, a portion of the field on the actual status report, Time Line indicates this condition by displaying the plus symbol (+) for truncated text fields or the asterisk symbol (*) for numeric fields.

Note: If, after entering the resource data fields, you want to move a resource data field ahead of the one that appears before it, highlight the data field you want to move forward and press Shift-up-arrow. If you want to move a resource data field behind the one that follows it, highlight the data field you move to move backwards and press Shift-down-arrow. (You need to use the arrow key on the numeric keypad for this.)

Tip

Remember to include the resource name as one of the resource data fields so you have a way to identify the data.

9. When you complete the Status Report Form, press F10. Time Line next displays the Page Break Form screen which closely resembles the screen you use to print the Tasks report (see fig. 8.11)

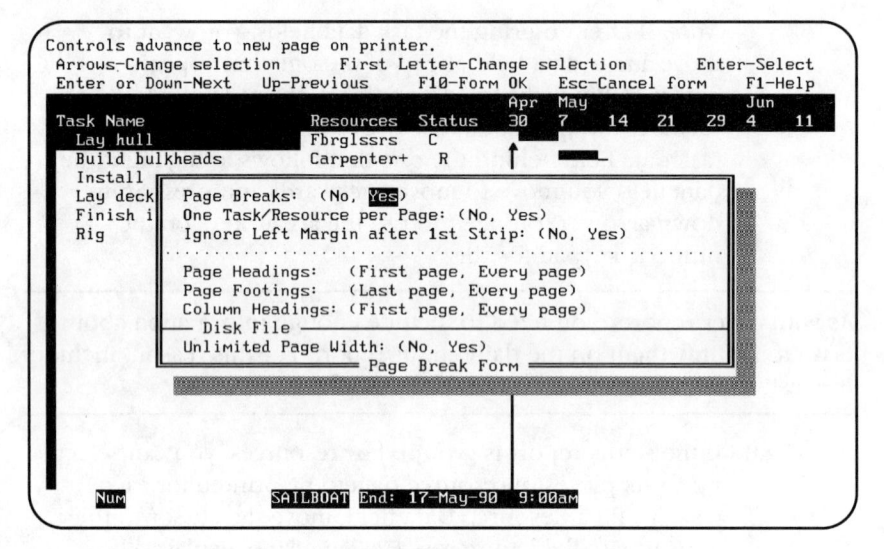

```
Controls advance to new page on printer.
  Arrows-Change selection     First Letter-Change selection      Enter-Select
  Enter or Down-Next    Up-Previous    F10-Form OK    Esc-Cancel form    F1-Help
                                              Apr  May                    Jun
Task Name                  Resources  Status   30   7    14   21   29    4    11
  Lay hull                 Fbrglssrs    C
  Build bulkheads          Carpenter+   R
  Install
  Lay deck   Page Breaks:  (No, Yes)
  Finish i   One Task/Resource per Page: (No, Yes)
  Rig        Ignore Left Margin after 1st Strip: (No, Yes)
             ...........................................................
             Page Headings:   (First page, Every page)
             Page Footings:   (Last page, Every page)
             Column Headings: (First page, Every page)
           ─ Disk File ─
             Unlimited Page Width: (No, Yes)
           ══════════════════ Page Break Form ══════════════════



  Num             SAILBOAT End: 17-May-90   9:00am
```

Fig. 8.11. A page from an example Status Report grouped by task.

Tip You can press F10 when the Page Break Form appears to accept the default settings.

10. With the cursor on the Page Breaks field, mark Yes if you want Time Line to break, or advance, to the top of the next page when it finishes printing one page. (With page breaks, Time Line doesn't print on the perforation.)

11. If you're going to tape the pages of the Status Report together, you can set the Ignore Left Margin After 1st Strip field to Yes so Time Line doesn't use a left margin on pages in strips 2, 3, 4, and so on.

12. If you set the Page Breaks field to Yes, Time Line allows you to specify whether you want Page headings and Column headings to appear on just the first page or on every page and the Page Footings to appear on just the last page or on every page.

13. Move the cursor to the Unlimited Page Width field. Mark Yes if you're going to create a disk file which you'll later print with one of the sideways printing programs.

14. Once you complete the Page Break Form screen, press F10 to initiate printing of the report. Figure 8.12 shows a page from an example Status Report grouped by task. Figure 8.13 shows a page from an example Status Report grouped by resource.

```
Schedule Name  :
Responsible    :
As-of Date     : 30-Apr-90  9:00a      Schedule File : SAILBOAT


Status Report for month of  2-Apr-90 through  1-May-90


                                Start      End
Task Name                       Date       Date
------------------------------  ---------  ---------
Lay hull                        30-Apr-90  7-May-90










TIME LINE Status Report Page 1
```

Fig. 8.12. A page from an example Status Report grouped by resource.

```
Schedule Name  :
Responsible    :
As-of Date     : 30-Apr-90  9:00a      Schedule File : SAILBOAT


Status Report for Fbrglssrs, month of  2-Apr-90 through  1-May-90


                                Start      End        Resource    Total
Task Name                       Date       Date       Name        Cost
------------------------------  ---------  ---------  ----------  ------------
Lay hull                        30-Apr-90  7-May-90   Fbrglssrs         960.00








TIME LINE Status Report Page 1
```

Fig. 8.13. A page from an example Status Report grouped by resource.

Printing an Assignment Report

As you would probably guess, the Assignment Report shows resource and cost assignments either by task or by resource. As with several of the other Time Line reports, you get the flexibility to choose the information you want on the report.

To print the assignment report, you follow these steps:

1. Activate the menu bar and select Reports and then Assignment. Time Line displays the Assignment Report Form (see fig. 8.14) which you use to control how the Assignment Report looks and what information it shows.

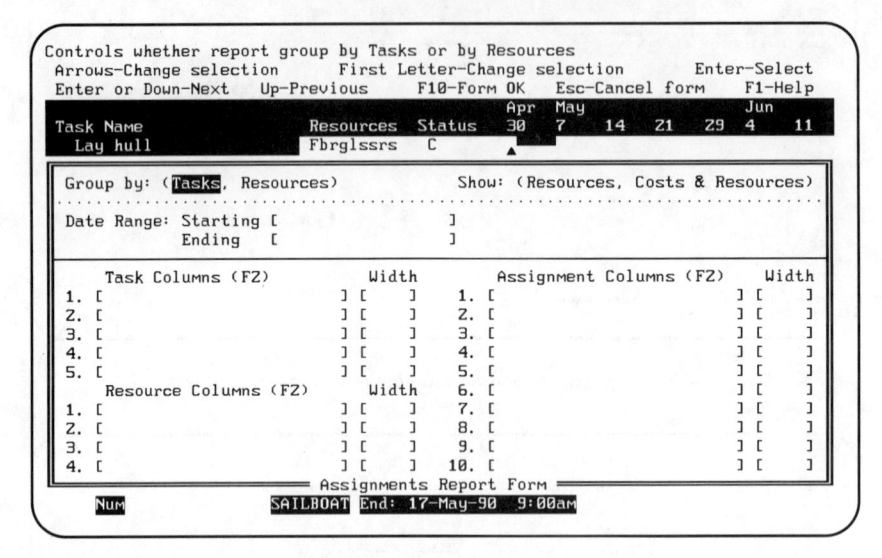

```
Controls whether report group by Tasks or by Resources
 Arrows-Change selection     First Letter-Change selection       Enter-Select
 Enter or Down-Next    Up-Previous      F10-Form OK   Esc-Cancel form    F1-Help
                                           Apr  May                    Jun
 Task Name                  Resources Status 30   7    14   21   29    4    11
   Lay hull                 Fbrglssrs   C
 ┌─────────────────────────────────────────────────────────────────────────┐
 │ Group by: (Tasks, Resources)         Show: (Resources, Costs & Resources)│
 │ ........................................................................│
 │ Date Range: Starting  [              ]                                   │
 │               Ending  [              ]                                   │
 │         Task Columns (FZ)        Width      Assignment Columns (FZ)  Width│
 │     1. [                    ] [        ]  1. [                    ] [    ]│
 │     2. [                    ] [        ]  2. [                    ] [    ]│
 │     3. [                    ] [        ]  3. [                    ] [    ]│
 │     4. [                    ] [        ]  4. [                    ] [    ]│
 │     5. [                    ] [        ]  5. [                    ] [    ]│
 │         Resource Columns (FZ)    Width    6. [                    ] [    ]│
 │     1. [                    ] [        ]  7. [                    ] [    ]│
 │     2. [                    ] [        ]  8. [                    ] [    ]│
 │     3. [                    ] [        ]  9. [                    ] [    ]│
 │     4. [                    ] [        ] 10. [                    ] [    ]│
 │══════════════════════════ Assignments Report Form ══════════════════════│
 │  Num              SAILBOAT End: 17-May-90   9:00am                       │
 └─────────────────────────────────────────────────────────────────────────┘
```

Fig. 8.14. The Assignment Report Form.

2. With the cursor on the Group by field, mark Task if you want a report that is arranged by tasks. Alternatively, mark Resource if you want a report that is arranged by resources.

3. If you set the Group by field to Resources, move the cursor to the Show field. Then mark Resources if you want the report to list only resources and mark Costs & Resources if you want the report to list costs along with the resources.

4. (Optional) If you want to limit the period of time reported on the assignment report to a certain range of dates, enter a starting and ending date in the date range fields. To enter the starting and ending dates, you can use any of the valid date formats. If you don't enter a start or end date the entire schedule prints—which means that it's as if you entered the start date as the first task's start date and the ending date as the last task's end date. You can use keywords in place of actual dates. Time Line accepts the keywords *today*, *tomorrow*, *yesterday*, and *asof*.

5. Select up to five pieces of task data to be printed for each assignment. To fill a Task Data field, move the cursor to the appropriate field and press F2. Time Line displays a box which lists each of the data fields Time Line collects or calculates for a task. Use the arrow keys to highlight the data field you want and then press Enter. Time Line next fills the Width column behind the Task Data field with the width of the actual data field, but you can change this to some smaller number if you don't want to see the entire field's contents. If you end up truncating, or cutting off, a portion of the field on the actual status report, Time Line indicates this condition by displaying the plus symbol (+) for text fields or the asterisk symbol (*) for numeric fields.

6. Select up to four pieces of resource data to be printed for each assignment. To fill a Resource Data field, move the cursor to the appropriate field and press F2. Time Line displays a box which lists each of the data fields, or pieces of information, Time Line collects or calculates for a resource. Use the arrow keys to highlight the data field you want and then press Enter. Time Line next fills the Width column behind the Resource Data field with the width of the actual data field, but you can change this to some smaller number if you don't want to see the entire field's contents. However, if you end up truncating, or cutting off, a portion of the field on the actual status report, Time Line indicates this condition by displaying the plus symbol (+) for text fields or the asterisk symbol (*) for numeric fields.

7. Select up to ten pieces of assignment data to be printed for each assignment. To fill an Assignment Data field, move the cursor to the appropriate field and then follow the same procedure as described in steps 5 and 6 for filling a task or resource data field.

Note: If, after entering the task, resource, or assignment data fields, you want to move a resource data field ahead of the one that appears before it, highlight the data field you want to move forward and press Shift-up-arrow. If you want to move a resource data field behind the one that follows it, highlight the data field you move to move backwards and press Shift-down-arrow. (You need to use the arrow keys on the numeric keypad for this.)

> ***Tip*** As noted earlier in the chapter for other reports, remember to include as task and resource data fields those pieces of data that let you identify the task or resource such as the task name or the resource name.

8. When you complete the Assignment Report Form, press F10. Time Line next displays the Page Break Form (refer to fig. 8.11).

9. With the cursor on the Page Breaks field, mark Yes if you want Time Line to break to the top of the next page when it finishes printing one page. (With page breaks, Time Line doesn't print on the perforation.)

10. If you're going to tape the pages of the assignment report together, you can set the Ignore Left Margin After 1st Strip field to Yes so Time Line doesn't use a left margin on pages in strips 2, 3, 4, and so on.

11. If you set the Page Breaks field to Yes, Time Line allows you to specify whether you want Page headings and Column headings to appear on only the first page or on every page and the Page Footings to appear on only the last page or on every page.

12. Move the cursor to the Unlimited Page Width field. Mark Yes if you're going to create a disk file which you'll later print with one of the sideways printing programs.

13. Once you complete the Page Break Form, press F10 to initiate printing of the report. Figure 8.15 shows a page from an example assignment report grouped by task.

Printing a Cross Tab Report

The Cross Tab Report cross-tabulates a piece of project data-you specify which piece—and then produces a report by using the results. Cross-tabulation refers to creating a table of data and then adding up the rows and columns of data. That may sound confusing, but an example will help clarify things. For instance, if you created a report that showed the total costs by task and by week such as that shown below, you would be cross-tabulating total costs by task and by week.

	Week 1	Week 2	Week 3	Total
Task 1	$3	$5	$4	$14
Task 2	1	1	2	4
Task 3	2	3	3	8
Total	$6	$9	$9	$26

```
Schedule Name  :
Responsible    :
As-of Date     : 30-Apr-90  9:00a      Schedule File : SAILBOAT


                                Resource    Total          Yet To Go      Complet
Task Name                       Name        Hours          Hours          Hours
--------------------------      ----------  -------------  -------------  -------
Lay hull                        Fbrglssrs         80             80
Build bulkheads                 Carpenter         24             24
                                Crane             32             32
Install engine                  Mechanic           4              4
                                Crane              4              4
Lay deck                        Fbrglssrs         80             80
                                Crane             40             40
Finish interiors                Carpenter         18             18
Rig                             Mechanic          24             24




TIME LINE Assignments Report Page 1
```

Fig. 8.15. *A page from an example Assignment Report grouped by task.*

By cross tabulating, you can then see the total costs of any particular task by week, the total costs of all tasks for a week, the total costs of any particular task, and the total cost of all tasks for all weeks.

To print a Cross Tab Report, follow the steps listed below:

1. Activate the menu bar and then select Reports and Cross Tab. Time Line displays the Cross Tab menu (see fig. 8.16) which you use to indicate whether you want a Task vs Time cross-tabulation as used in the earlier illustration, a Resource vs Time cross-tabulation, or a Task vs Time cross-tabulation.

2. Select the type of cross-tabulation you want. Time Line displays the Cross Tab Report Form you'll use to specify the piece of data you want cross-tabulated and to tell Time Line how you want the data cross-tabulated. Figure 8.17 shows the Cross Tab Report Form screen.

3. If you selected a Task vs Time or Resource vs Time cross-tabulation, move the cursor to the Date Range fields and enter the starting and ending dates of the period of time you want covered in the report. To enter the starting and ending dates, you can use any of the valid date formats. If you don't enter a start or end date the entire schedule prints—which means that it's as though you entered the start date as the first task's start date and the ending date as the last task's end date. You can use keywords in place of actual dates. Time Line accepts *today*, *tomorrow*, *yesterday*, and *asof*.

Part III: Managing the System

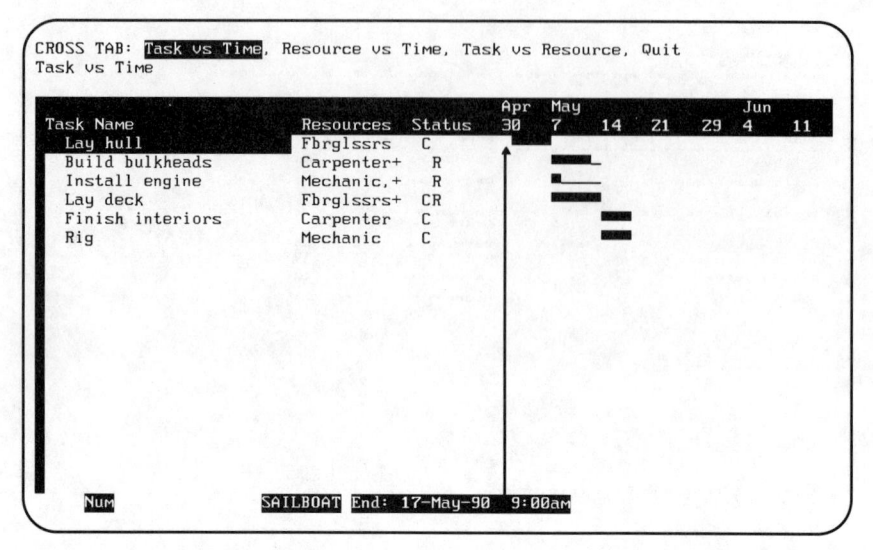

Fig. 8.16. The Cross Tab menu.

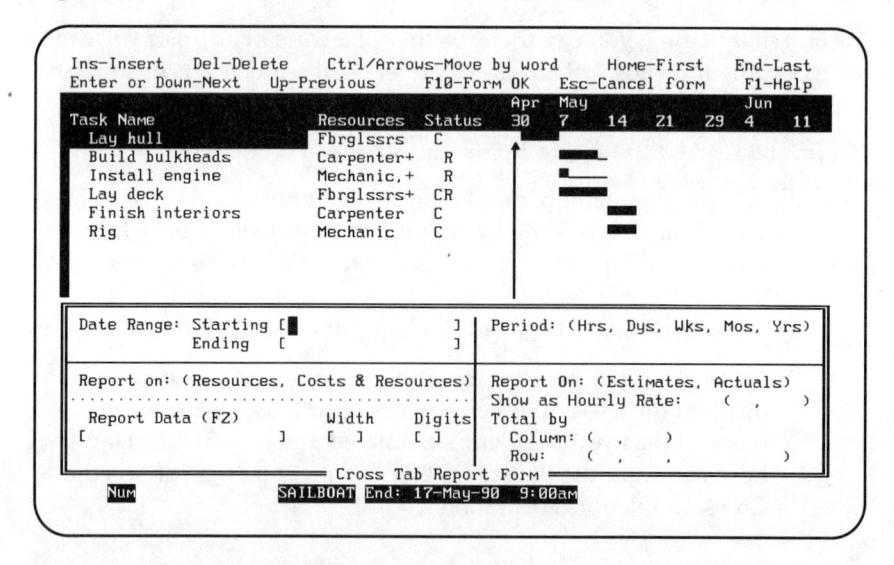

Fig. 8.17. The Cross Tab Report form.

4. If you selected a Task vs Time or Resource vs Time cross-tabulation, move the cursor to the Period field and mark the unit of time you want to use for the columns of the cross-tabulation.

5. Move the cursor to the Report On field. Mark Resources if the report should include only resources data; mark Costs &

Resources if the report should include both resources and costs.

6. Move the cursor to the Report Data field and press F2. Time Line displays a box which lists each of the data fields Time Line collects or calculates for a task or resource. Use the arrow keys to highlight the data field you want and then press Enter. Time Line next fills the Width column behind the Report Data field with the width of the actual data field and fills the Digits field with the default number of decimal places, but you can change these.

7. (Optional) Move the cursor to the Report On field. If you set the cost tracking switch to Yes on the Options Form, you can report on actual costs by marking Actual. (Chapter 4, "Managing Project and Task Details," describes the Options Form.

8. (Optional) If you are creating either a task vs time or resource vs time cross tabulation, you can direct Time Line to convert the data to hourly rates. To do so, move the cursor to the Show as Hourly Rate field and mark Yes.

9. If you want to have Time Line calculate column totals and print a totals column, move the cursor to the Total By Column field and mark Yes. If you don't, leave the Total By Column field set to No.

   Note: If column totals don't make sense, for example, because you're totaling percentages fields, Time Line won't let you set the Total by Column field to Yes.

10. If you want to have Time Line calculate row totals and print a totals row, move the cursor to the Total By Row field and mark Yes. You also have the option of directing Time Line to calculate cumulative totals, which you do by marking Cumulative. If you don't want Time Line to calculate totals, cumulative or non-cumulative, leave the Total By Column field set to No.

    Note: As with column totals, if row totals don't make sense, Time Line won't let you set the Total by Row field to Yes or Cumulative.

11. When the Cross Tab Report Form is complete, press F10. Time Line next displays the Page Control Form (refer to fig. 8.6).

Tip You can press F10 when the Page Control Form Appears to accept the default settings.

12. (Optional) With the cursor on the Page Breaks field, mark Yes if you want to control how Time Line advances to the next page. If you set the Page Breaks field to Yes, Time Line lets you force page breaks at specified outline levels (see step 13), and it prints page numbers.

13. (Optional) If you set the Page Breaks field to Yes, Time Line allows you to move the cursor to the Advance to New Page at Outline Level field. With this field set to 0, Time Line breaks to a new page only when the current page is full. With this field set to 1, Time Line breaks to a new page at every first, or main, level task. With this field set to 2, Time Line breaks to a new page at every second level task. (Second level tasks are those that are subtasks to the first level tasks.) Similarly, a setting of 3 means the page break occurs at every third level task and so forth.

14. (Optional) If you're going to tape the pages of the Tasks Report together, end to end, you can set the Ignore Left Margin After 1st Strip field to Yes so Time Line doesn't use a left margin on pages in strips 2, 3, 4, and so on.

15. (Optional) If you set the Page Breaks field to Yes, Time Line allows you to specify whether you want Page and Row headings to appear on just the first page or on every page and the Page and Row Footings to appear on just the last page or on every page.

16. (Optional) Move the cursor to the Row Spacing field. Enter 1 to print a single-spaced report, 2 to print a double-spaced report, 3 to print a triple-spaced report and so on.

17. (Optional) Move the cursor to the Column Spacing field. Enter the number of spaces you want Time Line to put between columns of data. You can enter a number from 1 to 77.

18. (Optional) Move the cursor to the Print Zeros as field. If when a cost amount is zero, you want Time Line to print the zero, mark Yes. If you instead want Time Line to leave the field blank, mark Spaces.

19. (Optional) Move the cursor to the Unlimited Page Width field. Mark Yes if you're going to create a disk file which you'll later print with one of the sideways printing programs.

20. Once you complete the Page Control Form, press F10 to initiate printing of the report. Figure 8.18 shows an example of a Task vs Time cross-tabulation report, using the sailboat project.

```
Schedule Name :
Responsible   :
As-of Date    : 30-Apr-90  9:00a      Schedule File : SAILBOAT


                           30-Apr-90      7-May-90       14-May-90          Total
                           ---------      --------       ---------          -----
Lay hull                      960.00                                        960.00*
Build bulkheads                             1,160.00                      1,160.00*
Install engine                                154.00                        154.00*
Lay deck                                    1,960.00                      1,960.00*
Finish interiors                                              270.00         270.00*
Rig                                                           324.00         324.00*
                           ==========    ==========     ==========     ==========
Total                         960.00        3,274.00          594.00  |    4,828.00*

TIME LINE Task vs Time Report showing Total Dollars
```

Fig. 8.18. An example of a Tasks vs Time cross-tabulation report.

Printing a Resource Report

The resource report prints information about resources and costs. Like several of the other Time Line reports, you choose what information you want to see on the report.

To print a Resource Report, you take the following steps:

1. Activate the menu bar and then select Reports and Resource. Time Line displays the Resource Report Form (see fig. 8.19) which you use to indicate which resource and cost information you want to see on the report.

2. With the cursor on the Report On field, mark Resources if you want the report to list only resources and mark Costs & Resources if you want the report to list costs along with the resources.

3. Select up to twelve pieces of resource data to be printed for each resource report. To fill a Column Data field, move the cursor to the appropriate field and press F2. Time Line

Part III: Managing the System

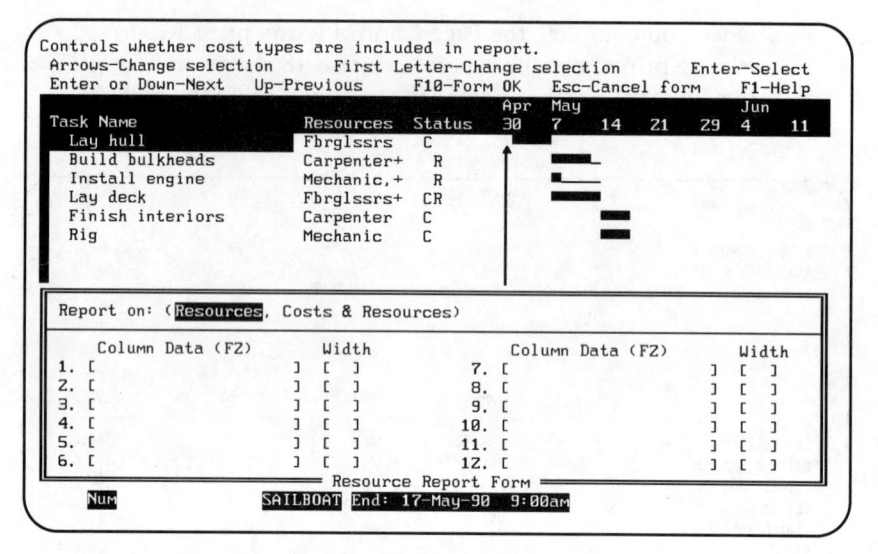

```
┌─────────────────────────────────────────────────────────────────────┐
│ Controls whether cost types are included in report.                 │
│ Arrows-Change selection    First Letter-Change selection  Enter-Select│
│ Enter or Down-Next    Up-Previous   F10-Form OK   Esc-Cancel form  F1-Help│
│                                        Apr  May              Jun    │
│ Task Name            Resources Status  30   7   14   21  29  4   11 │
│    Lay hull          Fbrglssrs    C                                 │
│    Build bulkheads   Carpenter+   R                                 │
│    Install engine    Mechanic,+   R                                 │
│    Lay deck          Fbrglssrs+   CR                                │
│    Finish interiors  Carpenter    C                                 │
│    Rig               Mechanic     C                                 │
│                                                                     │
│  ┌────────────────────────────────────────────────────────────────┐ │
│  │ Report on: (Resources, Costs & Resources)                      │ │
│  │                                                                │ │
│  │     Column Data (FZ)     Width        Column Data (FZ)   Width │ │
│  │  1. [            ]    [     ]      7. [            ]   [     ] │ │
│  │  2. [            ]    [     ]      8. [            ]   [     ] │ │
│  │  3. [            ]    [     ]      9. [            ]   [     ] │ │
│  │  4. [            ]    [     ]     10. [            ]   [     ] │ │
│  │  5. [            ]    [     ]     11. [            ]   [     ] │ │
│  │  6. [            ]    [     ]     12. [            ]   [     ] │ │
│  │════════════════════ Resource Report Form ══════════════════════│ │
│  │  Num         SAILBOAT End: 17-May-90  9:00am                   │ │
│  └────────────────────────────────────────────────────────────────┘ │
└─────────────────────────────────────────────────────────────────────┘
```

Fig. 8.19. *The Resource Report Form screen.*

displays a box which lists each of the data fields Time Line collects or calculates for a resource. Use the arrow keys to highlight the data field you want and then press Enter. Time Line next fills the Width column behind the Resource Data field with the width of the actual data field, but you can change this to some smaller number if you don't want to see the entire field's contents. However, if you end up truncating, or cutting off, a portion of the field on the actual status report, Time Line indicates this condition by displaying the plus symbol (+) for text fields or the asterisk symbol (*) for numeric fields.

Tip As noted earlier in this chapter, be sure to include the Resource Name as one of the data fields so you know which resource you're looking at.

   4. When the Resource Report Form is complete, press F10. Time Line next displays the Page Control Form (refer to fig. 8.6).

   5. (Optional) With the cursor on the Page Breaks field, mark Yes if you want to control how Time Line advances to the next page. If you set the Page Breaks field to Yes, Time Line lets you force page breaks at specified outline levels (see step 6), and it prints page numbers.

6. (Optional) If you set the Page Breaks field to Yes, Time Line allows you to move the cursor to the Advance to New Page at Outline Level field. With this field set to 0, Time Line breaks to a new page only when the current page is full. With this field set to 1, Time Line breaks to a new page at every first, or main, level task. With this field set to 2, Time Line breaks to a new page at every second level task and so on. (Second level tasks are those that are subtasks to the first level tasks.)

7. (Optional) If you're going to tape the pages of the Tasks Report together, end to end, you can set the Ignore Left Margin After 1st Strip field to Yes so Time Line doesn't use a left margin on pages in strips 2, 3, 4, and so on.

8. (Optional) If you set the Page Breaks field to Yes, Time Line allows you to specify whether you want Page and Row headings to appear on just the first page or on every page, and you want the Page and Row Footings to appear on just the last page or on every page.

9. (Optional) Move the cursor to the Row Spacing field. Enter 1 to print a single-spaced report, 2 to print a double-spaced report, 3 to print a triple-spaced report, and so on.

10. (Optional) Move the cursor to the Column Spacing field. Enter the number of spaces you want Time Line to put between columns of data. You can enter a number from 1 to 77.

11. (Optional) Move the cursor to the Print Zeros as field. If when a cost amount is zero, you want Time Line to print the zero, mark Yes. If you instead want Time Line to leave the field blank, mark Spaces.

12. (Optional) Move the cursor to the Unlimited Page Width field. Mark Yes if you're going to create a disk file which you'll later print with one of the sideways printing programs.

13. Once you complete the Page Control Form screen, press F10 to initiate printing of the report. Figure 8.20 shows an example of a Resource report.

Printing a Histogram Report

A Histogram report resembles the histogram screen view: It shows resource allocations, or assignments, using a bar chart. Mechanically, creating a histogram resembles creating a Resource vs Time Cross Tab report, which

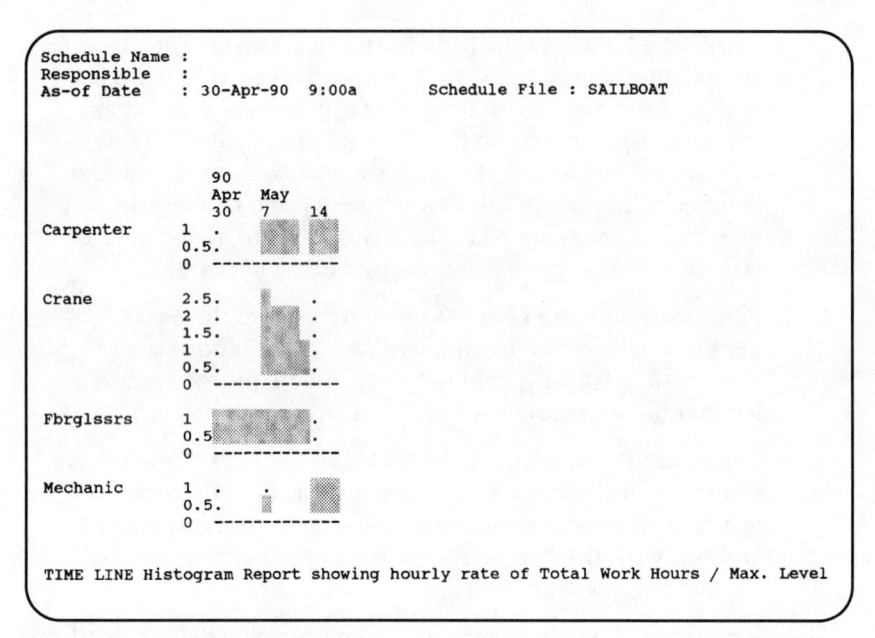

```
Schedule Name  :
Responsible    :
As-of Date     : 30-Apr-90  9:00a      Schedule File : SAILBOAT


                        90
                        Apr   May
                        30    7    14
           Carpenter  1   .
                      0.5.
                      0   -------------

           Crane      2.5.
                      2   .
                      1.5.
                      1   .
                      0.5.
                      0   -------------

           Fbrglssrs  1
                      0.5
                      0   -------------

           Mechanic   1   .
                      0.5.
                      0   -------------

TIME LINE Histogram Report showing hourly rate of Total Work Hours / Max. Level
```

Fig. 8.20. An example Resource Report.

isn't surprising because they both communicate the same information—in different ways.

To print a Histogram report, you take the following steps:

1. Activate the menu bar and then select Reports and Histogram. Time Line displays the Histogram Data Form, which you'll use to specify the resource data you want to see in a histogram. Figure 8.21 shows the Histogram Data Form screen.

Tip You can accept the default settings on the Histogram Data Form by pressing F10 when the screen appears. This lets you skip steps 2 through 9.

2. Move the cursor to the Duplicate On-screen Histograms field. If you want to have Time Line complete the Histogram Data Form so that your printed histogram matches the one Time Line displays on the screen, mark Yes. If you do set the Duplicate On-screen Histograms field to Yes, you'll be able to enter the Date Range fields (described in step 3) but no others.

3. Move the cursor to the Date Range fields and enter the starting and ending dates of the period of time you want covered in the histogram. Use any of the valid date formats. If you don't enter a start or end date the entire schedule prints. As elsewhere, you can use keywords in place of actual dates such as *today*, *tomorrow*, *yesterday*, and *asof*.

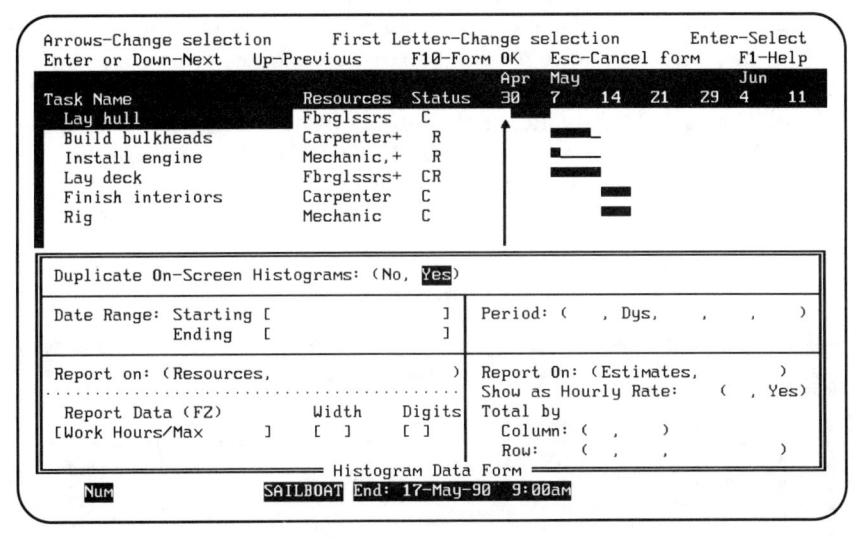

```
Arrows-Change selection     First Letter-Change selection      Enter-Select
Enter or Down-Next    Up-Previous      F10-Form OK   Esc-Cancel form    F1-Help
                                          Apr  May                     Jun
Task Name                 Resources Status 30   7    14   21   29   4    11
  Lay hull                Fbrglssrs  C
  Build bulkheads         Carpenter+ R
  Install engine          Mechanic,+ R
  Lay deck                Fbrglssrs+ CR
  Finish interiors        Carpenter  C
  Rig                     Mechanic   C

 Duplicate On-Screen Histograms: (No, Yes)

 Date Range: Starting [            ]    Period: (     , Dys,    ,     )
             Ending   [            ]

 Report on: (Resources,             )   Report On: (Estimates,       )
 ..........................             Show as Hourly Rate:  ( , Yes)
 Report Data (F2)      Width   Digits   Total by
 [Work Hours/Max   ]   [   ]   [   ]       Column: (    ,    )
                                           Row:    (    ,    )
                       ========== Histogram Data Form ==========
     Num              SAILBOAT End: 17-May-90  9:00am
```

Fig. 8.21. The Histogram Data form.

4. Move the cursor to the Period field and mark the unit of time you want to use for the columns of the histogram.

5. Move the cursor to the Report On field. Mark Resources if the report should include only resources data; mark Costs & Resources if the report should include both resources and costs.

6. Move the cursor to the Report Data field and press F2. Time Line displays a box which lists each of the data fields, or pieces of information, Time Line collects or calculates for a resource. Use the arrow keys to highlight the data field you want and then press Enter. Time Line next fills the Width column behind the Report Data field with the width of the actual data field and the Digits with the default number of decimal places, but you can change these if you want to use less space.

7. (Optional) Move the cursor to the Report On field. If you set the cost tracking switch to yes on the Options Form, you can report on actual costs by marking Actual. (Chapter 4, "Managing Project and Task Details," describes the Options Form.)

8. (Optional) You can direct Time Line to convert the data to hourly rates. To do so, move the cursor to the Show as Hourly Rate field and mark Yes.

9. (Optional) If you want to have Time Line calculate column totals and print a totals column, move the cursor to the Total By Column field and mark Yes. If you don't, leave the Total By Column field set to No. If column totals don't make sense, say, because you're totaling percentages fields, Time Line won't let you set the Total by Column field to Yes. (*Note:* Although Total by Row field shows on the Histogram Data Form Screen, it isn't used. So you won't be able to move the cursor to the field or make entries in it.) Time Line next displays the Histogram Report Form (see fig. 8.22).

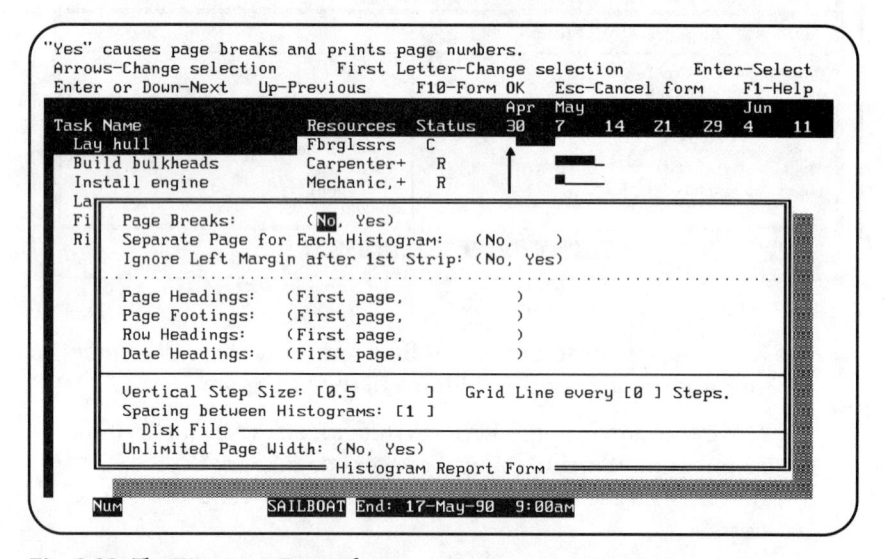

```
"Yes" causes page breaks and prints page numbers.
  Arrows-Change selection      First Letter-Change selection      Enter-Select
  Enter or Down-Next    Up-Previous      F10-Form OK    Esc-Cancel form    F1-Help
                                              Apr  May                  Jun
  Task Name                 Resources  Status  30   7    14   21   29   4    11
    Lay hull                Fbrglssrs    C
    Build bulkheads         Carpenter+   R
    Install engine          Mechanic,+   R
    La
    Fi    Page Breaks:         (No, Yes)
    Ri    Separate Page for Each Histogram:  (No,   )
          Ignore Left Margin after 1st Strip: (No, Yes)
          ..............................................
          Page Headings:   (First page,        )
          Page Footings:   (First page,        )
          Row Headings:    (First page,        )
          Date Headings:   (First page,        )

          Vertical Step Size: [0.5    ]   Grid Line every [0 ] Steps.
          Spacing between Histograms: [1 ]
          ── Disk File ──────────────────────────────────
          Unlimited Page Width: (No, Yes)
          ════════════════════ Histogram Report Form ════
   Num              SAILBOAT End: 17-May-90  9:00am
```

Fig. 8.22. *The Histogram Report form.*

10. (Optional) With the cursor on the Page Breaks field, mark Yes if you want Time Line to advance to the next page after it fills the current page. If you set the Page Breaks field to Yes, Time Line doesn't print on the perforation between sheets of continuous form paper. If you set the Page Breaks field to No, Time Line does print across the perforation—which makes it easy to tape or paste the individual sheets of a report together.

> **Tip**
>
> You can accept the default setting on the Histogram Report Form by pressing F10 when the screen appears. You can then skip steps 10 through 18.

11. (Optional) If you set the Page Breaks field to Yes, Time Line allows you to put each histogram on a separate page. To do so, mark the Separate Page for Each Histogram field as Yes.

12. (Optional) If you're going to tape the pages of the Tasks Report together, end to end, you can set the Ignore Left Margin After 1st Strip field to Yes so Time Line doesn't use a left margin on pages in strips 2, 3, 4, and so on.

13. (Optional) If you set the Page Breaks field to Yes, Time Line allows you to specify whether you want Page and Row headings, Page Footings, and Date Headings to appear on just the first page or on every page.

14. (Optional) Move the cursor to the Vertical Step Size field. Time Line lets you use the Vertical Step Size field to control the number of resource units that each vertical axis increment represents. The default value is .5 which is what the on-screen version of the Histogram uses. Smaller numbers result in more detail; larger numbers result a less detail.

15. (Optional) Move the cursor to the Grid Line field and indicate how often you want a horizontal grid line printed. 0 results in no gridlines. 1 results in gridlines being printed for each vertical axis increment. 2 results in gridlines being printed for every second vertical axis.

16. (Optional) Move the cursor to the Spacing Between Histograms field. Enter the number of spaces you want Time Line to put between the histogram columns.

17. (Optional) Move the cursor to the Unlimited Page Width field. Mark Yes if you're going to create a disk file that you'll later print with one of the sideways printing programs.

18. Once you complete the Histogram Report Form, press F10 to initiate printing of the report. Figure 8.23 shows an example of a Histogram report.

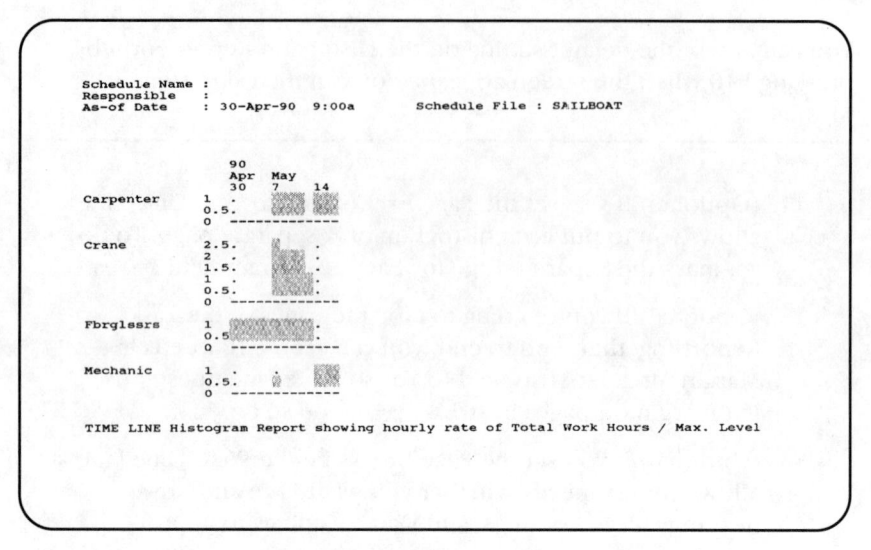

Fig. 8.23. An example of the Histogram report.

Printing a PERT and Tree Charts

PERT and Tree Charts are both easier to print. To print either chart, which roughly mirrors the on-screen versions of PERT and Tree charts, you follow these steps:

1. Activate the menu bar and select Reports. Then select PERT if you want to print a PERT chart and select Tree if you want to print a Tree Chart. Time Line next displays message box that asks whether you want to Go, Change Layout, or Quit (see fig. 8.24).

2. To print a chart, select Go. Time Line prints a PERT or Tree chart using the standard format. Figure 8.25 shows the standard PERT chart; and figure 8.26 shows the standard Tree chart.

As figures 8.25 and 8.26 show, the standard versions of the PERT and Tree charts show only the task names, but you can control which information Time Line shows for each of the task boxes in a PERT or Tree diagram. To do so, you follow these steps:

1. Activate the menu bar and select Reports and then PERT or Tree. Time Line displays the message box shown in figure 8.24.

Chapter 8: Printing Reports 239

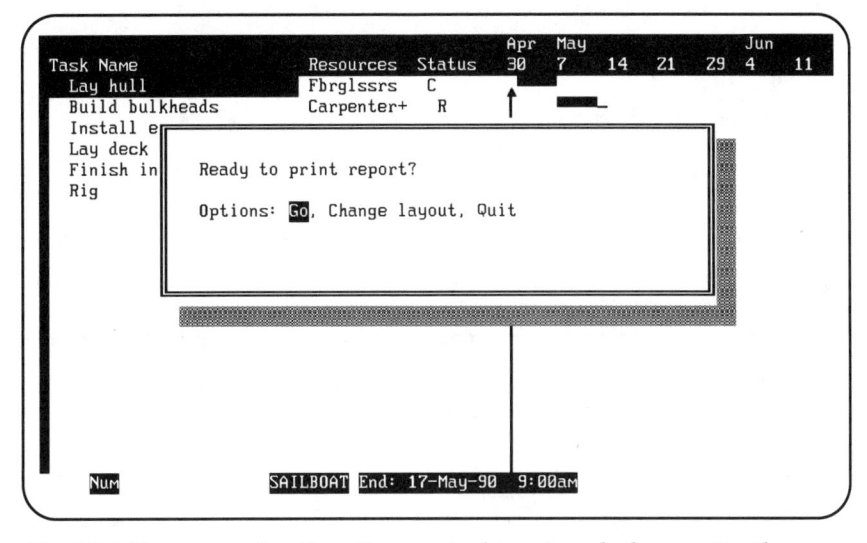

```
                                        Apr  May              Jun
Task Name              Resources Status  30   7   14   21  29  4   11
  Lay hull             Fbrglssrs   C
  Build bulkheads      Carpenter+  R
  Install e┌─────────────────────────────────────────┐
  Lay deck │                                         │
  Finish in│  Ready to print report?                 │
  Rig      │                                         │
           │  Options: Go, Change layout, Quit       │
           │                                         │
           └─────────────────────────────────────────┘


  Num           SAILBOAT End: 17-May-90  9:00am
```

Fig. 8.24. The message box Time Line uses to determine whether you Go, Change Layout, or Quit.

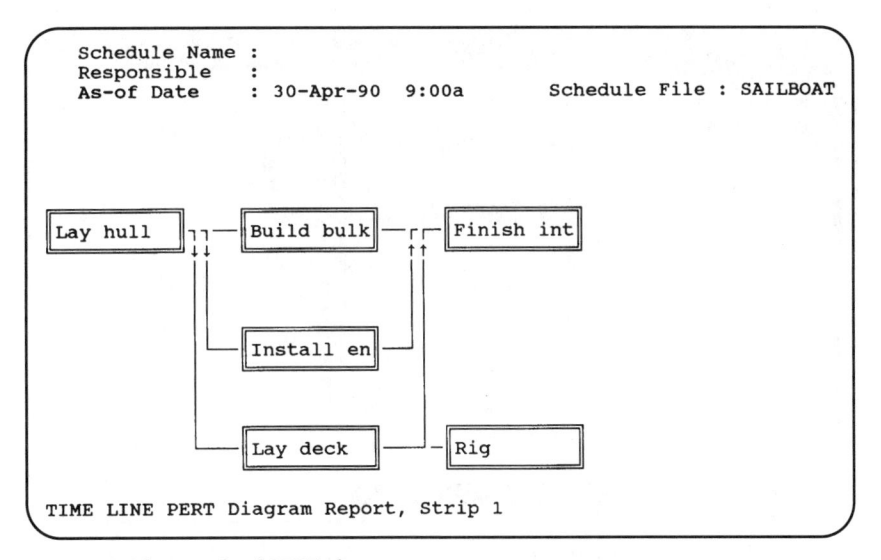

```
  Schedule Name :
  Responsible   :
  As-of Date    : 30-Apr-90  9:00a     Schedule File : SAILBOAT




  ┌────────┐    ┌──────────┐     ┌───────────┐
  │Lay hull│────│Build bulk│─────│Finish int │
  └────────┘    └──────────┘     └───────────┘


                ┌──────────┐
                │Install en│
                └──────────┘


                ┌──────────┐     ┌───────────┐
                │Lay deck  │─────│Rig        │
                └──────────┘     └───────────┘

  TIME LINE PERT Diagram Report, Strip 1
```

Fig. 8.25. The standard PERT chart.

    2. Select the Change Layout option. Time Line displays the Standard Layout box (see fig. 8.27) which lists several alternative formats for PERT and Tree charts. (*Note:* The same layouts are available for PERT and Tree chart screens.)

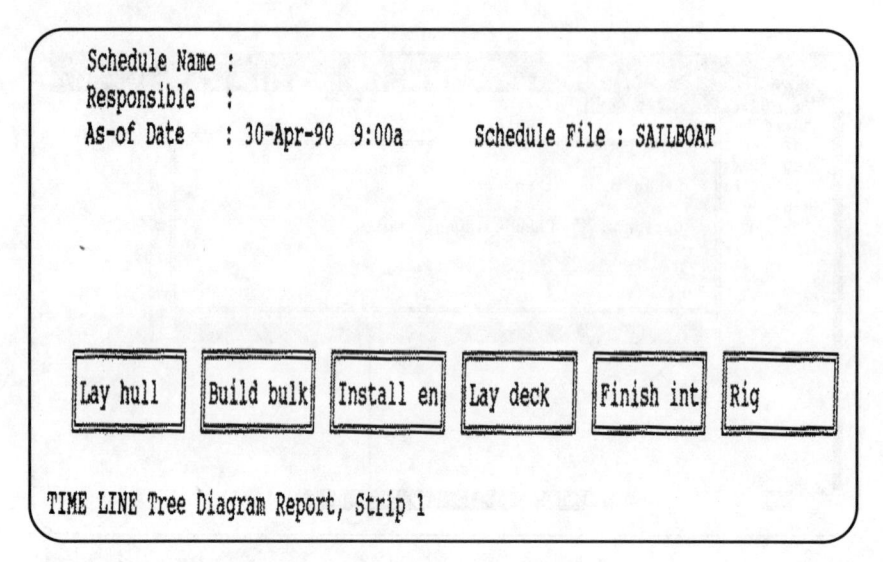

```
Schedule Name :
Responsible  :
As-of Date   : 30-Apr-90  9:00a      Schedule File : SAILBOAT




         ┌────────┐ ┌──────────┐ ┌──────────┐  ┌────────┐ ┌──────────┐ ┌─────┐
         │Lay hull│ │Build bulk│ │Install en│  │Lay deck│ │Finish int│ │ Rig │
         └────────┘ └──────────┘ └──────────┘  └────────┘ └──────────┘ └─────┘


TIME LINE Tree Diagram Report, Strip 1
```

Fig. 8.26. *The standard Tree chart.*

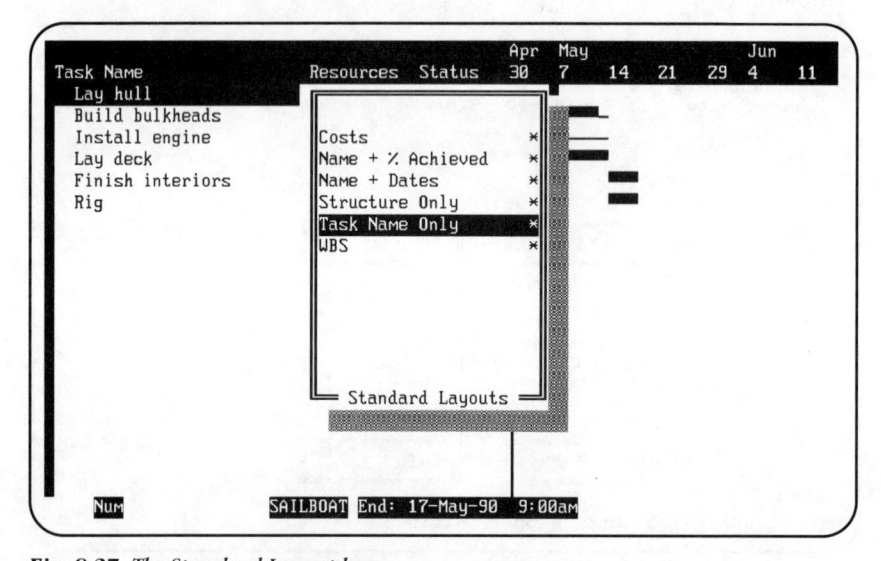

```
                                          Apr  May                 Jun
Task Name            Resources  Status    30   7    14   21   29   4    11
  Lay hull
  Build bulkheads
  Install engine    ┌─────────────────────────┐
  Lay deck         │Costs                  × │
  Finish interiors │Name + % Achieved      × │
  Rig              │Name + Dates           × │
                   │Structure Only         × │
                   │Task Name Only         × │
                   │WBS                    × │
                   │                         │
                   │                         │
                   │                         │
                   │══ Standard Layouts ═════│
                   └─────────────────────────┘


 Num         SAILBOAT  End: 17-May-90  9:00am
```

Fig. 8.27. *The Standard Layout box.*

> 3. From the standard layout box, mark one of the layouts and
>   then press Enter. These six variations differ only in the data
>   they print with the boxes that make up the PERT chart of the
>   Tree chart. The default layout is Task Name Only, but you
>   can choose one of the other by using the arrow keys to
>   highlight the option you want to use. The Costs layout, for
>   example, includes the total costs of a task. Name + %

Achieved shows the task name and the completion percentage for the task. (The other layout names are also similarly descriptive so I won't describe their names here. Refer to Chapter 7 if you have any questions.) Time Line then redisplays the message box shown in figure 8.24, from which you can print the chart.

The predefined layouts which Time Line provides—the six items listed in figure 8.24 will probably also provide all the variations you need as far as PERT and Tree Charts go, but you can also create customized PERT and Gantt Charts. To do this, you follow the same steps described in Chapter 7, "Customizing Gantt, PERT, and Tree Chart Screens," for creating custom PERT and Tree chart layout.

Printing Graphical Gantt and PERT Charts

The two textual report options, Reports Gantt and Reports PERT, produce Gantt and PERT charts that are often entirely adequate. These reports may show all the information you need, organize the information in the way you want, and present the information in as professional an appearance as you desire. But using the Graphics Gantt and Graphics PERT options, you can produce graphical versions of these two standard project management reports. I could spend several paragraphs describing the mechanical differences between the textual and graphical versions of these two charts, but you'll see the difference immediately by comparing the two approaches. Figure 8.28 shows a graphical version of a Gantt chart for the sailboat project. Figure 8.29 shows a graphical version of a PERT chart. Compare these graphical charts to the textual versions shown earlier in the chapter.

Simple Printing of Gantt and PERT Charts

Printing a graphical Gantt or PERT doesn't have to be difficult at all. In fact, producing these charts can be considerably easier than printing a textual report. The following steps explain how to create simple charts:

1. Activate the menu bar and select Graphics.

2. Select Gantt if you want to print a Gantt chart and Time Line displays the Graphics/Gantt Chart Form screen. Or select PERT if you want to print a PERT chart and Time Line dis-

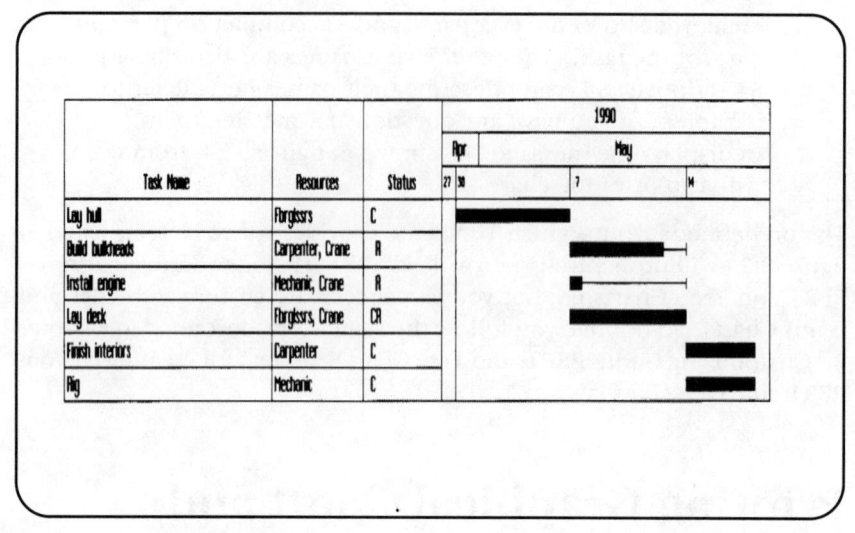

Task Name	Resources	Status	1990 Apr 27 30	May 7	14
Lay hull	Frgtsrs	C	■■■■■		
Build bulkheads	Carpenter, Crane	R		■■■——	
Install engine	Mechanic, Crane	R		■—	
Lay deck	Frgtsrs, Crane	CR		■■■■	
Finish interiors	Carpenter	C			■■
Rig	Mechanic	C			■■

Fig. 8.28. A graphical Gantt chart.

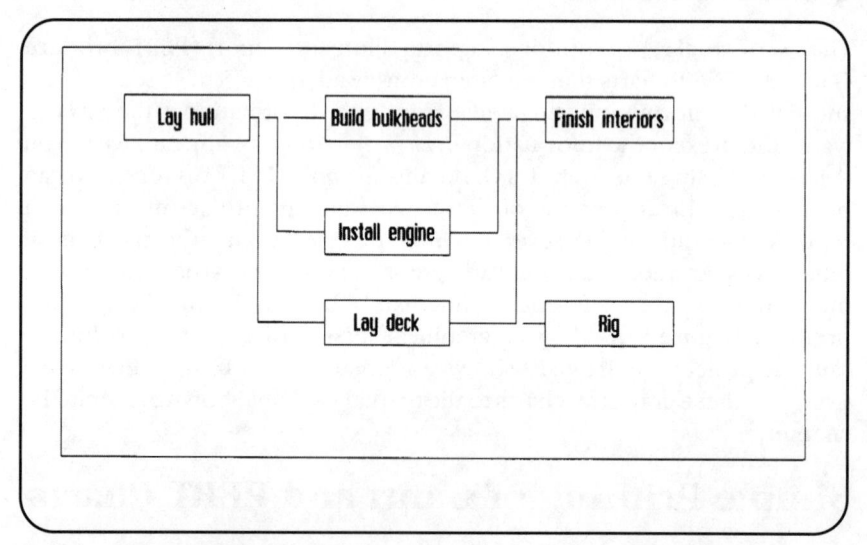

Fig. 8.29. A graphical PERT chart.

      plays the Graphics/PERT Chart Form screen. (I'll describe in the next sections how to complete the Graphics/Gantt Chart Form and the Graphics/PERT Chart Form.)

3. With the Graphics/Gantt Form or Graphics/PERT Form displayed, press F10 to initiate creation of the chart. Time

Line next displays a message box that tells you it's completing the Gantt or PERT chart layout. Then, after it completes the layout, it displays the Graphics/Chart Size Form.

4. With the Graphics/Chart Size Form displayed, press F10 to begin printing the chart. The screen will go blank and then you'll see a series of messages telling you that Time Line is creating a file, asking you to to wait one moment, and then asking you to "please wait." After a few seconds, you'll see the chart, the way it will appear when printed. The chart will probably be too large to fit on a single screen.

   To move back and forth across the chart, use the arrow keys or the Home and End keys. Home moves the chart so the first page shows, and End moves the chart so the last page shows. You can use the Shift key with the arrow keys to move farther in the direction of the arrow rather than using the arrow keys alone.

   To go to a specific part of the chart, press F5 which resizes the chart so it fits on a single screen. The various pages of the chart that will be printed show on the screen. Use the arrow keys to mark with the dashed lines box the page you want to view and then press Enter. Time Line redisplays the chart page you selected in its regular size.

   To resize the chart, use the + and – keys and also the combination Ctrl-Home. Ctrl-Home resizes the chart so it fits on one screen. The + key incrementally increases the size of the chart on the screen so you can more clearly see chart details. The – key incrementally decreases the size of the chart on the screen.

   Note: The + and – keys don't affect the ultimate size of the printed chart.

   To mark only certain pages for printing, press F8 when the page that you want to print is displayed on the screen. Time Line saves that page of chart in a file for later printing with the F10 key.

5. To print the chart, press F10. If you marked any of the pages for printing with the F8 key, F10 causes only the marked pages to print. *Note:* To abort the printing and quit the preview, press Esc.

Completing the Graphics/Gantt Chart Form

In the previous section, "Simple Printing of Gantt and PERT Charts," step 2 refers to the Graphics/Gantt Chart Form (see fig. 8.30). This screen gives you a series of options that let you customize the Gantt chart that gets printed. Perhaps the most important thing to remember about this form is that you don't have to use it—you can simply use the screen's default settings as those for creating a Gantt chart. But you can change the standard appearance of a Gantt chart by changing the default settings, and this flexibility often means you can produce Gantt chart that match exactly what you need.

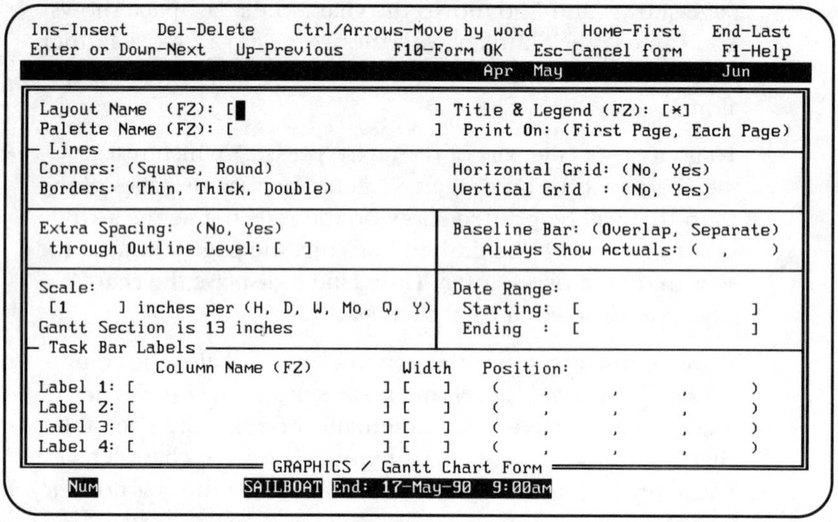

```
 Ins-Insert    Del-Delete     Ctrl/Arrows-Move by word      Home-First    End-Last
 Enter or Down-Next   Up-Previous      F10-Form OK    Esc-Cancel form     F1-Help
                                                 Apr   May                 Jun
  Layout Name  (F2): [                       ] Title & Legend (F2): [*]
  Palette Name (F2): [                       ]  Print On: (First Page, Each Page)
  Lines
  Corners: (Square, Round)                     Horizontal Grid: (No, Yes)
  Borders: (Thin, Thick, Double)               Vertical Grid  : (No, Yes)

  Extra Spacing:   (No, Yes)                   Baseline Bar: (Overlap, Separate)
   through Outline Level: [  ]                    Always Show Actuals: (  ,    )

  Scale:                                       Date Range:
   [1      ] inches per (H, D, W, Mo, Q, Y)     Starting:  [                    ]
  Gantt Section is 13 inches                    Ending  :  [                    ]
  Task Bar Labels
              Column Name (F2)            Width    Position:
  Label 1: [                          ] [   ]   (    ,     ,     ,     )
  Label 2: [                          ] [   ]   (    ,     ,     ,     )
  Label 3: [                          ] [   ]   (    ,     ,     ,     )
  Label 4: [                          ] [   ]   (    ,     ,     ,     )
                          GRAPHICS / Gantt Chart Form
      Num                 SAILBOAT End: 17-May-90  9:00am
```

***Fig. 8.30.** The Graphics/Gantt Chart Form.*

By this point, and if you're considering customizing a graphics report, you're probably proficient and perhaps even fluent with the mechanics of moving between fields, entering inputs, and marking choices. Accordingly, I'll simply describe in the paragraphs that follow exactly what the fields on the Graphics/Gantt Chart Form represent.

The Layout Name Field

The Layout Name field identifies the Gantt view layout Time Line will use to generate the Gantt chart. To see a list of the available layouts, press F2. Time Line then displays the Layout List box. Select the Gantt view layout you want to use from the Layout List box.

Note: Refer to Chapter 7, "Customizing Gantt, PERT, and Tree Chart and Screens," if you don't remember much about layouts. That chapter describes layouts, the Layout List box, and the steps for creating custom layouts.

The Palette Name Field

The Palette Name field identifies the colors that Time Line will use for the pieces of the Gantt chart. To see a list of the available palettes, press F2. Time Line then displays the Palette List box (not shown) which simply shows the predefined palettes. Choose a palette by highlighting one of those listed and pressing Enter. If you want to create or edit a palette, you do so in roughly the same way as you create or edit a layout. To edit a palette, highlight the palette you want to modify and then press F2. To create a palette from scratch, press Ins. In either case, Time Line next displays the Graphics/Gantt Palette Form (also not shown) which simply lists the parts of the Gantt chart and the default colors. You simply assign the colors you want. To assign colors, move the cursor to the field that identifies the chart part and press F2. Time Line displays a list of the available colors. Mark the color you want to use and then press Enter.

The Title & Legend Field

The Title & Legend field gives you an opportunity to specify what the Gantt Chart title should look like and whether a legend, or list of symbols and symbol explanations, should appear. The Title & Legend field works like the Layout and Palette fields: with the cursor positioned on the Title & Legend field, you press F2 to display a list box which shows the predefined Title & Legend settings. To edit a Title & Legend definition, highlight the definition you want to modify and then press F2. To create a definition from scratch, press Ins. Time Line displays the Graphics/Gantt Title Form (not shown) which simply gives you space to enter a title and notes and to specify whether you want a legend and, if you do, where you want it positioned.

Note: Because the Palette and Title & Legend Forms work similarly to the Layout Form screen, refer to Chapter 7's discussion of the Layout option if you have any trouble with creating or editing palette definitions or Title & Legend definitions.

The Print On Field

The Print On field lets you control whether the title, notes, and legend specified by the Title & Legend field prints on the first page or on each page.

If you set Print On to Each Page, Time Line also prints the first data column on each page. Data columns are specified by the layout. Typically, the first data column is either the Task name or the WBS Code field.

The Corners, Borders, Horizontal Grid, and Vertical Grid Field

The Corners field controls whether Time Line uses square or rounded corners for the border around the Gantt chart. The Borders field controls the type and thickness of lines that Time Line uses to draw the border about the Gantt chart: thin, thick, or double. The Horizontal Grid field lets you include thin, horizontal, dashed lines across the main part of a Gantt chart which may make it easier to tell which task bars go with which tasks. The Vertical Grid field lets you include thin, vertical dashed lines down the main part of the Gantt chart which may make it easier to tell when task bars start and stop.

Note: Gridlines tend to add visual precision to a Gantt chart at the expense of making it slightly less readable so you'll want to experiment with including and excluding gridlines.

The Extra Spacing and Through Outline Level Fields

The Extra Spacing and Through Outline Level fields let you control the spacing between the rows in the Gantt chart. If you want to put extra rows between the rows that actually show data or task bars, mark Yes. If you don't, mark No. If you do mark No, you can tell Time Line to use the extra row only through a certain level of tasks. If you enter a 0 in the Through Outline Level field, Time Line puts a blank row between every filled row. If you enter a 1, Time Line only puts a blank row before each first level task. (A first level task is a task that doesn't have a summary task about.) If you enter a 2, Time Line only puts a blank row before each first level task and before each second level—task which are the first level's subtasks. If you enter a 3, Time Line only puts blank row before each first, second, and third level task, and so on.

The Baseline Bar and Always Show Actuals Fields

If you created a baseline project schedule, you use the Baseline Bar and Always Show Actual fields to control how Time Line shows baseline information. (Refer to Chapter 6, "Monitoring Project Progress, Resources, and Costs" for information on setting and using baseline schedules.) With the Baseline Bar set to Overlap, Time Line shows the baseline schedule as thick shaded bars and shows the actual schedule as thin solid bars which overlap the thick shaded bars. (Baseline schedule milestones appear as big diamonds, and actual schedule milestones are displayed as little diamonds.) With the Baseline Bar set to Separate, Time Line shows the baseline schedule as a thick shaded bar and shows the actual schedule under the baseline schedule bars a thin line with triangles at either end. (Again, milestones are shown as diamonds, but this time an arrow points from the baseline milestone to the actual milestone.)

If you do set the Baseline Bar to Separate, you have the option of setting the Always Show Actuals field to No. Setting the Always Show Actuals to No field directs Time Line to print only the baseline bar if the baseline and actual bars are the same.

The Scale and Gantt Section Is Fields

For purposes of drawing a graphics Gantt chart, Time Line doesn't use the Layout's scale setting, but instead uses the Scale setting from the Graphics/Gantt Chart Form. The Graphics/Gantt Chart Forms Scale field lets you control how many inches Time Line uses to show a certain interval of time. You enter the number of inches and the time interval. So, for example, to specify that one inch should represent one month, you enter 1 in the Scale input field and then highlight Mo in the Scale per intervals settings. The settings you choose affect the width of the printed Gantt chart. These settings also determine the time units displayed on the horizontal time axis: Choose Hours to see hours, days, and months; Days to see days, months, and years; Weeks to see weeks, months, and years; Months to see Months and Years; Quarters to see quarters and years; and Years to see years.

As you enter Scale inputs, Time Line calculates the number of inches the actual task bars section of the Gantt chart takes based on your Scale inputs and enters this value in the Gantt Section Is field. You can use this information to get an idea of just how wide the printed Gantt chart will be.

Note: The printed Gantt chart will include both the task bar section of the Gantt chart, which is what is calculated in the Gantt Section is field, and the task data columns you specified on the Layout form. For more information on this topic, return to Chapter 7's discussion of the Layout option.

The Date Range Fields

The Data Range fields limit the period of time reported on the Gantt chart to a certain range of dates. Simply enter a starting and ending date. You can use any of the valid date formats. If you don't enter a start or end date, the chart's start date is the first task's start date and the ending date is the last task's end date. Your Date Range entries don't affect the task names printed on the Gantt Chart report so if you use the Date Range field, there may be tasks without task bars.

The Task Bar Labels Field

Task bar labels are individual pieces of task data that Time Line will print either to the left, to the right, directly above, or directly below the task bar to which they apply. Task bar labels give you the ability to include additional textual data in the middle of a Gantt chart. To see a list of the pieces of task data that Time Line collects, press F2 when the cursor rests on one of the Task Bar Label fields. Time Line will display a list of the data elements collected for a task. Using the arrow keys, mark the field you want to use and press Enter. More data elements exist than can appear in the list box at one time, so you can use the PgUp and PgDn keys to see different portions of the list.

Once you identify the data element you want to use for a task bar label, Time Line fills in the Width field with the actual maximum width of the data element, but you may want to limit the actual characters allowed for the label to something less than the maximum size of the data element. You can do this by changing the number Time Line inputs to something smaller. If Time Line can't fit a textual label into the allowed space, it truncates the label and indicates such with a + symbol at the end of the label. If Time Line can't fit a numeric value into the allowed space, it displays asterisks to show the value won't fit.

You also need to specify where you want the task bar label located. Do this by marking the Position field either Left. Right, Above, or Below.

Completing the Graphics/PERT Chart Form

Step 2 in the "Simple Printing of Gantt and PERT Charts" section also refers to the Graphics/PERT Chart Form (see fig. 8.31). This screen, like the Graphics/Gantt Chart Form described in the preceding section, gives you a series of options that let you customize the PERT chart that gets printed. As with the Graphics/Gantt Chart Form, you don't have to use the Graphics/PERT Chart Form because the screen's default settings work fine. The Graphics/PERT Chart Form, however, gives you the option of changing the standard appearance of a PERT chart. The paragraphs that follow describe how to fill the fields on the Graphics/PERT Chart Form.

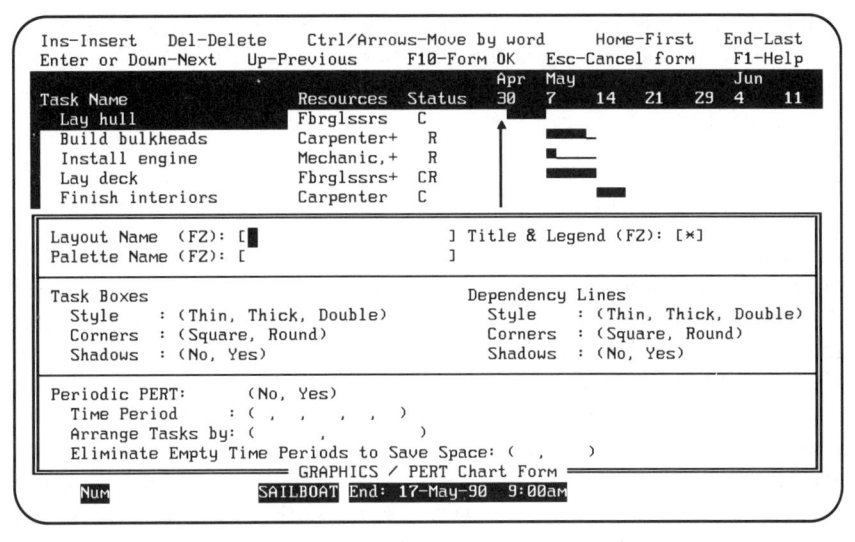

```
Ins-Insert    Del-Delete    Ctrl/Arrows-Move by word    Home-First    End-Last
Enter or Down-Next    Up-Previous    F10-Form OK    Esc-Cancel form    F1-Help
                                            Apr  May              Jun
Task Name              Resources  Status    30   7   14   21  29   4    11
   Lay hull            Fbrglssrs     C
   Build bulkheads     Carpenter+    R
   Install engine      Mechanic,+    R
   Lay deck            Fbrglssrs+    CR
   Finish interiors    Carpenter     C

Layout Name  (F2): [ ]              ] Title & Legend (F2): [*]
Palette Name (F2): [                ]

Task Boxes                          Dependency Lines
   Style   : (Thin, Thick, Double)     Style   : (Thin, Thick, Double)
   Corners : (Square, Round)           Corners : (Square, Round)
   Shadows : (No, Yes)                 Shadows : (No, Yes)

Periodic PERT:        (No, Yes)
   Time Period      : ( , , , )
   Arrange Tasks by : (     ,     )
   Eliminate Empty Time Periods to Save Space: (    ,    )
============== GRAPHICS / PERT Chart Form ==============
   NUM           SAILBOAT  End: 17-May-90  9:00am
```

Fig. 8.31. The Graphics/PERT Chart Form.

The Layout Name Field

The Layout Name field identifies the PERT view layout Time Line will use to generate the PERT chart. To see a list of the available layouts, press F2. Time Line then displays the Layout List box. Select the PERT view layout you want to use from the Layout List box.

Note: Refer to Chapter 7, "Customizing Gantt, PERT, and Tree Chart Screens," if you don't remember much about layouts. That chapter describes layouts and the Layout list box and explains how to create custom layouts.

The Palette Name Field

The Palette Name field identifies the colors that Time Line will use for the pieces of the PERT chart. To see a list of the available palettes, press F2. Time Line then displays the Palette List box (not shown) which shows the predefined palettes. Choose a palette by highlighting one of those listed and pressing Enter.

If you want to create or edit a palette, you do so in basically the same way you create or edit a layout. To edit a palette, highlight the palette you want to modify and then press F2. To create a palette from scratch, press Ins. In either case, Time Line next displays the Graphics/PERT Palette Form (also not shown) which simply lists the parts of the PERT chart and the default colors. You simply assign the colors you want. To assign colors, move the cursor to the field that identifies the chart part and press F2. Time Line displays a list of the available colors. Mark the color you want to use and then press Enter.

The Title & Legend Field

The Title & Legend field gives you an opportunity to specify what the PERT chart title should look like and whether a legend, or list of symbols and symbol explanations, should appear. The Title & Legend field works like the Layout and Palette fields: With the cursor positioned on the Title & Legend field, press F2 to display a list box which shows the predefined Title & Legend settings. To edit a Title & Legend definition, highlight the definition you want to modify and then press F2. To create a definition from scratch, press Ins. Time Line displays the Graphics/PERT Title Form (not shown) which simply gives you space to enter a title and notes and lets you specify whether you want a legend and where you want the legend positioned.

Note: Because the Palette and Title & Legend Forms work similarly to the Layout Form, you may want to refer to Chapter 7's discussion of the Layout option if you have any trouble with creating or editing Palette definitions or Title & Legend definitions.

The Task Box Style, Corners, and Shadows Fields

The Task Box Style, Corners and Shadows fields control how Time Line draws the boxes that represent tasks in a PERT chart. All of these fields are probably self-explanatory. The Style field controls whether Time Line uses thin, thick, or double (thin) lines to draw the boxes. Thin lines, by the way, are the thinnest lines your printer or plotter can draw. Thick lines are equivalent to four or five thin lines. Double lines use two thin lines with the gap between the two lines shaded.

The Corners field controls whether Time Line draws square or rounded corners on the boxes that represent tasks.

If you set the Corners setting to square, you have the option of directing Time Line to draw a shadow behind the box to give the illusion of three dimensionality.

The Dependency Line Style, Corners, and Shadows Fields

The Dependency Line Style, Corners and Shadows fields work like the Task

Box Style, Corners, and Shadows fields. The only difference is that the Dependency fields control how Time Line draws the lines between the boxes that show the dependencies. All of the these fields are probably self-explanatory, but if you have questions, refer to the earlier discussion of the Task Box fields.

The Periodic PERT Field

Normally, a PERT chart focuses on the tasks that make up a project and the relationships, or dependencies, between those tasks. It doesn't, however, visually incorporate the project's visual time scale. Time Line gives you the option of creating a periodic PERT chart which includes a horizontal time scale across the top of the page and then draws task boxes so the left edge of the task box aligns with the task's start date. To direct Time Line to draw a Period PERT chart, set the Periodic PERT field to Yes.

The Time Period Field

If the Periodic PERT field is set to Yes, Time Line lets you move the cursor to the Time Period field which you use to choose the time units for calibrating the horizontal timescale: Days, Weeks, Months, Quarters, or Years. Time Line uses one column for each time unit you specify, and the columns are wide enough to hold an entire task box. Accordingly, if your project covers a long time period and you use small time periods, a periodic PERT chart becomes very wide. The time unit you choose also effects which time intervals show on the horizontal time scale. If you choose Days, Time Line shows days, months, and years. If you choose Weeks, Time Line shows weeks, months, and years. If you choose Months, Time Line shows months and years. If you choose Quarters, Time Line shows quarters and years. If you choose Years, Time Line shows only years.

The Arrange Tasks by Field

With the Periodic PERT field is set to Yes, Time Line also lets you move the cursor to the Arrange Tasks by field which you use to indicate whether Time Line should use the actual or the baseline start dates for positioning the task boxes on the PERT chart. Actual, of course, indicates the actual start date; and baseline indicates the baseline start date.

The Eliminate Empty Time Periods to Save Space Field

There's one final field that applies when the Periodic PERT field is set to Yes:

the Eliminate Empty Time Periods to Save Space field. This field lets you direct Time Line to omit columns that represent time intervals during which no tasks start. Setting the Eliminate Empty Time Periods field to Yes should compress the timescale and, therefore, reduce the width of PERT chart. However, this field also makes the timescale more difficult to read because it doesn't include certain time intervals.

Completing the Graphics/Chart Size Form

Step 3 in the Simple Printing of Gantt and PERT Charts section refers to the Graphics/Chart Size Form screen (see fig. 8.32). This screen lets you change the default size of a graphical Gantt chart or a PERT chart. Now you don't have to change the default size, but often it's handy to do so. You might, for instance, want to shrink a chart so it fits on a single page. Or you might want to expand a chart so it's easier to read. The paragraphs that follow describe how to use the fields on the Graphics/Chart Size Form screen.

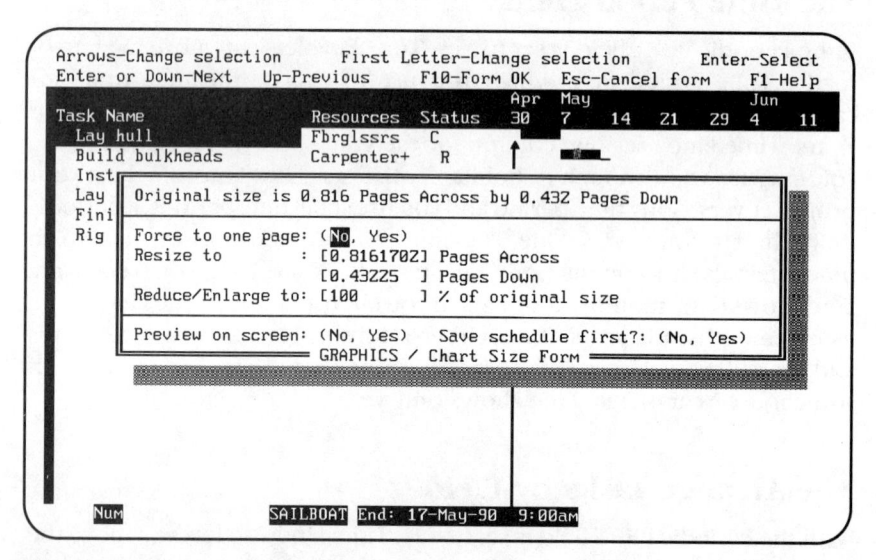

Fig. 8.32. The Graphics/Chart Size Form.

The Force to One Page Field

The Force to One Page field is self-explanatory. This field either shrinks or expands a Gantt chart or PERT chart so that the chart takes up a full page.

The Resize to Pages Across and Pages Down Fields

The original chart size, calibrated in pages, shows at the top of the Graphics/Chart Size Form. If you want to change the size of a chart without forcing it to fit on just one page, you can use the Resize fields to shrink or expand the chart so that it uses a certain number of pages for its width or a certain number of pages for its height.

The Reduce/Enlarge to Field

The Reduce/Enlarge to field lets you shrink or expand the chart to a certain percentage of the original size. (You may be familiar with the Zoom function that's available on many photocopier machines: The Reduce/Enlarge to field works the same way.)

Note: The Resize fields and the Reduce/Enlarge fields work in tandem. If you change the Resize fields, Time Line calculates the Reduce/Enlarge percentage that your Resize entries represent. And if you change the Reduce/Enlarge percentage, Time Line calculates the resulting size in Pages Across and Pages Down.

The Preview on screen Field

The Preview on screen field controls whether Time Line first displays the chart on the screen or instead prints the chart on your printer. The default setting is Yes, which gives you the option to review the chart prior to printing. Alternatively, you can skip the preview.

Chapter Summary

This chapter described how and why you use each of the Report and Graphics menu options to produce project management reports—activities that are usually of critical importance to projects. The reason for this is that Time Line reports help you to communicate complete project information to everyone involved in a project—an integral step in ensuring project success.

The next chapter covers an equally important topic: working with the Time Line files that contain the project, task, and resource information.

9

Working with the Time Line Files

As you use Time Line, you need to know how to work with the files that contain the project, task, and resource information. First, you obviously need to know how to save and later retrieve the projects. You also need to know how to create backup copies of the project files in case a file is irreparably damaged through either human or hardware error. As your use of Time Line becomes more frequent, you may also want to remove projects that you no longer need, use tasks or resources from existing projects to create entirely new projects, and even export and import files between Time Line and other application programs.

Covering the Basics of File Management

Several basic file management operations are important for everyone who uses Time Line. These basics include the following:

1. Saving a project for the first time (also covered in Chapter 3)
2. Resaving a project
3. Renaming and relocating project files
4. Retrieving a project file (also covered in Chapter 3)
5. Erasing files

6. Backing up and restoring project files

The next several pages cover these basic operations. If you already read Chapter 3, you can probably skip the sections on saving a project for the first time and retrieving a project because these techniques are described there.

Saving a Project for the First Time

After you finish creating a calendar, adding tasks, and defining task dependencies, you'll want to save the project. Saving a project simply takes a copy of the project file in memory and stores it on your hard disk. To save the project for the first time, take the following three steps:

1. Activate the menu bar and select the File option. Time Line displays the File menu (see fig. 9.1). Select the Save option from the File submenu.

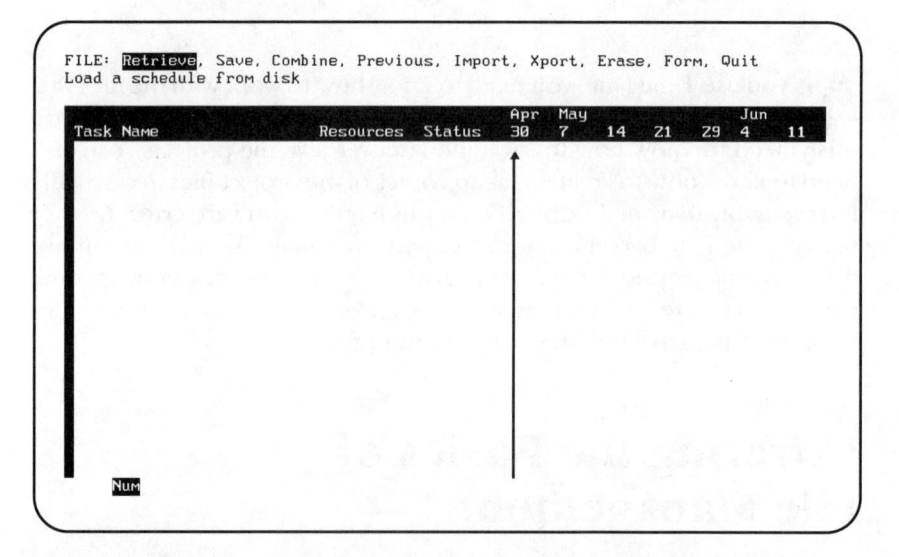

```
FILE: Retrieve, Save, Combine, Previous, Import, Xport, Erase, Form, Quit
Load a schedule from disk
```

                                                Apr May   Jun
Task Name   Resources   Status   30   7   14   21   29 4   11

Fig. 9.1. The File menu.

2. After you select the Save Option, Time Line displays the No Name box (see fig. 9.2). The No Name box gives you the choice of canceling the save operation, naming the schedule and saving it, or saving only the global options. By default, Time Line highlights the Name this Schedule option, so if you want to name and save the schedule, just press Enter. Alternatively, if you just want to save the options—the options include the printer and video configurations—use the arrow keys to highlight Options only and then press Enter.

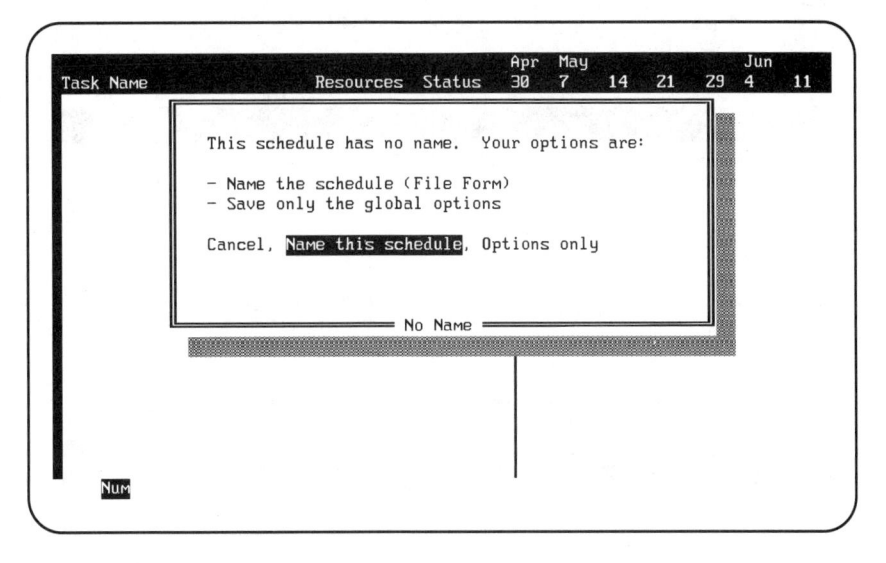

```
                                  Apr  May              Jun
    Task Name        Resources Status 30   7   14   21  29   4   11

         ┌─────────────────────────────────────────┐
         │  This schedule has no name. Your options are: │
         │                                         │
         │  - Name the schedule (File Form)        │
         │  - Save only the global options         │
         │                                         │
         │  Cancel, Name this schedule, Options only │
         │                                         │
         │                                         │
         │              ══ No Name ══              │
         └─────────────────────────────────────────┘

    NUM
```

Fig. 9.2. The No Name Box.

3. If you selected Name this Schedule in step 2, Time Line displays the File Save Form box at the bottom of the screen (see fig. 9.3). In the DOS file field, type the file name you want to use. Valid DOS file names can be up to eight characters long, using letters and numbers but not blanks, and can use several symbols including:

   ' ~ ! @ # $ % ^ & ( ) _ - { } '

   In the DOS file extension field, Time Line displays the characters T$0 which it will use as file extension. You can, however, choose to use another file extension by entering three different characters. File extensions can use all the same characters as file names.

3. In the Directory field, Time Line displays the default pathname used to store Time Line files, C:\TL4\DATA. You can change this if you want by replacing the default entry with some new entry. Whatever you enter, however, needs to be a valid pathname: The drive letter must represent a valid disk drive, the directory must already be defined on that disk drive, and the subdirectory must be defined and located in the directory.

4. When the File Save Form box is complete, press F10 to save the project using the specified name in the indicated directory. If you haven't recalculated the schedule since the last

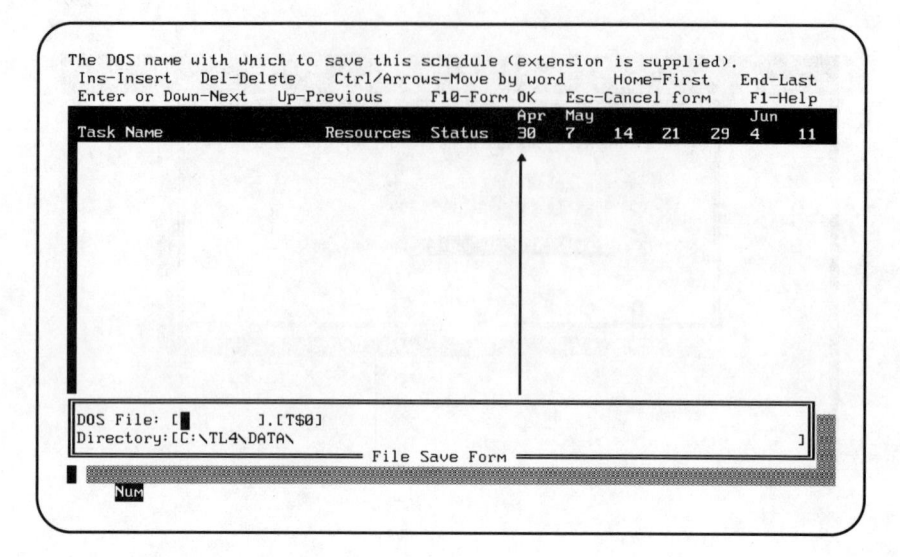

```
The DOS name with which to save this schedule (extension is supplied).
  Ins-Insert    Del-Delete    Ctrl/Arrows-Move by word    Home-First    End-Last
  Enter or Down-Next    Up-Previous    F10-Form OK    Esc-Cancel form    F1-Help
                                            Apr  May                    Jun
Task Name                    Resources Status 30   7    14   21   29   4    11











DOS File: [       ].[T$0]
Directory:[C:\TL4\DATA\                                                        ]
                        ══════ File Save Form ══════
  Num
```

Fig. 9.3. The File Save Form box.

change to the schedule, Time Line will ask whether you want to recompute the schedule before saving. Answer Yes or No depending on whether you want the project file to be up-to-date.

Resaving a Project

After you've saved a project file once, you follow a slightly different procedure to save it the second and all subsequent times. To resave a project, you follow these steps:

1. Activate the menu bar and select File Save. Time Line displays the Replace File box (see fig. 9.4) which indicates that the file you want to save already exists and which asks whether you want to replace the old version of the file, make a copy of the file under a new name, extract some of the tasks in the file to a separate file, or save only the global options.

2. You then have two options:

    A. If you want to replace the original copy of the file, use the arrow keys to highlight Replace and then press Enter. Time Line then resaves the project file under its original name.

Chapter 9: Working with the Time Line Files **259**

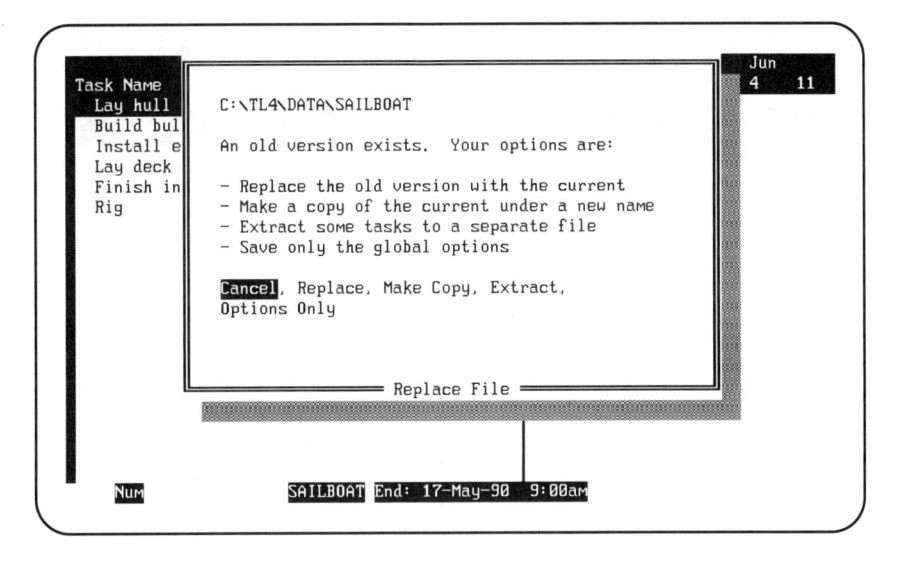

```
                                                              Jun
  Task Name                                                   4    11
   Lay hull    ┌──────────────────────────────────────────┐
   Build bul   │ C:\TL4\DATA\SAILBOAT                     │
   Install e   │                                          │
   Lay deck    │ An old version exists.  Your options are:│
   Finish in   │                                          │
   Rig         │ - Replace the old version with the current│
               │ - Make a copy of the current under a new name│
               │ - Extract some tasks to a separate file  │
               │ - Save only the global options           │
               │                                          │
               │ [Cancel], Replace, Make Copy, Extract,   │
               │ Options Only                             │
               │                                          │
               │══════════════ Replace File ══════════════│
               └──────────────────────────────────────────┘

  Num          SAILBOAT End: 17-May-90  9:00am
```

Fig. 9.4. The Replace File box.

    B. If you want to make a copy of the original file under a new name, use the arrow keys to highlight Make Copy and then press Enter. Time Line next displays the File Save Form box (refer to fig. 9.3). Enter the new name or directory and then press F10. Time Line saves the file using the name and directory you specified on the File Save Form box.

Renaming and Relocating Project Files

You use may want to use a file name or the location that differs from the original name and location. To do so, follow these steps:

1. Activate the menu bar and select File Form. Time Line displays the File Form box (see fig. 9.5).

2. The File Form specifies the file name and the directory that Time Line uses when you execute the File Save option to replace the original file. Enter the file name and directory you want to use and then press F10.

    Note: You can also specify how many old versions Time Line keeps around on disk. Time Line differentiates versions by their file extensions. The newest version uses the file extension T$0. The next newest uses T$1, the one after that uses T$2, and so on.

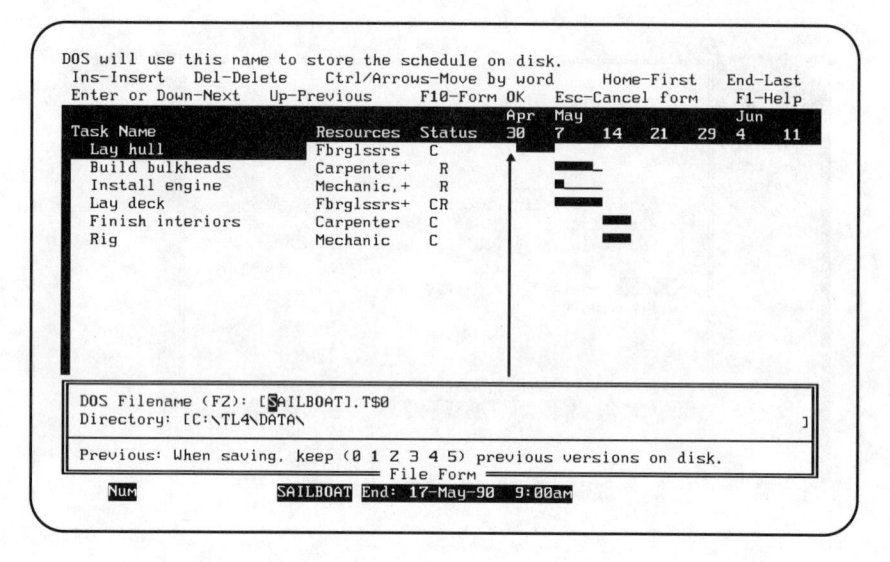

```
DOS will use this name to store the schedule on disk.
   Ins-Insert   Del-Delete   Ctrl/Arrows-Move by word    Home-First   End-Last
   Enter or Down-Next   Up-Previous    F10-Form OK    Esc-Cancel form   F1-Help
                                               Apr May              Jun
Task Name                  Resources Status  30  7   14   21   29   4   11
   Lay hull                Fbrglssrs   C
   Build bulkheads         Carpenter+  R
   Install engine          Mechanic,+  R
   Lay deck                Fbrglssrs+  CR
   Finish interiors        Carpenter   C
   Rig                     Mechanic    C




  DOS Filename (F2): [SAILBOAT].T$0
  Directory: [C:\TL4\DATA\                                             ]
  Previous: When saving, keep (0 1 2 3 4 5) previous versions on disk.
 ══════════════════════════════ File Form ══════════════════════════════
   Num                SAILBOAT End: 17-May-90  9:00am
```

Fig. 9.5. *The File Form.*

3. After you complete the File Form, follow the steps described earlier for resaving a file. When you resave the file, Time Line will use the new file name and directory as specified in the File Form.

Retrieving the Project

To retrieve a project file you've previously saved on your hard disk, take these steps:

1. Activate the menu bar and select File Retrieve. Time Line displays the Directory List box (see fig. 9.6). It shows all the projects in the default directory (C:\TL4\DATA) that have the file extension T$0, which Time Line uses to show the most recent versions of each project file.

Tip If you want to see more than just the most recent files, you can display all previous versions by activating the menu bar and selecting File Previous. Time Line then displays a Directory List screen which lists all the projects in the default directory with the file extension T$?, which includes T$0, T$1, T$2, and so on.

Chapter 9: Working with the Time Line Files

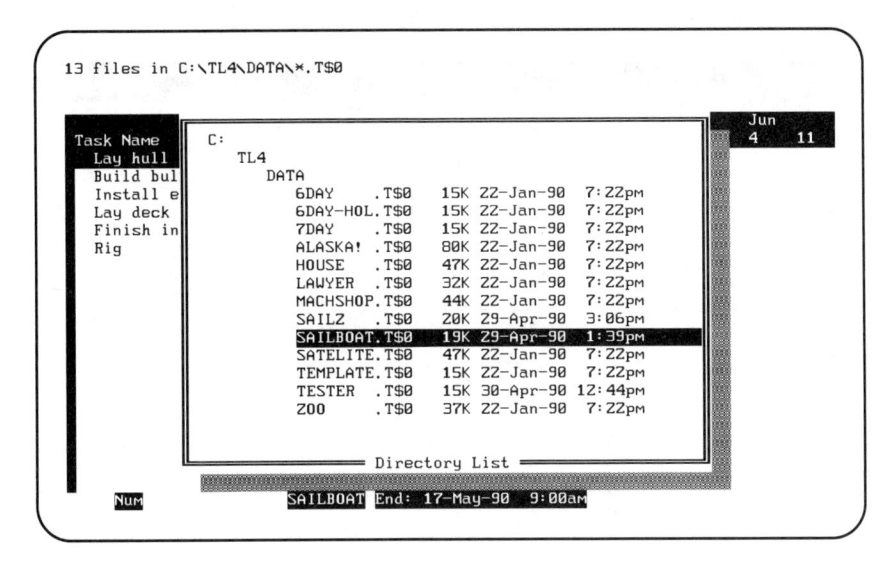

```
13 files in C:\TL4\DATA\*.T$0
                                                                    Jun
                                                                    4    11
Task Name    C:
  Lay hull     TL4
  Build bul        DATA
  Install e           6DAY       .T$0   15K 22-Jan-90   7:22pm
  Lay deck            6DAY-HOL.T$0      15K 22-Jan-90   7:22pm
  Finish in           7DAY       .T$0   15K 22-Jan-90   7:22pm
  Rig                 ALASKA!    .T$0   80K 22-Jan-90   7:22pm
                      HOUSE      .T$0   47K 22-Jan-90   7:22pm
                      LAWYER     .T$0   32K 22-Jan-90   7:22pm
                      MACHSHOP.T$0      44K 22-Jan-90   7:22pm
                      SAILZ      .T$0   20K 29-Apr-90   3:06pm
                      SAILBOAT.T$0      19K 29-Apr-90   1:39pm
                      SATELITE.T$0      47K 22-Jan-90   7:22pm
                      TEMPLATE.T$0      15K 22-Jan-90   7:22pm
                      TESTER     .T$0   15K 30-Apr-90  12:44pm
                      ZOO        .T$0   37K 22-Jan-90   7:22pm

                              Directory List
  Num              SAILBOAT End: 17-May-90   9:00am
```

Fig. 9.6. Time Line displays the Directory List when you select File Retrieve or File Previous.

2. (Optional) To change the disk, highlight the disk letter and press the – key. Time Line displays the other disks on your computer. Mark the disk for which you want to see directories and then press the + key.

3. (Optional) To change the directory, highlight the current directory and press the + key to cause Time Line to display a list of the directories at the same level as the selected directory. Highlight the directory from the list you want and then press the + key. Time Line then displays the files in the newly selected directory.

4. Use the arrow keys to highlight the project you want to retrieve. When the project is highlighted, press Enter. Time Line retrieves the project and then displays it.

5. If you previously retrieved a project or started to create a project, Time Line displays the message box (see fig. 9.7) that alerts you that retrieving a new file will erase the schedule already stored in memory. To continue, select Erase Schedule in Memory by typing an E or by using the arrow keys to highlight Erase Schedule in Memory and then pressing Enter.

Note: Erasing the schedule in memory doesn't erase the schedule saved on disk.

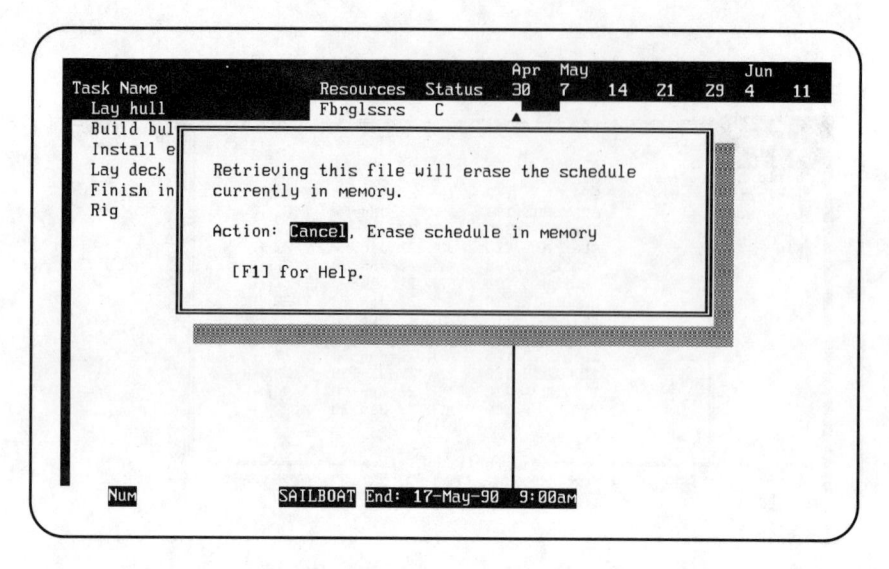

```
                                       Apr May              Jun
Task Name          Resources Status    30  7  14  21  29   4   11
Lay hull           Fbrglssrs  C
Build bul
Install e
Lay deck    Retrieving this file will erase the schedule
Finish in   currently in memory.
Rig
            Action: Cancel, Erase schedule in memory

            [F1] for Help.



Num            SAILBOAT End: 17-May-90  9:00am
```

Fig. 9.7. The message box that alerts you retrieving a new file will erase the schedule already stored in memory.

Erasing Files

Occasionally, you'll need to erase project files you've previously created. You might, for instance, want to get rid of old project files you know you'll never look at again. Or you might want to remove project files you've already stored on floppy disks or tape.

Tip Let me issue a caveat here: Be careful about erasing files. You should consider erasing as equivalent to permanently destroying the files. If you do unintentionally erase a file and don't have a backup copy of the file, you have two choices:

1. Re-create the project from scratch (which may not be all that difficult if you've only got a handful of tasks, dependencies, and relationships.)

2. Immediately turn off your computer without saving any files or running any other programs, run down to the local computer store, purchase one of the disk utilities packages (such as PC Tools Deluxe, Norton Utilities, or Mace Utilities) that let you undelete the files, and then try to undelete the files, using an undelete utility. For beginners, this may not be all that feasible but at least you should be aware that it is a possibility—especially if you've erased a project with many tasks, dependencies, and resources.

To use the Erase Option, you follow these steps:

1. Activate the menu bar and select File Erase. Time Line displays the Erase submenu (see fig. 9.8) which lists the five categories of files Time Line will list so you can erase them: Current Time Line Files (files that use the file extension T$0), Any Time Line files, Time Line Version 2 files, Time Line Version 3 files, and Any DOS Files.

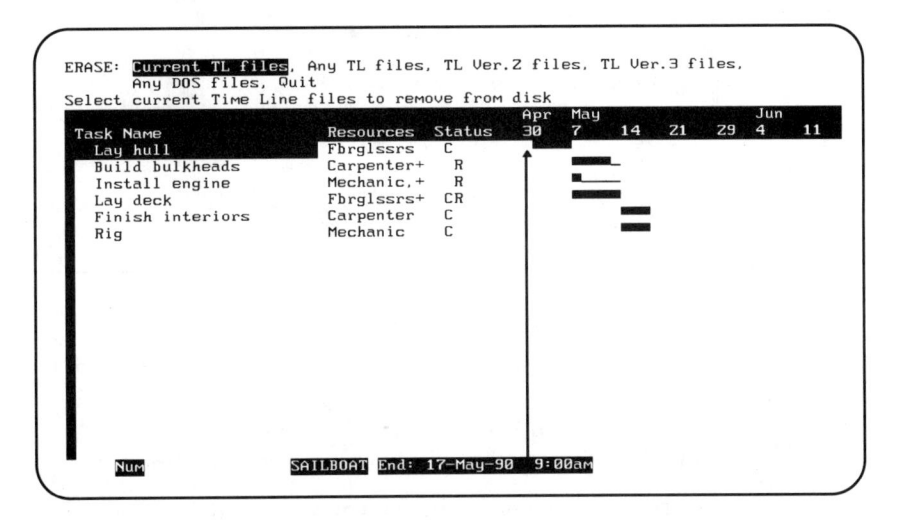

```
ERASE: Current TL files, Any TL files, TL Ver.2 files, TL Ver.3 files,
       Any DOS files, Quit
Select current Time Line files to remove from disk
                                          Apr  May              Jun
Task Name            Resources  Status    30   7    14   21  29  4   11
  Lay hull           Fbrglssrs    C
  Build bulkheads    Carpenter+   R
  Install engine     Mechanic,+   R
  Lay deck           Fbrglssrs+   CR
  Finish interiors   Carpenter    C
  Rig                Mechanic     C




 Num                 SAILBOAT End: 17-May-90   9:00am
```

Fig. 9.8. The File Erase submenu.

2. Highlight the option that describes the general category of Files you want to erase. Time Line displays the File Erase box (see fig. 9.9) which identifies the current disk and directory and then lists the files in that directory that fall into the erase category you chose.

3. (Optional) You can then change the disk or directory specification.

   A. (Optional) To change the disk, highlight the disk letter and press the – key. Time Line displays the other disks on your computer. Mark the disk for which you want to see directories and then press the + key.

   B. (Optional) To change the directory, highlight the current directory and press the + key to cause Time Line to display a list of the directories at the same level as the selected directory. Highlight the directory from the list you want and then press the + key. Time Line then displays the files in the newly selected directory that fall into the erase category you identified in step 2.

Part III: Managing the System

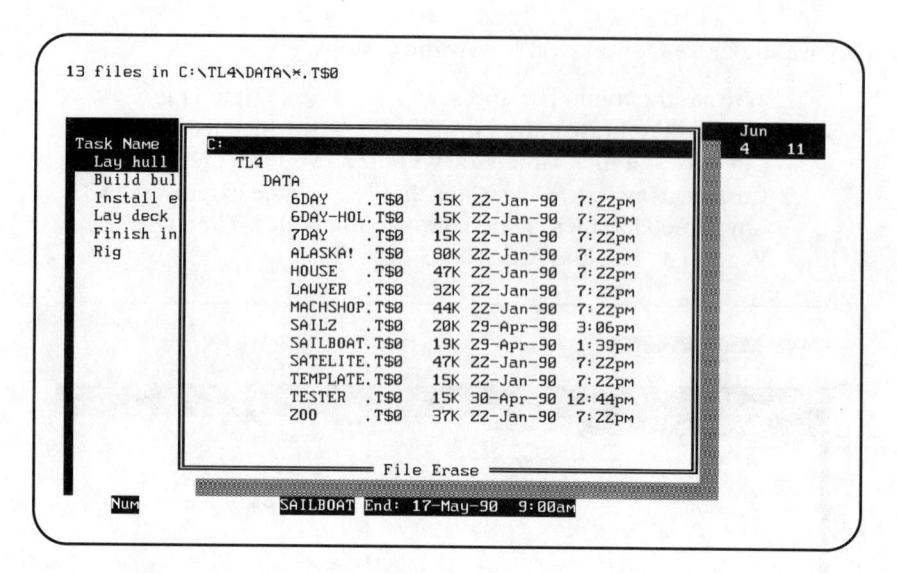

```
13 files in C:\TL4\DATA\*.T$0

Task Name        C:                                              Jun
  Lay hull          TL4                                           4    11
  Build bul           DATA
  Install e             6DAY      .T$0   15K  22-Jan-90   7:22pm
  Lay deck              6DAY-HOL.T$0    15K  22-Jan-90   7:22pm
  Finish in             7DAY      .T$0   15K  22-Jan-90   7:22pm
  Rig                   ALASKA!   .T$0   80K  22-Jan-90   7:22pm
                        HOUSE     .T$0   47K  22-Jan-90   7:22pm
                        LAWYER    .T$0   32K  22-Jan-90   7:22pm
                        MACHSHOP.T$0    44K  22-Jan-90   7:22pm
                        SAILZ     .T$0   20K  29-Apr-90   3:06pm
                        SAILBOAT.T$0    19K  29-Apr-90   1:39pm
                        SATELITE.T$0    47K  22-Jan-90   7:22pm
                        TEMPLATE.T$0    15K  22-Jan-90   7:22pm
                        TESTER    .T$0   15K  30-Apr-90  12:44pm
                        ZOO       .T$0   37K  22-Jan-90   7:22pm

                           ══════ File Erase ══════
  Num             SAILBOAT End: 17-May-90   9:00am
```

Fig. 9.9. The File Erase box.

> *Note:* As with other list boxes in Time Line, you use the arrow keys to move the highlight to different items on the list. If the list is too big to fit on just one screen, you can also use the PgUp and PgDn keys to display different portions of the list.

4. Use the arrow keys to mark the file you want to delete and then press Enter. Time Line displays a message box that asks you to confirm that you want to erase the file.

5. To erase the highlighted file, select Proceed. Time Line deletes the file from your hard disk and then redisplays the File Erase box.

6. If you want to erase another file, repeat steps 3 through 5, otherwise press Esc twice to return to the main Time Line screen.

Backing up Project Files

Time Line maintains several versions of a project file on your disk, but you need to know how to create backup copies of the file. Backup copies of files minimize—and come close to eliminating—the chance that you'll lose a project file because of a hardware failure, software bug, or human error.

Because Time Line doesn't provide a built-in backup function, you'll need to use the DOS backup function which you can do by following these steps:

1. (Optional) If you're currently in Time Line, move to the DOS prompt by activating the menu bar and then select Utilities, Exit to DOS, and Quick Exit (Chapter 10 describes the Utilities menu options in more detail).

2. Insert a blank, formatted disk into the A disk drive.

3. Type the following command at the DOS C:> prompt to backup the contents of the Time Line data directory to the A drive:

    backup c:\tl4\data*.t$0 a: /s

    DOS then copies all of the most recent project files in the data directory in the TL4 directory to the floppy disk drive in the A drive. The T$0 file extension is the one used for the most recent version of a project file.

    For example, if you wanted to copy the sailboat project files, you would type the following command instead:

    backup c:\tl4\data\sailboat.t$0 a: /s

4. Put the backup copy of the project file or files away in a safe place.

5. (Optional) If you exited to DOS from Time Line, type *exit* at the DOS prompt to return to Time Line.

Refer to the DOS users manual that came with your computer for help on using the BACKUP command and formatting floppy disks.   *Tip*

Backing up your files is that simple. But you also need to make two important decisions. First, you must decide how often you need to back up your files. Opinions vary regarding how frequent is frequent enough. My feeling is that you should backup your project management files immediately after you complete any session in which you enter or edit tasks, dependencies, or resources. After you've worked with the Time Line program for a while, however, you'll be able to judge for yourself what makes the most sense for your specific situation.

A related question involves the number of old backup copies you should keep. Usually two or three copies are adequate. (This rule of thumb is known as the "grandfather, father, son" scheme.) For example, suppose that you backup your project management files every day. On Thursday, a hard disk failure destroys, among other things, the file for a critical project you're managing. If you kept two backup copies in addition to the most recent backup copy, you have not only the Wednesday copy, but also the

Tuesday copy. So if the Wednesday copy is somehow damaged (an unlikely but still possible situation), you still have the Tuesday and Monday copies to restore. Obviously, the more recent a backup copy, the easier it is to recover because you'll need to re-enter the work you did since the backup occurred. But even using an old backup copy is easier than recovering with no backup files.

Be sure to keep the backup copy of your project file in a safe place. You should not keep all the backup copies in the same location. If your business suffers a fire, for instance, you might lose all copies—no matter how many backups you kept. Store at least one copy at an off-site location, such as your safety deposit box at the bank or at home.

Restoring Project Files

Eventually someone will trip over the computer power cord, or power outage will occur because of an electrical storm or a brownout. You may even be so unlucky as to have your computer malfunction or have someone spill the contents of a cup of coffee into you computer. In any of these cases, there's a chance you'll lose the project file or files stored on your hard disk. But thankfully, this loss only needs to be an inconvenience instead of a disaster if you've backed up your project file or files as described in the preceding section. If you did backup your files, you can restore them by following the steps listed below:

1. (Optional) If you're currently in Time Line, move to the DOS prompt by activating the menu bar and then select Utilities, Exit to DOS, and Quick Exit (Chapter 10 describes the Utilities menu options in more detail).

2. Insert your most recent backup disk in the A disk drive.

3. Type the following command at the DOS C:> prompt to restore the contents of the Time Line data directory from the floppy disk in the A: drive:

    restore a: c:\tl4\data\ a: /s

   DOS then copies all of the backup project files on the floppy disk drive in A to the data directory in the TL4 directory.

4. (Optional) If you exited to DOS from Time Line, type *exit* at the DOS prompt to return to Time Line.

5. Input the tasks, dependency, and resources changes you entered between the time you last backed up and the time you restored.

> Refer to DOS user manual that came with your computer for help or additional information on the RESTORE command.
>
> *Tip*

Advanced File Management Operations

Time Line provides three advanced file management tools for users who aren't afraid to go beyond the basics. If you're comfortable with the file operations described earlier in the chapter, you probably want to at least familiarize yourself with the three advanced file operations that Time Line provides. These three file operations are

1. Combining two project files

2. Exporting files to other application programs like Lotus 1-2-3 or dBASE III, and

3. Importing files from other applications programs like Lotus 1-2-3 or dBASE III

Combining Files

Combining files simply means copying part of another project file into the current project schedule. There are seven variations of the file combine operation. Each copies some portion or part of a source project file on disk into the project currently in memory. The seven file combine operations are

1. *Task/Resources/Costs*, which copies all the parts of a source project file

2. *Resources/Costs*, which copies only the resource and cost parts of a source project file

3. *Calendar*, which copies only the calendar information from a source project file (as long as the project file currently in memory is empty)

4. *Filters*, which copies the filters from a source project file

5. *Journal Notes*, which copies the notes in the journal list from a source project file

6. *Layouts*, which copies the layouts from the source project file

7. *Graph Palettes*, which copies the graphics color palettes from a source project file

I won't spend time here describing each of these parts because that's already been covered earlier in the book. If you would like a refresher about any of these, however, you might find it helpful to skim over earlier chapters. Chapter 3 describes how calendars are defined, Chapter 4 describes how to create and use journal notes, Chapter 5 describes how resources and costs are defined, Chapter 7 describes how to create and use filters and layouts, and Chapter 8 describes graphics color palettes.

To initiate a File Combine operation, follow these steps:

1. Activate the menu bar and then select File Combine. Time Line displays a Directory List box which shows the files in the current directory (see fig. 9.10).

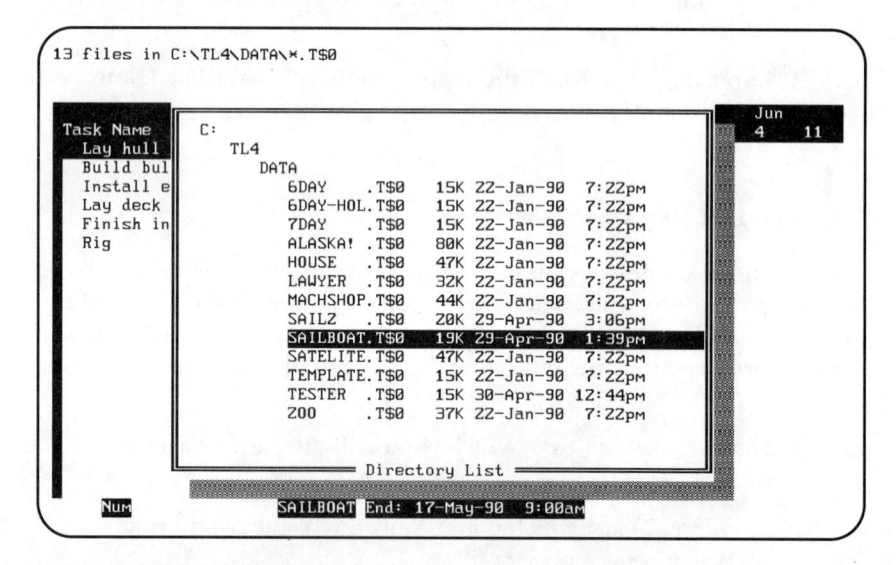

```
13 files in C:\TL4\DATA\*.T$0

                                                            Jun
Task Name   C:                                              4    11
  Lay hull     TL4
  Build bul       DATA
  Install e          6DAY     .T$0    15K 22-Jan-90  7:22pm
  Lay deck           6DAY-HOL.T$0    15K 22-Jan-90  7:22pm
  Finish in          7DAY     .T$0    15K 22-Jan-90  7:22pm
  Rig                ALASKA!  .T$0    80K 22-Jan-90  7:22pm
                     HOUSE    .T$0    47K 22-Jan-90  7:22pm
                     LAWYER   .T$0    32K 22-Jan-90  7:22pm
                     MACHSHOP.T$0    44K 22-Jan-90  7:22pm
                     SAILZ    .T$0    20K 29-Apr-90  3:06pm
                     SAILBOAT.T$0    19K 29-Apr-90  1:39pm
                     SATELITE.T$0    47K 22-Jan-90  7:22pm
                     TEMPLATE.T$0    15K 22-Jan-90  7:22pm
                     TESTER   .T$0    15K 30-Apr-90 12:44pm
                     ZOO      .T$0    37K 22-Jan-90  7:22pm

                     ════ Directory List ════

 Num              SAILBOAT End: 17-May-90  9:00am
```

Fig. 9.10. *The Directory List box.*

2. You then have the option of changing the disk and directory.

    A. (Optional) To change the disk, highlight the disk letter and press the - key. Time Line displays the other disks on your computer. Mark the disk for which you want to see directories and then press the + key.

    B. (Optional) To change the directory, highlight the current directory and press the + key to cause Time Line to display a list of the directories at the same level as the selected directory. Highlight the directory from the list you want and then press the + key. Time Line then displays the files in the newly selected directory.

3. Use the arrow keys to mark the source project file you want to use in the file combine operation and then press Enter. Time Line displays the File Combine box (see fig. 9.11). It asks which of the seven file combine operations you want to execute.

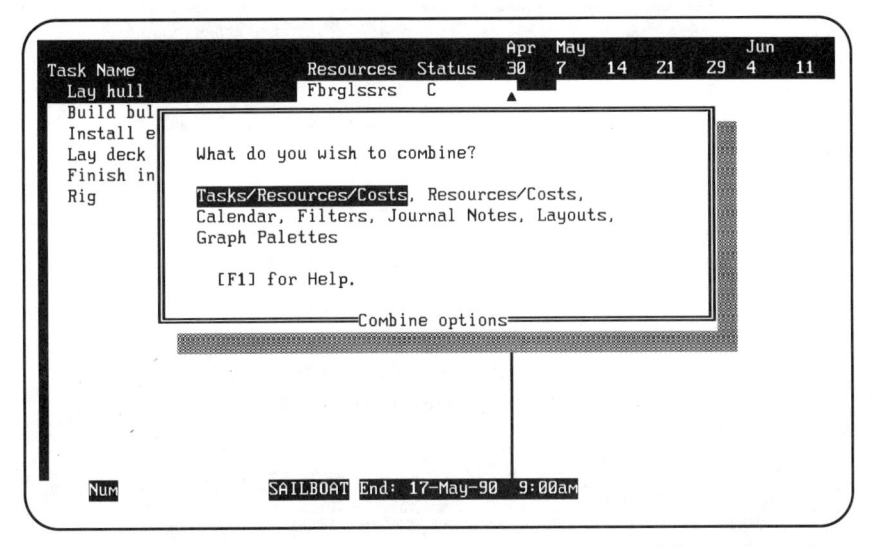

Fig. 9.11. The Combine Options box shows the seven varieties of the combine operation.

4. Use the arrow keys to highlight the type of file combine operation you want and then press Enter.

5. If you select the Tasks/Resources/Costs combine, Time Line next displays a message box (see fig. 9.12) that asks whether or not you want to create a top-level, or first level, task that acts as summary task of the tasks coming from the source project file. If you do, mark Yes and press Enter. (Time Line names a summary task created this way as Summary of and then the source file name.)

6. If you select the Tasks/Resources/Costs combine Time Line also asks, using the message box shown in figure 9.13, whether, if the calendars of the two projects differ, it should use the incoming tasks durations or their start and end dates to show when they occur and how long they will take to

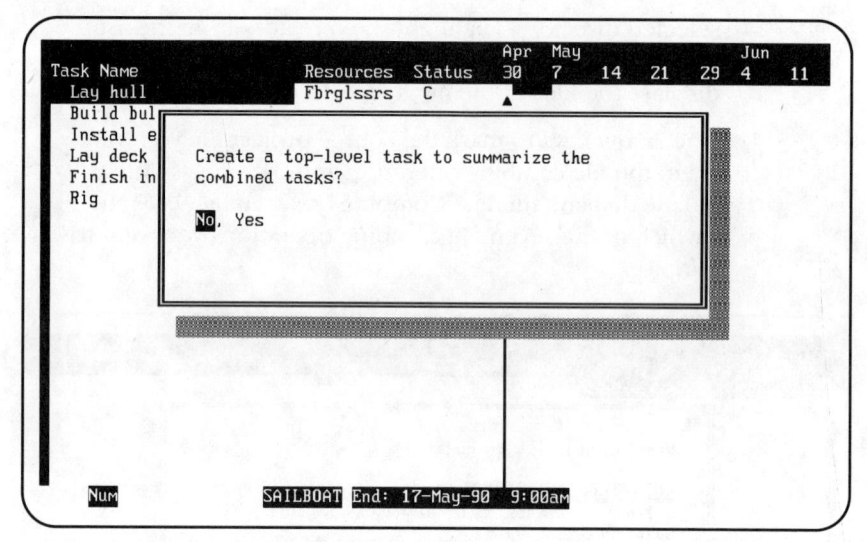

```
                                          Apr  May                  Jun
Task Name              Resources Status   30   7    14   21   29   4    11
  Lay hull              Fbrglssrs   C
  Build bul┌─────────────────────────────────────────────┐
  Install e│                                             │
  Lay deck │ Create a top-level task to summarize the    │
  Finish in│ combined tasks?                             │
  Rig      │                                             │
           │ No, Yes                                     │
           │                                             │
           └─────────────────────────────────────────────┘


Num              SAILBOAT End: 17-May-90  9:00am
```

Fig. 9.12. *The message box that asks whether you want to create a top-level summary task for the in-coming tasks.*

complete. Highlight the appropriate response, Durations or Start/End dates, by using arrow keys. Then press Enter. Time Line then completes the combine operation.

```
                                          Apr  May                  Jun
Task Name              Resources Status   30   7    14   21   29   4    11
  Lay hull
  Build bul┌─────────────────────────────────────────────┐
  Install e│                                             │
  Lay deck │ If the calendars of the combined and existing│
  Finish in│ schedules differ, should the incoming tasks'│
  Rig      │ Durations be preserved, or their Start and End│
           │ dates?                                      │
           │                                             │
           │ Durations, Start/End dates                  │
           │                                             │
           │   [F1] for Help.                            │
           │                                             │
           └═══════════════ Cal Differences ═════════════┘


Num              SAILBOAT End: 17-May-90  9:00am
```

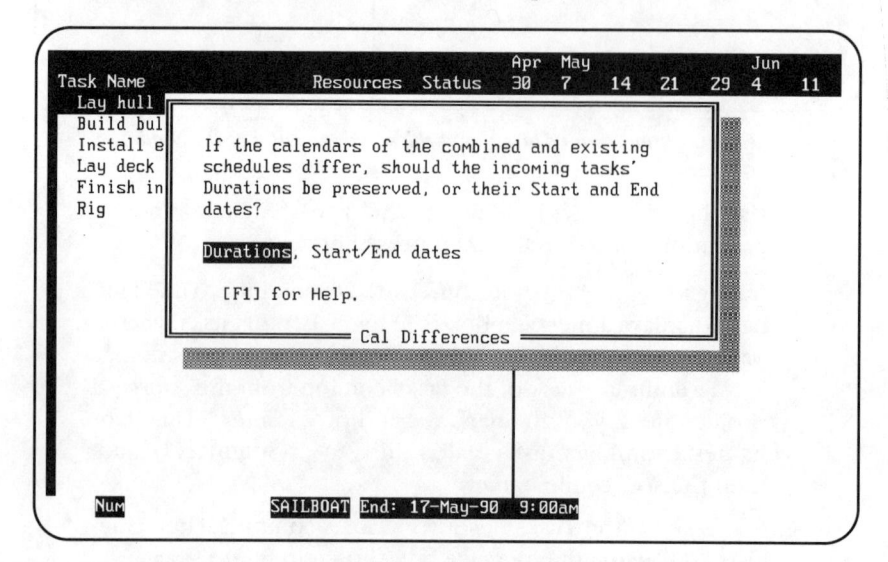

Fig. 9.13. *The Message box that asks what should be done if the calendar of the incoming tasks differs from the current project's calendar.*

Exporting Time Line Files

Time Line lets you export Time Line data to several popular spreadsheet and database files including Lotus 1-2-3 and Symphony files, Borland Quattro files, Microsoft Excel files, and Ashton-Tate dBASE III and dBASE IV files. Time Line also lets you export data to comma-separated value text files which can be used by mainframe and minicomputer applications as well as custom personal computer applications. Time Line only exports data tied to the tasks currently visible on the screen so that you can control the data exported using the Filter option (described in Chapter 7, "Customizing Screens").

Note: If you use another spreadsheet or database program, don't assume you can't export data from Time Line. Even if your spreadsheet isn't one of those identified in the preceding paragraph, there's a good chance that you can export the file using Time Line's 1-2-3 file format.

Similarly, if your database program isn't one of those listed, there's also a good chance that it will accept a database file using a dBASE file format which you can create by exporting from Time Line.

To export data from the current project schedule, follow these steps:

1. Activate the menu bar and select Files Xport Tables. Time Line displays the Export Form (see fig. 9.14) which you'll use to specify what data you want to export and how you want the exported data to be formatted.

```
Create an export file containing task data (name, duration, etc.).
 Arrows-Change selection     First Letter-Change selection    Enter-Select
 Enter or Down-Next     Up-Previous    F10-Form OK  Esc-Cancel form    F1-Help
                                                    Apr    May              Jun
┌─────────────────────────────────────────────────────────────────────────────┐
│ Export this data:                                                           │
│                                                                             │
│ Task         (No, All, Baseline, Gantt Layout)..........  [        ].WK1   │
│ Resource     (No, All, Baseline).......................  [        ].WK1   │
│ Assignment   (No, All, Baseline).......................  [        ].WK1   │
│ Dependency   (No, All).................................  [        ].WK1   │
│                                                                             │
│ Verify unique WBS codes for reimport?  (No, Yes)                            │
│                                                                             │
│ Export these cross tabs:                                                    │
│                                                                             │
│ Task vs Time        (No, Yes)..........................  [        ].WK1   │
│ Resource vs Time    (No, Yes)..........................  [        ].WK1   │
│ Task vs Resource    (No, Yes)..........................  [        ].WK1   │
│                                                                             │
│ Export Format     (FZ): [1-2-3 Release 2    ]  File Extension: [WK1]       │
│ Export Directory  (FZ):                                                     │
│   [C:\TL4\DATA\                                                        ]   │
│ ══════════════════════════ Export Form ═══════════════════════════════════  │
│ Num            SAILBOAT End: 17-May-90  9:00am                              │
└─────────────────────────────────────────────────────────────────────────────┘
```

Fig. 9.14. The Export Form.

2. If you want to export task information, mark the Task settings as either All, Baseline, or Gantt Layout. All causes Time Line to export all of the major task data fields. Baseline causes Time Line to export only the baseline task data fields. Gantt Layout causes Time Line to export only the task data fields that show in the current Gantt Layout. After you mark the Tasks field as All, Baseline, or Gantt Layout, Time Line displays the file name to the right of the Task setting with the default file name Time Line will use for the file it creates, TASKS. If you want to use some other file name, move the cursor to this field and enter the file name.

3. If you want to export resource and costs information, mark the Resource settings as either All or Baseline. Again, All causes Time Line to export all of the resource or cost data fields, and Baseline causes Time Line to export only the baseline resource or cost data fields. After you mark the Resources field as All or Baseline, Time Line fills the file name field to the right of the Resource export setting with the default file name Time Line will use for the file it creates, RESOURCE. Similar to the task export file, if you want to use some other file name, move the cursor to this field and enter the file name.

4. If you want to export resource and costs assignment information, mark the Assignment settings as either All or Baseline. Mark All if you want Time Line to export all of the resource or cost assignment data fields, and mark Baseline if you want Time Line to export only the baseline assignment data fields. If you mark the Assignment field as All or Baseline, Time Line fills the file name field to the right of the Assignment export setting with the default file name, ASSIGNMT. Just as for the task and resource export files, if you want to use some other file name, move the cursor to this field and enter the file name.

5. If you want to export task dependency information, mark the Dependency settings as All. If you mark the field as All, Time Line fills the file name field with the default file name, DEPEND. If you want to use some other file name, move the cursor to this field and enter the file name.

6. (Optional) For Time Line to export tasks successfully, it needs to be able to identify tasks uniquely and to arrange them correctly. WBS Codes provide the information Time

Line needs to both identify and arrange tasks. If you plan to later import the information you're now exporting, set the Verify Unique WBS for Reimport to Yes. With this field set to Yes, Time Line will review WBS codes when it exports and will alert you to WBS code errors such as missing codes or duplicate codes.

7. You can also create files that summarize the results of a cross-tabulation by using the Time Line export feature. As described in Chapter 8, "Printing Reports," Time Line can prepare three cross-tabulations: one that cross-tabulates a piece of task data in terms of tasks and time, another that cross-tabulates a piece of task data in terms of resources and time, and a third that cross-tabulates a piece of task data in terms of tasks and resources. Because I described cross-tabulation in detail in Chapter 8, I won't repeat those discussions here. If you want the results from a cross-tabulation exported to a file, indicate the kind of cross-tabulation you want. As for the other export files Time Line creates, you can replace the default file names which are TVST for tasks versus time, RVST for resources versus time, and TVSR for tasks versus resources.

When Time Line executes the export, it will display the Cross Tab Report Form (described in Chapter 8) to collect the information necessary to complete the cross-tabulation. You complete the screen as described in the "Printing a Cross Tab Report" section in Chapter 8.

8. To specify which file format you want Time Line to use for the file it creates, move the cursor to the Export Format field and press F2. Time Line displays a small list box (see fig. 9.15) which indicates the various file formats available: 1-2-3 Release 1A, 1-2-3 Release 2, Symphony Release 1.0, Symphony Release 1.1 & 2.0, Quattro, Excel, dBASE III and dBASE IV, Plain CSV (text), and, finally, Time Line CSV (text). The last two comma-separated formats don't show on the first page of the list box, so you need to press PgDn or use the down-arrow key to see them.

9. From the file format list box, use the arrow keys to highlight the file format you want Time Line to use for the export file it creates. Then press Enter. You simply choose the file format that the software application program you will later use to import the files needs or expects. For instance, if you want to

Part III: Managing the System

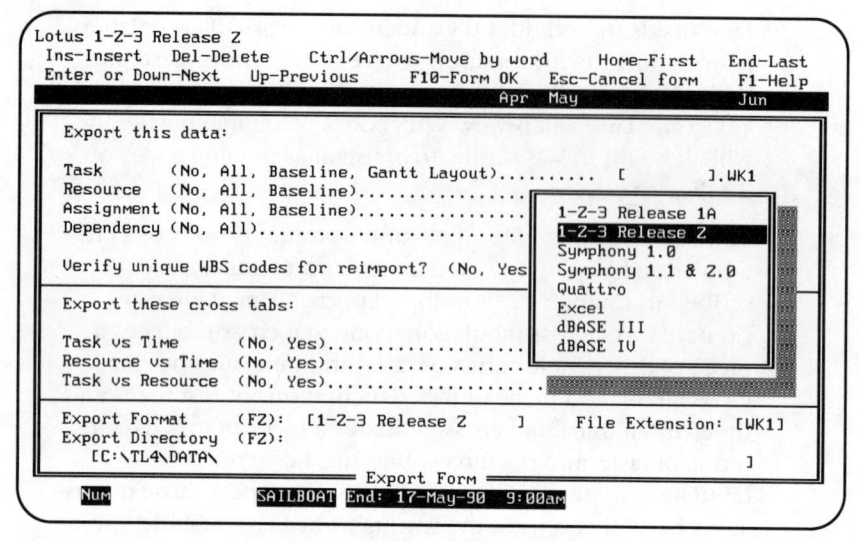

```
Lotus 1-2-3 Release 2
  Ins-Insert    Del-Delete    Ctrl/Arrows-Move by word    Home-First    End-Last
  Enter or Down-Next    Up-Previous    F10-Form OK    Esc-Cancel form    F1-Help
                                              Apr    May                  Jun
  ┌─────────────────────────────────────────────────────────────────────────┐
  │ Export this data:                                                       │
  │                                                                         │
  │ Task        (No, All, Baseline, Gantt Layout).......... [      ].WK1    │
  │ Resource    (No, All, Baseline)................                         │
  │ Assignment  (No, All, Baseline)................ ┌──────────────────┐    │
  │ Dependency  (No, All).......................... │ 1-2-3 Release 1A │    │
  │                                                 │ 1-2-3 Release 2  │    │
  │ Verify unique WBS codes for reimport? (No, Yes  │ Symphony 1.0     │    │
  │                                                 │ Symphony 1.1 & 2.0│   │
  │ Export these cross tabs:                        │ Quattro          │    │
  │                                                 │ Excel            │    │
  │ Task vs Time        (No, Yes)................   │ dBASE III        │    │
  │ Resource vs Time    (No, Yes)................   │ dBASE IV         │    │
  │ Task vs Resource    (No, Yes)................   └──────────────────┘    │
  │                                                                         │
  │ Export Format      (F2):  [1-2-3 Release 2     ]  File Extension: [WK1] │
  │ Export Directory   (F2):                                                │
  │       [C:\TL4\DATA\                                                   ] │
  │═══════════════════════════════ Export Form ═══════════════════════════  │
  │  Num                   SAILBOAT End: 17-May-90  9:00am                  │
  └─────────────────────────────────────────────────────────────────────────┘
```

Fig. 9.15. The List box that shows the valid export formats.

work with project data using Lotus 1-2-3 Release 2, highlight the second file format listed, 1-2-3 Release 2.

10. (Optional) To change the directory where Time Line creates the export file, move the cursor to the Export Directory field and press F2. Time Line displays the Directory List box.

    To change the disk, highlight the disk letter and press the key. Time Line displays the other disks on your computer. Mark the disk for which you want to see directories and then press the + key.

    To change the directory, highlight the current directory and press the + key to cause Time Line to display a list of the directories at the same level as the selected directory. Highlight the directory from the list you want and then press Enter.

11. When the Export Form screen is complete, press F10. Time Line begins the export process and creates each of the files you specified in the same order as the files are listed on the Export Form. As the export operation continues, Time Line displays message boxes that keep you apprised of the progress. As noted earlier in step 7, if you export cross tabulation files, before Time Line begins creating these files, it displays the Cross Tab Report Form screen which you use to specify the type of cross tabulation.

A Few Words on Exporting Time Line Files

Mechanically, exporting files isn't any more difficult than most of the things you'll do with Time Line. The eleven steps described in the preceding section are not, when you get right down to it, all that complex. There is, however, a challenge in exporting files: The challenge is to create files that contains the project information you want and—the *and* is important—that can be retrieved by the other software application program that you want to use. This, unfortunately, is sometimes more complex than simply completing the eleven steps described in the preceding section. In fact, I could literally write several chapters and perhaps even an entire book describing the little nuances and subtleties of exporting files for use with other applications. Most readers, however, don't need and won't want that sort of information, so I won't cover it here.

However, if you happen to be a reader who will be exporting files, let me suggest a few tactics:

> First, skim over this chapter's section on exporting to get a general feel for what you're about to do. You'll still need to follow the eleven steps described earlier and the more comfortable and confident you are with the general mechanics, the easier it'll be to work out the details of the export operation you want to perform.

> Second, pull out the Time Line user manual and review the specific sections on how to export to the particular file you're going to create and on the file format you're going to use. Also review the tables in the Appendix F of the User Manual. The tables list the data fields that Time Line collects and which can, in most cases, be exported for tasks, resources, assignments, and dependencies.

> Third, plan to spend some time experimenting with export operation to make sure things work as you intend them to work. Concentrate on making sure that you can use the exported data the way you want and that you actually export the data you need.

Importing Files

Time Line lets you import files that aren't in the Time Line version 4 file format for use with Time Line version 4.0. You can import files from previous versions of Time Line (version 2 and version 3 files), from several popular spreadsheet and database files, and even from ASCII text files. File importing can be extremely handy because it gives you the ability to use project management data created by some other software application in Time Line version 4.0.

Importing Time Line Version 2 and 3 Files

The first two options on the Import submenu (see fig. 9.16) relate to importing files created by the two previous versions of Time Line, version 2 and version 3. The steps for using either of these options should be quite familiar to you because they resemble retrieving an ordinary file. The only real difference is that instead of selecting File Retrieve, you select File Import Time Line Ver 3 or File Import Time Line Ver 2.

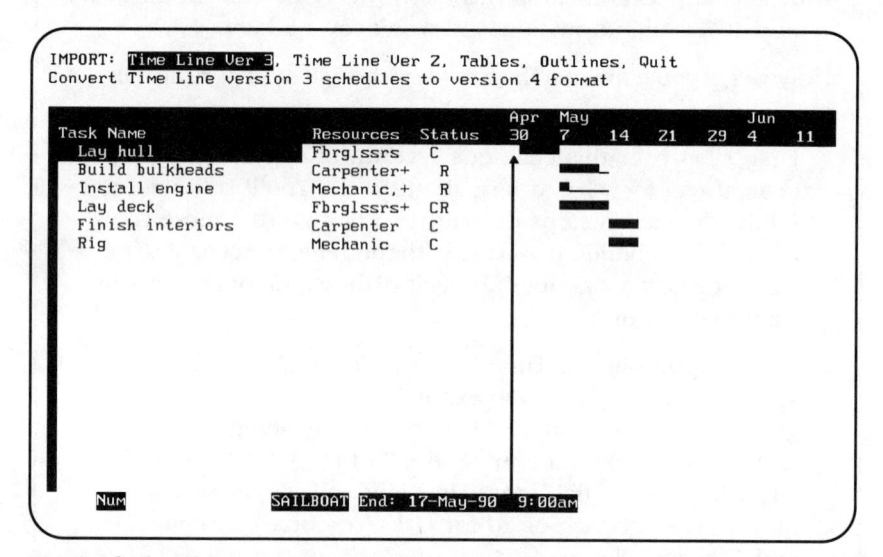

```
IMPORT: Time Line Ver 3, Time Line Ver 2, Tables, Outlines, Quit
Convert Time Line version 3 schedules to version 4 format

                                            Apr  May              Jun
Task Name              Resources  Status    30   7   14   21  29   4   11
  Lay hull             Fbrglssrs    C
  Build bulkheads      Carpenter+   R
  Install engine       Mechanic,+   R
  Lay deck             Fbrglssrs+   CR
  Finish interiors     Carpenter    C
  Rig                  Mechanic     C




 Num                SAILBOAT End: 17-May-90  9:00am
```

Fig. 9.16. The File Import submenu.

The precise steps for importing Time Line version 2 or version 3 files are

1. Activate the menu bar and select File Import. Time Line displays the Import submenu with its four options: Time Line Ver 3, Time Line Ver 2, Tables, and Outline.

2. To retrieve a version 3 file, select Time Line Ver 3. Or to retrieve a version 2 file, select Time Line Ver 2. Either way, Time Line displays the Directory List screen like the one shown earlier in figure 9.5. The Directory List screen shows all the projects in the default directory C:\TL4\DATA with the file extension T#0 if you selected the version 3 option and T@0 if you selected the version 2 option.

3. You then have two options:

   A. (Optional) To change the disk, highlight the disk letter and press the – key. Time Line displays the other disks on your computer. Mark the disk for which you want to see directories and then press the + key.

   B. (Optional) To change the directory, highlight the current directory and press the + key to cause Time Line to display a list of the directories at the same level as the selected directory. Highlight the directory from the list you want—such as TL3 or TL2—and then press the + key. Time Line then displays the files in the newly selected directory.

4. Use the arrow keys to highlight the project you want to retrieve. When the project is highlighted, press Enter. Time Line retrieves the project and then displays it.

5. If you previously retrieved a project or started to create a project, Time Line displays the message box that alerts you that retrieving a new file will erase the schedule already stored in memory. To continue, select Erase Schedule in Memory by typing an E or by using the arrow keys to highlight Erase Schedule in Memory and then pressing Enter.

Importing Spreadsheet and Database Files

Time Line also lets you import several popular spreadsheet and database files including 1-2-3 Release 1A and Release 2.0 files, Symphony Release 1, 1.1, and 2.0 files, Quattro files, Excel files, and dBASE III and dBASE IV files. And, as noted earlier, if you use another spreadsheet or database program, don't assume you can't import data from it into Time Line. Even if your spreadsheet isn't one of those identified, there's a good chance that it will create a spreadsheet file using a 1-2-3 file format which you can then import into Time Line. Similarly, if your database program isn't one of those listed, there's also a good chance that the program will create a database file using a dBASE file format which you can also import into Time Line.

One important thing to remember about importing files is that they must organize the data in a very specific, formal way so that Time Line correctly interprets the pieces of text, the numeric values, and the dates that make up a project schedule. The User's Manual gives detailed explanations of each of the fields that Time Line collects or calculates. It also describes how this information should arranged in a file so Time Line can import it. If you want to review that material, you can refer to the import sections in Chapter

19 and Appendix K of the User's Manual. I'm not going to repeat those discussions here, however, because there's actually a more convenient way to determine exactly what the information you want to import should look like: This shortcut is to simply retrieve one of the example project files that come with Time Line, export that project data using a file format like the one for which you're trying to import, and then review the export file to see what Time Line expects of an import file. This shortcut works because the files that Time Line creates in an export operation perfectly match what Time Line expects in files you ask it to import. (One aspect of spreadsheet files is easy to miss so I'll mention it here: The worksheet range in the import file that contains the data needs to be named TL_TABLE.)

Once the file you want to import is arranged so Time Line can recognize it, the steps for actually importing are straight-forward. To import a spreadsheet or database file, follow these steps:

1. Activate the menu bar and select Files Import Tables. Time Line displays the Import Form screen (see fig. 9.17) which you'll use to specify what type of data you want to import and where the files containing the data are located.

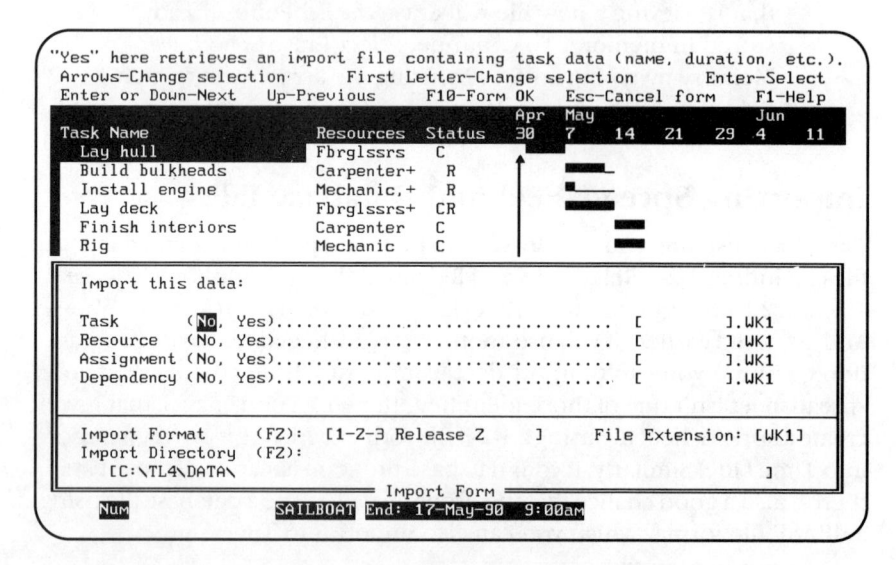

```
"Yes" here retrieves an import file containing task data (name, duration, etc.).
Arrows-Change selection     First Letter-Change selection     Enter-Select
Enter or Down-Next    Up-Previous     F10-Form OK    Esc-Cancel form    F1-Help
                                           Apr  May                    Jun
Task Name              Resources  Status   30   7    14   21   29   4    11
  Lay hull             Fbrglssrs  C
  Build bulkheads      Carpenter+ R
  Install engine       Mechanic,+ R
  Lay deck             Fbrglssrs+ CR
  Finish interiors     Carpenter  C
  Rig                  Mechanic   C

 Import this data:

  Task       (No, Yes).....................................  [           ].WK1
  Resource   (No, Yes).....................................  [           ].WK1
  Assignment (No, Yes).....................................  [           ].WK1
  Dependency (No, Yes).....................................  [           ].WK1

 Import Format    (F2):  [1-2-3 Release 2     ]    File Extension: [WK1]
 Import Directory (F2):
   [C:\TL4\DATA\                                                          ]
                           ═══════ Import Form ═══════
  NUM              SAILBOAT End: 17-May-90  9:00am
```

Fig. 9.17. The Import Form.

2. If you want to import task information, mark the Task settings as Yes. If you do mark the Tasks field as Yes, Time Line fills the file name field to the right of the the Task import setting with the default import file name, TASKS. If you used some other file name, move the cursor to this field and enter that file name.

3. If you want to import resource and costs information, mark the Resource settings as Yes. As with importing task data, if you mark the Resource field as Yes, Time Line fills the file name field with the default import file name, RESOURCE. So if you used some other file name, move the cursor to this field and enter that file name.

4. If you want to import resource and costs assignment information, mark the Assignment settings as Yes. If you do mark the Assignment field as Yes, Time Line fills the file name field with the default import file name, ASSIGNMT. If the file to be imported uses another name, move the cursor to this field and enter the file name.

5. If you want to import task dependency information, mark the Dependency settings as Yes. Time Line fills the file name field with the default import file name, DEPEND, but if you want to use some other file name, move the cursor to this file name field and enter it.

6. To identify the format of the file you want Time Line to import, move the cursor to the Import Format field and press F2. Time Line displays a small list box (refer to fig. 9.15) which indicates the various file formats available: 1-2-3 Release 1A, 1-2-3 Release 2, Symphony Release 1.0, Symphony Release 1.1 & 2.0, Quattro, Excel, dBASE III and dBASE IV, and Time Line CSV (text). The last format, Time Line comma separated values, doesn't show on the first page of the list box so you need to press PgDn or press the down-arrow key to see it.

7. From the file format list box, use the arrow keys to highlight the format of the file you want Time Line to import. Then press Enter.

8. (Optional) To change the directory where Time Line looks for the import file, move the cursor to the Import Directory field and press F2. Time Line displays the Directory list box. You then have two options:

> To change the disk, highlight the disk letter and press the – key. Time Line displays the other disks on your computer. Mark the disk for which you want to see directories, and then press the + key.

To change the directory, highlight the current directory and press the + key to cause Time Line to display a list of the directories at the same level as the selected directory. Highlight the directory from the list you want and then press Enter.

9. When the Import Form screen is complete, press F10. Time Line begins the import process and adds task, resources, assignments, or dependency data from each of the indicated files to the current project schedule. As the import operation continues, Time Line displays message boxes that keep you apprised of the progress.

Importing Outline Files

Time Line also allows you to import one final category of files: ASCII text files. This feature lets you use word-processing programs and outliner programs to create Time Line project schedules. This feature isn't for everybody. The ASCII files you import become quite cryptic if you try to describe a project completely. Nonetheless, it is helpful to know about this alternative method of creating project schedules.

Before Time Line can import an ASCII file, the ASCII file must follow several conventions. These conventions include the following:

- The file must be an ASCII file; the standard file formats used by a word processing or outliner program won't work.

- Time Line uses the current schedule settings to define such things as the calendar and hardware configuration.

- Each task must be entered on a separate line.

- The first piece of data on a line must be the task name.

- To enter additional pieces of data besides the task name, add an asterisk after the task name. Time Line considers the characters to the left of the asterisk to be part of the task name and the characters to the right of the asterisk to be task data.

- Separate with one space any additional pieces of task data that follow the asterisk.

- Time Line allows up to 250 characters on one line which is probably more than will fit on one line of your text editor.

Note: If the text wraps to the next line, Time Line interprets it as a new task.

- Time Line assumes the earliest date following the task name and asterisk is the task start date and that the latest date is the task end date. If only one date follows the task name and asterisk, Time Line assumes it is the task start date.

- Dates and times can be entered using any of the valid date and time formats.

- If you enter a time with no date, Time Line uses the project As-of date as the default date.

- Identify subtasks by indenting them underneath their summary task, and use spaces to indent a subtask because the Tab key may not work.

- Time Line will number tasks with WBS codes for you based on their order in the text file.

You can see that defining projects with an outline ASCII text file amounts to an entirely new way of describing projects. As an example of an outline that might be imported, you could type into an ASCII file (using a word processor or outliner) the following information about the familiar sailboat project, defining the project tasks and their start and end dates:

```
Lay hull            *2-Apr-90  11-Apr-90
Build bulkheads     *11-Apr-90 17-Apr-90
Install engine      *11-Apr-90 9:00am 11-Apr-90 2:00pm
Lay deck            *11-Apr-90 18-Apr-90
Finish interiors    *18-Apr-90 23-Apr-90
Rig
  Winches           *18-Apr-90 19-Apr-90
  Masts
    Main Mast       *19-Apr-90 9:00am 19-Apr-90 2:00pm
    Fore Mast       *19-Apr-90 2:00pm 20-Apr-90 9:00am
  Halyards          *20-Apr-90 23-Apr-90
```

If you wanted to add notes to the any of the tasks—which would be equivalent to entering text in Task Form Notes field, just insert an empty line under the task you want to describe with a note, type a dash (–), and then add a note. For example, to document the Lay hull task with the note "Depends on shipment of fiberglass" and the Fore Mast task with the note "Who should do work if mechanic is still sick then?", you would insert the second and twelfth lines that show in the outline that follows:

```
    Lay hull              *2-Apr-90  11-Apr-90
  -Depends on shipment of fiberglass
    Build bulkheads       *11-Apr-90 17-Apr-90
    Install engine        *11-Apr-90 9:00am 11-Apr-90 2:00pm
    Lay deck              *11-Apr-90 18-Apr-90
    Finish interiors      *18-Apr-90 23-Apr-90
    Rig
      Winches             *18-Apr-90 19-Apr-90
      Masts
        Main Mast         *19-Apr-90 9:00am 19-Apr-90 2:00pm
        Fore Mast         *19-Apr-90 2:00pm 20-Apr-90 9:00am
  -Who should do work if mechanic is still sick then
      Halyards            *20-Apr-90 23-Apr-90
```

Time Line also provides 17 special words or symbols that let you define additional task data fields, resources, assignments, and task dependencies. Table 9.1 summarizes these special features which essentially allow you to create complete project schedules without even using the Time Line Schedule options.

Table 9.1
Special Words and Symbols Available on an Outlined Project Schedule

Word or Symbol	Description
ALAP	Defines a task's type as "As Late As Possible"
ASAP	Defines a task's type as "As Soon As Possible"
DONE	Defines a task's status as "Done"
END	Indicates the date that follows this special word is the task end date
FIXED	Defines a task's type as "Fixed"
FUTURE	Defines a task's status as "Future"
JOIN	Defines dependencies. If JOIN is set with the $ symbol, it results in dependency definitions between any two tasks at the same level. In this case, the first task is the predecessor, and the second is the successor. If JOIN is set on a line for a specific task, the task with the JOIN special word is marked as a successor to the first task at the same level that precedes the successor task.
KEYWORD	Defines a keyword for tasks and resources

Table 9.1 Continued

Word or Symbol	Description
MILESTONE	Defines a particular task as a milestone even if it means overriding a Time Line rule that says tasks with durations or both an end and start date aren't milestones
NOJOIN	Mitigates the effect of a default ($) JOIN for a task that contains NOJOIN. Causes the task line that contains the UNJOIN special word not to be considered as a successor to the task immediately preceding it at the same level
OBS	Defines an OBS code for a task
PER	Calibrates the unit of time of a resource or cost. PER is followed by MINUTES, HOURS, DAYS, WEEKS, MONTHS, or YEARS — or their abbreviations, min, hr, dy, wk, mth, or yr. (Also see RATE which PER needs to be used with.)
PERCENT	Describes the percent of completion or the achieved percent of a task
PRIORITY	Defines the priority of a task
RATE	Gives the cost of a resource. If you don't enter a resource cost, Time Line enters the cost for you as $1 per hour. (Also see PER which RATE needs to be used with.)
STARTED	Defines the status of a task as "Started"
WBS	Lets you enter a WBS code for a task. You don't need to use this unless you want to control the WBS codes assigned: Time Line will automatically assign WBS Codes for you.
@	Defines a resource. (Also see RATE, PER and KEYWORD which are additional special words for describing a resource.); The line @Mechanic, for example, would define a resource named mechanic
$	Defines default characteristics for all the tasks that follow until the next $ symbol. Defaults can be overridden for a specific task by using another special word on the line defining that task

The following example shows a sample outline ASCII file that uses many of these special words or symbols. If you have questions about what a particular piece of task data actually signifies, you might find it helpful to refer back to Chapter 4, "Managing Project and Task Details." All the task data fields referred to in table 9.1 can also be entered using the large version of the Task Form which is described in Chapter 4. Similarly, If you have questions about what a particular piece of resource data signifies, refer back to Chapter 5, "Identifying and Allocating Project Resources and Costs." All the resource data fields referred to in table 9.1 can also be entered using the Resource Form screen, which is also described in Chapter 5.

```
Lay hull         *2-Apr-90 11-Apr-90 done
-Depends on shipment of fiberglass
Build bulkheads  *11-Apr-90 17-Apr-90 join done
Install engine   *11-Apr-90 9:00am 11-Apr-90 2:00pm
started percent 50
Lay deck         *11-Apr-90 18-Apr-90 future asap
Finish interiors *18-Apr-90 23-Apr-90 join future asap
Rig
  Winches        *18-Apr-90 19-Apr-90 future asap
  Masts* join
    Main Mast    *19-Apr-90 9:00am 19-Apr-90 2:00pm
future asap
    Fore Mast    *19-Apr-90 2:00pm 20-Apr-90 9:00am
join future asap
-Who should do work if mechanic is still sick then
future
    Halyards     *20-Apr-90 23-Apr-90 join future asap
```

Once you've defined that ASCII text file, actually importing the file is straight-forward. To import an ASCII text file, you follow these steps:

1. Activate the menu bar and select File Import Outlines. Time Line next displays the message box shown in figure 9.18, which asks whether you want import a text file from disk (one you've already created) or a text file from keyboard transfer (one you create from scratch as part of the import process.)

2. If you want to import a text file you've already created, highlight disk and press Enter. Time Line next displays the Text Import box which lists all the files in the selected directory with the file extension TXT (see fig. 9.19). You then have two options:

Chapter 9: Working with the Time Line Files

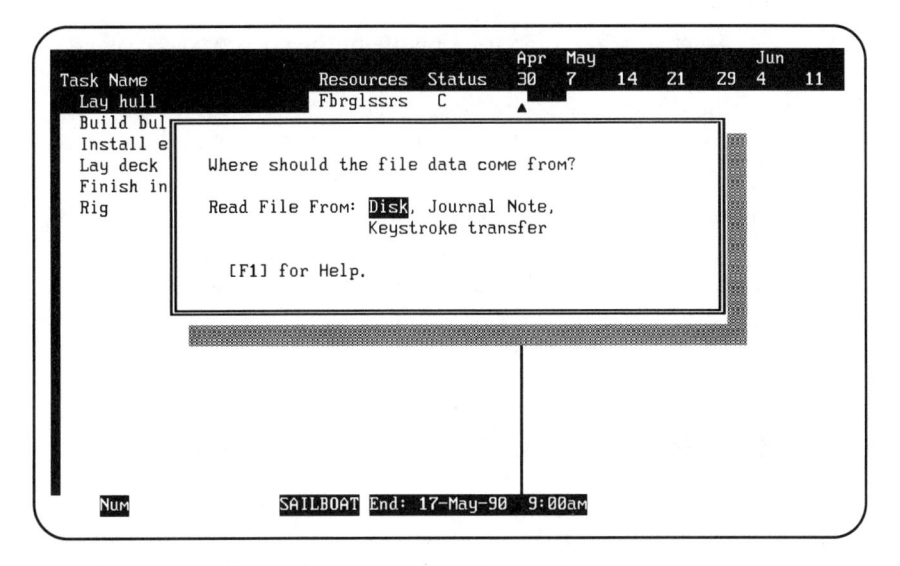

Fig. 9.18. The message box that Time Line uses to determine whether you want to import a text file disk or create one from scratch.

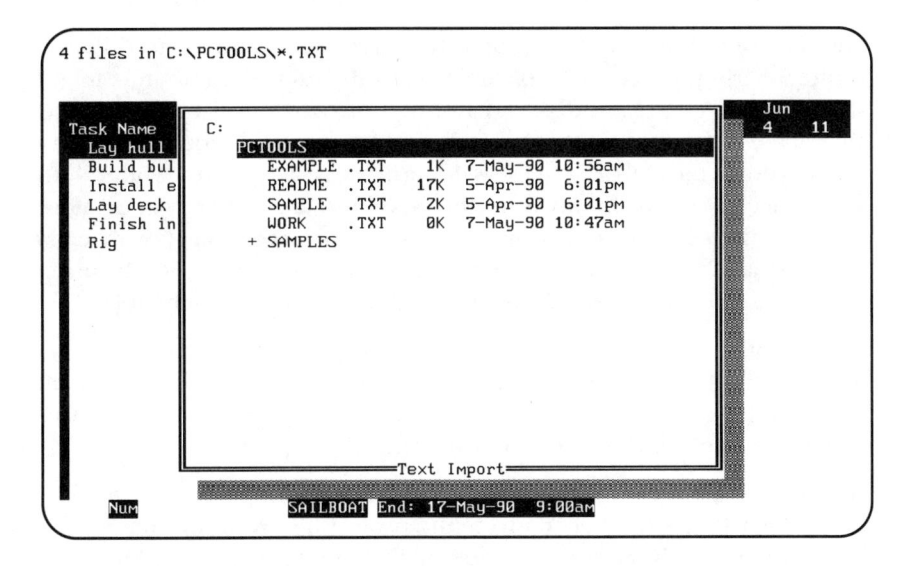

Fig. 9.19. The Text Import List box.

To change the disk, highlight the disk letter and press the – key. Time Line displays the other disks on your computer. Mark the disk for which you want to see directories and then press the + key.

To change the directory, highlight the current directory and press the + key to cause Time Line to display a list of the directories at the same level as the selected directory. Highlight the directory from the list you want and then press Enter.

3. Highlight the file you want to import and then press Enter. Time Line imports the text file. When it finishes, the program displays a note telling you it's done. Press F10 to continue.

4. Recalculate the schedule by pressing F9.

Working with Files on a Network

Working with Time Line project files on a network isn't really much different than working with the same files on a single, stand-alone personal computer. There are, however, a few minor differences related to locking and unlocking files. And knowing about these differences will make things easier if you happen to be using Time Line in a network environment.

The majority of personal computer networks really amount to disk and printer sharing devices. For example, several personal computers might share a single large hard disk and a printer or two. Most of the time, this shared use is transparent to you: You don't need to worry about what Mary is doing down the hall or what Joe is doing in the cubicle next to yours. With shared access to a disk, however, the possibility exists that two or more people may access the same project file. In fact, for large projects with many participants, there a good chance that more than one person will be using Time Line simultaneously to update or review the project schedule.

To deal with the possibility that two or more users might be simultaneously updating the same project, each unaware that someone is also working on the project, Time Line uses file locking. File locking results in only one user being able to make changes to a project file at a time.

Here's how file locking works in Time Line: When one user retrieves a project schedule—in effect copying the project file from the shared disk into his computer's memory—Time Line locks that project schedule's file. When the file is locked, only the user who first retrieved the file can save the file using the original file name. If another user retrieves a locked file, the user will be alerted that the file is already locked and that the user won't be able to save the file under the original name. This other user can, however, still view the project, print reports, make changes to the copy of the file in memory, and even save the file using a different file name. (*Note:* Time Line not only locks the current version of the file but also any previous versions of the file.)

Time Line unlocks a file when the first user to retrieve the file, the user who caused Time Line to lock the file in the first place, erases the schedule from memory using the Schedule Erase option, renames the file using the File Form option, or quits Time Line.

Chapter Summary

This chapter examined how you go about working with the files that Time Line creates and uses. First, the chapter described some basic file operations such as saving, retrieving, erasing, and backing up and restoring files—knowledge that is essential to protecting the work you do with Time Line. The chapter next described the advanced file operations that Time Line provides such as combining files, and exporting and importing project management data between Time Line and other software programs. Finally, this chapter also briefly overviewed the file locking and file unlocking Time Line uses when it runs on a network—information network users need to understand in order to work with files in that environment.

The next chapter, "Using Time Line's Utilities and Macros Features," describes Time Line features that make working with the Time Line program easier.

10

Using Time Line Utilities and Macro Features

This chapter in *Using Time Line* describes the menu options that appear under the Utilities main menu option. Essentially, the options on the Utilities menu are handy tools you can use to make working with Time Line easier. This chapter is broken into two sections: "Tapping the Time Line Utilities," which reviews how you use each of the Utilities menu options except macros, and "Speeding Things Up with Macros," which describes the Time Line macro capability.

Tapping the Time Line Utilities

With the Utilities menu, Time Line provides five tools you can use to make working with Time Line easier or more convenient: Macros, Exit to DOS, Stats, DOS Date and Time, and TL 3.0 Config (see fig. 10.1). These five tools don't relate to project management, but rather allow you to work with the Time Line program or your computer. The discussion of macros comes a little later in the chapter, but the other four options are described in the paragraphs that follow.

The Exit to DOS Option

The Exit to Dos option lets you temporarily step outside of Time Line and get back to DOS without quitting the Time Line program or having to save the project schedule you were working with. This means you can use DOS

```
UTILITIES: Macros, Exit to DOS, Stats, DOS Date/Time, TL 3.0 Config, Quit
Macros Menu

                                              Apr  May              Jun
Task Name              Resources  Status      30   7    14   21  29 4   11
```

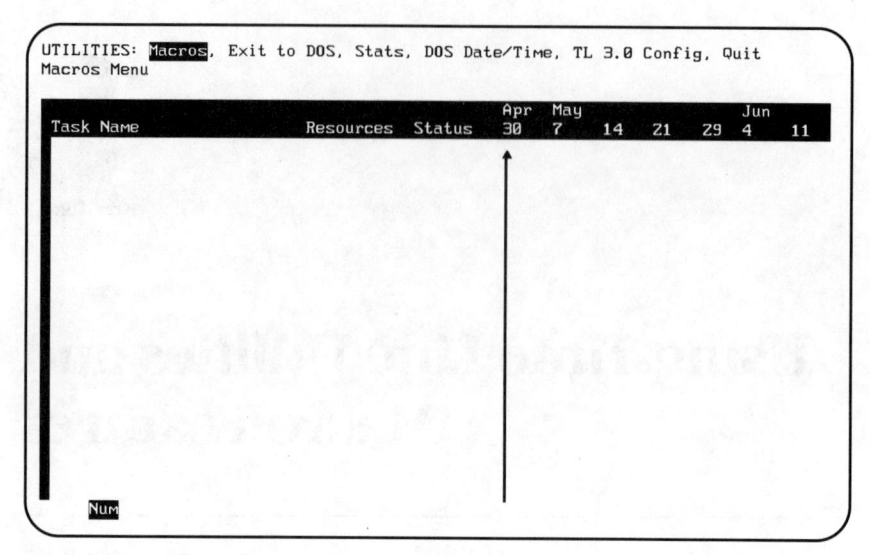

Fig. 10.1. The Utilities menu.

to do things like format a disk or make a copy of a file without saving your project, quitting Time Line, and when you're finished with DOS, having to restart Time Line and retrieve the project schedule you want to use.

To use the Exit to DOS option, follow these simple steps:

1. (Optional) Save your current project schedule before you exit just in case you forget to return to Time Line and save the schedule after using DOS. If you do forget to return and save the project schedule, you'll lose any changes or additions you made to the project schedule after you last saved it.

2. Activate the menu bar, select Utilities, and then select Exit to DOS. Time Line then displays Exit to DOS box in figure 10.2.

3. You then have two options, depending on which way you want to use DOS.

    A. If you want to return to DOS to perform various DOS commands before returning to Time Line, you have two choices: Proceed and Quick Exit.

    Proceed frees up as much memory as it can before providing you access to the DOS prompt. This process of freeing up memory takes a few extra seconds, but the additional memory gives you more flexibility to do things like run any of the DOS command and even small programs.

Chapter 10: Using Time Line Utilities 291

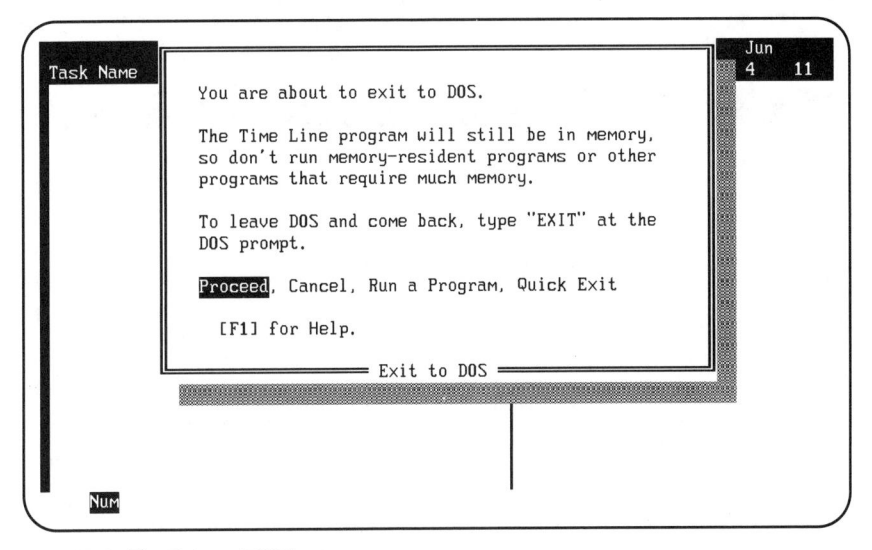

```
Task Name                                                      Jun
                                                               4    11
         ┌─────────────────────────────────────────┐
         │  You are about to exit to DOS.          │
         │                                         │
         │  The Time Line program will still be in memory,
         │  so don't run memory-resident programs or other
         │  programs that require much memory.     │
         │                                         │
         │  To leave DOS and come back, type "EXIT" at the
         │  DOS prompt.                            │
         │                                         │
         │  Proceed, Cancel, Run a Program, Quick Exit
         │                                         │
         │     [F1] for Help.                      │
         │                                         │
         │═══════════════════ Exit to DOS ═════════│
         └─────────────────────────────────────────┘

 Num
```

Fig. 10.2. The Exit to DOS box.

Quick Exit just provides you instant access to the DOS prompt. It doesn't, however, free up any memory which may mean that you have very little memory. With only a little memory, you probably won't be able to run any other programs, and you may not even be able to run certain DOS commands.

B. If you're exiting to DOS to run another program, you can use the Run a Program option. If you select Run a Program, Time Line displays the DOS Exit Form box shown in figure 10.3.

Enter the program name (and the path name) in the Program File field. For example, if you want to run Microsoft Word (which you start by typing *word*) and Word is stored in the Word directory on your C drive, you type *c:\word\word* to start the program.

Enter any parameters, or additional information, you include after the program name when you start the program. So if you're running a word processing program that lets you retrieve the document file by including the document file name after the program, you could enter that file name here. (Refer to your program's manual if you're not sure which parameters apply to the program you're loading.)

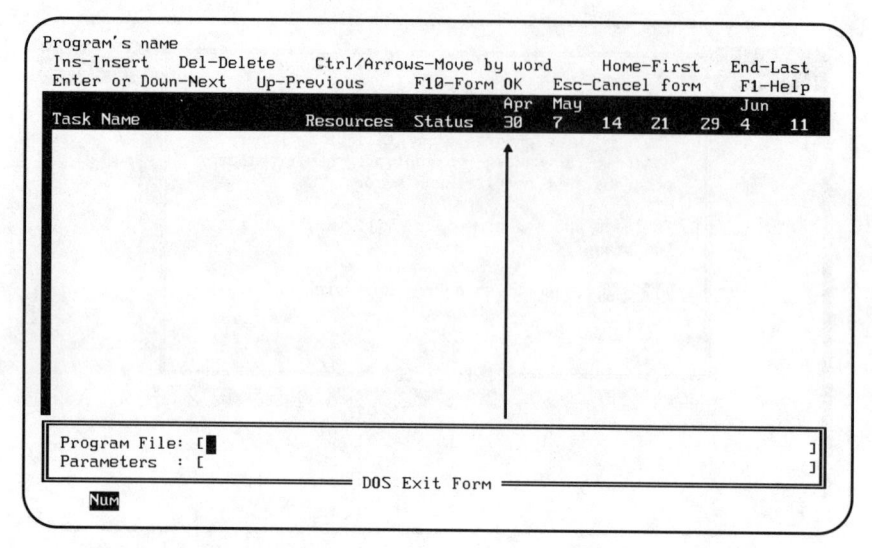

```
Program's name
 Ins-Insert    Del-Delete    Ctrl/Arrows-Move by word    Home-First    End-Last
 Enter or Down-Next    Up-Previous    F10-Form OK    Esc-Cancel form    F1-Help
                                          Apr  May                    Jun
Task Name                    Resources  Status  30   7    14   21   29  4    11




















 Program File: [                                                              ]
 Parameters  : [                                                              ]
                          ═══════ DOS Exit Form ═══════
NUM
```

Fig. 10.3. *The DOS Exit form.*

After you complete the DOS Exit Form box, press F10. Time Line first frees up memory just like the Proceed option and then starts the program you identify in the DOS Exit Form box. When you exit from the program, you return to Time Line automatically.

4. If you exited to DOS using either the Proceed or Quick Exit options, you need to type the word *exit* at the DOS prompt to return to Time Line.

Stats

The Stats tools gives you some basic information about your computer and which project schedule you've loaded into memory. If you select the option—which you do by activating the menu bar and selecting Utilities Stats—Time Line displays the Time Line Statistics screen shown in figure 10.4. To leave the screen, press Esc or select the Quit help option at the bottom of the screen.

The Time Line Statistics screen gives you a variety of information. At the top of the screen, Time Line indicates the project schedule file name, the directory from which you retrieved it, the directory where the actual Time Line program resides, and which version of DOS you're using. In roughly the middle of the screen, Time Line displays the name of the program user you identified during installation and gives the serial number of your copy.

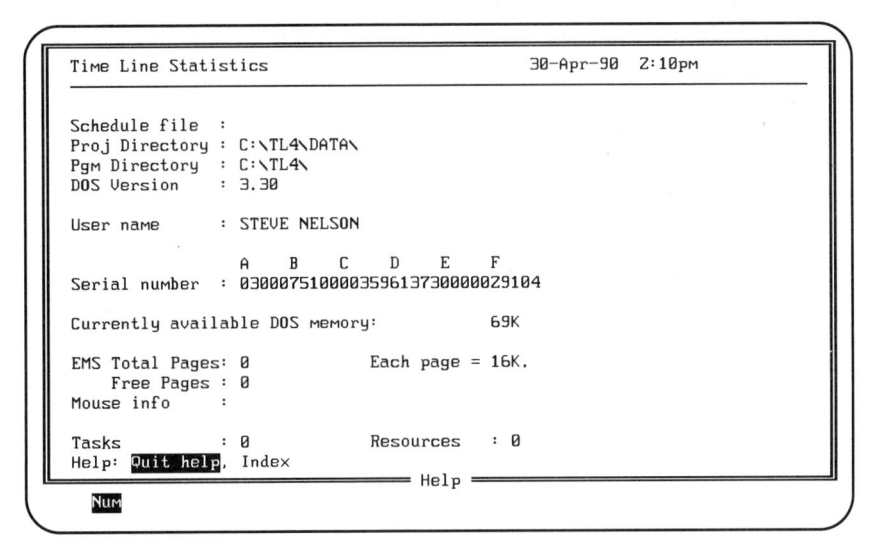

```
┌─────────────────────────────────────────────────────────────┐
│                                                             │
│  Time Line Statistics                  30-Apr-90  2:10pm    │
│  ─────────────────────────────────────────────────────────  │
│                                                             │
│  Schedule file  :                                           │
│  Proj Directory : C:\TL4\DATA\                              │
│  Pgm Directory  : C:\TL4\                                   │
│  DOS Version    : 3.30                                      │
│                                                             │
│  User name      : STEVE NELSON                              │
│                                                             │
│                   A   B   C   D   E   F                     │
│  Serial number  : 030007510000359613730000029104            │
│                                                             │
│  Currently available DOS memory:         69K                │
│                                                             │
│  EMS Total Pages: 0        Each page = 16K.                 │
│      Free Pages : 0                                         │
│  Mouse info     :                                           │
│                                                             │
│  Tasks          : 0        Resources    : 0                 │
│  Help: Quit help, Index                                     │
│                                 ══════ Help ══════          │
│   NUM                                                       │
└─────────────────────────────────────────────────────────────┘
```

Fig. 10.4. The Time Line Statistics screen.

At the bottom of the screen, Time Line shows the conventional DOS memory left, the total expanded memory your computer has, the available expanded memory, whether a mouse is installed, and how many tasks and resources the current schedule contains.

You can use this information on the Time Line Statistics screen in several ways. The project schedule file name and directory information lets you check which project file you actually retrieved. The user name shows who owns the copy of Time Line. The memory information at the bottom of the screen can be useful for monitoring available memory and making sure you don't run out.

DOS Date and Time

The DOS Date and Time option updates your system clock (which Time Line uses to determine the current date and time). In effect, the DOS Date and Time command is identical to the DATE and TIME commands you enter at the DOS prompt. If you discover while working with Time Line that the date or time is wrong, the DOS Date and Time option provides a quick way to update an incorrect system clock.

To use the DOS Date and Time option, activate the menu bar and then select Utilities and then DOS Date and Time. Time Line displays the Date Form shown in figure 10.5. With the cursor positioned on the Date field, you simply enter the date and time using any of the date and time formats that Time Line understands. Then press F10.

As you may recall, Time Line understands each of the following dates and times:

Dates:

11/26/91
11-26-91
26-Nov-91
Nov 26, 91
November 26, 1991
26-November-1991

Times:

5pm
5:00pm
17:00

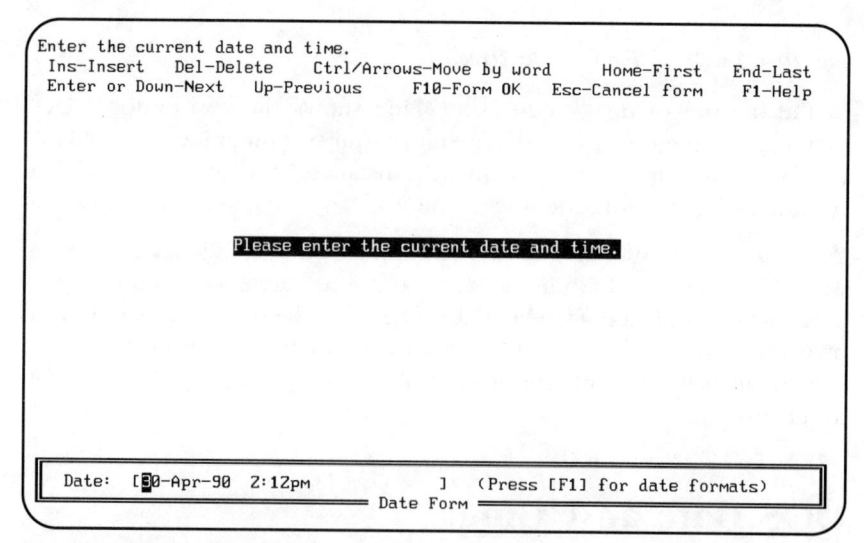

```
┌─────────────────────────────────────────────────────────────────────┐
│ Enter the current date and time.                                    │
│  Ins-Insert    Del-Delete    Ctrl/Arrows-Move by word    Home-First    End-Last │
│  Enter or Down-Next    Up-Previous    F10-Form OK    Esc-Cancel form    F1-Help │
│                                                                     │
│                                                                     │
│                                                                     │
│                                                                     │
│                Please enter the current date and time.              │
│                                                                     │
│                                                                     │
│                                                                     │
│                                                                     │
│     Date:   [30-Apr-90  2:12pm            ]   (Press [F1] for date formats) │
│                              ═══ Date Form ═══                      │
└─────────────────────────────────────────────────────────────────────┘
```

Fig. 10.5. The Date Form box.

TL 3.0 Config

If you used the previous version of Time Line, version 3.0, you can use the TL 3.0 Config option to copy the configuration settings from the Time Line version 3.0 configuration file. To use this option, activate the menu bar and select Utilities TL 3.0 Config. Time Line looks for the Time Line version 3.0 configuration file, TLCNFG3.DAT, in the Time Line program directory or its subdirectories. If the program can't find the file, it displays an error message in a box, alerting you to the predicament and instructing you to copy the old configuration file to the new Time Line program directory.

Speeding Things Up With Macros

Macros is the other tool that Time Line lists on the Utilities menu (refer to fig. 10.1). The rest of this chapter focuses on bringing you up to speed on this powerful tool so that you can make your use of Time Line faster and easier. For starters, I define macros and walk you through the steps for writing an initial simple macro. Then I'll talk about how to write working macros and use them in the project schedules you create. Finally, I'll cover some of the more advanced techniques experienced users can use to write sophisticated macros.

What Is a Macro?

Macros sound complex, but they really are not. In essence, macros amount to sequences of keystrokes that Time Line types for you. To tell Time Line to type this series of keystrokes, you press something called a *hotkey*, which is simply a combination of two keyboard keys. For example, you might decide to create a macro to type a lengthy word—like *hydroelectricity*—that you constantly use in task notes and journal notes for a dam project you're using Time Line to manage. By defining a hotkey combination of, say, Alt-h, you could simply press two keys, the Alt key and the h character key, instead of the sixteen character keys required to type out the word *hydroelectricity*. In this case, the macro speeds things up by letting you type fourteen fewer keys—a significant time savings if you otherwise would have had repeatedly to type the entire word.

By saving you keystrokes, then, macros save you time. That, in a nutshell, is the beauty of macros. But if all that macros do is provide a kind of writing shortcut, their usefulness would be limited. After all, there really aren't going to be that many long words you use so frequently that it would make sense to create macros for them. However, macros also let you abbreviate, or short-cut, the keystrokes you type to choose menu options, select screen options, and even fill form screens. And all this means that you can create macros that type out the series of keystrokes that do one of these other tasks. You could create macros, for example, that clear the current schedule filter, renumbers tasks with WBS codes, or quit the Time Line program.

Illustrating Some Simple Macros

To illustrate how simple this business of writing a macro can be, I'll describe how to write a couple of simple macros: one that types out the word *hydroelectricity* and another that clears the current filters. If you're sitting at your computer, consider following with the steps listed below. Along the way, I'll explain each in detail so you can later apply the information to writing your own macros.

To write simple macros, you tell Time Line to record the keystrokes you type. This means, of course, that before you can tell Time Line to record your keystrokes, you need to be someplace in Time Line where it's possible to type the keystrokes. So for the first example of creating a macro that types the word *hydroelectricity*, activate the menu bar, select Schedule Journal, and then press Ins to display the empty Journal screen into which you can type the keystrokes.

Next, follow the steps below to create the *hydroelectricity* macro:

1. Press Alt-R to tell Time Line to start recording keystrokes. Time Line displays the word Record in the lower left corner of the screen to remind you that it's recording (see fig. 10.6)

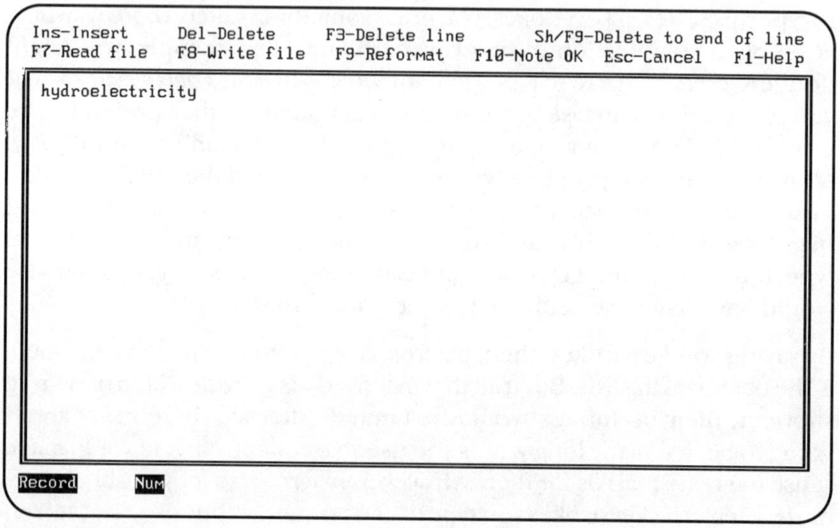

```
 Ins-Insert     Del-Delete     F3-Delete line        Sh/F9-Delete to end of line
 F7-Read file   F8-Write file  F9-Reformat   F10-Note OK   Esc-Cancel   F1-Help
 hydroelectricity




















 Record     Num
```

Fig. 10.6. Time Line displays the word Record *in the lower left corner of the screen when it's recording keystrokes.*

2. Type *hydroelectricity*. (Figure 10.6 shows the Journal Notes screen after you've completed step 2.)

3. Press Alt-R to tell Time Line to stop recording keystrokes. Time Line removes the word Record because it's stopped recording.

4. (Optional) To tell Time Line to run the macro you created, press Alt-P.

5. To leave the Journal notes screen, press Esc, select Proceed, and then press Esc again.

It's that simple. You've written your first Time Line macro. This kind of macro is called a *temporary macro* because it's only available until you leave Time Line or use the Alt-R hotkey to record another macro. If you want to create a permanent macro, you need to follow a slightly different procedure for recording your keystrokes and then save the macro to disk. But none of this is that much more difficult.

Suppose that you wanted to write a macro that clears the current filters that Time Line uses to determine which tasks to display on the Gantt chart screen. To clear the current filters, you would normally type a slash (/), then an S (for schedule), an F for filters, and a C for clear. (Chapter 7, "Customizing Gantt, PERT, and Tree Chart Screens," describes the Filters option in detail. If you're not familiar with the Filters option, don't worry about what the option does. Instead, focus on the fact that the macro is selecting a series of menu options.)

To write a permanent macro that clears the current filters, first make sure that either the Gantt chart or PERT chart is displayed on the screen and that the menu bar isn't already activated. The reason for this is that you need to be able to type the exact sequence of keystrokes that you want Time Line to record.

1. Activate the menu bar and select Utilities Macros Record. Or press the Alt = key combination. In either case, Time Line next displays the Primary Macro Form (see fig. 10.7).

2. With the cursor positioned on the Macro Name field, enter up to a 40 character name for the macro. The name you enter here is what Time Line uses to identify the macro so you can't use the name of another macro you've already created. You also can't use spaces so if you type a space, Time Line substitutes the underscore character for the space.

3. (Optional) Move the cursor to the Macro HotKey field and type the keys you want to use as the hotkey for the macro. Use the Ctrl or Alt key as the first key in the hotkey combination and then select another key. A word of warning: Don't

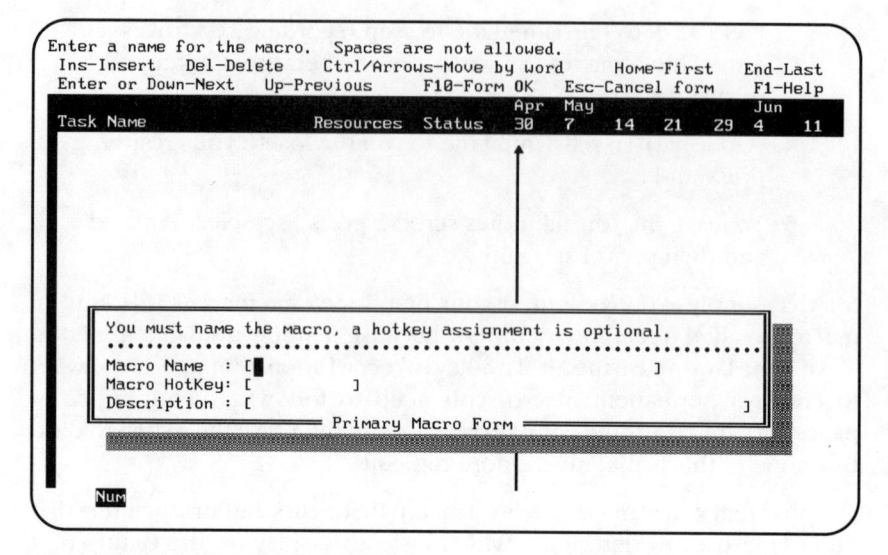

```
Enter a name for the macro.  Spaces are not allowed.
  Ins-Insert    Del-Delete    Ctrl/Arrows-Move by word    Home-First    End-Last
  Enter or Down-Next    Up-Previous    F10-Form OK    Esc-Cancel form    F1-Help
                                           Apr  May                      Jun
  Task Name                 Resources  Status  30   7    14   21   29   4    11
```

```
  You must name the macro, a hotkey assignment is optional.
  ...........................................................
  Macro Name   : [                                           ]
  Macro HotKey: [      ]
  Description  : [                                           ]
                    ══════ Primary Macro Form ══════
```

Fig. 10.7. The Primary Macro Form box.

use key combinations that are used by either Time Line or another program you run while using Time Line. You shouldn't, for example, use hotkeys that are combinations of Ctrl or Alt and function keys such as F1 or F2.

4. (Optional) Move the cursor to the Description field and enter a description of the macro (the description can be up to 60 characters long).

5. When the Primary Macro Form box is complete, press F10 to save the information and proceed with recording the keystrokes you want to turn into a macro. To indicate that it will record the keystrokes you type, Time Line displays the word Recording in the lower left corner of the screen.

6. Type the keystrokes you want Time Line to record. To have it record the keystrokes for clearing the current filters, for example, you type / (slash), S (Schedule), F (Filters), and then C (Clear).

7. To stop recording your keystrokes, press Alt- (the Alt key followed by the hyphen key). Don't, by the way, substitute the minus key on the keypad for the hyphen key, because the minus key doesn't work.

8. (Optional) To execute the macro, you have two choices:

If you gave the macro a hotkey, type the hotkey combination. Time Line executes the keystrokes that make up the macro.

Alternatively, you can activate the menu bar, select Utilities Macros, and then Macros List. (You can also press Alt-F6 to do this.) Time Line next displays the Macros List box shown in figure 10.8. The Macros List box shows the names of all the macros currently available. The macro notekey and the macro description of the highlighted macro also appears at the bottom of the Macros List box. Use the arrow keys to mark the macro you want to run and then press F10 or Enter. Time Line executes the keystrokes that make up the macro.

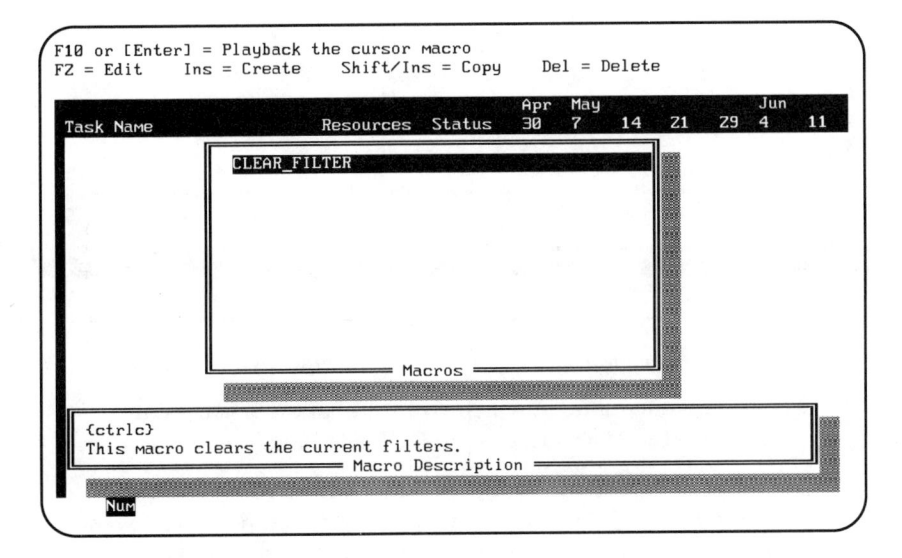

```
F10 or [Enter] = Playback the cursor macro
F2 = Edit    Ins = Create    Shift/Ins = Copy    Del = Delete

                                          Apr  May              Jun
Task Name              Resources  Status  30   7   14   21  29  4   11
                 ┌─ CLEAR_FILTER ──────────────────┐
                 │                                 │
                 │                                 │
                 │                                 │
                 │                                 │
                 │                                 │
                 │                                 │
                 │                                 │
                 │                                 │
                 └═══════════ Macros ══════════════┘

 {ctrlc}
 This macro clears the current filters.
 ══════════════ Macro Description ══════════════

 Num
```

Fig. 10.8. *The Macros list.*

9. (Optional) To stop a macro before the final keystroke, you can press Ctrl-Break.

Note: The ability to stop a macro with Ctrl-Break can be particularly handy when you've created a macro that doesn't work correctly and, therefore, won't stop on its own.

Saving and Reusing Macros

To reuse the permanent macros you create, you need to save them in a file on your disk just as you save project information in a file. You can probably already guess the steps:

1. Activate the menu bar and select Utilities Macros Save. Time Line displays the File Save Form (see fig. 10.9)—the same box you use to save regular project files. The difference for a macro file is that Time Line uses the file extension M$0 for macro files. (Time Line uses the file extension T$0 for project files.)

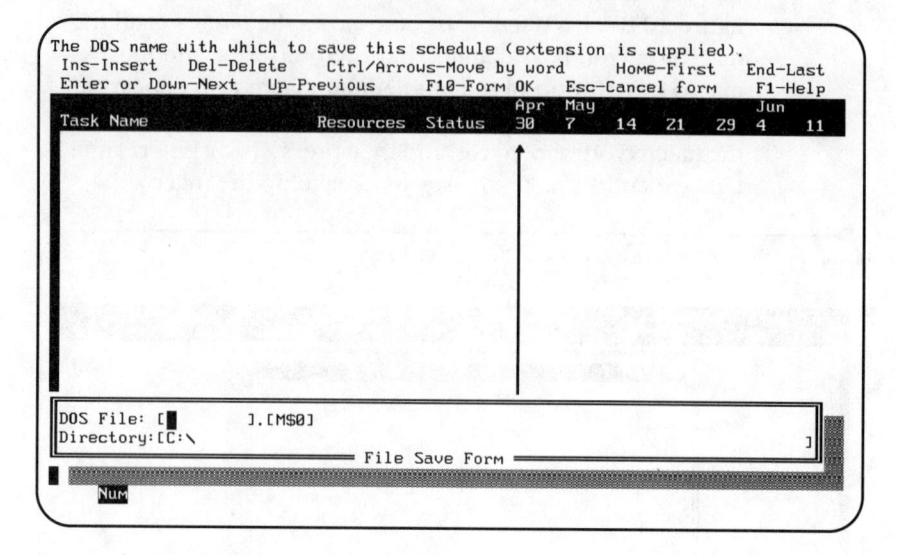

```
The DOS name with which to save this schedule (extension is supplied).
  Ins-Insert    Del-Delete    Ctrl/Arrows-Move by word      Home-First    End-Last
  Enter or Down-Next    Up-Previous        F10-Form OK    Esc-Cancel form    F1-Help
                                              Apr  May                    Jun
Task Name                    Resources Status  30   7    14    21   29    4    11












 DOS File: [█       ].[M$0]
 Directory:[C:\                                                                  ]
                            ════════ File Save Form ════════

  Num
```

Fig. 10.9. The File Save Form with the file extension set to save a macro file.

2. Enter the file name in which you want all the macros currently on the Macro List in the DOS File field.

3. Enter the path name to the directory where you want the macro file stored on your hard disk. For example, if you want to store the macro file in the same directory where the project files are stored, specify the directory as C:\TL4\DATA.

4. Press F10 when the File Save Form is complete.

5. If you previously saved a macro file using the file name entered in the DOS File field, Time Line displays a message that alerts you it's about to overwrite an existing macro file. To continue, select Proceed. To abort the save operation, select Cancel.

When you first start Time Line, and even after you load project schedule files, no macros are available. To use macros you've previously saved, you retrieve them from the disk by following the steps below:

1. Activate the menu bar and select Utilities, Macros, and then Load.

2. If there are already macros in memory, Time Line displays the Macros Exit box shown in figure 10.10.

   To replace the macros currently in memory with those from a macro file on disk, select Erase Current Macros.

   To add to the macros currently in memory those from a macro file on disk, select Add to Current Macros.

```
                                           Apr  May           Jun
Task Name              Resources Status    30   7   14  21   29   4   11
                                       ▲
       ┌─────────────────────────────────────────────────┐
       │  There are macros in memory.                    │
       │                                                 │
       │  Shall I: Erase current macros,                 │
       │           Add to current macros, Cancel         │
       │                                                 │
       │                                                 │
       └══════════════════Macros Exist═══════════════════┘

 NUM
```

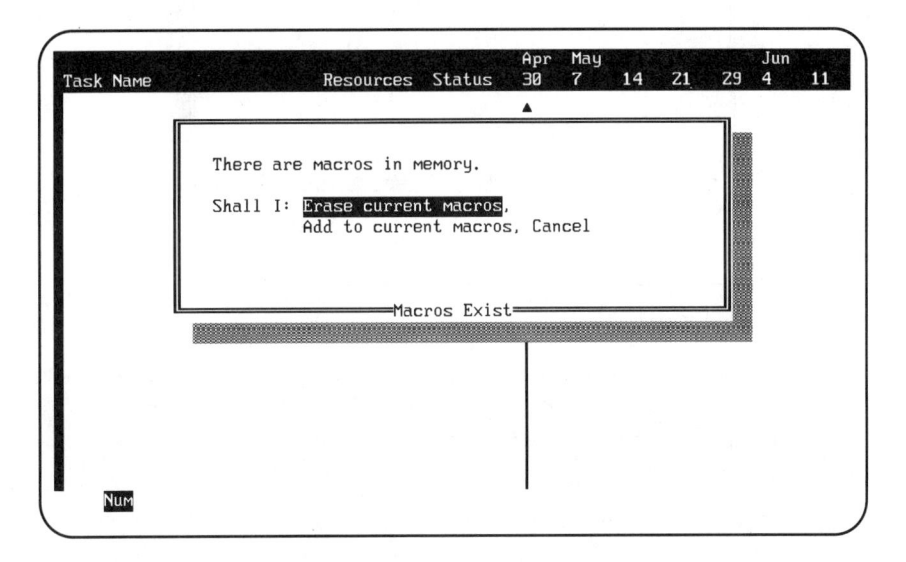

Fig. 10.10. The Macros Exist box.

3. Time Line next displays the Macro File list box (see fig. 10.11) which lists the macro files in the current directory. Use the arrow keys to highlight the macro file that contains the macros you want to use and then press Enter. (*Note:* The Macro File list box works just like the Project File list box described in Chapter 9, "Working with the Time Line Files," so refer there if you need more information.)

Note: If you use Time Line macro files, you should include them in your backup and restore operations, too. Backing up and restoring project files is described in Chapter 9.

Some Tips for Writing Simple Macros

You can write helpful macros that end up being very simple. Even so, however, there are some conventions you want to consider—conventions that should make it easier to construct and use the macros. These conventions, not all of which will apply in every situation, are itemized below:

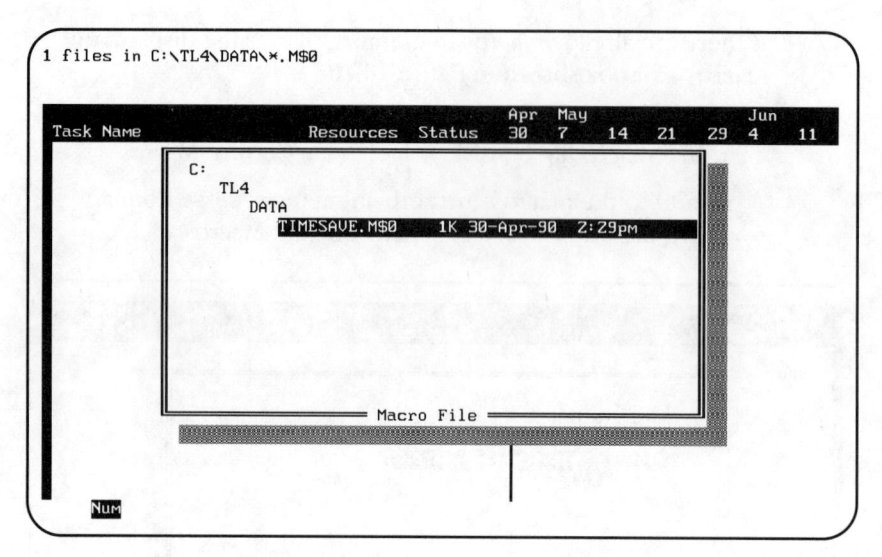

Fig. 10.11. The Macro File list box.

1. Take time to plan out your macro before you start recording. A few minutes spent sketching out what you want the macros to do can act as a blueprint you use to make sure that what you want to do is feasible.

2. If your macro activates the menu bar, start macros by pressing the Esc key several times. This assures that if the menu bar is already active when you start the macro, it is first inactivated.

3. Test your macro with example project files before you use it on a real project schedule. You can do anything in a macro that you can do with Time Line commands including such things as deleting tasks and resources, changing project options, and even erasing project and macro files. Even if your macro isn't supposed to change any data, verify that it doesn't before you run the macro on a schedule you don't want to corrupt or lose.

4. Remember that Ctrl-Break will stop a macro. If your macro doesn't stop on its own—which probably indicates you've got a macro bug—use Ctrl-Break to abort the macro.

5. Don't use as a macro hotkey a key combination that is already used by Time Line someplace else or a key combination used by a memory resident program that you use alongside Time Line. For the most part, this means you should use as hotkeys the Alt or Ctrl key and a letter, although there are some

letters you shouldn't use for your own macros because Time Line already uses these. Alt-P and Alt-R, for example, are used for temporary macros. And Alt-C and Alt-V can be used for cutting and pasting text on data entry screens.

6. You can put more than one macro in a macro file, which means you can use macro files as a way to group macros that you use together. That way if you want to start using the macros, say, that make it easier to create a project schedule, you can load one macro file that contains all the macros you need.

7. Give macros descriptive names and use the description field to document what the macro is supposed to do. It's easy to forget what a macro does if you haven't used it for several weeks or months—even if you spent considerable effort constructing it.

Reviewing the Other Macro Menu Options

Besides those options already discussed, Time Line also provides several other Macro menu options you will find useful from time to time (see fig. 10.12). The options include: Halt, Insert, Erase, and Configure. The paragraphs that follow describe how each option works and explains why you use the option.

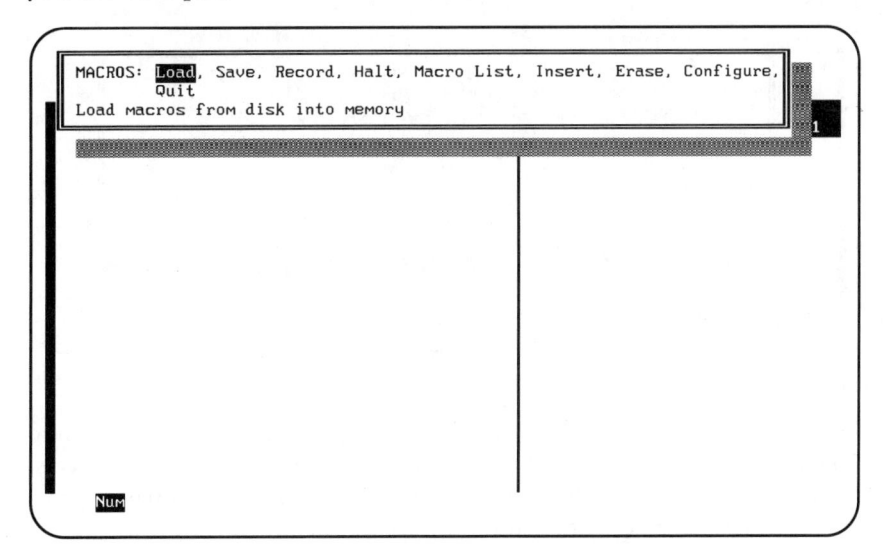

Fig. 10.12. The Macros submenu.

The Erase Option

The Erase option removes the macros currently in memory. This option does not delete macro files from your disk—instead, Erase only removes the macros currently in memory. In effect, Erase gives you a way to disable the macros in a macro file you previously loaded. When you select Erase, Time Line displays a message that alerts you that the program is about to erase all the macros in memory ands asks you to confirm that this is what you want done. Remember when you are using the Erase option that if you erase a macro before you save it, it is gone for good. The only way to make the macro available again is to recreate it from scratch.

The Configure Option

The Configure option lets you change the hotkey combinations that Time Line itself sets up for certain macro tasks. The option also lets you control the speed with which Time Line runs a macro. When you select the Configure option from the Macros menu, Time Line displays the Macros Configuration box (see fig. 10.13).

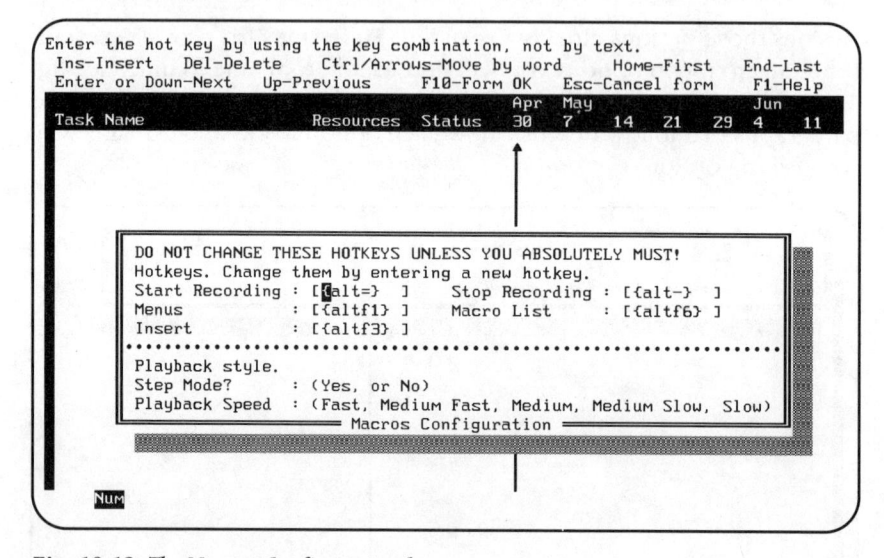

Fig. 10.13. The Macros Configuration box.

The top portion of the Macros Configuration box defines four hotkeys Time Line provides as substitutes for selecting one of the Macro menu options. Most of these have already been introduced in the preceding paragraphs. The two that haven't—Alt-F1 and Alt-F3—may be obvious to you:

- Alt-F1 is equivalent to activating the menu bar and selecting Utilities Macros

- Alt-F3 is equivalent to activating the menu bar and selecting Utilities Macros Insert (The Insert option is described a little later.)

You can change the hotkey Time Line uses for one of these functions if you find that the Time Line hotkey conflicts with the hotkey used by some other program you're running alongside Time Line—say as a memory resident program. To do so, simply type the keys you want to use for the hotkey.

The bottom portion of the screen controls how fast Time Line runs a macro. The Step Mode field causes Time Line to run macros one keystroke at a time—which can be very helpful for debugging, or unraveling, macros that don't seem to work right. The Playback Speed field provides five gradations that give you the ability to control how fast Time Line types the keystrokes. Usually, Fast is the preferred setting because the reason you're using macros in the first place is to speed things up.

When you've made the necessary changes to the Macros Configuration box, press F10 to save those changes and begin using them.

The Halt Option

The Halt option turns off the recording of keystrokes. Functionally, it's equivalent to pressing Alt-R when you're creating a temporary macro or Alt and - (hyphen) when you're creating a permanent macro. One important difference, however, between the Halt option and these other ways to stop keystroke recording is that if you select the Halt option, the keystrokes leading up to the keystroke where you select Halt also get recorded. For example, to select Halt, you would press / (slash) U (Utilities) M (Macros) H (Halt), so Time Line would end up recording the first three keystrokes you type. For this reason, you probably won't want to use Halt and will instead use Alt-R for temporary macros and Alt - (hyphen) for permanent macros.

The Insert Option

The Insert option provides a series of advanced macro functions that, in essence, let you perform some rudimentary programming with the Time Line macros features. To be candid, the features provided by the Insert option are not for most users. The capabilities are for those users who want to customize the operation of Time Line so it better meets their requirements.

In all, the Insert menu option accesses a submenu with seven additional macro options: Macro, Secondary Macro, Input Pause, Choices, Dialog, Pause, and Link (see fig. 10.14). You can also access these options when you're recording a macro or editing a macro. (Editing a macro is described later in this chapter.)

```
INSERT: Macro, Secondary Macro, Input Pause, Choices, Dialog, Pause,
        Link, Quit
Insert a macro from memory into the current macro.
```

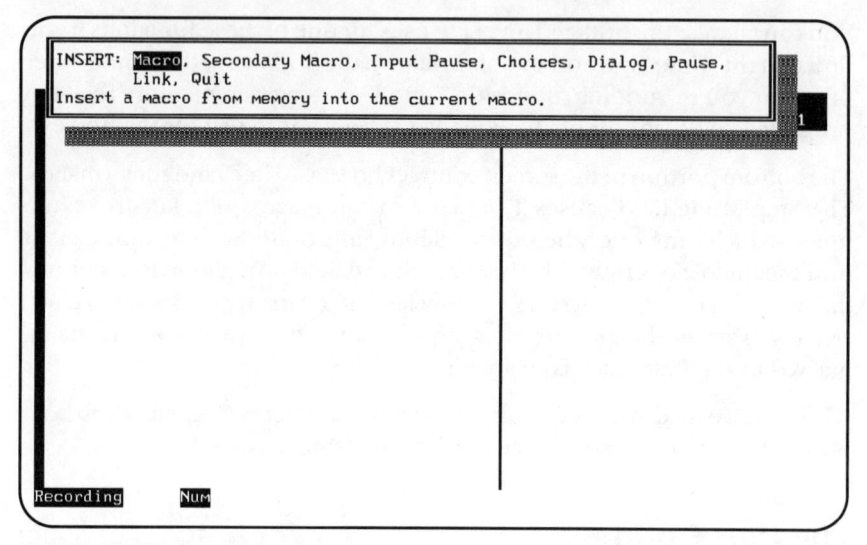

Fig. 10.14. The Insert submenu.

The Macro Option

Macro lets you run a macro from inside another macro. Suppose, for example, that you've written a macro named CLEAR_FILTER and you want the macro to run another macro named RECALC that recalculates the project schedule. At the point in the CLEAR_FILTER macro that you want to run the RECALC macro, you would select the Insert menu option. Pressing Alt-F3 provides a quick way of selecting the Insert menu option. Then you would select the Macro option from the Insert submenu. Time Line displays the Macro List box which lists all the macros currently in memory. You would simply highlight the macro you want to run, in this example RECALC, and then press Enter. The RECALC macro would then be run by the CLEAR_FILTER macro at the point in the sequence of keystrokes where you inserted it.

The Secondary Macro Option

Secondary Macro is a little complicated. Secondary macros give you a way to collect keystrokes while a macro runs and then repeat these keystrokes later during the macro. To initially cause the macro you're recording to later pause and collect these keystrokes, you select the Secondary Macro option. Time Line displays the Secondary Macro Form box (see fig. 10.15). This box looks and works like the Primary Macro Form box: You enter a macro name and, optionally, a hotkey and description. To cause the macro you're recording to later type the keystrokes collected, you use the Insert Macro option. Time Line displays the Macros List, and you select the Secondary Macro option.

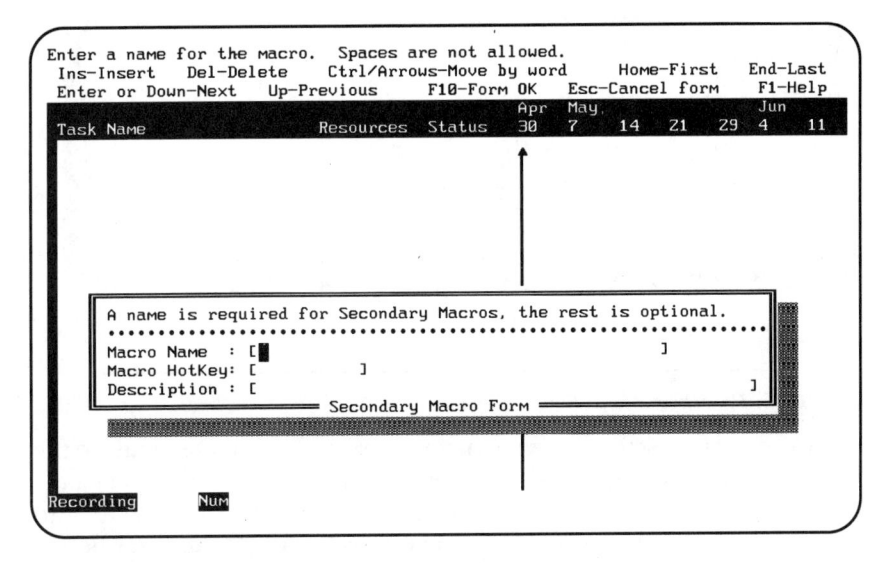

Fig. 10.15. The Secondary Macro Form box.

The Input Pause Option

The Input Pause option stops the macro so that the user can enter data. The Input Pause option, for example, gives you a way to stop a macro while a user enters or edits data on a Time Line Form screen. The macro resumes when the user presses F10. To use this feature in a macro you're recording, select Input Pause option at the point in a macro where you want the macro to stop so someone can enter or edit data. Time Line will display the message `Input: F10 = Resume Macro` at the bottom of the screen to remind the user to press F10 to continue the macro's execution.

The Choices Option

The Choices option lets you display a menu from which the user can select an option. Each option on the menu simply starts another macro. To use this feature in a macro you're recording, select Choices at the point in a macro where you want to display a menu that shows choices for the macro that is to be executed next. Time Line displays the Macro Menu Form box shown in figure 10.16.

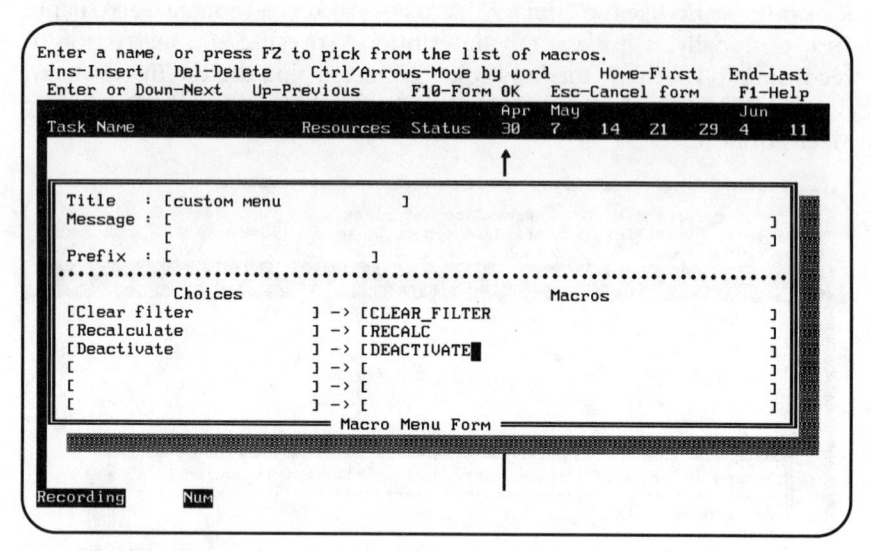

```
Enter a name, or press F2 to pick from the list of macros.
  Ins-Insert    Del-Delete    Ctrl/Arrows-Move by word      Home-First    End-Last
  Enter or Down-Next    Up-Previous    F10-Form OK    Esc-Cancel form    F1-Help
                                           Apr  May                  Jun
  Task Name              Resources  Status  30   7   14   21   29   4    11

        Title   : [custom menu              ]
        Message : [                                                       ]
                  [                                                       ]
        Prefix  : [                ]
        ...............................................................
              Choices                              Macros
        [Clear filter       ] -> [CLEAR_FILTER                            ]
        [Recalculate        ] -> [RECALC                                  ]
        [Deactivate         ] -> [DEACTIVATE                              ]
        [                   ] -> [                                        ]
        [                   ] -> [                                        ]
        [                   ] -> [                                        ]
                              ===== Macro Menu Form =====

  Recording        Num
```

Fig. 10.16. The Macro Menu Form screen.

The top half of the screen provides fields for you to give a screen title to the menu, create a message to be displayed with the menu, and give a name, or prefix, to the menu that the macro you're recording can use to refer to the menu. The bottom half of the screen provides two columns: Choices and Macros. Enter in the Choices column the names of the menu options you want on the menu. Enter in the Macros column the macros that should be run when the choice is selected. (Remember that Alt-F6 displays the Macros List from which you can select macros.) Figure 10.17 shows the menu created by the Macro Menu Form screen in figure 10.16.

The Dialog Options

The Dialog option lets you insert a message in a macro. This option gives you the ability to provide instruction and to report on the progress of the macro to the user running the macro. To use this feature in a macro you're recording, select the Dialog option at the point in a macro where the message box is to appear. Time Line then displays the Message Form box (see fig. 10.18). Enter the title and the message text in the appropriate fields. Figure 10.19 shows the message box defined when the Message Form box is completed as shown in figure 10.18.

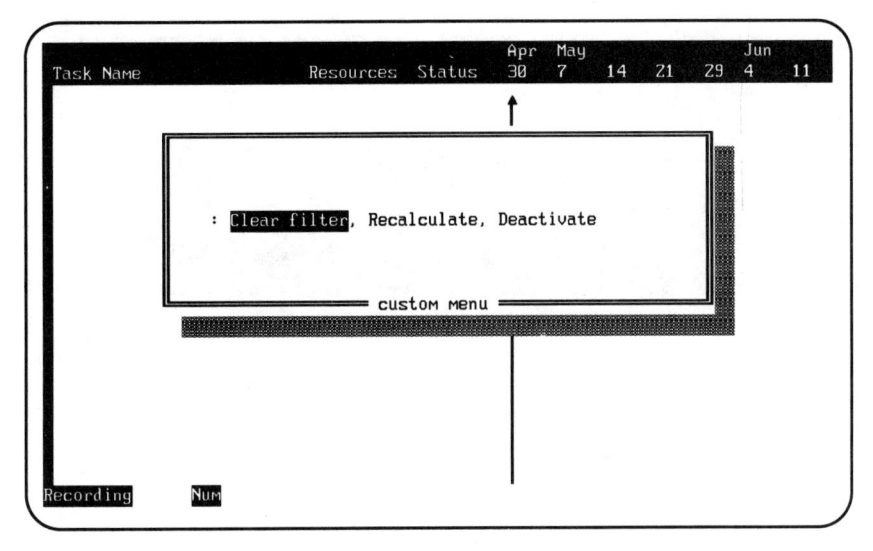

Fig. 10.17. An example macro menu.

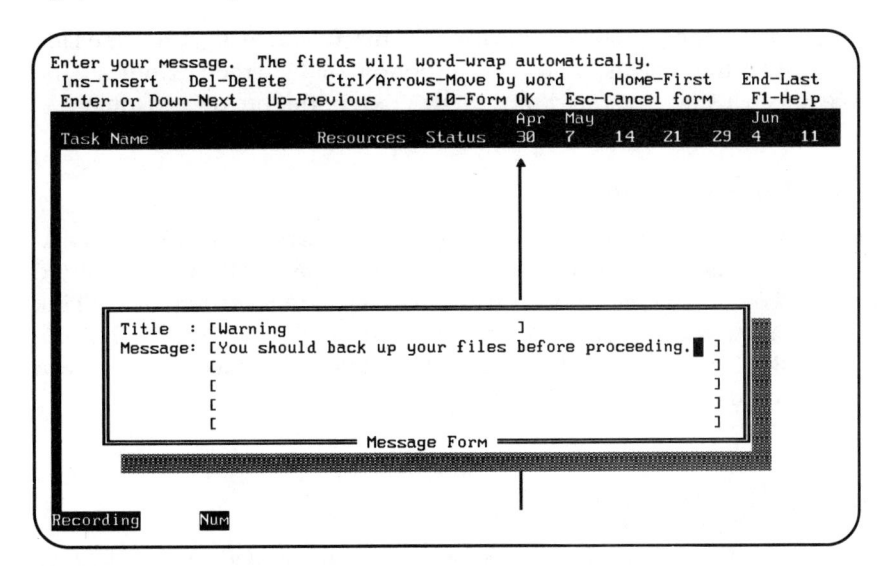

Fig. 10.18. The Message Form box.

The Pause Option

The Pause option stops the macro so that the user working with Time Line can enter data—or execute Time Line menu options. This option resembles the Input Pause command except that the user can execute Time Line commands. To use this feature in a macro you're recording, select Pause

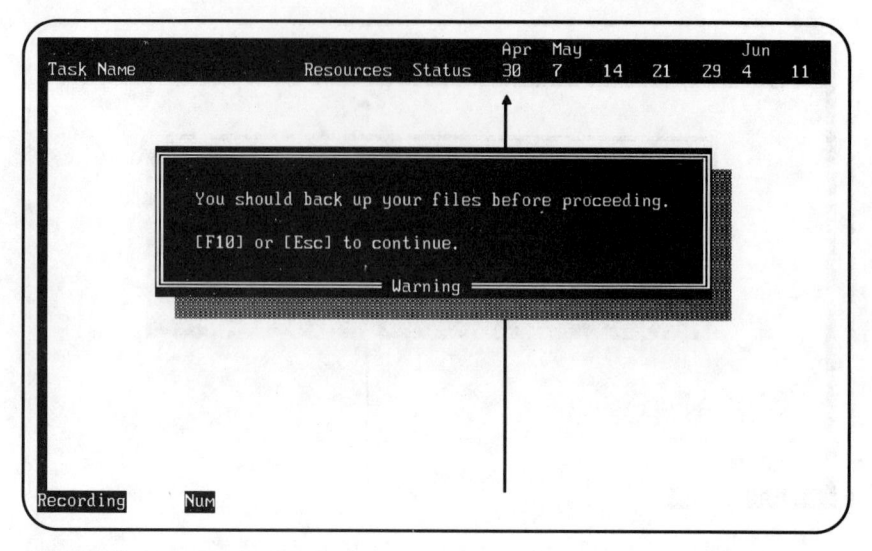

Fig. 10.19. An example message box.

option at the appropriate point. When the macro is actually run, Time Line will display the message, Pause at the bottom of the screen to indicate the macro is pausing. To restart the macro's execution, press Ctrl-Home.

The Link Option

The Link option lets you use a macro that's not currently in memory. Link, in effect, causes Time Line to load a macro file and retrieve the needed macro from it. To use this feature in a macro you're recording, select Link option at the point where the macro should be run. Time Line displays the Macro File list you use to identify the file and then the Macros List box you use to identify the macro.

Editing Macros

The discussion to this point has assumed you're using Macro record feature to construct macros. Although the record feature saves you time and trouble by recording the keystrokes for your macro as you create it, you do need some way of changing macros that don't get recorded quite right. So not surprisingly, Time Line provides a way to edit the sequences of keystrokes it collects. This editing can include deleting certain keystrokes, changing other keystrokes, and even wide scale additions of keystrokes.

Chapter 10: Using Time Line Utilities 311

To edit a macro you've previously created, follow these steps:

1. Activate the menu bar and select Utilities Macro Macro List.

2. Use the arrow keys to highlight the macro you want to change.

3. With the macro you want to change highlighted, press F2. Or if you want to edit a copy of an existing macro, press Shift-Ins. Time Line displays the macro editor screen which shows the name (and the hotkey, if there is one) on the bottom border of the screen (see fig. 10.20).

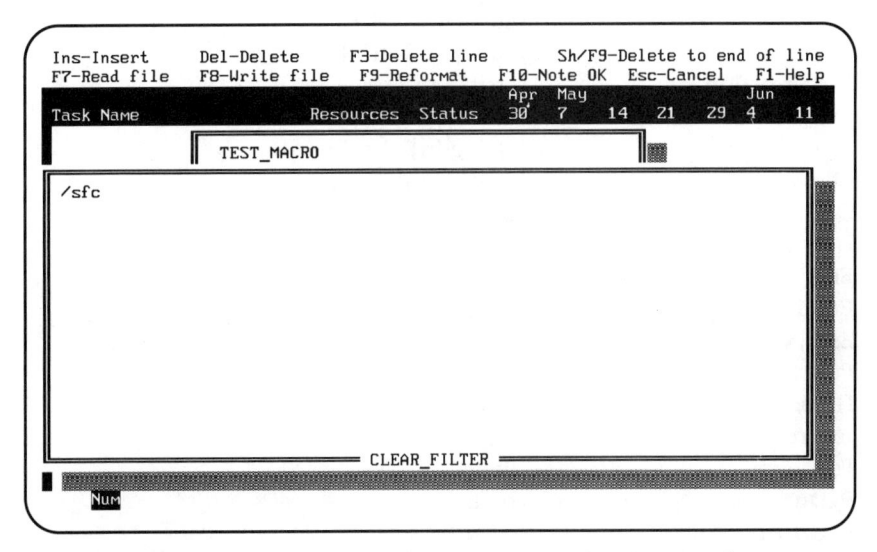

```
Ins-Insert      Del-Delete     F3-Delete line       Sh/F9-Delete to end of line
F7-Read file    F8-Write file  F9-Reformat    F10-Note OK  Esc-Cancel    F1-Help
                                             Apr  May                 Jun
        Task Name              Resources  Status  30   7    14   21   29  4    11

                  TEST_MACRO

 /sfc




                              CLEAR_FILTER

 Num
```

Fig. 10.20. The macro editor screen showing the macro that activates the menu bar and then selects Schedule Filter Clear.

4. Edit the keystrokes the same way you would edit any other text.

5. Press F10 to save your changes.

Most of the keys on a keyboard have a single character, number, or symbol equivalent, which is how they show up on the macro editor screen. Pressing the slash key to activate the menu, for example, shows up as /. And pressing the A key shows up as just an A in the macro. There are, however, a few keys that don't have one character equivalents such as the tab key or the Ins key. Time Line uses short words inside the brace symbols ({ }) to represent these. Table 10.1 summarizes these short words.

**Table 10.1
How Time Line Represents
Keyboard Keys and Key Combinations
without One Character Equivalents**

Keyboard Key	Macro Equivalent
Alt Letter keys	{alta} to {altz}
Alt Function keys	{altf1} to {altf10}
Alt Top row numbers	{alt1} to {alt10}
Backspace	{bks}
Ctrl Letter keys	{ctrla} to {ctrlg}
	{ctrli} to {ctrll}
	{ctrln} to {ctrlz}
Ctrl Function keys	{ctrlf1} to {ctrlf10}
Ctrl Number pad keys	{ctrllft}, {ctrlrgt}
	{ctrlpgdn}, {ctrlpgup}
	{ctrlhome}, {ctrlend}
Delete	{del}
Down arrow	{dn}
End	{end}
Enter	{enter}
Escape	{esc}
Function keys	{f1} to {f10}
Home	{home}
Insert	{ins}
Left arrow	{lft}
PgDn	{pgdn}
PgUp	{pgup}
Right arrow	{rgt}
Shift Function keys	{capsf1} to {capsf10}
Shift Tab	{revtab}
Tab	{tab}
Up arrow	{up}

In addition, the Insert options, which amount to special programming commands, are represented by still other words in braces or strings of several words in braces symbols. Table 10.2 summarizes how Time Line represents these. If you have questions about the arguments of the insert programming commands—these are shown in italics—refer to the earlier discussions of the Insert options. When there are arguments, they correspond to fields you fill on the screen for that Insert option.

Chapter 10: Using Time Line Utilities

Table 10.2
How Time Line Represents the Insert Options

Insert option	Syntax	Notes
Macro	{macroname}	The *macroname* argument is the actual name of the macro that should be run
Secondary Macro	{beginput}{macroname}{endinput}	The *macroname* argument is the actual name of the macro that's being partially defined. This is the statement that will result in Time Line stopping to collect whatever keystrokes the user enters. To subsequently run the macro, use the Macro programming command.
Input Pause	{beginput}{endinput}	Input Pause uses no arguments
Choices	{begmenu}*title*|*message*|*choice1,choice2....*|{*macroname1*}{*macroname2*}...{endmenu}	You can enter up to six complete sets of menu choices and macros.
Dialog	{begmsg}*title*|*message*{endmsg}	The message text can be up to 255 characters in length. Time Line will split the message into five 51-character lines in a message box.
Pause	{pause}	Pause uses no arguments
Link	{beglink}*drive\path\file name\macro*{endlink}	The *drive, path* and file name needs to be entered just as you would for completing the Link option, for example, C:\TL4\DATA\MACRO1.M$0. The macro name follows

Table 10.2 Continued

Table 10.2—_continued_

Insert option	Syntax	Notes
		this, separated from drive, path and file name by a slash. So if the macro name was CLEAR_FILTER, the complete link statement argument would look like: *C:\TL4\DATA\ MACRO1.M$0\ CLEAR_FILTER.*

Some Tips for Writing More Complex Macros

In addition to the tips listed earlier, there are some conventions you may want to consider as you write more complex macros. Again, not all of these will apply in every case, but it's a good idea to have them in the back of your mind as you construct complex macros:

1. Break large macros into several smaller macros and then create a new macro that runs each of the smaller macros. Smaller macros are generally easier to write and easier to debug. In addition, Time Line limits macros to 1,500 characters in length so by using this approach you shouldn't ever need to worry about this size limit.

2. You don't have to construct macros by recording the keystrokes, although this is usually the easiest way. You can also construct them by typing the keystrokes right in the macro editor window screen. This process is explained earlier in the chapter in the section "Editing Macros."

3. You can create looping macros by having a macro run itself, but there's no way to stop a looping macro like this automatically. (This capability does exist in other programming languages and in the macro feature of some software programs.) To stop a looping macro in Time Line, you press Ctrl-Break. You will probably need some method of stopping a looping Time Line macro—such as pausing the macro occasionally to see whether it is done.

Chapter Summary

This chapter describes how you can use the options on the Time Line Utilities menu. In essence, the Utilities menu is like a tool box and the individual menu options like tools. You probably won't ever use all the tools. Some you'll reach for more than others. But together the tools will make working with Time Line faster and easier.

This chapter concludes the discussion of Time Line's features. There is one other topic that is important to cover, however: preventing system disasters. Accordingly, Chapter 11 describes how to minimize or eliminate the risk of a system disaster that could ruin your project management system and files.

11

Protecting against System Disasters

System disasters affect more than your Time Line program and data files—they may affect every software program and data file on your computer. Many Time Line users feel that there isn't anything in the computer more important than their Time Line program and their data files. After all, the data that Time Line collects and processes is, for many users, essential to project success. So it's important for Time Line users to understand both the reasons for and some of the precautions against some of the more common and the more dangerous system errors. If you're an experienced computer user, you can probably skip this chapter. If you're new to computers or want to make sure you're playing it safe, you will benefit from quickly skimming the chapter.

The chapter is broken into three sections:

1. Defining a Few Basic Terms

2. Preventing Hardware Disasters

3. Preventing Software Disasters

One other thing—the information in this chapter doesn't apply only to Time Line program and data files. This information is covered here in the interest of protecting your project management system and records, but the information also applies to your other software and data files, as well.

Defining a Few Basic Terms

Before you begin looking into ways you can prevent system disasters, you need to understand a few computer terms:

Term	Description
Files	Files are the basic storage tool of computers. For example, if you looked in the Time Line directory, TL4, you would see a list of files. (You can try this yourself by typing DIR C:\TL4 at the C:> prompt.) In essence there are two types of files: program files and data files.
Program files	Program files store the instructions, or software, that tell your computer what to do. You can usually tell program files by their extensions because program files are named with EXE, COM, or BAT file extensions.
Data files	Data files store information. So, for example, the task and resource information you enter actually is stored in data files.
Software	The instructions that tell your computer what to do. Often people segregate software into *system software* (which generally controls the physical components of your computer system) and *application software* (which uses the operating software to create and process data). DOS, which is an acronym for Disk Operating System, is an example of system software. Time Line is an example of application software.
Hardware	Hardware refers to the actual, physical components of your computer—things like the monitor, keyboard, printer, disk drives, memory and microprocessor chips, and so forth.

Preventing Hardware Disasters

Computers, like people, don't always operate perfectly. And although you probably shouldn't worry about your personal computer breaking down, you do need to be prepared for it. Better yet, you can work to prevent it.

Dealing with Dirty Power

The electric power you use to run your computer and everything else in your home or office may itself pose a danger to your computer and the data you store on and with it. The danger comes from dirty electrical power: power that surges and sags in strength. Now most of the time, these fluctuations won't cause a problem. But if the surge is severe enough, it may cause your computer to reset itself. In effect, then, the power surge causes your computer to temporarily turn itself off which means, at the very least, you will lose the project information you have entered as part of the current session of Time Line. Unfortunately, the situation can get worse than that: if a power surge causes your computer to reset at the same time it's writing or reading data from your hard disk or a floppy disk, the data on the disk may be damaged.

To prevent this particular disaster, you can use a simple device called a *surge protector* or *surge suppresser*. You plug the surge protector into the wall socket, and then you plug your computer into the surge protector. The surge protector removes power surges, protecting your computer from receiving a power surge. Talk to your local computer supplier to see which type of surge protector is best for your system. You shouldn't have to pay much more than about $50.

Hard Disk Failures

Hard disks are remarkably reliable when you consider the fact that while your computer runs the actual disk is constantly spinning. Sooner or later, however, the disk will probably fail. And this is the first thing to know about hard disk failures: eventually, you too will suffer from one. So remember to back up regularly—that way, you minimize the time you lose re-entering transactions. (Chapter 9, "Working with the Time Line Files," describes how to back up your files.)

The other thing about hard disk failures—and, in fact, any other hardware failure—is that "later" is better than "sooner." So consider two preventative measures. First, don't turn on and off your machine several times a day. Instead, just leave it running. Your computer won't use much electrical power—probably about the same as your desk lamp. And by leaving the computer running all day—even while you're out running errands, going to lunch, or working with customers—you minimize the most wearing and stressful operation your computer goes through: being turned on.

A second preventative measure relates to the fact that heat really isn't good for your computer. So keep the room your computer is in at a comfortable temperature for your computer's sake if not for your own. And don't stack books, the user manual, or even this book on top of the computer or blocking it's ventilation holes. Some of the circuitry like the microprocessor need to stay below a certain temperature in order to work right. And I've even heard horror stories about the personal computer circuit boards—the laminated cardboard boards that the electronic circuitry plugs into—delaminating when temperatures become extreme.

Floppy Disk Problems

You will undoubtedly use floppy disks to store the back up copies of the Time Line files—even if you have a hard disk on your computer. For this reason, we need to include a little information about preventing floppy disk failures.

Floppy disks are amazingly durable. As long as you treat them with a reasonable degree of care, you really shouldn't have problems. There are, however, a few things you should consider. Floppy disks store data on a thin plastic disk that's coated with a material that can store magnetic charges. Magnetic charges on the disk's surface represent the binary digits, or bits, which are the basic building blocks of program and data files. This isn't so important to remember except that it explains why you want to treat floppy disks in a certain way.

First of all, because the actual disk is plastic, you don't want the diskette to get very cold or very hot. A very cold diskette—such as one subjected to temperatures below freezing—gets brittle and may change shape. A very hot diskette—one exposed to temperatures of 140 degrees—may warp or even melt. In either case, because the actual plastic disk becomes damaged, there's a good chance you'll also lose the data on the disk. You shouldn't, therefore, leave diskettes in your car if it's parked outside and the temperature is below freezing. You shouldn't leave diskettes on the dashboard of your car on a hot, sunny day. And you shouldn't set a steaming mug of coffee on top of the diskette.

A second set of problems relates to the fact that the information on the diskette is stored as a series of magnetic charges on the disk's surface. Because of this, you don't want to do things that change or foul the charges. Don't, for example, store diskettes next to a magnet even if the magnet is only a small one for holding paper clips. And don't store diskettes next to appliances that generate magnetic fields such as refrigerators, televisions, and telephones. You also don't want to touch the actual disk surface (which you can see through the opening on the plastic sleeve of the disk), spill things on the disk, or write on the diskette with something sharp.

Reviewing and Preventing Software Disasters

Software poses as many potential dangers to your computer and to your use of Time Line as does the hardware. There is, for example, the possibility of accidentally deleting files, of somehow "catching" a computer virus, and the myriad of difficulties that can come from working with beta software, freeware, and shareware. Because all these things can damage your computer, the Time Line data files, and your ability to use Time Line, it also makes sense to spend a few paragraphs talking about them.

Recovering Deleted Files

You can use a variety of ways to delete files: using the DOS DEL or ERASE commands, with Time Line, and with other application programs such as Lotus 1-2-3 and Microsoft Word. Because there are so many ways to delete files, it's not impossible to accidentally delete files—much as it's not impossible to accidentally throw out an important project document. So you should know that if you do accidentally delete a file, you can recover the file as long as your understand what happens when you delete a file and which tools you can use to recover, or undelete, previously deleted files.

When DOS deletes a file, it doesn't actually remove the file from the hard disk or floppy disk. Instead, it erases the first letter of the file's name on its list of files and file locations. Now at this point in time, the file and the file name—minus it's first letter—are still there. But DOS considers the deleted file gone. So you can still recover the file although you won't be able to use DOS to do so. However, there are several relatively inexpensive software programs that provide an undelete file feature. These include PC Tools Deluxe, Norton Utilities, and Mace Utilities. So if it was really important, you could trot down to the local software store, purchase one of these utilities—I'd recommend PC Tools Deluxe—and use it to undelete a deleted project file. Whichever software program you picked, the process would work the same way. Say, for example, that you picked PC Tools Deluxe. PC Tools Deluxe would look at DOS's list of files and file locations and give you a list of the files on the list that have had their first letters erased. So a Time Line data file might appear as

SAILBOAT.T$0

would instead appear on a list as

?AILBOAT.T$0

You would follow the program's directions for undeleting the files which simply means you would type the first letter of the file names that were deleted—in this example, you would type the letter S.

One important caution is needed with regard to keeping open your options to recover a previously deleted file. Once DOS marks a file as erased in its list of files and file locations, it assumes that the portion of the disk that contains the deleted file can be used to store other program and data files. So if you create any new data files, increase the size of existing data files, or install new program files—such as the software program you use to recover the deleted files, you may, in fact, over-write the file or files you want to recover. For this reason, if you do accidentally delete your files and will recover the deleted files using one of the popular software programs available, do so immediately. And don't do anything that changes or adds to the files on the hard disk or floppy disk that contains the deleted files.

Protecting against Viruses

Viruses have been around for quite a while—probably for almost 20 years now. Some say their existence and danger have been exaggerated. Others counter by pointing to the widely reported examples of viruses that you may have read about in your local newspaper. But whatever the truth, it makes sense to understand a thing or two about viruses and about how to protect yourself from them.

What Are Viruses?

Viruses are actually small software programs. Sometimes they do rather innocuous things like displaying political or supposedly humorous messages randomly or on specific dates—such as April 1—as you work on your computer. Often times, they operate more nefariously. A virus, for example, might secretly and slowly destroy program and data files bit by bit. And because the corruption of your data files is so slow, you don't notice the virus's effect until it's too late and the virus has infected even your backup copies of data files. Another virus might incrementally use more of your computer's power so it operates slower and slower—as you scratch your head and wonder why, for example, Time Line just doesn't work as snappy anymore. In each of these cases, however, it's clear that you don't want your machine infected. And in most cases, the steps for making sure your machine isn't infected or for disinfecting your machine aren't all that difficult as long as you understand where viruses come from and how you can detect and get rid of them.

Where Do Viruses Come From?

Because a virus is actually a software program, in order for your machine to be infected, the virus program file somehow needs to be copied to your computer. Usually, that means the virus program file is copied to your computer from an infected floppy disk. For this reason, the basic rule is that you shouldn't blindly copy program files from floppy disks.

I never worry about copying program files as part of installing a software program from a major software company. Software companies, for the most part, thoroughly test all the parts of a program long before you ever install it. But—and this is conjecture—I would be leery about copying program files from a floppy disk that comes from a friend or a friend of a friend. So, even aside from the legal and moral issues, you shouldn't copy pirated software because even though the original software is fine, the pirate copy floppy disk may be infected.

And, although not everybody will agree with me, I don't think you should use the free software that people pass around because, it's just too difficult to assure that the program files aren't infected. If you do insist on using these programs, consider contacting the original writer to confirm that the program files you're copying are, in fact, the ones he wrote. You might also confirm that the file date and file size, which shows when you list the program files using the DOS DIR command are the same as the original program files he created.

Detecting Viruses and Disinfecting Disks

If you have, in the past, indiscriminately copied program files to your hard disk, there's a possibility that your machine is already infected. Predictably, the steps for curing your machine really depends on the virus. Different viruses behave differently, but you should be on the watch for several things. First of all, keep a sharp eye out for program files that you don't understand or don't seem related to the software programs you use. If you find a suspicious-looking file, refer to the appropriate software user manual to confirm that it is indeed a valid program file. (Program files use the file extensions COM, EXE, or BAT.) If you find a program you know you don't use, remove it from the disk.

A second thing to watch for are increases in the file size of program files. Some viruses don't actually appear as a separate program file but rather append themselves to existing program files. Accordingly, if for no apparent reason, you see program files increasing in size, consider the possibility that the existing program file is being contaminated by a virus. You should be able to check quite easily with the software manufacturer if you have questions about this possibility. For the obvious reasons, any software manufacturer would be extremely interested if there were a virus specifically infecting one of their programs.

A third thing to watch for are hidden files. There may be two or three hidden files on a disk. PC DOS uses the two hidden files IBMBIO.COM and IBMDOS.COM. MS-DOS uses the two hidden files IO.SYS and MSDOS.SYS. (*Note:* File extensions on PC DOS hidden files are COM, not SYS.) If you use labels in your disk naming conventions, you may have a third hidden file. But there really shouldn't be other hidden files on your disks. And if there are, it's either because you hid them using one of the software programs mentioned earlier such as PC Tools Deluxe or Norton Utilities or someone else hid them—and that someone may just be the creator of a virus.

To check for the presence of hidden files, use the DOS CHKDSK command. To use the CHKDSK command, type *chkdsk* followed by the drive letter and a colon, and press Enter. (So, to look for hidden files on the floppy disk in drive A, for example, you would type *chkdsk a:* and press Enter.) DOS then displays information about the disk including the number of hidden files. (For an example of the other information that the CHKDSK command displays, refer to the DOS users manual that came with your computer.)

Working with Beta Software

Beta software is the pre-release software that software manufacturers distribute to small groups of users—usually experienced and sophisticated users—to test the software before it's actually released to the software-buying public. Now although in some people's minds there is a certain prestige to working with beta copies of software—particularly beta copies of popular programs—it's probably not something that you want to do on any machine that stores something as important as the system you're using to manage a project of critical importance. There's a reason that companies release beta copies of software products: the product may have programming bugs, or errors, that mean the program unexpectedly aborts or that it may damage or destroy data files. A related point is that you shouldn't, for the same reason, ever use a beta copy of the software in place of an actual released-to-the-public version.

Chapter Summary

This chapter covered a topic that most of us aren't used to thinking about: preventing system disasters. However, if you're going to use a computer as a tool for managing important projects, it makes sense to understand both how to prevent hardware disasters and how to prevent software disasters.

This chapter also concludes *Using Time Line.* Through this and the previous ten chapters I've tried to deliver information that will make it easier for you to succeed at projects by using Time Line as a project management tool. Hopefully, we—the publisher, editor, and I—have succeeded in our project, producing a book that makes it easier and more likely you'll succeed at your own projects. Good luck!

Index

A
activating menu bar, 95
actual costs, monitoring, 168
Add (Tasks menu) option, 65
allocating resources, 21, 139-143
    displaying allocations, 143-146
Always Show field, 106
American Standard Code for Information Interchange *see* ASCII
Any DOS Files (Erase menu) option, 263
Any Time Line files (Erase menu) option, 263
applications software, 318
Arrow keys, Notepad Navigation, 116
As-of date settings
    Current Time, 119
    Manual, 119
    selecting, 119
    Start/day, 119
    Start/week, 119
ascending sort order, 178
ASCII files
    importing, 280-286
    retrieving text, 117
    saving, 117
Assignment text report, 25, 202
    printing, 223-226
Assist menu options
    Help, 84
    New Schedule, 86-87
    Tutorial, 88
 Update, 171
    automatic recalculation, 120
    correcting, 130

B
backing up files, 264-266
BACKUP (DOS) command, 264-266
Baseline Gantt chart layout, 193
baselines, 160
benchmark, 159
beta software, 324
Both Verify and Renumber (WBS Manager menu) option, 103
brace symbols ({ }), 311
budgeting costs, 153-157

C
C/SSR Support Gantt chart layout, 194
calculating
    finish dates, 15-19
    slack time, 19
    start dates, 15-19
Calendar (Schedule menu) option, 59
Calendar file combine operation, 267
Calendar menu options
    Dates, 61
    Settings, 62
    Workhours, 59
Calendar Settings screen, 62-64
    Format End Dates field, 64
    Precision field, 64
    Standard Week Begins field, 63
    Standard Workday field, 62
    Standard Workweek field, 63
    Standard Year Begins field, 64
calendars
    adding tasks, 65-68
    creating, 59-64
    deleting tasks, 68-69
    editing tasks, 68-69
    erasing, 76
canceling macros, 302
characters
    deleting, 116
    inserting, 116
charts
    Gantt, 23-24, 80-81, 95, 143-144, 193-194
    histogram, 25, 144-146

layout, 192-193
PERT, 22, 72-75, 82, 93, 125
printing
    Gantt charts, 241-253
    PERT charts, 241-253
Tree, 22, 95
CHKDSK (DOS) command, 30
Choices (Macro menu) option, 307-308
choosing commands from menus, 59
circular dependencies
    correcting, 129
    loop, 130
Combine (File menu) option, 268
combining files, 267-271
commands
    choosing from menus, 59
    DOS
        BACKUP, 264-266
        CHKDSK, 30
        DEL, 321
        ERASE, 321
        RESTORE, 266-267
        TYPE, 41
Configure (Macro menu) option, 304-305
Configure menu options, 42
    Date Format, 42, 52
    Disk File, 42, 53
    Graphics, 42
    Mouse, 42, 54
    Printer, 42
    Video, 42
Configure Video screen, 44
configuring
    printers, 49-51
    Time Line, 42
Copy (Task menu) option, 115
Cost Assignment Form screen, 168
costs, 150-151
    actual, 168
    budgeting, 153-157
    fixed, 169
    identifying, 151-155
    recording, 168
    variable, 170
Costs PERT/Tree chart layout, 195
Critical Path filter, 182
Cross Tab text report, 202
    printing, 226-231
cross-tabulations, 273-274
Ctrl-← key, Notepad Navigation, 116
Ctrl-→ key, Notepad Navigation, 116
Ctrl-S key, scrolling DOS TYPE command, 41
Current time (As-of date settings) option, 119
Current Time Line Files (Erase menu) option, 263
Currently Scheduled filter, 183
cursor movement key combinations, 69
custom filters, 186-189
custom layouts, 196-200

D

data files, 318
database files, importing, 277-280
Date Display, selecting, 119
Date Formats (Configure menu) option, 42, 52
dates
    formats, 294
    selecting, 119
Dates & Durations Gantt chart layout, 194
Dates (Calendar menu) option, 61
Dates screen, 62
defaults
    ASCII file format, 53
    dates, 119
    directory, 34-35
    Force Future Tasks, 121
    Options Form, 117
    Outline, 121
    Prefix field, 104
    recalculation, 120
    Redo, 121
    Separate by entry, 106
    Task Form screen, 120
    times, 119
    Undo, 121
DEL (DOS) command, 321
deleting
    characters, 116
    files, 262-264
    filters, 190
    layouts, 200
    subtasks, 97
    summary tasks, 97
    tasks from calendars, 68-69
    to end of line, 116
dependencies, 11, 71-72
    circular, 129
    correcting, 129
    identifying, 127
    partial, 125
    PERT charts, 72-75
    standard, 125
Dependency Form screen, 126
Dependency List box symbols, 128
descending sort order, 178
Detail text report, 202
    printing, 214-217
Dialog (Macro menu) option, 308
Directory List box, 113
Directory List screen, 260
Disk File (Configure menu) option, 42, 53
displaying resource allocations, 143-146
documenting
    filters, 187
    projects, 122
    tasks, 66
DOS commands

Index 329

BACKUP, 264-266
CHKDSK, 30
DEL, 321
ERASE, 321
RESTORE, 266-267
TYPE, 41
DOS Date and Time utility, 293-294
duplicating tasks and subtasks, 115
duration of tasks, 13

E

early start dates, 15
editing
   filters, 190
   layouts, 200
   macros, 310-312
   tasks in calendars, 68-69
   with Journal box, 124
effort-driven scheduling, 149-150
electricity
   dirty power, 319
   power surges, 319
End key
   Notepad Navigation, 116
Erase (File menu) option, 263
Erase (Macro menu) option, 304
Erase (Schedule menu) option, 76
Erase (WBS Manager menu) option, 107
ERASE (DOS) command, 321
Erase menu options
   Any DOS Files, 263
   Any Time Line files, 263
   Current Time Line Files, 263
   Time Line Version 2 files, 263
   Time Line Version 3 files, 263
erasing
   files, 262-264
   projects, 76
   WBS Codes, 106
executing macros, 298-299
Exit to DOS utility, 289-292
Export Form screen, 272-275
   Assignment settings, 272
   Dependency settings, 273
   Resource settings field, 272
   Task settings field, 272
exporting files, 271-276

F

File (main menu) option, 76, 78
File menu options
   Combine, 268
   Erase, 263
   Form, 259
   Retrieve, 78, 260
   Save, 76, 256
   Xport Tables, 272

files
   ASCII
      retrieving text, 117
      saving, 117
   backing up, 264-266
   combining, 267-271
   data, 318
   erasing, 262-264
   exporting, 271-276
   extensions, 113
   formats, 53
   graphics, 51
   importing, 276-286
   program, 318
   READ.ME, 40
   recovering deleted, 321-322
   relocating, 259-260
   renaming, 259-260
   resaving, 258-259
   restoring, 266-267
   retrieving, 78-79, 260-262
   saving, 76-78, 256-258
Filter Form screen, 186-189
   Achievement field, 187
   Critical Path field, 187
   Data Fields, 189
   Dates field, 187
   Filter Name field, 186
   Notes field, 187
   Resource Keyword Contains field, 189
   Resources fields, 189
   WBS field, 188
filtering tasks, 181-190
filters
   custom, 186-189
   deleting, 190
   documenting, 187
   editing, 190
   naming, 186
   predefined
      Critical Path, 182
      Currently Scheduled, 183
      Resource Problems, 183
      Updating, 183
      WBS Errors, 183
Filters (Schedule menu) option, 182
Filters menu options
   Highlight, 184
   Select, 182
finish dates, 15-19
floppy disks, 320
Form (File menu) option, 259
Form (Report menu) option, 205
Form (Task menu) option, 117
Form (WBS Manager menu) option, 103
formatting
   dates, 52
   files, 53

G

Gantt Chart (Graphics menu) option, 80
Gantt Chart text report, 202
    printing, 209-211
Gantt charts, 23-24, 95
    layouts
        Baseline, 193
        C/SSR Support, 194
        Dates & Durations, 194
        Resources, 194
        Standard, 194
        Tracking, 194
        Updating, 195
        WBS Errors, 195
    printing, 80-81, 241-253
    resource allocations, 143-144
    screen, 190-192
Getting Started screen, 41
Go (Sort menu) option, 181
Graph Palettes file combine operation, 268
Graphics (Configure menu) option, 42
Graphics (main menu) option, 80
graphics plotters, 51
graphics printers, 51
Graphics Setup Form screen, 50
Graphics/Chart Size Form screen, 80, 252-253
    Force to One Page field, 252
    Pages Down Field, 253
    Preview on screen field, 253
    Reduce/Enlarge to field, 253
    Resize to Pages Across field, 253
Graphics/Gantt Chart Form screen, 244-248
    Always Show Actual field, 246
    Baseline Bar field, 246
    Borders field, 246
    Corners field, 246
    Data Range field, 247
    Extra Spacing field, 246
    Gantt Section Is field, 247
    Horizontal Grid field, 246
    Layout Name field, 244
    Palette Name field, 245
    Print On field, 245
    Scale field, 247
    Task Bar Label field, 248
    Through Outline Level field, 246
    Title & Legend field, 245
    Vertical Grid field, 246
Graphics/PERT Chart Form screen, 248-251
    Arrange Tasks by field, 251
    Corners field, 250
    Dependency Line Style, 250
    Eliminate Empty Time Periods to Save Space field, 252
    Layout Name field, 249
    Palette Name field, 249
    Periodic PERT Chart field, 251
    Shadows field, 250
    Task Box Style field, 250
    Time Period field, 251
    Title & Legend field, 250

H

Halt (Macro menu) option, 305
hardware requirements, 318
    DOS versions, 29
    floppy disk drives, 29
    hard disk, 29, 319-320
        free space required, 29
    memory, 29-30
    monochrome/color monitor, 29
heading keywords (reports), 208
help, 82-88
Help (Assist menu) option, 84
Highlight (Filters menu) option, 184
highlighting tasks, 184
histogram charts, 25, 144-146
Histogram text report, 202
    printing, 233-237
holidays, 62
Home key, Notepad Navigation, 116
hotkeys, 295

I

identifying costs, 151-155
identifying resources, 20, 135-138
Import Form screen, 278-280
    Assignment settings field, 279
    Dependency settings field, 279
    Import Directory field, 280
    Import Format field, 279
    Resource settings field, 279
    Task settings field, 279
Import menu options
    Import Time Line Ver 2, 276-277
    Import Time Line Ver 3, 276-277
importing files, 276-286
    1-2-3 Release 1A, 277
    1-2-3 Release 2.0, 277
    ASCII files, 280-286
    dBASE III, 277
    dBASE IV, 277
    earlier Time Line versions, 276-277
    Excel, 277
    Quattro, 277
    Symphony, 277
Input Pause (Macro menu) option, 307
Insert (Macro menu) option, 305-306
inserting characters, 116
Install program, 31-32, 37
Installation complete screen, 39
installing Time Line
    adding as a user, 32

Index 331

adding authorized users, 33
changing printers, 32
checking memory, 30
copying program files, 38
default directory, 34-35
graphics devices, 34-35
    plotters, 34-35
    printers, 34-35
    printing reports, 35
    printing text reports, 36
monitors, 37
on a LAN, 32
print options, 47
printers, 46-49
    printing text reports, 36
serial numbers, 34
setting date, 30
setting time, 30
time requirements, 31
user names, 34
video controller cards, 45

J

Journal box, 124
Journal Notes file combine operation, 268

K

key combinations, 69

L

Last Manual Order (Sort menu) option, 181
late start dates, 15
Layout Form option, 162
layouts, 192-193
    Baseline, 193
    C/SSR Support, 194
    Costs, 195
    custom, 196-200
    Dates & Durations, 194
    deleting, 200
    editing, 200
    Name + Achieved, 195
    Name + Dates, 195
    Resources, 194
    Standard, 194
    Structure Only, 195
    Tracking, 194
    WBS, 195
    WBS Errors, 195
leveling resources, 138
    automatically, 148-149
    manually, 147-148
Link (Macro menu) option, 310
links, 11
    in tasks, 113
    removing, 114

List option, 127
Load (Macro menu) option, 300
loop, circular dependency, 130

M

Macro (Macro menu) option, 306
Macro menu options
    Choices, 307-308
    Configure, 304-305
    Dialog, 308
    Erase, 304
    Halt, 305
    Input Pause, 307
    Insert, 305-306
    Link, 310
    Load, 300
    Macro, 306
    Macros List, 299
    Pause, 309
    Record, 297
    Save, 300
    Secondary Macro, 306-307
macros, 295
    brace symbols ({ }), 311
    canceling, 302
    creating menus, 307
    editing, 310-312
    executing, 298-299
    hotkeys, 295
    messages in, 308
    nesting, 306
    pausing, 309
    recording, 296-299
    removing from memory, 304
    saving, 299-301
    temporary, 297
    writing, 301-303
Macros List (Macro menu) option, 299
main menu options, 59
    File, 76, 78
    Graphics, 80
    Reports, 82
    Schedule, 59, 65
Manual (As-of date settings) option, 119
manual recalculation, 130
menu bar, 55, 59
    activating, 95
messages in macros, 308
Method setting, 48
milestones, 13
    tasks, 99
monitoring
    projects, 159
    resources, 21-22
    time on tasks, 21-22
mouse
    double-clicking, 55

N

scrolling, 55
Mouse (Configure menu) option, 42, 54
Mouse Control Form screen, 54
moving tasks, 71
   * Ctrl-PgDn, 99
   * Ctrl-PgUp, 99
   Ctrl-PgDn key, 98
   Ctrl-PgUp key, 98
   End key, 98
   Home key, 98

N

Name + Achieved PERT/Tree chart layout, 195
Name + Dates PERT/Tree chart layout, 195
naming filters, 186
nesting macros, 306
networks, 286-287
New Schedule (Assist menu) option, 86-87
No Name box, 55
note descriptions
   indenting, 124
   moving, 124
   outdent, 124
   unindenting, 124
Notepad Navigation keys, 116
notepads
   deleting text, 117
   documenting filters, 187
   documenting tasks, 66
notepads box, 115
Notes (Task menu) option, 115
numbering tasks, 106

O

OBS Codes, 110
OBS Codes (Task Form screen) option, 101
on-line help, 82-88
Options Form screen, 117-118, 121, 148
Organizational Breakdown Structure, *see* OBS
Other key (Sort menu) option, 180

P

parallel communications, 48
partial dependencies, 125
paths, PERT charts, 13-15
Pause (Macro menu) option, 309
pausing macros, 309
PERT Chart text report, 202
   printing, 238-241
PERT charts, 11-12, 93, 125
   drawing, 121
   layouts
      Costs, 195
      Name + Achieved, 195
      Name + Dates, 195
      Structure Only, 195
      WBS, 195
   paths, 13-15
   printing, 82, 241-253
   task dependencies, 72-75
   task durations, 13-15
   vs. tree charts, 22
PgDn key, Notepad Navigation, 116
PgUp key, Notepad Navigation, 116
power surges, 319
predecessor tasks, 11, 72-75
Primary key (Sort menu) option, 178
Primary Macro Form screen, 297-298
   Description field, 298
   Macro HotKey field, 297
   Macro Name field, 297
primary sort key, 177
Printer (Configure menu) option, 42
printing charts
   Gantt charts, 80-81, 241-253
   PERT charts, 82, 241-253
printing reports
   Assignment text report, 223-226
   Cross Tab text report, 226-231
   Detail text report, 214-217
   Gantt Chart text report, 209-211
   Histogram text report, 233-237
   PERT Chart text report, 238-241
   report heading keywords, 208
   Resources text report, 231-233
   Status text report, 218-223
   strips, 203-204
   Tasks text report, 211-214
   Tree Chart text report, 238-241
Proceed (WBS Manager menu) option, 107
Program Evaluation and Review Technique, 11
   See also PERT
program files, 318
project management
   components, 10
   monitoring time on tasks, 21-22
   PERT charts, 11-12
   resources, 19-21
   tasks, 10, 11
projects
   adding notes, 123-125
   backing up, 264-266
   combining, 267-271
   controlling notes, 117
   defining levels, 117
   defining tasks, 117
   deleting notes, 124
   describing, 117
   documenting, 122
   editing notes, 124
   entering descriptions, 118
   erasing, 76, 262-264
   monitoring, 159
   monitoring time, 163

Index

outlining notes, 124
recalculating time, 164
recording time, 163
recording with Responsible field, 119
relocating, 259-260
renaming, 259-260
resaving, 258-259
restoring, 266-267
retrieving, 78-79, 260-262
saving, 76-78, 256-258
schedules, 164

R

READ.ME file, 40-41
recalculating project time, 164
recalculation
   automatic, 120
      correcting, 130
   manual, 120
      correcting, 130
Record (Macros menu) option, 297
recording macros, 296-299
recovering deleted files, 321-322
Redo feature, 75
   defaults, 121
   limits, 121
relocating files, 259-260
removing
   macros from memory, 304
   text from notepad, 117
renaming files, 259-260
Renumber (WBS Manager menu) option, 110
renumbering tasks, 110
Report Form screen, 205-207
   Format field, 205
   Margins field, 206
   Print Names of Currently Active Filters field, 207
   Print Options Form Notes field, 207
   Report Heading field, 207
   Send Output To field, 205
reports
   Assignment text report, 202, 223-226
   Cross Tab text report, 202, 226-231
   Detail text report, 202, 214-217
   Gantt Chart text report, 202, 209-211
   Histogram text report, 202, 233-237
   PERT Chart text report, 202, 238-241
   report heading keywords, 208
   Resources text report, 203, 231-233
   Status text report, 203, 218-223
   strips, 203-204
   Tasks text report, 203, 211-214
   Tree Chart text report, 203, 238-241
Reports (main menu) option, 82
Represent As field, 112
resaving projects, 258-259
Resource Assignment Form screen, 140, 166

Resource Problems filter, 183
Resource text report, 203
resource usage
   monitoring, 166
   recording, 166
Resource/Cost Form screen, 136-138
   Cost Rate field, 138
   Default Assignment field, 137
   Full Name field, 137
   Keyword field, 137
   Level this Resource field, 138
   Maximum for Leveling field, 137
   Notes field, 137
   Resource Name field, 136
   Resource Type field, 137
resources
   allocating, 21, 139-143
      displaying allocations, 143-146
   assignment reports, 25
   costs, 150-151
   effort-driven scheduling, 149-150
   identifying, 20, 135-138
   leveling, 138
      automatically, 148-149
      manually, 147-148
   monitoring, 21, 22
Resources Gantt chart layout, 194
Resources List (Schedule menu) option, 135, 152-153
Resources text report, 203
   printing, 231-233
RESTORE (DOS) command, 266-267
restoring files, 266-267
Retrieve (File menu) option, 78, 260
retrieving projects, 78-79, 260-262

S

Save (File menu) option, 76, 256
Save (Macro menu) option, 300
saving
   macros, 299-301
   options, 55
   projects, 76-78, 256-258
   text in ASCII files, 117
   text in notepad to ASCII files, 117
Schedule (main menu) option, 59, 65
schedule links, 111
Schedule menu options
   Calendar, 59
   Erase, 76
   Filters, 182
   Resources List, 135, 152-153
   Sort, 177, 178
   Task Form, 92
   Tasks, 65
Schedule Name (Options Form) option, 118

Using Time Line

screens
   Calendar Settings, 62-64
   Configure Video, 44
   Cost Assignment Form, 168
   Dates, 62
   Dependency Form, 126
   Directory List, 260
   Export Form, 272-275
   Filter Form, 186-189
   Gantt chart, 190-192
   Graphics Setup Form, 50
   Graphics/Chart Size Form, 80 252-253
   Graphics/Gantt Chart Form, 244-248
   Graphics/PERT Chart Form, 248-251
   Import Form, 278-280
   Installation complete, 39
   Mouse Control Form, 54
   Options Form, 117, 121, 148
   Primary Macro Form, 297-298
   Report Form, 205-207
   Resource Assignment Form, 140, 166
   Resource/Cost Form, 136-138
   Setup Communications Form, 47
   Task Form, 65-68, 92, 140, 149, 155
   Time Line, 55
   Time Line Statistics, 293
   Workhours, 60
Search (Task menu) option, 70-71
searching tasks, 70-71
searching with WBS Codes, 102
Secondary key (Sort menu) option, 179
Secondary Macro (Macro menu) option, 306-307
secondary sort key, 177-178
Select (Filters menu) option, 182
selecting dates, 119
selecting tasks, 70-71
Separate by field, 106
serial communications, 48
Settings (Calendar menu) option, 62
Setup Communications Form screen, 47
slack time, 15
   calculating, 19
software, 318
   beta versions, 324
Sort (Schedule menu) option, 177-178
Sort menu options
   Go, 181
   Last Manual Order, 181
   Other key, 180
   Primary key, 178
   Secondary key, 179
sorting tasks, 177-181
   ascending sort order, 178
   descending sort order, 178
   primary key, 177
   secondary key, 177-178
sound, 121
spreadsheet files, importing, 277-280

standard dependencies, 125
Standard Gantt chart layout, 194
start dates, 15-19
Statistics utility, 292-293
Status text report, 203
   printing, 218-223
strips (printing reports), 203-204
Structure Only PERT/Tree chart layouts, 195
submenus, 59
subtasks, 11
   changing to tasks, 96
   collapsing, 97
   deleting, 97
   dependencies
      defining, 95
      identifying, 93
   hiding, 97
   moving
      Ctrl-PgDn key, 98
      Ctrl-PgUp key, 98
      End key, 98
      Home key, 98
   moving copies, 115
   unhiding, 97
successor tasks, 11, 72-75
summary tasks, 91, 157
   deleting, 97
surge protectors, 319
system clock, DOS Date and Time utility, 293
system software, 318

T

Task Form (Schedule menu) option, 92
Task Form screen, 65, 92, 140, 149, 155
   default Task Form, 120
   Driven by field, 149
   Duration field, 67-68
   End Date field, 68
   Force Future Tasks, 121
   Keywords option, 101
   Notes field, 66
   OBS Codes, 101
   Start Date field, 68
   Status field, 68
   task name field, 65-66
   Type field, 67
   WBS Codes, 101
Task menu options
   Add, 65
   Copy, 115
   Form, 117
   Notes, 115
   Search, 70-71
tasks
   ALAP, 66
   allocating resources, 139-143
   ASAP, 66

Index

creating schedule links, 111
defining using links, 113
dependencies, 11, 71-72
    correcting, 129
    deleting, 129
    identifying, 127
    PERT charts, 72-75
documenting notes, 115
duplicating, 115
duration, 13-15
entering keywords, 101
extracting from projects, 102
filtering, 101, 181-190
Fixed, 66
highlighting, 184
identifying levels, 105
linking to other files, 110
links, 11, 113
making copies, 115
milestones, 13, 99
    adding, 100
    creating, 99
    defining, 99
moving, 71
moving between, 95, 98
moving copies, 115
notepads, 115
numbering, 101, 104-106
numbering with WBS Manager, 103
PERT charts, 11-15
predecessor, 11, 72-75
project management, 10
removing links, 114
renumbering, 110
renumbering with WBS Codes, 110
searching, 70-71
selecting, 70-71
slack time, 15
sorting, 101, 177-181
subtasks, 11
    creating, 92
    dependencies, 93
    duplicating, 115
    moving copies, 115
successor, 11, 72-75
summary, 91, 157
    deleting, 97
timing, 12-15
    early finish dates, 15
    early start dates, 15
    late finish dates, 15
    late start dates, 15
unlinking from supporting task/project, 114
WBS Codes
    entering, 102
    searching for tasks, 102
zero duration, 99
Tasks (Schedule menu) option, 65
Tasks text report, 203
    printing, 211-214
temporary macros, 297
text reports
    Assignment, 202, 223-226
    Cross Tab, 202, 226-231
    Detail, 202, 214-217
    Gantt Chart, 202, 209-211
    Histogram, 202, 233-237
    PERT Chart, 202, 238-241
    Resource, 203, 231-233
    Status, 203, 218-223
    Tasks, 203, 211-214
    Tree, 203, 238-241
Time Line Statistics screen, 293
Time Line Version 2 files (Erase menu) option, 263
Time Line Version 3 files (Erase menu) option, 263
timing tasks, 12-15
    early finish dates, 15
    early start dates, 15
    finish dates, 15-19
    late finish dates, 15
    late start dates, 15
    monitoring time, 21-22
    start dates, 15-19
TL 3.0 Config utilities, 294-295
Tracking Gantt chart layout, 194
Transfer (WBS Manager menu) option, 109
Tree chart text report, 203
    printing, 238-241
Tree charts, 95
    layouts
        Costs, 195
        Name + Achieved, 195
        Name + Dates, 195
        Structure Only, 195
        WBS, 195
    vs. PERT charts, 22
Tree text report, 203
Tutorial (Assist menu) option, 88
TYPE (DOS) command, 41

U

Undo feature, 75
    default, 121
    limits, 121
Updating filter, 183
Updating Gantt chart layout, 195
utilities, 289
    DOS Date and Time, 293-294
    Exit to DOS, 289-292
    Statistics, 292-293
    TL 3.0 Config, 294-295

V

Video (Configure menu) option, 42

video components, 43
video controller card, 45
Video Options Menu Option, 44
viruses, 322-324

W

WBS PERT/Tree chart layouts, 195
WBS Code Prefix (WBS Manager menu) option, 104
WBS Codes
   creating, 104
   duplicating subtasks, 115
   duplicating tasks, 115
   erasing, 106
   renumbering, 110
   transferring, 109
   verifying, 107
WBS Errors field, 108
WBS Errors filter, 183
WBS Errors Gantt chart layout, 195
WBS Manager
   creating numbering schemes, 103
     menu options, 102
       Both Verify and Renumber, 103
       Erase, 107
       Form, 103
       Proceed, 107
       Renumber, 110
       Transfer, 109
       Verify Number Blank Tasks, 103
   removing WBS Codes, 103
   reviewing WBS Codes for errors, 103
   transferring contents, 103
Welcome screen, 30
Work Breakdown Structure, *see* WBS Codes
Workhours (Calendar menu) option, 59
Workhours screen, 60
working day, 60
working hours, 60
workweeks, 62
writing macros, 301-303

X

Xport Tables (File menu) option, 272

Free Catalog!

Mail us this registration form today, and we'll send you a free catalog featuring Que's complete line of best-selling books.

Name of Book _____

Name _____

Title _____

Phone ( ) _____

Company _____

Address _____

City _____

State _____ ZIP _____

Please check the appropriate answers:

1. Where did you buy your Que book?
   - ☐ Bookstore (name: _____)
   - ☐ Computer store (name: _____)
   - ☐ Catalog (name: _____)
   - ☐ Direct from Que
   - ☐ Other: _____

2. How many computer books do you buy a year?
   - ☐ 1 or less
   - ☐ 2-5
   - ☐ 6-10
   - ☐ More than 10

3. How many Que books do you own?
   - ☐ 1
   - ☐ 2-5
   - ☐ 6-10
   - ☐ More than 10

4. How long have you been using this software?
   - ☐ Less than 6 months
   - ☐ 6 months to 1 year
   - ☐ 1-3 years
   - ☐ More than 3 years

5. What influenced your purchase of this Que book?
   - ☐ Personal recommendation
   - ☐ Advertisement
   - ☐ In-store display
   - ☐ Price
   - ☐ Que catalog
   - ☐ Que mailing
   - ☐ Que's reputation
   - ☐ Other: _____

6. How would you rate the overall content of the book?
   - ☐ Very good
   - ☐ Good
   - ☐ Satisfactory
   - ☐ Poor

7. What do you like *best* about this Que book?
   _____
   _____

8. What do you like *least* about this Que book?
   _____
   _____

9. Did you buy this book with your personal funds?
   - ☐ Yes   ☐ No

10. Please feel free to list any other comments you may have about this Que book.
    _____
    _____
    _____

— **Que** —

Order Your Que Books Today!

Name _____

Title _____

Company _____

City _____

State _____ ZIP _____

Phone No. ( ) _____

Method of Payment:

Check ☐   (Please enclose in envelope.)

Charge My: VISA ☐   MasterCard ☐

American Express ☐

Charge # _____

Expiration Date _____

Order No.	Title	Qty.	Price	Total

You can **FAX** your order to **1-317-573-2583**. Or call **1-800-428-5331, ext. ORDR** to order direct.
Please add $2.50 per title for shipping and handling.

Subtotal _____
Shipping & Handling _____
Total _____

— **Que** —

BUSINESS REPLY MAIL
First Class Permit No. 9918   Indianapolis, IN

Postage will be paid by addressee

que®

11711 N. College
Carmel, IN 46032

NO POSTAGE
NECESSARY
IF MAILED
IN THE
UNITED STATES

BUSINESS REPLY MAIL
First Class Permit No. 9918   Indianapolis, IN

Postage will be paid by addressee

que®

11711 N. College
Carmel, IN 46032

NO POSTAGE
NECESSARY
IF MAILED
IN THE
UNITED STATES